Managing Human Resources

Managing Human Resources

Third Edition

edited by

Alan Cowling

Professor and Director of Research,
Middlesex University Business School

and

Chloë Mailer

Freelance Consultant

A member of the Hodder Headline Group
LONDON • SYDNEY • AUCKLAND

First edition published in Great Britain 1981
Second edition 1990
Third edition published in Great Britain 1998 by Arnold,
a member of the Hodder Headline Group,
338 Euston Road, London, NW1 3BH
http://www.arnoldpublishers.com

British Library Cataloguing-in-Publication Data
A catalogue record for this book is available from the British Library

ISBN: 0 340 69253 7

Publisher: Nicki Dennis
Production Editor: Liz Gooster
Production Controller: Rose James
Cover designer: Terry Griffiths

Typeset in 10 on 12pt Times by Phoenix Photosetting, Chatham, Kent
Printed and bound by JW Arrowsmith, Bristol

Contents

Biographical notes

Wendy Banfield
Wendy Banfield is Senior Lecturer in HRM at Middlesex University Business School teaching International HRM, International Business Organisation and Employee Resourcing. A Fellow of IPD, she is also Programme leader of the IPD Professional Postgraduate Diploma in Personnel Management. Following a degree in History, and a Postgraduate Diploma in Personnel Management from Aston University, she worked in personnel roles in both domestic and international companies before becoming a consultant, then joining the business school. She took an MBA at Henley, the Management College. She is particularly interested in ethical and cultural issues in international business.

Brenda Barrett
Brenda Barrett is Professor of Law in Middlesex University Business School. She studied law at Oxford and was called to the Bar at Gray's Inn. Her PhD was on employer's liability and, while she has many years of experience of lecturing and publishing on employment law generally, her special area of expertise is the law of occupational health and safety. Her research and publications on health and safety have given her a sufficient reputation for the United Nations to fund her in 1997 to visit China as an international expert.

Alan Cowling
Alan Cowling is Professor of Human Resource Management at Middlesex University Business School. His work experience has included managerial appointments with Cadbury Brothers, British Gas, and a subsidiary of GEC. His qualifications include an Oxford MA and a PhD in Employee Relations from City University, and he has researched and published widely on human resource management issues. He is a past Vice-President of the Institute of Personnel and Development.

Peter Critten
Peter Critten is Senior Lecturer at Middlesex University Business School specialising in HRD and Organisation Development. His background is in the design and evaluation of training systems mainly in service industries and in former Industrial Training Boards. In recent years, in association with the University's National Centre for Work Based Learning Partnerships, he has published guidelines to Health Care Practitioners on using portfolios for professional development and has a research interest in how portfolios can be used for both individual and organisation development.

Delia Goldring
Delia Goldring has a wide range of experience as a human resources practitioner in a variety of industries over a 20-year period. She is currently Director of Human Resources Jewish Care for a major social services agency based in the South East of England, from 1984 to 1996 she was Senior Lecturer at Middlesex University Business School in addition to running a successful human resources consultancy practice.

Phil James
Phil James is Professor of Employment Relations at Middlesex University Business School. Prior to joining the university he had worked as a researcher and editor at Industrial Relations Services, and taught at Birmingham University. Phil has researched and published widely in the fields of employee relations and occupational health and safety, and is a member of the editorial advisory board of the *Human Resource Management Journal*.

Jacqui Kasket
Jacqui Kasket is Senior Lecturer in Human Resource Management at Middlesex University Business School specialising in Training and Organisation Development. She has over 25 years practical experience in both the public and private sector, working as a trainer and internal and external consultant. Her early career includes posts as a line manager and personnel manager, before specialising in training and development.

Anna Kyprianou
Anna Kyprianou is Principal Lecturer in Human Resource Management at Middlesex University Business School. She has lectured in organisational behaviour and training and development for over twelve years, and is actively involved in training and development research and consultancy in business organisations.

John Lane
John Lane is an Occupational Psychologist and a partner in John Lane Associates (JLA), a consultancy specialising in selection and development. John has had careers in both Sales and HRM and now is Associate Senior Lecturer at Middlesex University. He has published a number of articles in leading professional journals.

Chloë Mailer
Chloë Mailer is a freelance consultant and writer with practical experience of human resource management in industry. A graduate of the Universities of St Andrews and Glasgow, she was a management adviser with The Industrial Society and editor of *Industrial Society*. Currently she is a management studies tutor in Further Education in Kent as well as acting as editorial consultant on this publication.

Tanya Pyne
Tanya Pyne is an Occupational Psychologist with expertise in the design and validation of selection methods. Tanya is currently employed at Middlesex University Business School in a research capacity where her primary interest is in the performance and development of staff in the National Health Service.

Allan Williams
Allan Williams is Professor of Organisational and Occupational Psychology, and Director of the Centre for Personnel Research and Enterprise Development at the City University Business School. Prior to holding his present post of Deputy Dean at the School, he was Pro-Vice-Chancellor of the University. He has researched, consulted and published widely in the HRM and organisation development areas. He is co-author of *Changing Culture*, published by IPD, and of *The Competitive Consultant*, published by Macmillan.

Preface

It is pleasing to record that the second edition has proved to be as popular as its predecessor, finding a place on many reading lists and managers' bookshelves. The third edition represents a thoroughgoing revision, providing both updated information and a revised structure that reflects the profound changes which have taken place over the last six years.

This decade has seen no let up in the pace of change affecting organisations and individuals. Britain has emerged from a period of recession, and many organisations have undergone profound structural and cultural changes. The now notorious 'three Ds' of downsizing, delayering, and decentralisation have been adopted by many organisations in response to intense competition and pressures to reduce costs. The drive for a transformation in the quality of production and improved customer service has led to a recognition by progressive firms of the importance of front-line staff and the need for continuous improvement. Not all change has been sensibly brought about, however, and unimaginative cost cutting has led all too often to anxiety and stress, demotivated employees, a loss of core competency, and an inability to respond to market opportunities. While successful organisations have continued to value, develop, and make good use of their human resources, thus achieving the benefits that accrue from the emphasis on the 'productivity through people' theme first heralded in the 1980s, others have pursued short-term policies and have therefore failed to capitalise on the contribution people can make to growth and bottom-line results.

In response to continuing economic pressures many human resource (HR) departments have slimmed further. While some have continued the trend to decentralise their operations, begun in the 1980s, others have done the reverse, attempting to turn themselves into in-house consultancy services. Traditional HR responsibilities, such as recruitment, training, and pay have been increasingly contracted out. Work 'competencies' have received great attention, and are increasingly being used as the basis for selection, training, and remuneration. At the same time the term 'competency' has come to have a variety of meanings, some based on rigorous definitions and procedures, some idiosyncratic and riddled with jargon. In general, reward management has assumed a greater significance during this decade, and employment law has settled down into a post-Thatcher era of generally accepted regulatory controls.

A team of authors has contributed to this new edition. Experts in their respective fields, they cover the wide-ranging field of contemporary human resource management, addressing themselves to line managers as much as to human resource specialists. Many contributed to the previous edition. New contributors reflect the surge of interest in equal opportunities, learning organisations, and the internationalisation of HR practice.

AGC
CJBM

Preface to first edition

This book has been written for students of management and practising managers interested in the management of human resources, and is concerned with the policies, procedures and practices which can lead to the effective recruitment, integration and deployment of the human resources of an enterprise. It is designed as a sequel to an earlier book, R. L. Boot, A. C. Cowling and J. K. Stanworth *Behavioural Sciences for Managers*, Edward Arnold, 1977, which introduces management readers to the behavioural sciences.

Managing Human Resources has been written with a variety of potential readerships in mind. It should prove particularly useful to students taking Part 2 of the Diploma in Management Studies, Stage 2 of the Diploma in Personnel Management, and Human Resources options on MBA courses. It should also interest practising managers who find themselves unable to undertake formal courses of study but who are concerned to review the latest developments in theory and practice relevant to the management of the personnel they control. It is addressed especially to the line manager, on the assumption that line managers bear the primary responsibility for managing personnel, but includes a discussion of the role of the personnel department, and the support personnel managers can provide for line managers and the goals of the organisation.

The term 'human resources' was chosen because it reflects a commendable modern emphasis in management terminology on treating employees as a valuable resource requiring expert selection and development rather than the more traditional view of employees as expendable units of labour to be indiscriminately hired and fired in the market place.

The need for this type of approach has been reinforced in recent years by the high cost of employing people and the effect of both government legislation and trade union pressures which render arbitrary dismissal an expensive procedure.

A gulf sometimes exists between theory and practice in the management of human resources, which this book attempts to overcome by describing both practical techniques and procedures and relevant theory and research. Techniques are not decried, as is the fashion in some quarters, because the writers appreciate from first hand experience that they provide the means by which busy managers can give effect to good policies and procedures. At the same time, care has been taken to present the best techniques available, and to supply constructive criticism, where it has been felt to be relevant. The general emphasis and direction in this book is therefore a *technological* one, that is to say, it is concerned with the practical application of sound theory. It takes as its model the attention given in countries such as Germany and Japan to practical technology and the practical skills of *getting things done*. We hope that it will help readers not only to master the best procedures and practices currently available, but also to go on to forge new and instructive methods which will serve them well in the rapidly changing circumstances in which managers have to operate.

Acknowledgement is due here to the five specialist contributors each of whom we invited to participate in the book because of his or her particular expertise in what has become a very wide-ranging subject. We feel sure that this will enhance the reader's appreciation and understanding of the subject matter as well as ensuring that only the most relevant policies and practices are outlined.

Ensuing chapters in this book concentrate on such key processes as employment, training, development, manpower planning, and remuneration. Because the study of industrial relations now represents a major subject in its own right it is left for detailed treatment in a separate book. However a chapter on labour relations at *plant level* is included. Each chapter takes account of the limitations imposed by financial restraints and organisational policies at the place of work. The growing importance of legislation is reflected in the final chapter, which not only gives an overview of the manner in which legislation now has to be taken into account in the management of human resources in the UK, but also quotes many relevant legal decisions invaluable to both student and manager alike.

AGC
CJBM

Preface to second edition

Since *Managing Human Resources* was first published in 1981 it has been adopted on a range of management and business studies programmes, as well as finding its way on to the bookshelves of practising managers. The first edition was written primarily for line managers and students preparing for line management positions, rather than for personnel specialists. There existed then, and still exists, a sufficiency of specialist personnel texts, but too few texts addressed to the needs of managers outside as well as inside the personnel function with a major responsibility for people. The second edition has this same objective and is addressed to all who have to manage human resources within work organisations.

Since 1981 significant changes have taken place. In 1981 western economies were struggling with economic recession and rising unemployment, while the business ethos was still largely that of the 1970s, influenced by the concept that big is beautiful! In many ways 1981 marked a watershed in thinking about organisations and for the next five years private companies re-learned the message of the need to be closer to the customer and for leaner and fitter organisations. Emphasis began to be placed on enterprise cultures and in the public sector, privatisation and competitiveness. Many large centralised bureaucracies have now been slimmed down and overlarge head offices have dispersed.

As organisations have attempted to assess their competitive advantage, assessing their strengths, weaknesses, opportunities and threats they have come to reappraise the significance of their most valuable resource, the people they employ, appreciating that their strategy now requires in most cases a higher calibre of human resource. There has also been the realisation that manpower costs could cripple revival and that the solution lay in lower wage costs together with higher productivity and a better motivated and trained work-force. As a result, in many firms wage costs per unit of output have fallen as productivity has risen and at the same time higher levels of remuneration, frequently linked to performance and value added, have been implemented.

These and other changes are reflected in this new second edition. In addition the content looks ahead to the challenges posed by the 1990s. European trends including the 1992 harmonisation proposals and the continuing economic threat from Japan and the Far East mean that human resources must be more cost effective. Demographic change, political pressures for equality of opportunity and new concepts of career and career planning that no longer assume life-time employment will also need to be taken on board by managers. In addition, research and practice are now producing new and better human resource techniques and practices. All these developments are reflected in this second edition which aims to take the effective management of human resources forward to meet the next century.

AGC
CJBM

List of abbreviations

AC	Appeal Cases
ACAS	Advisory, Conciliation and Arbitration Service
AEEU	Amalgamated Engineering and Electrical Union
AFTA	ASEAN Free Trade Association
All ER	All England Reports
APEC	Asia Pacific Economic Cooperation
APL	accreditation of prior learning
ASEAN	Association of Southeast Asian Nations
ASSET	Accreditation for Social Services Experience and Training
BARS	Behaviourally Anchored Rating Scales
CAC	Central Arbitration Committee
CCETSW	Central Council for Education and Training in Social Work (1988 Social Care Council)
CCT	compulsory competitive tendering
CPD	continuous professional development
CPIS	computerised personnel information systems
CRE	Commission for Racial Equality
EAT	Employment Appeal Tribunal
ECJ	European Court of Justice
EOC	Equal Opportunities Commission
EPOS	electronic point of sale
ER Act	Employment Rights Act 1996
EU	European Union
EWS	effective worker standard
GPMU	Graphical, Paper and Media Union
HCN	host country national
HR	human resources
HRM	human resource management
ICR	Industrial Cases Reports
ID	industrial democracy

IDS	Incomes Data Services
IES	Institute of Employment Studies
IMS	Institute of Manpower Studies
IPA	Institute of Practitioners in Advertising
IPD	Institute of Personnel and Development
IRLR	Industrial Relations Law Reports
ISPP	Intergovernmental Social Policy Protocol
ISR	International Survey Research
ITB	Industrial Training Board
LSL	lower standard of living
MCI	Management Charter Initiative
MNE	multinational enterprise
MSC	Manpower Services Commission
MSF	Manufacturing, Science and Finance
NAFTA	North American Free Trade Agreement
NDC	National Disability Council
NVQ	National Vocational Qualifications
OD	organisational development
OECD	Organisation for Economic Cooperation and Development
OPQ	Occupational Personality Questionnaire
PBR	payment by results
PDP	personal development plan
PMTS	Predetermined Motion Time Systems
PPP	Premium Payment Plan
QB	Queen's Bench
QWL	quality of working life
SEA	Single European Act 1986
SWOT	strengths, weaknesses, opportunities and threats
TCN	third country national
TULR(C) Act	Trade Union and Labour Relations (Consolidation) Act 1992
WLR	Weekly Law Reports

Introduction

Alan Cowling

Financial resources can be managed, and are managed, to good effect. Physical and technological resources can likewise be managed to good effect and so can human resources. Human resources are composed of individuals working for an organisation, employed these days on a variety of contracts, some as 'core' long-term staff, some as temporary staff, some as contracted staff, but collectively making up the most important of an organisation's resources. People are the only resource that can put financial, physical, and technological resources to best use. Managed well, success should follow; managed badly, failure will sooner or later result. To describe people as resources is not to dehumanise them, as some have asserted, but to recognise that they are valuable, and therefore should be treated as human beings. Old-fashioned terminology such as 'labour' or 'personnel' unfortunately did not always command such respect.

The first edition of this book, as outlined in the original preface (1980), sought to pioneer the idea in Britain that employees could and should be managed as a valuable resource. Today most managers are comfortable with the term 'human resources'. A few still prefer to refer to 'people' or 'employees' or 'staff', and to use the term 'personnel management'. At one level the terminology is less important, because it is practice that really counts. But at another level it does matter because ways of managing people at work have come a long way in the last 15 years, and a refusal to use the modern term 'human resources' can be an indication of a failure to recognise and utilise recent developments. A greater danger lies in the adoption of the new terminology while sticking with outdated policies and procedures, and too many examples of this are still to be found in companies today.

The term 'human resources' gained popularity in the United States some 15 to 20 years ago, and subsequently crossed the Atlantic a few years later. Recognition in the United States by leading organisations and writers on management of the importance of the contribution that could be made by employees to achieving corporate goals (including in the case of 'for profit' organisations to market share and the 'bottom line', and in 'not for profit' organisations to the quality of service), created great interest in new ways of managing people at work. This interest was heightened by an appreciation of the attention paid by Japanese corporations to employees and corporate value systems,[1] and evidence that the most successful corporations in the West also paid careful attention to the management of human resources.[2]

Before these developments, the term 'personnel management' was widely used to describe the process of managing people at work. Personnel management was not perceived as having strategic significance, nor indeed as a special concern of line management. Rather, it was seen as a necessary function. The primary concern of the personnel department was to cope with hiring and firing, signs of trade union militancy, organisation of training programmes, administration of wages, and the delivery of welfare programmes. The 1966 edition of *Functions of a Personnel Department*, published by the then Institute of Personnel Management, stated that:

the term personnel management is used in its broadest sense to describe the function of management primarily concerned with what is commonly called the human factor. The personnel department is a division within the management structure where men and women are employed to help to evolve and to help in carrying out various policies of a company in matters affecting its employees.[3]

Today the management of human resources is generally accepted to be a primary responsibility of all managers, line or staff, facilitated and supported by a lean and competent human resource department. The thinking that has helped to bring about this change can be traced back to that doyen of management writers, Peter Drucker. In his classic text *The Practice of Management*, written over 40 years ago, he charged management with three functions: economic performance, managing managers, and managing workers and work. 'Man alone of all the resources available to man', he said, 'can grow and develop', and then added, 'It implies the consideration of human beings as a resource . . .'.[4]

A significant and more recent contribution towards understanding human resource management (HRM) has been made by the Harvard Business School, who in 1980 introduced a human resource management syllabus onto their MBA programme. A research colloquium organised by Harvard in 1984 bringing together leading academics and business men considered the future character of HRM, which led to the analytical framework illustrated in Figure 0.1.

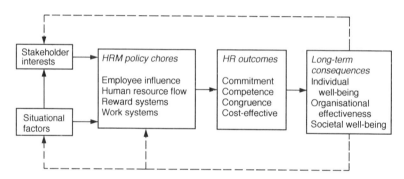

Figure 0.1 Harvard framework for human resource management

The concepts contained in Figure 0.1, such as 'stakeholder interests', 'situational factors', and 'HR outcomes of commitment, competence, congruence and cost effectiveness', are still in the process of being worked through by contemporary organisations.[5]

In further developing this line of thinking in the USA, Walton has contrasted old and new assumptions and approaches to the management of human resources, underlying the radical move from old-fashioned 'control-based' policies to new 'commitment-based' policies and systems.[6] This is illustrated in Table 0.1.

These new philosophies and policies on managing human resources have been more readily accepted by senior practising managers in the UK than by academics. Senior managers have had to respond to a shift to a global market and greater international competition, and the consequent need for a better educated and trained workforce, total quality practices, and lean decentralised organisation structures. Academics strongly influenced by the legacy of an industrial relations philosophy which emphasised conflict and espoused a pluralistic view of the workforce have had difficulty in coming to terms with a new scenario based on a unitary frame of reference.[7,8] Fortunately such introspection has now largely given way to studies of these new organisational developments, leading to the development of a recent literature which recognises the significance of new-style HR policies, and helps our understanding of the circumstances in which they may or may not succeed.[9,10,11]

Table 0.1 Contrast between control-based and commitment-based HRM systems

Policy area	HRM System	
	Control-based	*Commitment-based*
Job design principles	• Sub-division of work • Specific job responsibility • Accountability for specific job responsibility • Planning separated from implementation	• Broader jobs • Combined planning and implementation • Teams
Management organisation	• Top-down control and co-ordination • Management prerogative • Status symbols • Hierarchy	• Flat structure • Shared goals for control and co-ordination • Status minimised
Compensation	• Fair day's work for fair day's pay • Job evaluation • Individual incentives	• Reinforcing group achievements • Pay geared to skill and other contribution criteria • Gain-sharing, stock ownership, profit sharing
Assurance	• Labour a variable cost	• Mutual commitment • Avoid unemployment • Assist re-employment
Employee voice	• Unionised (damage control, bargaining, appeals process) • Non-union (open door policy, attitude surveys)	• Mutual mechanisms for communications and participation • Mechanisms for giving employee voice on issues
Labour management relations	• Adversarial	• Mutuality • Joint problem-solving and planning
Management philosophy	• Management prerogative • Management's exclusive obligation to shareholders	• Emphasis on claims of all stakeholders • Fulfilment of employee's needs is a goal not an end

Source: Walton, Towards a strategy

The chapters in this book successively outline recent thinking on human resource policies and practices, applying a critical approach. The authors aim to provide a good understanding and a sound knowledge base that will contribute to greater competence at work. Reference is made to the respective roles of line managers and human resource specialists as appropriate, but there is an assumption throughout that responsibility is shared for the effective management of human resources.

References

1. Pascale R, Athos A. *The art of Japanese management*. Harmondsworth: Penguin, 1982.
2. Peters T, Waterman R. *In search of excellence*. New York: Harper & Row, 1982.
3. Moxon G. *Functions of a personnel department*. London: Institute of Personnel Management, 1966: 3.
4. Drucker P. *The practice of management*. London: Heinemann, 1961.
5. Lundy O, Cowling A. *Strategic human resource management*. London and New York: Routledge, 1996.
6. Walton RE. Towards a strategy of eliciting employee commitment based on policies of mutuality. In: Walton RE and Lawrence PR eds. *HRM trends and challenges*. Boston: Harvard Business School Press, 1985.
7. Keenoy T. Human resource management: rhetoric, reality, and contradiction. *The International Journal of Human Resource Management* 1990; **1**(3): 363–84.
8. Storey J. Introduction: from personnel management to human resource management. In: Storey J ed. *New perspectives on human resource management*. London and New York: Routledge, 1989.
9. Guest D. Personnel management: the end of orthodoxy? *British Journal of Industrial Relations* 1991; **29**(2): 149–75.
10. Storey J. The take-up of human resource management by mainstream companies: key lessons from research. *The International Journal of Human Resource Management* 1993; **4**(3): September: 529–53.
11. Schuler R. Strategic human resource management: linking the people with the strategic needs of the business. *Organisational Dynamics* 1992; Summer: 18–31.

1 Developing a strategy for human resources

Alan Cowling

One issue dominates the subconscious thinking of both individuals and organisations – survival. And for organisations to survive in today's environment they must be successful. Survival and success dominate the thinking of chief executives, top management, and strategic planners. 'Strategy' is a concept borrowed from the military, where it denotes the art of war, and hence military survival. In business it denotes the art of economic survival.

When developing their strategies, companies in the private sector normally place their emphasis on financial, marketing, and operational considerations. In the public sector strategies have additionally had to take account of political matters. Until recently it was rarely thought necessary to consider human resource when strategies were developed. While the need for a productive and cooperative workforce was generally acknowledged, it was assumed that this could be comfortably achieved subsequent to the development of corporate strategy.

As indicated in the introduction to this book, the strategic significance of human resources has been increasingly recognised by Western corporations over the last decade. Factors that have contributed to this recognition have included the manifest success of Japanese industry that has paid great attention to people, their values and their skills, technological change which has increased the need for a well-educated and highly skilled workforce, and the positive example provided by a number of world-class Western organisations that have a coherent strategy for human resources.

1.1 The nature of corporate strategy

Faulkner and Johnson see corporate strategy as being concerned with the long-term direction and scope of an organisation.[1] It is crucially concerned with how an organisation positions itself in its environment and in relation to its competitors. By taking a long-term perspective in preference to a short-term tactical manoeuvre, competitive advantage is promoted.

The application of strategy to the public sector and 'not for profit' organisations maintains this long-term perspective, but has to be framed in different terms: the emphasis is not on achieving competitive advantage but on providing a public service of appropriate quality within budgeted cost restraints (although the distinction between public and private organisations has been blurred in recent years by government pressures for 'internal markets' and competitive tendering). The Local Government Board recommended in their 1991 report that 'Authorities adopt a strategic approach . . . traditional structures, practices and procedures are being re-examined to find new ways of improving service to their communities.'[2]

The best manner in which to formulate and execute strategy has been the subject of considerable debate. Whittington found 37 books in print bearing the title *Strategic Management*.[3] Until recently a rational planned approach has been the norm, with an emphasis on 'aims' and 'missions', and a systematic evaluation of alternative ways of achieving these. This has then been followed by selection and statement of the best way forward, and detailed plans extending several years into the future. Once approved by the chief executive these plans are 'cascaded' down through the organisation in hierarchical fashion.

In what has become a classic definition, Chandler in 1962 defined strategy as 'the determination of the long-term goals and objectives of an enterprise, and the adoption of courses of action and the allocation of resources of action and the allocation of the resources necessary to carry out these goals'.[4] Popular approaches in the 1970s and 1980s placed emphasis on an appraisal of strengths, weaknesses, opportunities, and threats (as typified by SWOT analysis and the Boston Consulting Group's portfolio) as an aid to determining strategy. Both approaches appealed to top management in Western organisations, convinced that they held a monopoly of intelligence and wisdom.

Research has challenged both the validity and practicality of this approach.[5,6] All too frequently, decision-making in boardrooms has been found to reflect power structures and group dynamics rather than rational analysis. The ability to predict events several years into the future has also been questioned, given the rapidity of change in the contemporary business environment. In consequence, authorities such as Mintzberg advocate an incremental approach which treats strategy formulation and implementation as a 'craft', and he comments that 'formulation and implementation merge into a fluid process of learning through which creative strategies emerge'. In his view, effective strategies combine deliberation and control with flexibility and organisational learning. Ansoff, however, considers this 'emergent' approach as unsuited to a turbulent environment, as strategies are produced that are out of date before they can be implemented.[7] Johnson and Scholes[8] see corporate strategy as 'the matching of the activities of the organisation's activities to its resource capability', as shown in Figure 1.1.

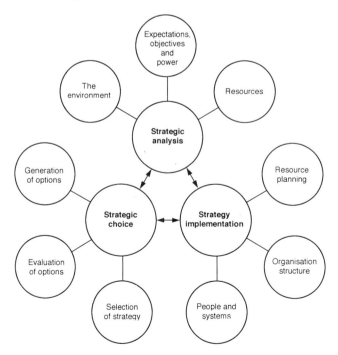

Source: Johnson, Scholes, *Exploring corporate strategy*

Figure 1.1 The elements of strategic management

1.2 Corporate strategy and human resource strategy

A human resource strategy can likewise be developed as a matching process, concerned with the manner and extent to which the stock of manpower should be varied to match predicted changes in the environment, and integrated continuously into corporate plans.

The model in Figure 1.1 highlights five areas where the analysis and planning of human resources are significant in the strategic management process, namely, 'environment', 'organisation structure', 'people and systems', 'resources', and 'resource planning'. The relevant aspect of the environment in this context is the labour market, which determines the supply of labour and impact on wage costs and employee attitudes. A good organisation structure is a strategic imperative, because without it the organisation will lack synergy. The right people and systems will deliver high productivity and quality, building on the human resources put in place by careful human resource planning. These factors will be considered in some detail later in this book.

While conventional wisdom now supports the integration of human resource strategy and corporate strategy, the evidence unfortunately is that only limited progress has so far been achieved. In a study of European companies Chris Brewster found the highest degree of integration among firms in Sweden, Norway, and France, and the lowest degree of integration in Germany and Italy.[9] The UK lagged behind Switzerland, Spain, Finland and the Netherlands in this respect. In a study in the USA, Paul Butler found variable degrees of integration in a sample of large corporations, and commented that

> In companies with two-way linkage, top management and corporate planners recognise that business plans affect – and are affected by – human resources . . . in these firms, consequently line managers, business planners, and human resources staff members relate to one another as strategic partners.[10]

Corporate strategy can also be envisaged as taking place at lower levels in the organisation. John Purcell has identified three levels of strategic decision-making.[11] At the top of the organisation 'first-order' strategies consist of decisions on long-term goals and the scope of activities, 'second-order' strategies lead to decisions on the way the enterprise is structured to achieve its goals, and human resource management decisions are included in 'third-order' strategies tied to annual budgets, where mechanisms for making things happen are put into place. Research by Shaun Tyson using this taxonomy and based on a sample of 30 large British companies found 'strong' evidence that divisional management creates detailed strategies, and in many cases the role of main boards was to coordinate and shape these strategies in support of the published vision and values.[12] HR directors were found to play an important role at divisional level, even though main boards frequently did not include an HR director, and Tyson concludes that HR divisional directors play an important role in the development of second- and third-order strategies. It is interesting to compare this apparent subordination of HR strategy to second- or third-level decision-making with the Japanese approach as expounded by Kenichi Ohmea that 'The Japanese company starts with people, trusting their capabilities and potential.'[13]

A comprehensive model of strategic human resource management has been developed by Olive Lundy, as illustrated in Figure 1.2.[14]

This model indicates progressive stages in developing a human resource strategy that is integrated with corporate strategy, and subsequently finds expression in third-order strategies, processes, and actions in key HRM areas such as selection, performance assessment, training and development, rewards and employee relations.

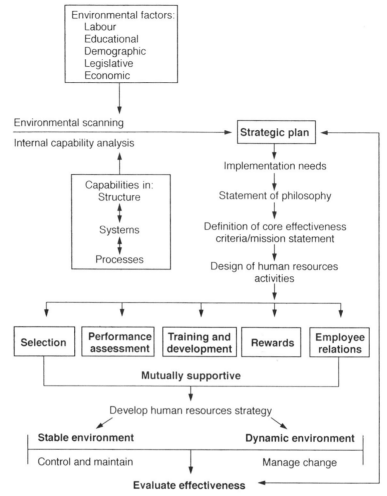

Source: Lundy, Cowling, *Strategic Human Resource Management*

Figure 1.2 Strategic human resource management: a comprehensive model

1.3 Structure and strategy

Designing and revising the structure of an organisation are key aspects of first-order strategy. Decisions on structure are normally taken at the highest level, usually by the chief executive advised by the board of directors. Advice is frequently taken from management consultants, but rarely from the human resource department, principally because the HR department is perceived by most chief executives as lacking the necessary expertise and influence in this area.

Creating the right kind of organisation and ensuring that it is properly staffed requires considerable planning. Organisations cannot be changed overnight, and it is important to get the structure right. 'Structure follows strategy' has been a much quoted maxim of corporate planners in the past. The first priority has therefore usually been to decide on a strategy encompassing markets, products, services and finance, leaving structure to later on, on the grounds that it can be designed subsequently in furtherance of the desired strategy. However, thinking is changing on this order of priorities and structure is now becoming a primary concern. Asked to state his order of priorities on this issue Tom Peters assigned top weighting to structure, followed by systems and people.[15] Strategy, he argues, should then be set subsequently at strategic business unit level. 'Top management', he adds, 'should be creative of a general business mission.'

To decide on the most appropriate structure, a number of basic questions have to be answered, including the following:

- How centralised or decentralised should we be in our operations and decision-making?
- How many layers do we really need?
- How formal or informal should our manner of operations be?
- Should staff report to only one supervisor?
- What should be the spans of control?
- Should staff be grouped by specialism, or in project or process teams?
- Can business processes be re-engineered, creating new and better ways of working together?

A range of options is available once these questions have been answered.

Option 1 Traditional hierarchical structures

Traditional hierarchical structures are based on theories developed in the first quarter of this century in accordance with so-called 'scientific management' principles. These principles have influenced the design of most medium to large-scale organisations for the first 60 years of this century.

- Decision-making is located at the top of the organisation.
- All staff report to only one superior.
- Spans of control are limited where possible to less than 10 people.
- Commands and official information must be transmitted through 'proper' channels of information, from the top to the bottom of the organisation.
- Staff are grouped by specialism into departments and sections.
- Authority derives from status in the organisation's hierarchy.
- Jobs are precisely defined in written job descriptions.
- The so-called line departments are those which directly generate revenue (e.g. sales and production), whereas the so-called 'staff' departments provide a support and advisory service to the line departments (e.g. human resources and accounts).

This model assumes that employees at work are dominated by their individual interests and not by group considerations, and the primary source of their motivation is money. Because it treats the organisation as if it were a machine it is frequently termed 'mechanistic'.

A version of this option is a 'bureaucratic' structure, widespread in the past in public sector organisations. To the above principles it adds a degree of impersonality whereby staff are selected by a central unit, possess security of tenure, and are expected to work strictly within the limits of their job descriptions. The advantages of this type of structure are stability, conformity and control; the disadvantages are inflexibility, inability to change, poor communications, and lack of cooperation between departments and different levels in the organisation.

Option 2 'Organic' structures

An 'organic' structure is in many ways the opposite of a 'mechanistic' structure, and has influenced thinking on the design of organisations for the last 30 years as the limitations of the traditional model were exposed.[16]

- Decision-making is delegated to those with relevant knowledge, irrespective of formal status.
- Staff do not have precise job descriptions, and adapt their duties to the needs of the situation.
- Information is informal, and all channels of information are used.
- There is high interaction and collaboration between staff, irrespective of status or department.
- There is an emphasis on flexibility, cooperation, and informality.

Because of its inherent flexibility, it is not possible to capture an organic structure in an organisation chart or simple diagram. The possible advantages of this type of organisation are flexibility, capacity for change, good communications and concerted team effort. The possible disadvantages are lack of structure and inability to mass-produce articles requiring repetitive and boring work routines.

Option 3 Matrix structures

Matrix structures are an attempt to overcome the rigidities imposed on organisations by an exclusive allegiance to one department and 'one boss'. Individual members of staff are allocated to a specialist department, representing their 'home' base, but spend most of their time working in mixed teams with staff from other specialist departments on projects, under the day-to-day control of one or more project leaders. There can be further dimensions to a matrix, as when staff also report to a geographically located head office, as in a multinational organisation. A matrix 'project' structure is depicted diagrammatically in Figure 1.3.

   The advantages are good team working, good communications, and a focus on the tasks to be accomplished. The disadvantages are possible confusion created by different reporting relationships, lack of job security when projects are completed, and lack of career development as specialisation gives way to team working.[17]

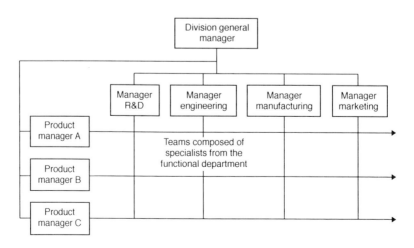

Figure 1.3 A simple matrix organisation structure

Option 4 Process-based structures

Chiefly under the recent impact of process re-engineering projects (sometimes termed 'business process re-engineering', or BPR), organisations have formed work teams around the basic processes essential to their business. This can then lead to a radical redesign of the organisation.[18]

An example of the redesign of an individual process is provided in the provision of mortgages. In a bank or building society the 'process' of providing a mortgage can be carefully mapped out from start to finish, leading to the elimination of stages that slow down the execution of the process and of any unecessary paperwork. Applied throughout an organisation, this can lead to a totally new structure, as is illustrated in Figure 1.4, based on work undertaken in the former National and Provincial Building Society.

This is sometimes termed a 'horizontal' organisation, for as Figure 1.4 illustrates, the result is a replacement of the traditional hierarchical structure by one based on work flows. Transition to this type of structure can be painful because it requires a radical change in the manner in which people work together, but it can result in a leaner and more effective organisation, provided the process is well managed, particularly the human resource aspects.[19]

1.4 Variations on the basic models

Each model is capable of being varied to some degree by different measures. Let us consider some of these.

Divisionalisation

An organisation can be split up into divisions. Divisions can be based either on geography, e.g. a 'Midlands' or 'Northern' division, or by product and market, e.g. a 'Chemicals' or 'Petroleum' division. Divisions are coordinated from a central headquarters.

The possible advantages of divisionalisation are that staff are closer to their customers and centralised bureaucracy can be reduced, allowing staff to work better together for a common purpose. The possible disadvantages are loosening of control and a weakening of identification with the present organisation.

Decentralisation

Decision-making is delegated as far down the organisation as possible. This enables decisions to be made by those with relevant technical expertise, and who are closer to customers. One version of decentralisation in the private sector is the creation of strategic business units, or 'SBUs'.

The possible advantages of decentralisation are that decisions are made at the point of operation and delivery, and the possible disadvantages are that the centre may lose control and there may occur a degree of anarchy.

Delayering

The number of levels between top management and the shop floor are drastically reduced, frequently with a target of less than five layers. Possible advantages include improved communications, cutting out of bureaucratic layers that slow down decision-making, cost savings, and better relationships between management and workers. Possible disadvantages include negative impact on career prospects as promotion prospects are restricted, and stress created by enlarged job boundaries.

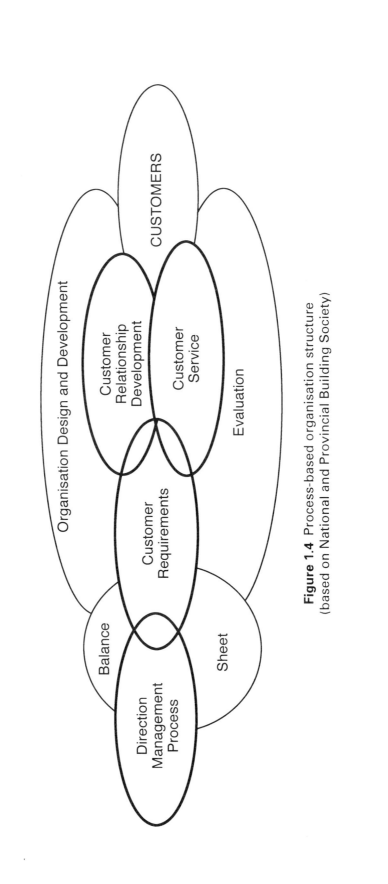

Figure 1.4 Process-based organisation structure (based on National and Provincial Building Society)

Inverting structures and including customers

In order to make the point that organisations exist to serve customers, and that head office staff exist to support the operating line management, organisation structures are now sometimes portrayed in an inverted form, as shown in Figure 1.5.

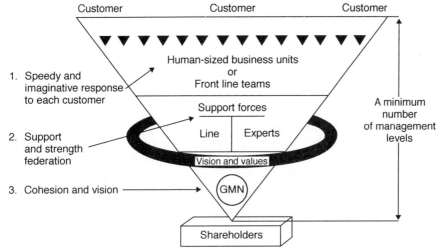

GMN = general managers network

Figure 1.5 Inverted organisation structure, emphasising customers and values

1.5 Factors influencing the choice of organisation structure

There is no one correct model with universal applicability. Organisations must introduce the structure most relevant to achieving their corporate goals, and to the prevailing circumstances, and must be prepared to change these structures as circumstances change. Some indicators which should assist in making this choice are provided below.

Stability of the environment

The environment relevant to the organisation should be analysed in terms of factors such as markets, clients, economic and financial circumstances, technology, legal constraints, power and politics. Stability in the environment indicates a stable formalised organisation structure; change in the environment indicates a more flexible decentralised form of structure. Today most organisations are facing change and require flexible structures.

Size

Sheer size has frequently in the past led to centralisation and bureaucracy. Because bureaucracy mitigates against successful change, many organisations now aim to decentralise into smaller accountable operating units and divisions.

Culture

Cultures are difficult to change, although change may be essential. The prevailing culture (i.e. norms and values attached to work) and the practical problems of changing it must be taken into account when planning change to structures. Culture is examined in more detail in the next section.

Internal labour market

The complexity and nature of work and the levels of education and professionalism of the workforce are important. A highly qualified professional workforce can by and large be left to get on with things; indeed, full professionals expect a high degree of autonomy, and prefer to work within a looser organisation structure. However, clear objectives and effective leadership are still necessary.

Technology of operations

Technology is changing fast, and a case in point is information technology, which can facilitate decision-making. An example of this is electronic point of sale (EPOS) in stores and supermarkets. Information on precisely what is being purchased is immediately transmitted to warehouses and head office, permitting centralisation of purchasing decisions.

Power

The five factors already discussed are rational factors. Power is not a rational factor, but is so important it must be mentioned. Internal power and politics, with individuals or groups attempting to gain or maintain control of an organisation, mean that structures are designed which reinforce the position of the most powerful group or groups. However, should this conflict too much with the rational needs of the organisation to survive and change in a dynamic environment, the power elite may lose their jobs.

1.6 Culture

Culture is now treated as a first-order strategy in many large organisations, and clearly involves human resources. 'Culture' became something of a buzz word during the 1980s in management circles, when it became fashionable to talk about changing an organisation's culture. The primary cause of the interest in culture was the success of Japanese manufacturers, and the assumption that their superiority was in part due to a supportive national and corporate culture. The book which more than any other publication helped to foster this interest in corporate culture was *In Search of Excellence*, by Tom Peters and Robert Waterman.[20] Based on a study of so-called 'excellent' American corporations, Peters and Waterman concluded that the key to excellence lay in achieving a state of shared values among all employees in an organisation. They also concluded that Western management had been placing far too much emphasis on what were perceived as the 'hard' factors of strategic decision-making, namely, structure, systems, and strategy. Excellent American (and Japanese) firms, however, placed equal emphasis on the 'soft' factors of staff, style and skills, with a special emphasis on shared values. This is illustrated in Figure 1.6 describing McKinsey's 7S model adapted and used by Peters and Waterman.

A number of the American companies portrayed as 'excellent' in 1982 could no longer be deemed to be excellent a few years later. For example, Walt Disney went through a period of producing unsuccessful films, Caterpillar lost a major share of its market for heavy plant machinery, Atari, well known for its computer games, suffered severe losses, and the jury is still out in the case of IBM. However, these failures did not diminish the interest in corporate culture as a key to achieving success.

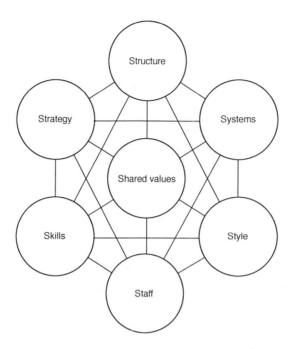

Figure 1.6 McKinsey's 7S framework

As well as placing an emphasis on shared values, Peters and Waterman promulgated a number of 'rules of thumb' for achieving excellence, many of which have passed into the vocabulary of managers everywhere. These include:

- a bias for action;
- close to the customer;
- autonomy and entrepreneurship;
- productivity through people;
- hands on, value-driven;
- stick to the knitting;
- simple form, lean staff;
- simultaneous loose-tight properties.

While these can be deemed to be simple 'motherhoods', they do underline certain home truths, for example, that productivity can only come through people. Whether these home truths have been fully understood and applied by top management in the UK is another matter. Only a handful of British companies reach international standards of excellence and quality.

A major criticism of the Peters and Waterman approach is that it fosters a continuation of the 'one best way' of managing philosophy perpetrated by scientific management writers in the first half of this century.[21] All the evidence from major studies of the connection between ways of organising and management, from Joan Woodward's classic study in the 1960s until the present day, show clearly that what may be the right approach for one organisation may be the wrong approach for another.[22]

Two well-known definitions of organisation culture illustrate alternative approaches relevant to strategy formulation:

Corporate culture is the pattern of basic assumptions that a given group has invented, discovered or developed in learning to cope with its problems of external adaptation and internal integration.

(Schein)[23]

The way we do things around here.

(Marvin Bower, managing director of a firm of management consultants (quoted by Deal and Kennedy))[24]

So management may attempt to change 'the way things are done around here' by direct intervention, orders, rewards, and personal example. Or they may attempt to alter patterns of basic assumptions by, for example, informing, educating, and advising.

Roger Harrison[25] described four types of prevailing organisation culture:

1. role culture;
2. power culture;
3. achievement culture;
4. support culture.

A role culture emphasises order, stability and control, and is based on a quest for security. Typical of a role culture might be an old-fashioned public sector bureaucracy. A power culture emphasises strength, decisiveness, and determination, and is based on a quest for control. Power cultures are found in some large private sector organisations where a handful of senior executives exert a large amount of power in an autocratic manner, and in privately owned smaller organisations where the controlling family may wield considerable power. Achievement cultures emphasise success, growth and distinction, and are based on self-expression. They may be found in some modern progressive organisations that encourage autonomy and self-expression. Support cultures are based on mutual service, integration and values, and are based on a sense of community. Charles Handy adapted this approach to come up with four types of organisation culture which correspond to conceptual 'maps' of organisation structures.[26] These are Power Cultures, Role Cultures (similar to Harrison's categories), Task Cultures and Person Cultures. Task Cultures place emphasis on the successful achievement of tasks and Person Cultures refer to organisations designed to create space for individuals to operate in and be creative.

Both these approaches link the predominating value system or culture to the design of the organisation, suggesting a match between structure and culture. This provides a useful reminder that if an organisation makes major changes to its structure it will need to promote a new and more congruent culture, and vice versa.

1.7 Human resource planning

First-order strategy is implemented through second- and third-order strategies. Third-order strategies in the HR area then find expression in human resource planning. It is frequently said of the Japanese that their success comes about through careful planning.[27] When the Nissan plant in the North East of England decided to build the new Micra model, they took on new employees up to nine months before production got under way in order to ensure that adequate training and team developments had taken place. This followed very careful selection of new employees.

This process has traditionally been referred to as manpower planning, but is now generally termed human resource planning. It aims to provide answers to questions such as:

- How many employees will we need next year?
- What skills and competencies will we need?
- What employee relations will we need?

- What is our current stock of human resources and skills?
- At what rates do we lose staff because of turnover?
- What sort of age structure do we have, and do we want?
- Should we train our staff, or buy them in?

The penalties for not carrying out human resource planning can be costly. Heavy costs can arise from not having staff ready and trained to operate new equipment and machinery, having to buy in staff at short notice, hire temporary staff, being faced with the consequences of a spate of unanticipated retirements, and probably most important of all, being unable to deliver a quality service to customers.

The simplest way of tackling human resource planning is by thinking of it in terms of demand and supply. Demand can be forecast from corporate plans. Supply can be forecast by working out the stock of manpower currently employed, calculating the likely shortfalls and surpluses, and planning accordingly.

Forecasting the likely demand for human resources should be a cooperative exercise between the corporate planners, line managers, and the HR department. Departmental heads should estimate their staffing needs and staffing budgets, a process which normally takes place at least once a year in medium and large organisations. Corporate planners then look at these estimates across the board and propose modifications to take account of forecast changes in markets and technology. At this stage the HR function can make an input in terms of proposed organisation change programmes and on the basis of information held on staffing needs.

Demand forecasting can normally be carried out with some degree of precision up to a year ahead, in other words, for as long ahead as markets and services to clients can be accurately forecast. However, longer-term forecasts of two to five years are also needed in order to plan expansion, recruitment, and 'downsizing' programmes and the appropriate training programmes for apprentices, graduates, and multi-skilling initiatives. These longer-term forecasts can be revised every year on a 'rolling' basis.

The supply side of human resource planning starts by ensuring accurate and up-to-date information is available on the current labour force. This requires good personnel records which provide easily retrievable data on human resources. Organisations employing more than 50 staff should as a rule use computerised personnel information systems (CPIS) to facilitate data retrieval and analysis.

1.8 Human resource information

Data on individual employees should include all the obvious information required for day-to-day purposes such as grade or status, address, sex, date of birth, insurance number, payroll number, next of kin, marital status, employment record, educational qualifications, ethnic origin, disabilities and fluency in foreign languages.

Keeping records accurately and up-to-date is essential. Employees are notoriously lax in notifying changes in their personal situation. One way of counteracting this is to supply individual employees with a print-out of their personal information at least once a year so that they can check and correct it if necessary.

Computerised personnel information systems facilitate the analysis of trends and the presentation of 'snapshots' or profiles of sections of the workforce. An example is provided by age profiles. These indicate whether an organisation, a department, or a group of employees sharing a common skill are 'top heavy' with a high proportion of staff rapidly approaching retirement age, 'bottom heavy' with a high proportion of young and less

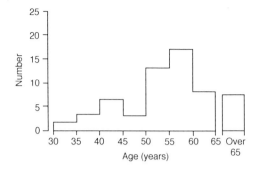

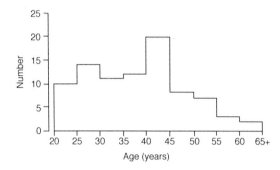

Figure 1.7 Two age profiles demonstrating
a lack of balance and a need for planning

experienced staff, or well balanced in their age distribution. Examples are shown in Figure 1.7.

It may of course be advantageous to have a top heavy group of employees if 'downsizing' is being planned, because they can be offered early retirement coupled with an early pension (in accordance with current income tax regulations). A bottom heavy profile may or may not be advantageous, depending on current circumstances; younger employees may be more energetic, but less experienced and more prone to leave.

Forecasts of labour wastage and absenteeism also need to be taken into account at this stage. Both these issues are examined in detail in the next chapter, in the context of recruitment and retention.

1.9 Putting the plan together

An examination of supply forecasts in the light of demand forecasts will indicate the areas where special initiatives are required to achieve balance. It is normal to draw up plans for action under a conventional list of functional headings, for example:

- Recruitment and selection: in which key areas should recruitment take place over the next twelve months?
- Training: what are the training and development priorities, and how should they be phased?
- Redundancies: where are redundancies likely to occur, and how should we set about consulting interested parties and arranging our placement or retraining activities?
- Employee relations: how should we maintain good relations with various worker representative groups and improve consultation and communication?
- Motivation: what new reward management initiatives and other measures to improve motivation are called for?

- Productivity and flexibility: what measures to improve productivity and flexibility, such as team working, are called for?
- Performance management: how can performance be managed better? Do appraisal schemes require review?
- Management development: what management development programmes are needed to develop appropriate competencies in managers in pursuit of new performance targets?

Clearly, there is overlap between these areas, but that is the way it should be. Human resource plans must be integrated into a concerted drive by line and HR managers to achieve organisational goals.

1.10 References

1. Faulkner D, Johnson G. *The challenge of strategic management.* London: Kogan Page, 1992.
2. Local Government Board. *Strategies for success.* London: HMSO, 1991.
3. Whittington R. *What is strategy, and does it matter?* London: Routledge, 1993.
4. Chandler AD. *The history of the American industrial enterprise.* Cambridge, MA: MIT Press, 1962.
5. Quinn JB. *Strategies for change: logical incrementalism.* Homewood, II: Richard D. Irwin, 1980.
6. Mintzberg H. Crafting strategy. *Harvard Business Review* 1987; July–August: 66–75.
7. Ansoff HI. Critique of Henry Mintzberg's 'The design school – reconsidering the basic premises of strategic management'. *Strategic Management Journal* 1991; **12**(6): 449–61.
8. Johnson G, Scholes K. *Exploring corporate strategy.* Hemel Hempstead: Prentice-Hall, 1989.
9. Brewster C, Larsen HH. Human resource management in Europe: evidence from ten countries. *International Journal of Human Resource Management* 1993; **3**(3): 409–34.
10. Butler PF. HR and strategic planning in eight top firms. *Organizational Dynamics* 1995: Summer.
11. Purcell J. The impact of corporate strategy on human resource management. In: Storey J ed. *New perspectives on human resource management.* London: Routledge, 1989.
12. Tyson S. *Human resource strategy.* London: Pitman, 1995.
13. Ohmae K. *The mind of the strategist.* London: Penguin, 1983: 224.
14. Lundy O, Cowling A. *Strategic human resource management.* London: Routledge, 1996.
15. Peters T. *Liberation management.* London: Macmillan, 1992.
16. Burns R, Stalker GM. *The management of innovation.* Welwyn Garden City: Tavistock Publications, 1961.
17. Bartlett CA, Ghoshal S. Matrix management: not a structure, a frame of mind. *Harvard Business Review* 1990; July–August: 138–45.
18. Hammer M, Champy J. *Re-engineering the corporation.* London: Brealey, 1994.
19. O'Brien R, Wainwright J. Winning as a team of teams – transforming the mindset of the organisation at National and Provincial Building Society. *Business Change and Re-engineering* 1993; **1**(3), Winter: 19–25.
20. Peters T, Waterman RH. *In search of excellence.* New York: Harper & Row, 1982.
21. Wilson D, Rosenfeld R. *Managing organisations.* London: McGraw-Hill, 1990.
22. Woodward J. *Industrial organisation: theory and practice.* London: Oxford University Press, 1965.
23. Schein E. *Organizational culture and leadership.* San Francisco: Jossey-Bass, 1985.
24. Deal TE, Kennedy A. *Corporate culture: the rites and rituals of corporate life.* Reading, MA: Addison Wesley, 1982.
25. Harrison R. How to describe your organization. *Harvard Business Review* 1972; Sept.–Oct. 119–28.
26. Handy C. *Understanding organisations.* Harmondsworth, Penguin, 1993.
27. Wickens P. *The Road to Nissan.* London: Macmillan, 1987.

SECTION I
MANAGING EMPLOYMENT

Introduction

Finding the right people is too important to be left to chance or to out-dated practices. 'Hire and fire' policies result in low levels of performance by demotivated employees who lack both the competencies needed to carry out tasks effectively, and the stability in employment that are the foundation of good customer relations. The same is true of 'crisis-management' recruitment procedures which attempt to replace key staff by desperate appeals to employment agencies, glossy but meaningless job advertisements, and employment interviews based on the maxim that 'I can spot winners as soon as they walk through the door'. Employees drive the modern business by creating products and services which can satisfy customers, and therefore there can be no substitute for carefully planned recruitment procedures, scientifically based selection methods, and those positive employment policies which motivate and retain high performers.

In the next two chapters valid and reliable methods of recruiting, selecting, and retaining employees in a manner consistent with the goals of the enterprise are outlined. The successful selection of employees is shown to be the fruitful culmination of carefully planned and well-researched recruitment procedures and the practical application of the latest developments in occupational psychology.

'Best practice' techniques of employment interviewing and psychometric testing are described and the most effective ways of retaining employees explored. The importance of job satisfaction is highlighted, and ways of developing 'psychological contracts' between employer and employed which lead to high levels of motivation are analysed.

2 Recruitment and retention

Alan Cowling

Renewing and retaining the stock of human resources are a primary task for organisations, and include all the considerations and activities involved in the sequence of attracting, selecting, starting new employees, and retaining the best. Done well, it can have an immediate and beneficial impact on performance when talented staff are taken on to carry out urgent and important tasks beyond the capacity of existing staff. Long-term benefits come about through recruitment over time of new employees with relevant aptitudes, abilities and motivation, capable of being developed into a high performance workforce. Because organisations consist of people, and because it is people, and only people, who can achieve success or failure, the success of an organisation is determined sooner or later by the calibre of its recruits and by the effectiveness of its recruitment and selection policies.

The process of recruitment encompasses a number of stages. Of primary concern is the development of a reputation as a good employer who attracts good quality applicants. Because selecting the best applicants merits a chapter on its own, a chapter on selection and occupational testing follows this chapter, and ideally the two should be read in conjunction.

Recruiting staff is, however, only one side of the coin. Retaining them is the other. Losing good staff represents a major loss of the investment that has gone into recruiting and training them, as well as having a serious impact on the work of their teams and departments. A positive policy on retention is therefore vital, and steps to achieve this are outlined later in this chapter.

2.1 Recruitment policy

The aim of a policy on recruitment should be to locate and attract good quality applicants and to make valid, reliable, and cost-effective decisions about whom to select. The first consideration is the best way to attract good quality applicants.

Whether good quality applicants apply for vacant positions depends on a number of factors. Among the most significant are the following:

- the reputation of the company as a good employer;
- how well the vacancy has been advertised;
- the attractiveness of the salary and conditions of service;
- whether potential applicants think they can do the job;
- whether the job looks interesting and satisfying.

The first consideration is the manner in which an organisation gains a reputation as a good employer. Large UK organisations such as Marks & Spencer, ICI, British Gas, and the National Health Service enjoy differing reputations as employers. Small firms likewise enjoy differing reputations in their local labour markets. While it takes years to build up a reputation as a good employer, reputations can be lost in months or even weeks by injudicious employment decisions, such as the well-publicised sacking of a group of employees carried out in a harsh and unsupportive manner.

The head of external liaison for British Airways has been quoted as saying that potential employees are as likely to be influenced by the overall image of a company as by the salary mentioned in an advertisement.[1] In a reported survey of 1000 employees, staff were asked to identify the five most important things they looked for in a job: 66 per cent said having an interesting and enjoyable job, 52 per cent said job security, 41 per cent said feeling they had accomplished something worthwhile, and 37 per cent said basic pay. Other staff surveys have found similar results.[2]

Recruitment policies need to be reviewed at regular intervals to ensure that they are offering the conditions and job opportunities that good applicants are looking for. Steps to follow in offering competitive salaries are examined in Chapter 12.

2.2 The labour market

To be effective, recruitment must take account of labour markets at both local and national levels. At local levels, this means gathering information about the supply and demand for recruits within an area defined by daily travel-to-work patterns. Manual workers are frequently reluctant to work more than five miles from where they live, while white-collar staff will travel further, either by public transport, if it is good, or by their own transport. Within this local labour market area the supply and demand for staff will be influenced by expansion and contraction by other employers, the rate at which local schools and colleges send young people into the labour market, new housing developments, and changes in public transport patterns. At national level demographic change and the entry of more women into the labour market are currently significant factors. Some companies rely on large intakes of school leavers every summer. Engineering companies may depend on an intake of new engineering graduates every autumn. From time to time various skill shortages affect the national labour market, especially during economic upturns, causing employers to complain bitterly, even though some of these skill shortages are a direct consequence of employers cutting back on training programmes in previous years.

Demographic change is the easiest national trend to anticipate because it is so well documented, yet employers are still caught out. The recent decline in the number of school leavers has been caused by the drop in birth rates 15 to 20 years ago. Because this decline has coincided with economic recession it has not had as much impact as was anticipated.

The current evidence is that while fewer young people are entering the labour market, more women are seeking employment, particularly on a part-time basis. Women are making up an increasing proportion of the labour force, although nearly half the women are in part-time jobs. More men are also in part-time jobs. In 1986, less than 8 per cent of mature men were in part-time work: ten years later it was nearly 20 per cent, according to the Government's Labour Force Survey. The cumulative drop in the workforce over the 5-year period 1990–95 amounted to 492 000 people. The number of men in the labour force fell by 498 000 and the female workforce grew by 6000. Since 1971 the number of women in the labour market has risen by almost a third, from 9.4 million to 12.1 million in 1995. The male workforce is, at 15.6 million in 1995, effectively the same as in 1971.

It is forecast that the current population bulge of workers in the 25–44 age range will gradually work its way upwards, creating an older workforce. There will be a fall of 1.2 million in the under-35 range. Fewer people are expected to enter employment in the next five years, partly for demographic reasons, partly because more young people will stay on in education.[3] Over the five years from 1995 to the end of the century, the UK labour force is projected to increase by 807 000, and by the year 2006 to rise by some 1.5 million. Most of this rise is forecast to be among women.

In the UK full-time workers have the longest working week of any state in the European Union. More than a third of male workers clock up over 48 hours a week. The European average working week for men is 41.1 hours, compared with the British figure of 45.4 hours. If staff shortages are anticipated, companies have a variety of options to consider, of which putting up rates of pay is only one, and may be self-defeating as other employers follow suit. Other options include:

- improved training;
- improved retention of staff;
- improved relations with local schools and colleges;
- more flexible use of labour;
- a more positive attitude to minority ethnic groups;
- employment of older workers.

2.3 Employment costs and the recruitment process

Employing people costs money. A decision to employ someone is equivalent to an investment decision costing thousands of pounds. In addition to basic salary, indirect benefits such as insurance, holidays, and occupational pensions can add another 30 per cent to employment costs. Then there is the cost of providing office or factory space, equipment and machinery. Add to this the cost of recruiting, selecting and training each new employee, and the costs mount up again. A basic annual salary of £15 000 becomes a cost of over £20 000 a year, plus possibly a further £5000 in equipment and support services. Initial recruitment and selection costs can easily add at least another £1000 per head. Because employees can no longer be hired and fired at whim, and are protected by employment legislation, employment costs should be treated as quasi-fixed costs in accounting terms, rather than variable costs.

Consider also the likely results of a bad selection decision. One 'bad apple' can soon upset others in the barrel. A bad employee can upset colleagues, customers, supervisors and subordinates. The result is further cost. Good selection pays a dividend; poor selection costs money.

All of this adds up to the need to give careful consideration before proceeding with employment. Is it essential to fill the vacancy? Can the work be redistributed? Are there suitable internal candidates? Does our human resource plan support recruitment at this time? A sensible sequence for tackling recruitment and selection that takes account of these important questions is provided in Figure 2.1.

2.4 Advertising for staff

There are many sources of potential recruits, ranging from respondents to factory gate notices, relatives and friends of existing employees, Job Centres, advertisements in the media, and employment agencies. Some offer free services, such as Job Centres, others, like advertising, are expensive. Over a period of time the HR department builds up a record of the cost and effectiveness of different sources of applicants to determine which offer best value for money.

Advertising for staff is big business. Nearly £470 million was spent by employers and their agencies in 1987, before the onset of the subsequent economic recession, and the figure is now considerably higher.[4] As a result, a sophisticated and thriving business has grown up. If use is going to be made of advertising agencies, care has to go into their

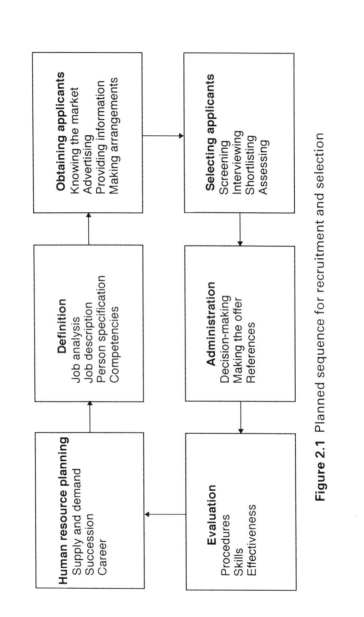

Figure 2.1 Planned sequence for recruitment and selection

selection. The professional body for UK advertising agencies is the Institute of Practitioners in Advertising (IPA), who operate a register of members. If a large-scale advertising campaign is planned, selected agencies can be asked to make presentations to the company, with the most convincing one then appointed. If occasional press advertisements are planned, then it is a good idea to appoint an agent to advise on the advertisement, to set it in copy form, and to place it in the desired newspapers or journals. Agencies book space in advance in the press, and it is frequently impossible to place an advertisement at short notice unless one goes through an agent. Agencies take a commission from the press, and therefore can frequently offer a good value service to employers.

What does a good advertisement include by way of information? More importantly, what do potential recruits want to see in advertisements? Evidence from surveys indicates that these are the priority items:

- place of work;
- salary;
- closing date for applications;
- how to apply;
- relevant experience;
- qualifications;
- duties;
- responsibilities;
- something about the organisation.

Advertising for staff is a form of selling – selling the job and selling the company in order to achieve the desired response.[5] It is therefore a good idea to start by asking the question: why might somebody want to do this job? Selling points can then be listed. A typical list might be: job interest, training provided, remuneration, technology, location. Following this, decisions can be made on the main headline, sub-headings and copy. The instructions on how to apply need to be clear. Today styles of advertising tend to be colloquial. Pomposity is avoided and language is kept simple and factual. Synergy with the overall corporate advertising style is desirable. Recording and analysing the results of advertising campaigns enable further advertising to concentrate on those channels that have demonstrated their success.

2.5 Short-listing

For most vacancies the objective of a recruitment campaign is to create a short-list of suitable candidates who match the requirements of the job specification. Provided an outline of essential and desirable requirements has been listed in the manner recommended (in the next chapter), a simple matching process can be carried out, matching the applicant's profile against those required by the job. If large numbers apply, however, this can be time-consuming, and an indication that the advertisement was too loosely worded.

The matching process is facilitated if application forms are designed so that the headings match job specifications. They also need to be designed with an eye to the organisation's current information systems, because personal data on the application form can be used for record purposes should the applicant be appointed and commence work. Factors such as education, qualifications, work experience, training, and special skills feature on most application forms, plus space for statements on health and disabilities. Personality, however, remains a contentious area. Space is normally provided for a description of leisure interests; this may provide some indication of personal characteristics, especially with school and college leavers (the subject of personality in the context of psychometric testing is addressed in the next chapter). It is also useful to leave free space for candidates to indicate why they think they are suitable for the position. Larger organisations employing a range of staff may need more than one application form. Forms for relatively straightforward work, such as manual work, can be kept simpler than the forms needed for more demanding professional and supervisory positions.

2.6 'The psychological contract'

The culmination of a recruitment process is normally a contract of employment. In the UK a legal contract has to be issued within strict time limits in the great majority of cases, and the manner in which this has to be drawn up is examined in some detail in Chapter 9. However, new employees commence employment with a wider set of expectations than those encompassed in the formal contract of employment. Employers in turn have a set of expectations concerning the behaviour of employees that is wider than the formal contract. Expectations on both sides are shaped by societal norms, local culture, and custom and practice. Western society is individualistic, and hence the employment relationship focus is normally on an individual's relations with his or her employer. Therefore the set of expectations on both sides is termed a 'psychological contract'. The significance of this 'contract' lies in the impact it can have on behaviour, job satisfaction, motivation and performance, and hence on the successful implementation of corporate strategy. This is brought out in Figure 2.2.

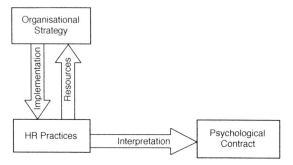

Source: Robinson, Kraatz, Rousseau, Changing obligations

Figure 2.2 Psychological contract, HR practices and organisational strategy

Various definitions exist. Most refer to something that is essentially subjective, based on people's perceptions, and mention such matters as loyalty, trust and recognition. It is generally accepted that mutual obligations are the essence of this psychological contract.[6] Obligations have been usefully defined as follows:

> beliefs, held by an employee or employer, that each is bound by promise or debt to an action or course of action in relation to the other party. These obligations may derive from explicit or implicit promises of future exchange or reciprocity. Each party possesses his or her own perception of the mutual obligations defining a relationship.[7]

Interest in this matter has been heightened by the recent debate over whether loyalty still exists within corporations, and whether mutual trust between employers and employees has been undermined by corporate downsizing and delayering. While some observers lament the passing of loyalty and trust, others welcome a new era in which change is the order of the day, and employees can take control of their own careers.

Recent research in the UK indicates that a higher level of confidence in management prevails than recent events may have led one to expect. A survey carried out on behalf of the IPD in 1996 of a random sample of working people found that 82 per cent considered their employers to be fair, 72 per cent were positive on the issue of trusting their employers, and 67 per cent expected to still be with their companies in five years' time. The overall results lead to the conclusion that the psychological contract is still perceived in traditional terms by most working people. Perceptions were most positive in those companies that had implemented modern 'high commitment' HRM policies, and least positive amongst the semi-skilled and un-skilled, and those on temporary contracts.

Middle management has attracted considerable attention in this context because it has been perceived as hardest hit by company downsizing and delayering exercises. A research study in the UK found that in spite of recent events, most middle managers still felt a sense of commitment to their employers. What they want is more variety at work, more responsibility, and the resources to help them meet these new demands. Looking ahead, the study concluded that the changing balance of core and peripheral workers currently taking place will influence both legal and psychological employment contracts. A new model of employment relationships has been proposed by Peter Herriott to cater for the three emerging types of employment relationships, one that will satisfy both organisational and individual needs, as illustrated in Table 2.1.[8]

Table 2.1 New model of employment relationships

Contract	Individual offers	Organisation offers	Risks
Development (core)	Flexibility Continuous added value Commitment, not dependence Innovation	Security Employability Use of skills core to the organisation's purpose Continuous development	Exploitation of security needs Life imbalance Insufficient security to allow for risk-taking Generality of skills will reduce their external market value
Autonomy (project)	Ready access to specific skills Experience gained in a wide range of organisations High performance with low management	Autonomy to exercise skills Freedom in how individuals work Challenge Experience that increases employability	Performance delivery undermined by: inadequate resources, poor management or organisational politics/culture Constraints on how they work
Lifestyle (part-time)	Flexibility in matching demand and resourcing Performance levels to match customer expectations Performance levels of full-time employees	Willingness to balance work and other role demands	Pay and conditions exploitation Lack of career development

Source: Herriott and Pemberton, A new deal for middle managers

Evidence from the USA also indicates some deterioration in psychological contracts.[9] This has led to exhortations to employees to build their own identities and careers instead of subordinating their needs to the corporation, and to employers to take responsibility for helping their workers to maintain employability.[10] In this vein, Rosabeth Moss Kanter[11] supports a model company employment statement that promises to:

- recruit for the potential to increase in competence, not simply for narrow skills to fill today's slots;
- offer ample learning opportunities, from formal training to lunchtime seminars – the equivalent of one month per year;
- provide challenging jobs and rotating assignments that allow growth in skills even without promotion to better jobs;
- measure performance beyond accounting numbers and share the data to allow learning by doing and continuous improvement;
- retrain employees as soon as jobs become obsolete;
- recognise individual and team achievements, thereby building external reputations and offering tangible indicators of value;
- provide three-month educational sabbaticals or external internships every five years;
- find job opportunities through the network of suppliers, customers, and venture partners;
- tap our people's ideas to develop innovations that lower costs, serve customers, and create markets – the best foundation for business growth and continuing employment.

2.7 Retention

Positive staff retention policies, if they are to be effective, must be based on measurement and analysis. Staff wastage can be measured in a number of ways, making use of information from the HR records database. The most commonly used measure is crude labour turnover on an annualised basis: the number of employees who have left in a calendar year, expressed as a percentage of the average number of employees during that year, as shown below:

Staff turnover of clerical officers employed in a local authority
Average number employed during the year   = 1000
Number who left employment during the year   = 100
Turnover is $\dfrac{100 \times 100}{1000} = 10\%$

This turnover figure can and should be calculated for departments and skill groups as well as for the organisation as a whole. Where considerable variations between departments are revealed, there needs to be a follow-up study to find out why some departments are showing relatively higher figures. High turnover is frequently an indication of low morale, poor supervision, unsatisfying work, or poor working conditions. However, this statistic can be misleading unless a stability figure is calculated at the same time. This is because it provides no indication as to whether a range of jobs in a department are experiencing turnover, or only a few jobs. Thus in the illustration provided above, the 100 leavers might have all been in the same job, lasting only a day or two before departing, or in 100 different jobs. A stability index is calculated by expressing the number of employees in a department or job category with more than twelve months' service as a percentage of the average number employed:

Stability of clerical officers employed in a local authority
Average number employed during the year   = 1000
Number with one or more years' service   = 950
Stability is $\frac{950}{1000} = 95\%$

Taken together, in this case these two statistics show that turnover is only a problem in a few of the clerical posts in the example. But for human resource planning purposes more than one year's figures are required to establish a trend and provide confidence in predictions of what might happen over the next one to three years. Contextual data also need to be collected, such as levels of unemployment and relative pay rates.[12] The likely impact of labour wastage on the stock of manpower over the next few years can then be used to predict the numbers likely to remain voluntarily in post. It can also be used as an input into more sophisticated modelling of the flows of manpower between grades. This can be of assistance in calculating likely promotion rates, and for career planning purposes. Computer-based mathematical models assist this process. Most models assume a traditional hierarchical graded organisation structure to predict flows into and out of grades within an organisation, as illustrated in Figure 2.3.

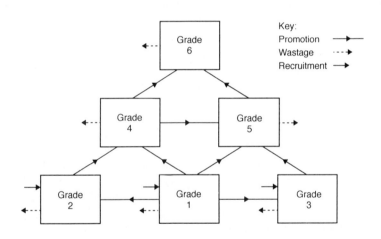

Figure 2.3 Model of manpower flows in a traditional organisation structure

Recent years have seen a shift away from hierarchical structures with a large number of levels to organisations based on smaller operating units with few layers, as already outlined in the previous chapter. This trend to simpler structures with lean staffing levels makes the need for planning even more important but turns the emphasis from quantitative to qualitative changes in the workforce. Forecasts are needed for both the numbers likely to remain in employment, and whether staff will possess the attitudes and skills that a changing environment will demand. Because of this, many organisations now place emphasis on multi-skilling and flexibility, enabling employees to tackle a range of tasks and to respond flexibly to as yet unforeseen demands from customers or their public masters.

2.8 Measuring absenteeism

Human resource management is concerned with achieving and retaining a committed and productive labour force, and high levels of absenteeism, like wastage, indicate a failure to achieve these goals. Additionally, human resource planning requires forecasts of attendance as well as wastage, and measures of absenteeism over a number of years are needed in order to measure trends and to make sensible forecasts.

Three measures of absenteeism are useful – *percentage of lost working days, days lost per working year* and *average length of absence*. Percentage of lost working days is calculated by expressing the number of days actually lost as a percentage of the number of days which should have been worked in a year. The most frequently used formula is:

$$\frac{\text{Number of days lost}}{\text{Total number of working days}} \times 100$$

Some organisations prefer to simply state the number of working days lost in a year per category of employee. The third measure is achieved by dividing the number of days lost by the number of absences to calculate the average length of each absence.[13]

An example of the first measure, expressed as a national problem, is provided by an Industrial Society survey which showed the national UK sickness absence rate running at 3.97 per cent, with absence rates in the public sector of 4.57 per cent, compared with 3.87 per cent in the private sector.[14] The same report estimated that workers in the UK take 200 million days off on sick leave each year at a total cost of £9 billion. Evidence from the Health and Safety Commission shows sick absence costing Britain £25 billion a year.[15] Days lost through sickness varies considerably by industry. Transport workers on average lose 20 days a year, manual workers in London boroughs 19.3 days a year, coal miners 9 days a year, shop workers 7 days a year, and financial services staff 5 days a year, with a national average of 7 days a year. The OECD (Organisation for Economic Cooperation and Development) has reported that Britain had the worst absenteeism in the industrialised world, losing 113 million working hours each year compared, for example, with France's 51 million. The Labour Force Survey conducted by the Office of National Statistics in 1995 showed 275 000 public sector workers, 4.5 per cent of the 5 959 000 total, absent from work for at least one day in a particular week singled out for measurement that summer. This figure was 50 per cent greater than the comparable figure in the private sector. Sick leave in the Civil Service totalled 3.6 million working days in 1994.

Measurement reveals the size of the problem. Yet it is a problem which many organisations do not take seriously, to their cost. It may be that because most absenteeism is put down to sickness, there is a feeling that little can be done. However, this is not the case. Some organisations achieve far better absenteeism levels than others.

2.9 Controlling absenteeism and wastage

Absenteeism and labour wastage represent a decision by the employee not to turn up for work. If reasons can be found why employees are not turning up for work or are quitting their jobs, a search for solutions can commence.

Some non-attendance is involuntary. Employees may be genuinely too ill to come to work or may have suffered a major domestic crisis. Therefore there is a basic minimum level below which it is unreasonable to expect non-attendance to fall. As noted, the national average for sickness-related absenteeism is 7 days a year. Some organisations achieve considerably lower figures. Research and common sense both point to a number of factors which influence non-attendance. These include penalties for non-attendance, the expectation that non-attendance is being closely monitored, the commitment of employees to the work they are doing, the degree of job satisfaction achieved at work, and relationships with fellow workers and bosses. A list of relevant factors provided in a model devised by Steers and Rhodes in 1978, and still relevant today, is shown in Figure 2.4.[16]

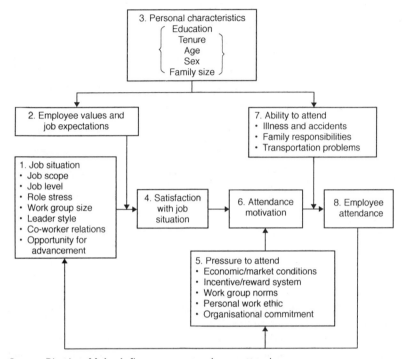

Source: Steers, Rhodes, Major influences on employee attendance

Figure 2.4 Factors influencing attendance and absenteeism

If measurement indicates that there is a problem, the first stage is to locate where it exists, i.e. in which departments, or categories of employee. The second stage is to try to find out the cause or causes of the problem by interviews with staff and supervisors and use of questionnaires. Steps to tackle the problem can then be initiated, and followed up to see if they are working. An example of a successful scheme, which had the desired effect of reducing absenteeism to a satisfactory level, is provided in Figure 2.5.

Controlling labour wastage requires a similar approach, namely, measurement, location of the problem, finding the reasons, implementing measures, and reviewing progress. The most significant difference, however, lies in the difficulties in establishing why people are leaving. When people give in their notice it is important that they should be interviewed by their head of department, and in some cases, by an HR executive. They may also be asked to state their reason for leaving in writing or by ticking the reason on a short-list of possible reasons. However, the fact is that leavers are frequently reluctant to tell the truth, the whole truth, and nothing but the truth about their reasons for leaving. They may not wish to upset people, or may be afraid to tell the truth, or not wish to jeopardise the reference they may need from their employer. Following up staff after they have left usually results in a very poor response. There is no easy solution to this problem, although a trained interviewer can usually get somewhere near the truth.

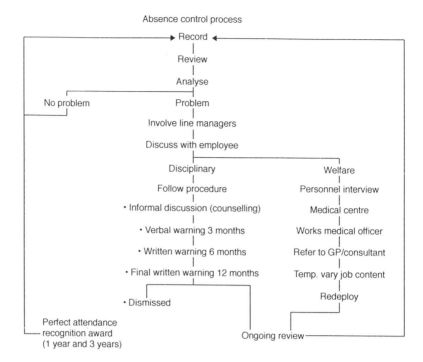

Figure 2.5 Example of company absence control procedure

A more positive way of tackling labour wastage is to focus on why people stay, rather than why they leave. As the overriding objective is to achieve high levels of productivity and motivation, it is important to find out why staff stay, and what they find good about the job, as well as their criticisms. Regular attitude surveys are of great assistance and enable management to deal not only with complaints, but more importantly, to enhance the positive aspects of employment packages.

Improved retention is achieved by paying attention to the factors that enhance employment, both financial and psychological. Unfortunately evidence is building up that levels of job satisfaction in the UK have declined over the past 20 years. A large-scale survey by International Survey Research (ISR) showed only 53 per cent of British workers responding favourably to questions on terms and conditions of employment in 1995, compared with 64 per cent in 1975. Employee satisfaction with pay and benefits had deteriorated over the last ten years by 14 per cent, with colleagues and managers by 15 per cent, and with opportunities for personal and career development by 17 per cent. The survey covered 17 European countries, and showed the British as second only to the Hungarians in their overall level of job dissatisfaction.[17] There is clearly a lot more to be done to improve job satisfaction and employee retention in the UK.

2.10 References

1. Olins R. Polishing up the image in the skills crisis. *Sunday Times* 5 November 1989.
2. Industrial Society Press. *Blueprint for success: a report on involving employees in Britain.* London: May, 1989.
3. *Social trends.* London: HMSO, 1996.
4. Wheeler D. How to recruit a recruitment agency. *Personnel Management* April 1988.
5. Arkin A. Sold on interest. *People Management Review* 1996; 13 June: 9–13.

6. Rousseau DM. Psychological and implied contracts in organizations. *Employee Rights and Responsibilities Journal* 1989; 2: 121–39.
7. Robinson SL, Kraatz MS, Rousseau DM. Changing obligations and the psychological contract: a longitudinal study. *Academy of Management Journal* 1994; **37**(1): 137–52.
8. Herriot P, Pemberton C. A new deal for middle managers. *People Management* 1995; 15 June: 32–4.
9. Robinson *et al.*, Changing obligations.
10. Heckscher C. *White collar blues: management loyalties in an age of corporate restructuring.* New York: Basic Books, 1995.
11. Kanter RM. Creating a habitat for the migrant manager. *Personnel Management* 1992; October: 38–40.
12. Bevan S. *The management of labour turnover.* IMS Report no. 137, Brighton: Institute of Manpower Studies, 1987.
13. IDS Study *Controlling absence.* Study 498, London: Incomes Data Services, January 1992.
14. Industrial Society. *Wish you were here.* London: March 1993.
15. Thomson A. Unhealthy trends in Britain's sick leave. *The Times* 12 June 1991.
16. Steers RM, Rhodes SR. Major influences on employee attendance: a process model. *Journal of Applied Psychology* 1978; August: 393.
17. Whitfield M. Britain grapples with changing job market. *People Management* 1996; December: 10–11.

3 Selection methods

John Lane and Tanya Pyne

3.1 Introduction

The process of selection is perhaps the most important of activities in managing human resources. To say an organisation is only as good as the people in it is a cliché, but like most clichés it is substantially true. Choosing the right person for the job enhances organisation efficiency by ensuring the job is well done. More than this, effective selection can help enable 'promotion from within' and make management development policies practical realities. In this latter context selection must be seen in the light of the company's manpower plan which follows from its business plan.

The importance of good selection is highlighted by the effects of making wrong choices, for example:

- increased recruitment costs from having to readvertise a vacancy and time spent screening application forms, writing letters, setting up initial interviews and other assessment methods;
- the damaging effect on team morale – caused by staff instability – can be aggravated by diminishing respect for a management which has demonstrably showed lack of judgement through its selection methods;
- while the vacancy remains or the wrong person is in the job, the job is not being properly done, creating an opportunity cost to the organisation which can be substantial.

The chances of picking the right person at the outset are greatly influenced by the choice of assessment available to management and the degree of accuracy employed to assess knowledge, competencies and personality traits.

Selection is essentially a two-way process where the employing organisation seeks to assess the suitability of applicants in terms of what it requires. Applicants make similar judgements on their own criteria, i.e. what they want from the job and from the organisation.

Selection is very much a process concerned with making a prediction from data obtained about candidates from methods of assessment such as cognitive tests and personality measures about how they will perform once in the job. From the individual's point of view the process is similar except that the prediction is based upon the perceived demands of the job, e.g. effort, abilities, pressures, etc. and the self-assessed abilities and motivations of any individual.

The assessment applicants make has been described as their self-efficacy;[1] this is the confidence they have in their own abilities to do the job successfully. Applicants are unlikely to take a job unless they feel they can do it. Similarly, a potential employer would only offer a job if it was felt that the candidate would be successful in it. Unfortunately both individuals and organisations can make predictions often based on insufficient evidence or data and sometimes these predictions are wrong – resulting in further recruitment costs; the opportunity costs of a vacancy not filled; the (often negative) impact on team morale and the effect on the individual.

How well methods of assessment, including self-efficacy, actually work depends on their predictive validity and the concept of validity as a whole which has a fundamental impact on the efficiency of the selection process. Since the purpose of assessment is to discriminate between job applicants – on legal grounds – in terms of their suitability for the job, the assessment methods used are all forms of tests. The term 'tests' is used to refer to the generality of assessment methods.

3.2 Validity

The validity of an assessment method, e.g. psychometric tests, interview, work sample, assessment centre ratings, concerns what the test measures and how well it does so. The word 'valid' is meaningless in the abstract, i.e. without specific reference to the particular use for which the test is being considered. All procedures for determining validity are concerned with performance on the test and other independently observable or specified behaviours. There are four types of validity, as follows:

1. content-related validity
2. criterion-related validity
3. construct-related validity
4. face validity.

Content-related validity

If a test samples and measures the knowledge, skills or behaviours required to perform the job successfully then the test has content validity. Content validity is usually determined by a detailed job analysis, with each duty or task described – together with the associated knowledge and skills required to perform it. The most important and the most frequent activities should be identified so that the job analysis provides an accurate picture of the whole and also provides a weighting for the skills and knowledge required when compiling the Person Specification.

There should be a direct relationship between job content and test item. For example, when recruiting secretaries for whom spelling might be an important ability, a preferred method of testing this would be to dictate a passage involving words typically used in the job and then checking for errors of spelling, rather than use a multiple choice test with the instruction to 'Underline the correctly spelled word'. Content validity can also play an important role in deciding issues of unfair discrimination.

Criterion-related validity

This kind of validity is a measure of the relationship between performance on a test and performance on a criterion or set of job performance criteria – these might be competencies, performance ratings or objective measures.

This type of validity is in many ways the most important to successful selection given that the selection process is essentially predictive. There are two types of criterion-related validity – *concurrent validity* and *predictive validity* – and these are now explained.

Concurrent validity: The concurrent validity of a test is established by selecting a large sample (about 100) of existing job holders and asking them to complete the test. These job holders are then assessed on their work performance – the assessment usually being done by immediate managers, who do not have prior knowledge of individual test results. Performance criteria might be 5- or 7-point rating scales or sometimes job holders are grouped into high, medium and low performers. Scores on the test are then matched against performance and a test is said to have concurrent validity if there is a statistically significant relationship between test scores and performance.

Predictive validity: Predictive validity refers to the extent to which scores on a test actually predict performance criteria. For example, to establish the predictive validity of a test of numerical reasoning ability job applicants would take the test but the results would not be used to influence the hiring decision. Instead, applicants would be selected by whatever existing assessment methods currently apply. At a later stage, perhaps after 6 months or so of being in employment, performance criteria ratings would be obtained and matched against the scores the former applicants (now employees) obtained on the numerical reasoning test. If there is a close relationship between test score and job performance then the test can be said to have significant predictive validity.

Concurrent vs predictive validity: Since selection involves prediction, it follows that organisations would carry out a predictive validity study before introducing any new methods of assessment. There is no doubt that such studies provide the best evidence for adopting or rejecting an assessment technique. In practice, however, they are rarely used, for a number of reasons.

First, the costs involved; it might be that in the case quoted above the numerical reasoning test was a poor predictor of performance. While it could be argued that this is still important knowledge it is not always easy to convince organisations of this. A further problem is sample size: for a validation study to have any statistical credibility this should be around the 100 mark. So with a predictive validity study we are looking for 100 applicants for the same or similar jobs who are subsequently hired. Except in 'start up' situations, it may take all but the very largest employers many years to reach a figure of 100 new starters, by which time many of the early starters may have left, performance criteria may be changed, the job may have become more/less difficult due to the economic environment, technology may have changed the job, etc. Such difficulties make predictive validity studies a comparatively rare event except in the largest and most stable organisations.

Concurrent validity studies, on the other hand, are somewhat easier to conduct. The problem of sample size is still an issue, tending to make it difficult for small to medium-sized firms to carry them out. It is a relatively large organisation which will employ 100 people all engaged in the same or broadly similar jobs. However, given sufficient people, the time factor is not an issue. Other factors, however, which need to be considered, perhaps principally the need to allay the employees' fears that they are completing tests for the sole purpose of research into a new assessment method and not as criteria for 'selection' for redundancy or some other unwelcome change.

Several factors limit the extent to which concurrent validity can be used as an indicator of predictive validity. First, if a test has content validity, i.e. it measures ability needed in the job, then experience in the job may improve performance on the test, producing average test scores less likely to be attained by job applicants – thus potentially good employees may be wrongly rejected. Second, the conditions in which job seekers as against existing staff compete may also make a difference to comparable results. For example, a test involving problem-solving may be done less well by people with higher anxiety levels (job seekers) than by existing staff for whom the outcome is not pass or fail. Nevertheless, concurrent validity studies are easier to undertake than predictive studies and many organisations do carry them out and use the results as best evidence about validity prior to 'going live', using a new assessment method as a selection tool.

The criteria problem

There are some problems associated with defining and measuring performance criteria. Since criterion-related validity is a measure of the relationship between scores or performance on an assessment method and how well people actually do the job – the performance criteria – it follows that if it is not possible to obtain criteria which permit accurate evaluation between people and which reflect the real purpose of the job, then the results of validation studies are devalued. Job criterion measures fall broadly into two categories:

1. objective criteria
2. subjective criteria.

Objective criteria: Objective criteria measures generally refer to performance outputs or aspects of the job which can be objectively measured. Some examples are the volume, quantity or calls to order ratio for sales people; the number of times the telephone rings before it is answered as a measure of the efficiency of a switchboard operator; delivering a project on time, within budget and up to quality might be criterion measures for evaluating the performance of a project manager.

The problem of using such measures as indicators of job success is that there is a tendency to select those aspects of a job more easily measurable but not necessarily of fundamental importance to the core of a job. For example, with the telephone operator, the manner in which a telephone is answered might be more important to the image of an organisation than the fact that the telephone was answered after 3–4 rings. Of course, a best position is where the telephone is answered promptly and in the right manner, but where measurable criteria are in place, concentration tends to be placed on them sometimes to the detriment of 'softer' but equally important criteria.

A further issue is the extent to which 'outside' factors, i.e. outside the control of employees, affect performance. For example, decreases in labour turnover may reflect high unemployment and lack of job opportunities elsewhere rather than the efficiency of management policy on employee retention. In the same way, changes in exchange rates may have substantial effects on the volume of export sales but nothing whatsoever to do with the quality or abilities of export sales people, making individual assessment on sales criteria very difficult. Such situations in themselves render so-called objective assessment open to subjective influence. An assessor might attribute improvements in export sales in some individual cases to changes in exchange rates, yet in other cases to improvements in selling ability – in the former attributing changes to the situation and in the latter making attributions to the person. Ways of establishing more reliable objective criteria are discussed later.

Subjective criteria: Perhaps the most frequently used example of subjective criteria is based often on competencies and/or overall performance and invariably using a 5- or 7-point rating scale. It is not the intention here to review or discuss the somewhat exhaustive findings on the bias inconsistency and error associated with such ratings. Perhaps the best-known of these errors is the 'halo' effect, defined by Saal *et al.* (1980)[2] as a 'rater's failure to discriminate between conceptually and potentially independent aspects of the ratee's behaviour' (in the case of performance criteria, raters may not be able to make distinct judgements between a ratee's position with regard to separate competencies), thus, for example, the individual rated, say, 5 on 'managing people' will be likely to be judged similarly on 'problem solving' or 'planning and organisation'. A further error comes from leniency or severity meaning a tendency to assign a higher or lower rating than performance warrants.[3] Finally there is a tendency for raters to rate around the mid-point of the scale – ignoring the outer limits – an error of central tendency leading to restriction of range.

Rater characteristics also affect ratings; Herriot (1984)[4] reports sex and occupation interaction in such a way that female workers are rated less favourably when in traditional masculine occupations. Ethnic origin and gender also interact: Herriot also cites incidences where the more white men there were as assessors in an assessment centre, the lower black women were rated.

Clearly all inadequacies in being able accurately to measure the efficiency of one employee against another can have serious effects on the results of any criterion validity study and, more importantly, can make selection more like a lottery than a systematic, logical process.

Construct-related validity

The construct-related validity of a test is the extent to which the test is measuring some theoretical ability, construct or trait. As an example, take a personality trait such as extroversion and assume the task is to construct a set of interview questions which will give an accurate measure of the trait. The construct validity of the interview can be established by having all the interviewees complete a personality test which measures 'extroversion'. If interviewees are defined as extroverts via the interview and as extroverts via the personality measure then the interview can be said to have construct validity. Establishing construct validity may involve quite extensive studies and a large number of people to achieve statistical respectability.

Face validity

Finally, an assessment method will have face validity if questions or test items are seen by candidates to be reflective of the nature of the job. Thus in devising a test for would-be accountants, face validity would be enhanced if terms used in the accounting profession featured in the test, e.g. profit, depreciation, costs, budget, etc. While there is no evidence that face validity affects candidates' performance, the use of job-relevant items and questions will serve to give applicants more information about the job, thus facilitating the self-selection process mentioned above.

3.3 Correlation

Construct- and criterion-related validity are assessed and expressed by a correlation coefficient while content and face validity are assessed by more qualitative means. The *correlation coefficient* (denoted by 'r') indicates the strength of the relationship between two (or more) variables and takes on values ranging from −1.0 (perfect negative relationship) to 0 (no relationship), and to +1.0 (perfect positive relationship). This is linear correlation which assumes a straight line relationship between the variables. Some examples may help to clarify this, as shown by Figures 3.1–3.3.

Changes in room temperature and changes in the mercury level of a thermometer would represent a correlation of +1.0 as temperature increases and the mercury level moves up the scale. Zero correlation might be indicated by changes in body temperature and times of the day – assuming the body remains still and is healthy – the body will maintain a constant temperature regardless of time. A negative correlation occurs when decreases in one variable are associated with increases in another; for example, number of days training in interview techniques and volume of staff turnover within the first three months of employment, the implication being that more effective assessment leads to lower staff turnover.

The coefficient of correlation under certain measurement conditions represents the slope of a straight line with a value of r = 1.0 being perfect correlation shown by a 45° line going through the origin of the graph. A line with a slope of 0 would be horizontal, indicating a correlation coefficient of 0. Correlation analysis provides a line which provides the best mathematical fit to the data – even though as can be seen in Figure 3.2 the fit is still poor.

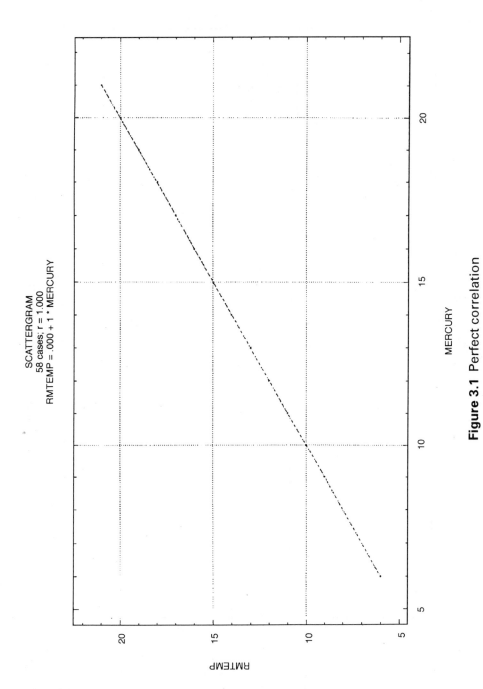

SCATTERGRAM
58 cases; r = 1.000
RMTEMP = .000 + 1 * MERCURY

MERCURY

RMTEMP

Figure 3.1 Perfect correlation

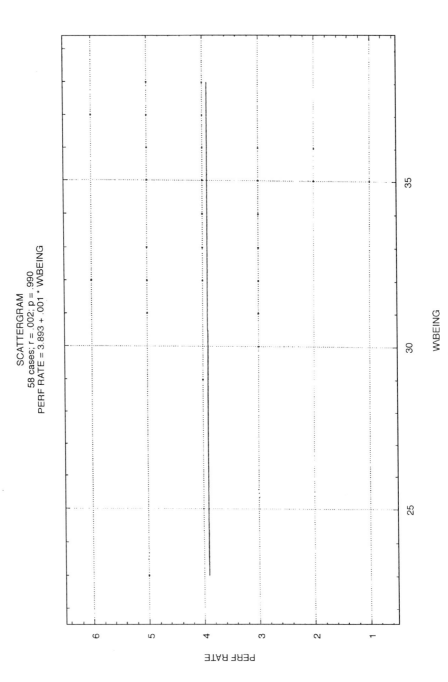

Figure 3.2 Zero correlation

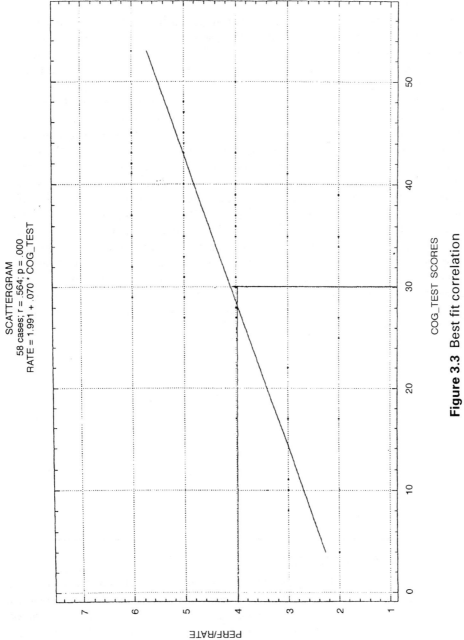

SCATTERGRAM
58 cases; r = .564; p = .000
RATE = 1.991 + .070 * COG_TEST

Figure 3.3 Best fit correlation

Figure 3.1 gives an example of perfect correlation, r = 1.0. All the points representing room temperature and levels of mercury lie on the straight line. Note that where r = 1.0 there is perfect prediction, thus if room temperature moves to 10° from 15° then the mercury level will do likewise. Regrettably, correlation of this magnitude is never encountered in the selection field.

Figure 3.2 represents a zero correlation between performance ratings for 58 middle managers in a wholesale newspaper firm and their scores on the personality trait of 'sense of well-being'. Note the straight line is horizontal. It can be seen that the dots where the variables have been plotted against each other are almost randomly distributed and bear no obvious relationship to the horizontal line. In terms of prediction the graph is of no use; changes in performance ratings have no bearing on difference in 'personal well-being'.

Figure 3.3 represents a scattergram showing the relationship between scores on a test of verbal and numerical ability and overall performance ratings for 58 managers employed in a leading grocery organisation. Note the scatter points are distributed around the straight line rather than on it, emphasising that the line is one of 'best fit' with a correlation coefficient of r = 0.564, which represents high criterion-related validity. Even so, it was decided that the cut-off point on test score is 30, with a corresponding performance rating of 4. Thus anyone scoring less than 30 would be rejected. (All the points in the area less than 30 but not more than 4 represent rejections – in spite of satisfactory ratings.) These scores are termed 'false negatives'. Similarly, there would have been a number of 'false positives' shown by the points in the area exceeding 30, but less than 4. These people would have been recruited only to have turned out unsuccessful, given a criterion of minimum performance rating of 4. Fortunately, in the majority of cases the predictions would have been accurate. From such examples it can be seen that the greater the value of r, the greater the degree of accuracy in prediction, as Table 3.1 shows.

Table 3.1 The correlation coefficient and forecasting accuracy

Value of r_{xy}	Percentage reduction in errors of prediction of y from x
0.0	0.0
0.2	2.0
0.25	3.2
0.35	6.3
0.40	8.3
0.45	10.0
0.50	13.4
0.60	20.0

3.4 Measuring validity

Construct- and criterion-related validities are measured by a correlation coefficient. In the case of criterion-related validity the variables are scored on the assessment method and on some criterion measures. The resulting correlation is known as a *validity coefficient*. With construct-related validity, the correlation may be between scores on two similar tests, e.g. if scores on two tests of general cognitive ability correlate with a validity coefficient of r = 0.8, then it can reasonably be assumed that both tests are measuring the same type of ability.

Construct-related validity may also be assessed using factor analytical statistical techniques which are beyond the scope and purpose of this book. Content-related validity is assessed through qualitative means, using observation and interpretation. For example, comparing job analysis and person specifications with test questions will provide evidence that the assessment method is designed to measure the competencies, knowledge, etc. required to do the job. A similar situation occurs with face validity.

3.5 Reliability

Reliability is a key concept used in the evaluation of methods of assessment. It is defined as 'the consistency of scores obtained by the same person when re-examined with the same test on different occasions or different sets of equivalent items (questions) or under other variable examining conditions'.[5]

Consistency or stability is another necessary condition for test validity. A test is of no value if someone, for example, is classified as an extrovert on first being tested but emerges as an introvert if the same personality test is completed a week later. Any criterion-related validity study using such data would be seriously flawed. Perhaps more graphically, if a rule measures a piece of cloth as 1 metre on one occasion but as 1.1 metres on another, then the ruler is of very limited use as a measure – the same principle applies with tests.

Measuring reliability

The most widely used measure is known as test–retest reliability. Here the same people complete the same test on two occasions, the two sets of scores are then correlated and the resulting coefficient is known as a 'reliability coefficient'. The time interval between tests has a bearing on the value of the reliability coefficient – the longer the interval, the lower the coefficient.

Another method of assessing reliability and consistency is using parallel or alternate forms of test. The same people can be tested on one form of the test and then tested on an equivalent form. The resulting correlation of the two sets of scores is the reliability coefficient. The time interval between tests has a bearing on the reliability coefficient and as with test–retest reliability this should be stated when reliability coefficients are quoted.

Split-half reliability

Another form of reliability is internal consistency, also known as split-half reliability. Here a single test is divided into two halves, e.g. a test of 100 questions would be split into the equivalent of 2 tests of 50 items each. The scores from each half would then be correlated and a coefficient of reliability obtained. There is no time element involved so stability is not assessed. The reliability coefficient is more a measure of the degree to which the test is measuring the same characteristic or ability – consistency, in fact. Tests are generally split on an odd/even question basis.

Before leaving reliability, it is worth pointing out that reliability tends to increase with the length of a test.

3.6 Improving criterion-related validity

Applying meta-analytical techniques (a process whereby the results of many separate studies can be combined), Schmidt, Hunter and Urry (1976)[6] demonstrated that the validity of tests of cognitive abilities, verbal, numerical and reasoning aptitudes can be widely generalised across occupations and job functions, suggesting that jobs in advanced technological societies require a common core of cognitive abilities to perform them successfully and that these skills are predictive of performance in different fields of activities.[7]

The results of this research suggest that tests of cognitive abilities can be successfully introduced as an aid to selection for many kinds of jobs, in many occupations. It is vital to ensure any such tests have content and predictive validity since poor evidence to support this can lead to breaches of equal opportunity legislation.[8]

With regard to the criterion-related validity of personality measures, it has been shown that validity is significantly increased where a logical link can be established between a personality trait and a specific job activity, e.g. conscientiousness and planning ability. Validity coefficients as high as 0.3 have been reported in such cases.

The accuracy of self-efficacy expectations is likely to be improved where there is a clear understanding of what the job entails, the particular difficulties, most frequent and important activities, not forgetting cultural aspects of the organisation. This kind of information can be communicated via initial recruitment advertisements, job descriptions, interviews and most importantly by allowing job applicants to speak to existing job incumbents, at the actual workplace to find out what the job really entails. Such 'realistic job previews' apart from fulfilling the purpose of permitting more accurate self-efficacy expectations have also been shown to reduce labour turnover.[9]

Since estimates of self-efficacy are likely to be overstated (high self-confidence is often a desirable trait), to reduce the effects of this a simple questionnaire can be constructed on key activities of the job as shown below.

> On a scale of 1 to 10 where 1 = very little confidence and 10 = absolute confidence please indicate your level of confidence.
>
> Rate 1–10
>
> Reducing costs whilst maintaining quality _____
> Improving management development strategies _____
> Reducing labour turnover _____
> Improving the cost per recruit _____

This completed questionnaire can then be used as part of a structured interview with questions such as 'You are extremely confident about reducing labour turnover – what do you see as the issues involved and what is the basis for your confidence?' Such questions can produce unique and revealing insights into candidates' perceptions of the job – which can then be checked against received wisdom and candidates' self-perceptions and the evidence for them.

3.7 Choosing performance criteria

Job analysis can identify key activities and major responsibilities which are important in deciding the basis on which individual performance is judged. In terms of objective measures, it is advisable to sample criteria over a long rather than short period of time. Lane and Herriot (1990)[10] found that the predictive validity of self-efficacy ratings increased, the longer the time period over which changes in gross profit and admissions were measured. Common sense confirms this view, for example, assignment or examination marks taken over all subjects over an entire year will be a more reliable measure of ability than one result only.

Choose measures over which individuals have substantial control, in other words, measures which when changed reflect variations in job holder performance rather than in other external factors over which the job holder has limited, if any, control.

Accuracy of performance ratings can also be improved by ensuring the rater has had relevant contact with the ratee,[11] watching the job being done, perhaps. Finally, the rating process can usually be improved with training. Appropriate training could include improving observational skills, strengthening rater knowledge of job requirements and analysis of common rater errors.

Selection tools

As discussed earlier, the validity of any selection method is clearly dependent on the reliability of the particular test being used and the degree of appropriateness of the purpose for which the test is being used. With this in mind, Robertson and Smith (1989)[12] calculated the approximate validity coefficients commonly used as a yardstick with which to compare the validity of the various assessment techniques currently in use to determine selection decisions. These are shown with their respective validity coefficients in Table 3.2.

Table 3.2 Average validity coefficients for selection methods

Selection method	Validity coefficient
Assessment centres	0.41–0.43
Work samples	0.38–0.54
Cognitive tests	0.25–0.45
Interviews	0.14–0.23
Personality tests	0.15

Source: Smith and Robertson 1989

3.8 Psychometric tests

Psychological or psychometric tests refer to standardised tests constructed to measure mental abilities or attributes. Within the context of occupational selection, tests of cognitive abilities and personality measures are frequently included in the selection process. The use of psychometrics for selection and development is somewhat patchy in UK organisations. A number of research surveys show variation in the purpose and extent to which tests are being used within organisations.[13] Psychometric tests have increasingly gained in popularity in Britain in recent years for staff selection and development purposes with personality tests and cognitive tests now being used for a range of positions from junior clerical to senior managers and in a variety of environments including manufacturing, service industry and managerial environments.[14]

Cognitive tests

Cognitive tests or ability tests can be split into two major categories: attainment and aptitude tests. *Attainment tests* are measures of learned or acquired knowledge. Traditional examinations to assess the level of knowledge acquired by students in a specific subject fall into this category. In an occupational setting such measures may be useful in order to establish that the employee has a sufficient grasp of a specific subject to be able to undertake the demands of the job. Professions such as medicine and law require their practitioners to undertake a series of attainment tests in order to gain professional qualifications. Such qualifications assure an employer that a potential employee has the essential knowledge and/or skills to work to a minimum standard of competence.

Aptitude tests concern an individual's ability to acquire skills or knowledge in the future. They may be designed to measure either general ability levels or a specific aptitude. All such tests are designed to be carried out in a standardised fashion; tests are strictly timed so that all candidates have the same length of time available in which to complete the tests. The environment must be suitable with minimum distractions to candidates in order to ensure that they perform at their optimum level. Test instructions are delivered to all candidates in an identical fashion, and scoring is carried out in an objective manner with the use of pre-coded scoring systems. Many tests can now be scored by computer scanner to calculate performance levels. The advantages of such standardised systems include the fact that all candidates are tested under the same circumstances, asked the same questions and given identical tasks to do. The objectivity of scoring systems eliminates the opportunity for personal biases and interpretation of individual testers to influence the performance rating of the candidate. Scores on these tests are interpreted using norm tables which allow us to compare an individual's performance against a group of their peers, e.g. fellow school leavers or graduate applicants. Using this system of scoring, one test can thus be suitable for use at a variety of achievement levels. A range of tests is available for different levels of occupations. In particular there is a wide range of verbal and numerical tests, some of which are job-specific and aim to test people using the type of information they are likely to deal with in the job, e.g. technical or sales-oriented.

General ability or *general intelligence tests* aim to assess a candidate's intelligence level by examining a cross-section of mental areas including verbal ability, numerical ability, the ability to recognise and interpret shapes, and so on, using pen and paper-based exercises. These tests are used in a variety of situations from educational to occupational settings. In the case of selection, general ability or general intelligence tests are often used where specific job measures are not important or not available and the candidate's potential to benefit from, e.g., a management training course is more important than their current levels of knowledge in a particular area.

Specific ability tests

Specific ability tests aim to test just one area of an individual's ability and appropriate tests are chosen according to the specific abilities required to do the job in question. The most common groups of such tests are the following.

Verbal ability tests: These generally aim to test either the level of verbal understanding or the verbal critical reasoning skills of the candidate. They normally consist of either a series of words from which a meaning needs to be decided or else require the candidate to read a passage of information and then answer a series of questions based on the text. These tests do not aim to measure attainment but level of language fluency. In selection they are used for a wide range of jobs – from those which demand that candidates understand basic written literature such as health and safety directions, to senior positions where an aptitude for interpreting detailed information from complex reports is of importance.

Numerical ability tests: These tests examine the numerical strengths of candidates; normally they involve a series of mental arithmetic tasks to be calculated in a short period of time. Numerical critical reasoning tests use graphs or charts from which candidates interpret statistical information and deduce conclusions from the information provided.

Diagrammatic ability tests: These tests usually consist of a series of abstract shapes and diagrams which candidates are required to follow and interpret. They are used in assessing those who are likely to have to follow instructions in diagrammatic format such as electricians or those having to work from engineering or architectural plans.

Spatial ability tests: Candidates are required to visualise and mentally manipulate 2- and 3-dimensional shapes, often being asked to recognise patterns or changes in series of pictures. Such tests are used primarily in selection of technical staff.

Mechanical ability tests: The ability to demonstrate mechanical reasoning aptitude is tested using a series of pictures which require candidates to interpret the meanings of the pictures and the likely outcome of certain mechanical interactions. A basic knowledge of physics may facilitate the interpretation of such diagrams. Performance on these tests may be somewhat influenced by previous experience as well as mechanical aptitude.

Manual dexterity tests: Manual dexterity is usually assessed by setting candidates a physical task requiring them to assemble a number of components in a short period of time. Speed and precision are usually the focus for such tests although many dexterity tests reflect the specific requirements of the job, e.g. a mechanic might be asked to assemble part of a car engine.

Personality questionnaires

Judgements about personality are made on a daily basis as we attempt to understand and mentally categorise the people we come into contact with. We assign certain attributes to individuals on the basis of their physical appearance such as their height, weight and skin colour, and we also associate certain stereotypical characteristics to features such as nationality or regional accents. Most of the assumptions we make about people on first meeting them are based on very little real information, are open to our personal biases and are often quite inaccurate. A more structured attempt to measure scientifically or compare people has been devised in the form of 'paper and pen' personality tests which attempt to compare individuals objectively along a number of dimensions.

Personality measures originated in the clinical environment where they were used as diagnostic tools and as measures of mental stability. The Woodworth Personal Data sheet was the first widespread personality measure to be used in an occupational environment. This questionnaire was used in the First World War as a screening device to sift out those individuals mentally unsuited to service in the army. In essence it was a standardised psychiatric interview which could be administered in a self-completion format to many individuals at once.

There are many psychological approaches and theories as to the nature and definition of personality. Apropos selection, the trait and type theories assume a number of stable and enduring dimensions of an individual's personality which can be measured and assessed to establish suitability for specific job requirements. Personality tests used in an occupational environment are standardised self-completion questionnaires. Typically they present a number of statements about preferred ways of behaving and ask the candidate to indicate whether or not each statement is likely to reflect their behaviour. There are no right or wrong answers to the questions; respondents' answers are used to build up a profile about their preferred mode of behaviour in a number of circumstances. Examples of the typical items found in personality questionnaires can be seen below:

	True	False	Undecided
(i) I enjoy being the centre of attention	☐	☐	☐
(ii) I like solving technical problems	☐	☐	☐
(iii) I prefer to work on my own than with a group	☐	☐	☐

The traits being measured by personality inventories vary somewhat in both definition and number, though five core traits known as 'the Big Five' are generally found in most of the commonly used personality questionnaires, these include: *extroversion, agreeableness, conscientiousness, neuroticism* and *intellect*. The 16PF, one of the most widely used personality tests in Britain, was designed by Cattell to measure 16 personality factors or traits. Scores are assembled to produce a profile on the 16 scales including traits such as reserved–outgoing, tough-minded–sensitive, practical–imaginative and submissive–dominant. Norms, or average test scores, are available for a variety of professions including accounting, engineering and chemists. Other tests such as the Occupational Personality Questionnaire (OPQ) – developed specifically for the UK selection market – measure a number of traits in three broad dimensions: *relationships with people*; *thinking style* and *feelings and emotions*. Other versions of the OPQ have been designed to assess job-specific characteristics such as those traits identified as relevant to a sales job or customer service positions. Questionnaires can be administered either in the traditional pen and paper format or on computer. Scores from the OPQ can either be interpreted by a qualified administrator or can be fed into a computer software expert system which produces a personality profile and detailed report.

Personality tests give an insight into the way in which individuals perceive themselves. A number of obvious problems such as candidates' desire to shape their answers according to the requirements necessary to gain employment are associated with the use of personality questionnaires. Research has shown their predictive validity to be quite low compared with other psychometric tests; however, when used in conjunction with other selection tools such as cognitive tests, and an exploratory feedback interview (from an appropriately qualified individual), the personality profile can provide a good starting-point for further discussion. It may be very useful in flagging up issues to be addressed in interview which might not otherwise have been discussed.

3.9 Other kinds of test

Work samples

The only certain way of knowing how an individual will perform in a job is to employ them. Given the impracticality of employing all applicants, a realistic alternative is to allow candidates to demonstrate their relevant skills, knowledge or abilities by carrying out a sample of the work. Occupational fields such as advertising, art or architecture have long required applicants to show portfolios or samples of their work as part of the screening process. Work sample tests may be assessments of a practical skill such as a word processing test to assess speed and accuracy for an office post, or a wiring test for an electrician.

In-tray/in-basket exercises

For jobs which are less easily measured such as managerial posts, 'in-tray' or 'in-basket' tests are commonly used to assess candidates' ability to cope with typical contents of a manager's daily work. Such tests require candidates to demonstrate abilities relevant to the particular job such as prioritisation of tasks, critical analysis of reports and written communication ability. The advantage of these tests is that they can be designed to reflect the requirements of the job very closely and this will increase the content and predictive validity of the tool. The materials used in this kind of test normally reflect the nature of the materials a post holder would be expected to deal with daily, e.g. a human resources manager might have to consider problems including selection issues, staff shortages and a formal disciplinary process, while a purchasing manager might have to deal with balancing budgets, stock control issues and purchasing decisions.

Trainability tests

Some positions are not suited to work samples, for instance apprenticeship jobs where it is expected that the successful candidate will acquire the necessary skills 'on the job'. Technical apprentices are typically trained by a combination of structured training and working with an experienced job holder. In such cases the ability to learn quickly and an aptitude for the relevant skills are the most important determinants of success in the job. Trainability tests typically involve a 'mock' training session similar to the type the job holder would receive in the post. After a standardised training session where all applicants receive the same information and tools, a task, e.g. wiring a light, is set, and candidates are assessed on their performance in a number of criteria such as accuracy, speed, tidiness of workmanship, correct use of materials, etc.

3.10 Assessment centres

The selection methods above describe individual selection tools, however, it is widely recognised that multiple assessment methods are more reliable than any single method alone. The assessment centre is a technique which employs a number of assessment tools in an attempt to gather a wide spectrum of knowledge about candidates and achieve more valid selection decisions. Assessment centres were first used in the 1930s by the German Army and were later adopted by the American and British Armies who still use them to select entrants to the military. The first widespread use of assessment centres for graduate recruitment was by AT&T, the American telecommunications company, in the 1950s. Since then assessment centres have gained in popularity for both selection and development purposes and at the end of the 1980s it was estimated that about a third of large organisations in Britain were using assessment centres for selection purposes.[15]

The exercises included in the assessment centre process depend on the nature of the job vacancy. Typically they include the use of psychometric tests, group exercises, presentations, written tasks, 'in-tray' or 'in-basket' tests and work samples. Candidates' performance on the various tests and exercises is observed by several raters (normally including relevant line managers as well as HR staff). To increase inter-rater reliability and the overall effectiveness of the assessment centre process, assessment criteria need to be clearly defined and observers trained in the use of the rating scales. An example of the type of scales commonly used in this process can be seen in Table 3.3.

Table 3.3 Example of rating scales used by observers in assessment centre process

	Group discussion exercise
Analytical skills	1 (weak)–2–3–4–5–6–7 (strong)
Team working skills	1 (weak)–2–3–4–5–6–7 (strong)
Leadership skills	1 (weak)–2–3–4–5–6–7 (strong)

Studies examining the comparable validity of assessment methods rate assessment centres as one of the strongest methods of predicting the performance of a candidate, but they are time-consuming to organise and run as well as being a very costly method of selection. Consequently, the use of assessment centres is largely restricted to graduate and senior management positions.

3.11 The interview

The most commonly used method to select employees is still the interview; very few people in the UK are hired without having at least one face-to-face interview with their employers and many organisations still use the interview as their only tool of assessment. The traditional interview method has been given poor reviews as a way of predicting the best person for a job. A number of research studies examining the validity of the selection interview have found it to be considerably weaker than alternative methods such as cognitive tests or assessment centres.[16] The interview as it is normally carried out is unreliable as an assessment method. The information obtained about candidates is often inconsistent and interviewers frequently rate the same candidates quite differently (poor inter-rater reliability). Other factors contributing to the interview's poor predictive validity include the fact that in structured interviews, material is not consistently covered and the degree or depth of information obtained may depend both on the interpersonal rapport between interviewers and candidates and on the level of nervousness of the interviewee. Other factors to be considered are the likelihood that interviewers will form their impressions of the candidate in the first few minutes of their meeting rather than over the full course of the interview, coupled with the fact that less favourable information tends to have more impact on interviewers than favourable information.[17] Despite this, however, few people would be prepared to hire an individual they have not actually had a chance to meet and assess for themselves. Since the interview is unlikely to be abandoned as a selection tool, it is worthwhile trying to improve its reliability and predictive validity. Research shows that structured interviews developed as a result of a thorough job analysis can increase the validity of the interview to as high as r = .35. Several types of interview methods have been developed to try to assess the criteria identified as important to job performance.

Situational interviews

The situational interview is a type of structured interview which includes a set of questions (based on the job analysis) asking candidates to predict how they would behave in various situations likely to occur in the job, for example, in a customer service role, applicants might be asked how they think they would deal with an aggressive customer in a certain situation. All applicants would be asked such standardised questions as part of the overall interview. The consistency of this approach enables more valid comparison and discrimination between candidates.

Competence-based interviews

While the situational interview asks candidates to predict how they would act in the future, competence-based interviews ask applicants to reflect on their behaviour in the past and to describe an occasion on which they have used a specific ability, for example, how they have managed a situation with an aggressive customer in a previous job.

These structured, job-related interview techniques allow greater comparability between competing candidates than the traditional interview style affords. Additional factors such as training of interviewers, identification of important assessment criteria and agreement of expected standards can also increase the inter-rater reliability between interviewers.

Finally, as with all assessment tools, the validity is likely to increase when the interview is used in conjunction with other information about the candidate such as a personality profile or assessment centre results.

3.12 Choosing a selection method

Torrington and Hall[18] point out that although the search for the perfect method of selection continues, HR managers continue to use a variety of imperfect methods in order to cope with the demands of the job. All too often pressures to fill a position rapidly or with minimum expense lead to less than ideal selection processes. For a job vacancy to be filled as suitably as possible, a number of steps are important in order to determine the most appropriate selection criteria and selection methods. In a typical graduate or managerial vacancy, screening and selection of candidates will occur over a number of phases. Figure 3.4 illustrates an example of a typical graduate selection process.

STAGE 1: Preparation for selection
- ▶   Carry out thorough job analysis
- ▶   Produce job description
- ▶   Develop person specification
- ▶   Identify selection criteria
- ▶   Identify/develop appropriate assessment measures.

STAGE 2: Recruitment
- ▶   Advertisement
- ▶   Use of recruitment agencies.

STAGE 3: Selection process
- ▶   Assessment stage 1: Screening for essential qualifications and experience demanded by person specification using application forms or CVs.
- ▶   Assessment stage 2: Further screening for appropriate aptitudes or personality profile using psychometric tests and/or assessment centre methods such as work samples, presentations, etc.
- ▶   Assessment stage 3: Short-listing of candidates who have met previous selection criteria; may involve interview and/or final tests. Candidates may be invited to visit work location and gain realistic preview of job in question.
- ▶   Assessment stage 4: Selection decision based on determining the most suitable candidate for the job.

STAGE 4: Selection decision
- ▶   Job offer
- ▶   Probation (normally between 3 months and 1 year).

Figure 3.4 Typical graduate selection procedure

As discussed, the complexity, cost and length of a selection process are usually dependent on the level of the job and the calibre of candidate required. The amount of time, effort and money invested in the selection procedure normally reflects the likely impact or value of the potential job holder. For example, those in a position to influence the overall performance of the organisation such as a senior manager or a Chief Executive generally merit more resources than those in junior positions. Some professions, e.g. the military and aviation, have traditionally attracted a great deal of interest in methods for selecting appropriate entrants, where the impact of poor selection decisions may result in disastrous consequences in terms of risk to human life.

Factors which have added greater pressure for the need for effective selection in the 1990s and have influenced the increasing trend towards adopting psychometric measures include:

- The high cost of recruitment and selection processes, coupled with additional cost in terms of lost revenue for lower performance levels during training and 'settling in' periods for new staff, ensure the need to try to make a good selection decision and to avoid unnecessary staff turnover.
- Reduced mobility of staff as a result of current labour market trends, meaning that staff are less likely to leave a job of their own accord and, as a result, poor selection choices may impact on the organisation for a long time.
- Legislation, for example equal opportunities and sex discrimination laws, which encourage employers to avoid using unfair or discriminatory selection practices.[19]

While these factors are important elements for organisations to consider and clearly emphasise the significance of the cost of 'mistakes' in the selection process, we must not lose sight of the fundamental reason for trying to ensure the most effective selection procedures: to identify the best person for the job.

3.13 References

1. Bandura A. *Social foundation of thought and action*. Englewood Cliffs, NJ: Prentice Hall, 1986.
2. Saal F, Downey R, Lahey M. Rating the ratings: assessing the psychometric quality of rating data. *Psychological Bulletin* 1980; **88**: 413–28.
3. Saal F, Landy F. The mixed standard rating scales: an evaluation. *Organisational Behaviour and Human Performance* 1977; **18**: 19–35.
4. Herriot P. *Down from the ivory tower: graduates and their jobs*. Chichester: John Wiley, 1984.
5. Anastasi A. *Psychological testing*. New Jersey: Macmillan Publishing Company, 1990.
6. Schmidt F, Hunter J, Urry V. Statistical power in criterion-related validity studies. *Journal of Applied Psychology* 1976; **61**: 473–85.
7. Anastasi, *Psychological testing*.
8. Kellet D, Fletcher S, Callen A, Geary B. Fair testing: the case of British Rail. *The Psychologist* 1994; **7**(1): 26–9.
9. Premack S, Wanous J. A meta-analysis of realistic job preview experiments. *Journal of Applied Psychology* 1985; **70**: 706–19.
10. Lane J, Herriot P. Self ratings, supervisor ratings, position and performance. *Journal of Occupational Psychology* 1990; **63**(1): 77–88.
11. Landy F, Farr J. Performance rating. *Psychological Bulletin* 1980; **87**: 72–109.
12. Robertson I, Smith M. Personnel selection methods. In: Smith M and Robertson I eds. *Advances in selection and assessment*. Chichester: John Wiley, 1989: 89–112.
13. Bevan S, Fryatt J. *Employee selection in the UK*. Falmer: Institute of Manpower Studies, 1988; Mabey B. The majority of large companies use psychological tests. *Guidance and Assessment Review* 1989; **5**(3): 1–4; Mabey B. The growth of test use. *Selection and Development Review* 1992; **8**(3): 6–8. Williams R. Psychological testing and management selection practices in local government: results of a survey, June 1991. Luton: Local Government Management Board, 1991; Shackleton V, Newell S. Management selection: a comparative study of methods used in top British and French companies. *Journal of Occupational Psychology* 1991; **64**(1): 123–37.
14. Williams R. Occupational testing: contemporary British practice. *The Psychologist* 1994; **7**(2): 11–13.

15. Mabey, The majority of large companies.
16. Arvey R, Campion J. The employment interview: a summary and review of recent literature. *Personnel Psychology* 1982; **35**: 281–322; Schmitt N, Coyle B. Applicant decisions in the employment interview. *Journal of Applied Psychology* 1976; 61: 184–92; Hunter J, Hunter R. Validity and utility of alternative predictors of job performance. *Psychological Bulletin* 1984; **96**: 72–98.
17. Lane J. Methods of assessment. *Health Manpower Management* 1992; **18**(2): 4–6.
18. Torrington D, Hall L. *Personnel management: A new approach*, 3rd edition. Hemel Hempstead: Prentice Hall, 1995.
19. Sparrow P, Hiltrop J. *European human resource management in transition*. Hemel Hempstead: Prentice Hall, 1994.

SECTION II
TRAINING AND EMPLOYMENT

Introduction

While the importance of training and development is widely recognised, many employers in the UK still prefer to leave this task to others rather than incur the costs of training their own employees. Fortunately most successful companies realise the benefits of investing in their human resources in a manner which enhances their competitive advantage, quality of service, and the motivation of their employees. Recent years have seen a range of new approaches to training and development. These include competency-based training, team working, an extended range of national vocational qualifications, a move from standard packaged training programmes to tailor-made courses, and the development of work-based learning. Other recent trends include support for continuous professional development (CPD), flexible and distance learning packages, renewed emphasis on the benefits of creating 'learning organisations', computer-aided learning (including use of CD-ROMs), and measures to encourage employees to take 'ownership' of their own development.

The chapters in this section describe and comment on these and other recent developments. Building on modern principles of training and their application within manufacturing and the service sector, this section progresses to an in-depth examination of contemporary approaches to organisation development, and concludes with new and exciting ways of creating 'learning organisations', and the possibilities opened up by transformed cultures and those enriched work-based value systems which can lead to the personal growth of employees as well as enhanced organisational effectiveness.

4 Training
The essential ingredient

Anna Kyprianou and
Jacqui Kasket

'Training is a continuing investment in the most valuable of all our national resources – the energies of our people'[1] and many consider it, along with education, to be imperative to the industrial success of the UK. This chapter examines training from a number of different perspectives. First, it attempts to place the importance of training into a broader national context and to highlight its benefits to both organisations and individuals. It goes on to use a training framework to explore how organisations can systematically train their employees.

4.1 Training: the broader national perspective

The relationship between training, education and industry is one which has generated a great deal of debate and controversy. The idea that there is a relationship between education, training and industrial performance is not a new one: Baron Lyon Playfair (1851, 1870) drew attention to the comparative weakness in his reports on technical education, and by 1903, Marshall noted the insecurity of Britain's position. In 1964, the Industrial Training Act was introduced and the Industry Training Boards were created. Further legislation in 1973 set up the Manpower Services Commission, one of whose aims was to develop human resources 'to contribute fully to economic well being'. The MSC (later known as the Training Commission and the Training Agency) scored initial successes in improving industrial training in the UK, however, the underlying problems still remained. Education and training were once seen as vehicles for improving and enhancing organisations as well as society at large. Today, they are frequently regarded as an expensive commodity whose worth is often linked with the lack of the UK's industrial performance.

Throughout the 1980s and 1990s, the debate about education and training in Britain was related to the perceived need to enhance the nation's economic competitiveness which, it was felt, had long been neglected.[2] 'We in Britain have over the years consistently under-invested in human capital'[3] and 'we have not sufficiently recognised its [training] importance in the past. This we must remedy and ensure that the skills of our people are fitted for the challenge of the years ahead'.[4]

The contribution of education and training to Britain's competitiveness has been accepted by both ministers and industrialists, and this has given the debate a new impetus. Britain's poor economic performance is now firmly blamed on 'low investment' in education and training. There is a consensus in the growing body of competitive education and training research that Britain provides significantly poorer education and training for its workforce than its major international competitors.[5]

The combination of poor performance during compulsory schooling years and a high percentage of students leaving school at 16 has meant that the average British worker enters employment with relatively few qualifications. This lack of initial qualifications does not seem to be compensated by increased employer-based training. Indeed, quite the reverse seems to be true; British firms offer a lower quality and quantity of training than those of its major competitors. The 'Training in Britain Survey' (1989) found that of those employers that did train (1 in 5 didn't), no more than 48 per cent of the workforce was covered. In other words, more than half the workforce did not benefit from any form of training. By 1995 of the 22 million employees in the UK about 1 in 4 received job-related training. Of those employees receiving no training, approximately 47 per cent reported that they had never been offered training by their current employer on or away from the job. This group represents 1 in 3 (34 per cent) of all employees. France and Germany have already achieved the equivalent of our (old) Lifetime Target 3 (50 per cent of the workforce qualified to at least NVQ 3 or equivalent) and are aiming for 80 per cent by the year 2000. Japan achieved this in 1986. Although it is difficult to prove a direct empirical relationship between education and training and economic performance, no-one would dispute that a qualified engineer is more likely to produce a complex piece of equipment than an unskilled employee. However, do marginal differences in the quantity and quality of education and training affect performance?

There are those who would argue that the expansion of British industry has been hindered by the failure of the education and training system to produce sufficient quantities of skilled labour (producing skills shortages). Furthermore, the ability of the British economy and organisations to adapt to longer-term shifts in international competition has been impeded by the lack of qualified personnel.

The notion of 'skills shortages' is not a new phenomenon. In 1968, the Donovan Commission held that 'the lack of skilled labour has constantly applied a brake to our economic expansion since the war'.[6] 'This view was held throughout the 1970s, 1980s and 1990s. A series of studies in the 1980s demonstrated the strong positive correlation between industrial productivity and skills levels.[7] So why has Britain failed to train?

It is true that there was a gradual expansion of educational provision during the post-war period, but this was not reflected in training provision, due largely to the fact that training was left in the hands of industry.

4.2 Training and industry

Why did industry and organisations fail to rise to the training challenge? One explanation is that organisations consider it cheaper for them to hire already skilled workers than to train their own and risk them being poached by other companies – this is likely to be the major reason for under-investment in training.

A major study undertaken in the mid-1980s revealed that there were additional reasons why employers did not train as extensively as their international counterparts.[8] Few employers felt that training was sufficiently central to their business for it to be a main component in their strategy. The majority of employers believed that the amount of training they did was about right. Training was rarely seen as an investment, there seemed to be little analysis of training needs or any subsequent evaluation of the little training that did take place. Training was not seen as a major contributor to competitiveness. The reluctance to invest in training was put down to uncertain future markets, technological developments, poaching and demarcation.

There were few external pressures for organisations to invest in training (for example, from competitors, employees, unions, external commentators, government). In Germany, by contrast, there is a strong formalised tradition of training backed by legislation monitored for content and with recognised qualifications. Likewise in France, legislation stipulates a minimum expenditure on training that each organisation must undertake, together with statutory rights for individuals to training leave. In the USA, training is less formalised –

the pressure comes from individuals. Nevertheless, the recent Presidential Commission on Skills has given renewed impetus to training in core skills. The driving force for training in these countries is either strong cultural pressure or a clear legislative structure. The conclusion to be drawn from this evidence is that if Britain's performance on training is to improve, this can only be achieved by a major change in employer and employee attitudes to training: 'To compete internationally the UK needs a highly motivated and well qualified workforce. We need . . . employers who see the importance of developing the skills of their employees, and people in the labour force who take their development seriously.'[9]

4.3 Making the case for training: benefits for the employer and the individual

Effective training is said to contribute significantly to the improvement of competitiveness, productivity and the quality of services to customers.[10] The tangible benefits of training to employers are numerous. A recent survey[11] identified the following: training costs less in the long run than recruiting fully trained workers. Evidence suggests that 'recruited fully trained workers' tend to leave much sooner than employees the organisations had trained themselves. Training also imparts the 'right attitude' to employees and 'attitudes' are often just as important as skill and knowledge acquisition. The long-term benefits of training outweigh the short-term costs. For example, higher skill and knowledge levels, lower labour turnover, reduced recruitment costs and a greater commitment to the organisation. Improved efficiency results from savings from material costs due to reduced wastage; improved delivery performance; improved quality, reliability and range of products or services to customers; more efficient scheduling of work and improved responsiveness to specific customer requirements; a more flexible and adaptable workforce generally, with faster adaptation to new technologies in particular.[12]

Given the breadth of these benefits, it is hard to understand why so many organisations fail to train their employees systematically. While most employers would agree that training is 'a good thing', there are some factors which deter them from investing in training. These include the perceived costs of training and a real concern about employees leaving once trained.

Many individuals consider training an important aspect of their working lives. Economic and other reasons are often given for wishing to undertake training. A survey carried out in 1994 of individuals' attitudes to learning[13] found that over two-thirds of respondents thought people given training find their jobs more interesting. More than half thought that those who received training at work got promotion or better pay, and over three-quarters felt that they were more marketable and employable as a result of training. Furthermore, the Employment in Britain Survey[14] found that training provision was near the top of people's preferences about what a job should offer.

Since training provides so many benefits to both employers and employees, there is a clear need for organisations to invest in training, to harness the interests of individuals, as well as improve the operation of the training market making it easier for them to define and obtain from internal and external providers the training they require.

Thus far, 'training' has been referred to as a generic term but it can take a multitude of guises. Let us consider the term 'training' in more depth.

4.4   Towards a definition of training

Training is a subject which everyone knows something about, but it still poses problems when one attempts to provide a hard-and-fast definition. Numerous definitions of training have appeared over the years. For example, in the 1970s training was considered to be: 'the systematic development of the attitude, knowledge and skill behaviour pattern required by an individual in order to perform adequately a given task or job'[15] or 'a sequence of experiences or opportunities designed to modify behaviour in order to attain a stated objective'[16] or 'any activity which deliberately attempts to improve a person's skill at a task'.[17]

By 1981, there was already a change in emphasis:

> a planned process to modify attitude, knowledge or skill behaviour through learning experience to achieve effective performance in an activity or range of activities. Its purpose in the work situation is to develop the abilities of the individual and to satisfy the current and future manpower needs of the organisation.[18]

> a planned effort by an organisation to facilitate the learning of job-related behaviour on the part of its employees.[19]

> the systematic acquisition of skills, rules, concepts or attitudes that result in improved performance in another environment.[20]

Ultimately, training includes all forms of planned learning experiences and activities whose purpose is to effect changes in performance and other behaviour through the acquisition of new knowledge, skills, beliefs, values and attitudes. Defined in this way, training reflects activities that are intended to influence the ability and motivation of individual employees. In other words, training can prepare people to work and help increase their worth to their employer and to themselves.[21]

While most training would fall into the broad statement above, it can include a range of activities. These include:

- *Traditional training:* training given to promote the learning of specific, factual and narrow range of content to facilitate or improve human performance on the job, for example, technical skills training.[22]
- *Education:* learning experiences that improve overall competence in a specific direction.[23] This is typically associated with secondary and higher education in particular fields of study.
- *Vocational education:* a set of learning experiences that are broader in scope than training but narrower than general education, for example, apprenticeship training.
- *Management development:* organisationally provided educational activities focused on improving managerial performance through training in technical, human relations and organisational decision-making skills.[24]
- *Organisational development:* organisationally provided educational activities focused on changing employees' beliefs, values, attitudes and behaviour that hinder human interactions and thus human problem solving and decision-making in various departments, divisions or the total organisation.[25]

Common to all these activities is the underlying assumption that organisations and the people within them develop by learning irrespective of the approach adopted. A further basic principle is that for training to be worthwhile, it is imperative that learning takes place.

4.5 Training and learning

'Learning is a relatively permanent change in behaviour that occurs as a result of practice or experience.'[26] Therefore, we can say that the learning experience goes to the heart of all training activities, and that training, if it is to be successful, depends on an understanding of the learning process.

The trainee will bring to any learning situation a range of knowledge, skills and attitudes previously acquired. The trainer must build on these attributes, which will vary from person to person, so that each trainee can gain new knowledge, skills and attitudes. However, no two trainees will necessarily learn in the same way. In practice, the trainer will try to provide a learning situation that appears to meet the needs of the greatest number of trainees. Trainees may also vary in the degree of motivation they possess and in their level of self-esteem. Those with low motivation/self-esteem will normally take longer to complete a training programme than the well-motivated trainee.

Learning theories can be complex and diverse with distinct paradigms. Common themes shared by most learning theorists are that motivation goes to the core of learning be it *extrinsic motivation* or *intrinsic motivation*. Extrinsic motivation refers to factors 'extrinsic' to the job itself, but whose absence leads to job dissatisfaction, e.g. company policy, supervision, working conditions, pay, interpersonal relations, etc., sometimes known as hygiene factors. Intrinsic motivation refers to factors 'intrinsic' to the job itself which are strong determinants of job satisfaction, e.g. achievement, recognition, the work itself, responsibility and advancement.[27] Ultimately, whatever the source of motivation, the individual needs to be convinced of the need for training, for without such commitment, learning will be at best a very slow process. Other individual differences such as personality, intellectual ability, age, and the learning environment also affect individual learning and the rate at which people learn.

Kolb and the learning process

People learn in different ways. People have styles of learning which influence not only how they learn in a particular situation but also how they manage, solve problems, and make decisions in their work. However, several attempts have been made to extract a general model of the learning process from the apparent diversity of learner behaviour. According to Kolb (1974),[28] learning is viewed as a circular and perpetual process, whose key stages are experience, observation of and reflection on experience, analysis of the key learning points arising from experience, and the consequent planning and trying out of new or changed behaviour (see Figure 4.1).

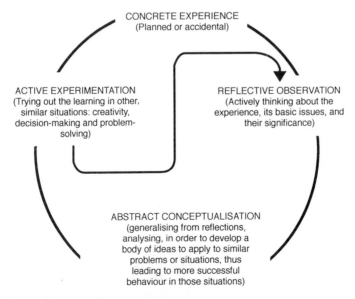

Source: Kolb, Rubin, McIntyre, *Organisational psychology*

Figure 4.1 The learning process

Honey and Mumford[29] refined Kolb's categories and used them in selecting the type of trainee (identified by learning style) most likely to benefit from a certain type of programme. They found that people's predominant learning styles tended to fall into one of the following four categories: activists, reflectors, theorists, pragmatists. These relate to the four different learning processes described by Kolb in 1974.

Activists involve themselves fully in new experiences. They enjoy the here and now and are happy to be dominated by immediate experiences. They are open minded, not sceptical and this tends to make them enthusiastic about anything new. They revel in short-term crisis fire fighting. They often tackle problems by brainstorming. They tend to be bored with implementation and longer-term consolidation.

Reflectors collect and analyse data about experiences and events, so they tend to postpone reaching definitive conclusions for as long as possible. They prefer to take a back seat in meetings and enjoy observing other people in action. When they act, it is as part of a wide picture which includes the past as well as the present, and others' observations as well as their own.

Theorists tend to be detached, analytical and dedicated to rational objectivity rather than anything subjective or ambiguous. Their approach to problems is consistently logical. They prefer to maximise certainty and feel uncomfortable with subjective judgements, lateral thinking and anything flippant.

Pragmatists are keen on trying out ideas, theories and techniques to see if they work in practice. They don't like 'beating around the bush' and tend to be impatient with ruminating and open-ended discussions. They are essentially practical, down-to-earth people who like making practical decisions and solving problems. Their philosophy is 'if it works it's good'.

In any organisation there will be a mix of activists, reflectors, theorists and pragmatists: people whose way of learning and approach to problems and decision-making is primarily, even completely, characterised by the forms of behaviour described under these headings. What is important is to identify the different learning styles and approaches so that these can be matched to needs, and so that those dominated by one style more than any other can improve their effectiveness by developing a wider range of styles to suit their present and future roles and tasks.

The concept of *learning styles* is an important development because it helps to throw some light on how people actually learn. It indicates that there are varying approaches which can be related to different training methods.

In summary, learning theories and the application of learning principles are the cornerstone of training. Silverman (1970)[30] succinctly identified ten basic generalisations from learning theory which are particularly pertinent to the training situation. These are as follows:

1. Trainees learn best by making active responses. People learn best by doing and getting involved, not just listening.
2. The responses that the trainee makes are limited by their abilities and by the sum total of their past responses.
3. Learning proceeds most effectively when the trainee's correct responses are promptly reinforced.
4. The frequency with which a response is reinforced will determine how well it will be learned.
5. Practice in a variety of settings will increase the range of situations in which learning can be applied.
6. A motivated trainee is more likely to learn and to use what they have learned than an unmotivated trainee.

7. The trainee should be encouraged to find summarising or governing principles to help to organise what they are learning.
8. The trainee should be assisted to learn to discriminate the important stimuli in every situation so that they can respond appropriately.
9. The trainee will learn most effectively when they can learn at their own pace.
10. There are different kinds of learning and they may require different learning conditions.

These and other issues relating to learning must be borne in mind when designing training as the success of any training can only be gauged by the amount of learning that occurs and is transferred to the job. Too often, unplanned, uncoordinated and haphazard training efforts significantly reduce the learning that could have occurred.

4.6 A systematic training approach

Training and learning will take place, especially through informal workgroups, whether an organisation has a coordinated training effort or not. But without a well-designed systematic approach to training, what is learned may not be what is best for the organisation.

Figure 4.2 shows the relevant components of the four major phases typically adopted in a training system. This provides a useful framework for the systematic application of learning at the workplace. This crude systematic approach forms the basis of many of the subsequent models of the training process. It is simple, logical and illustrates the dependency relationship between the different steps. However, there are those who feel that this is too mechanistic and clear-cut, suggesting, for example, that needs may be identified at the evaluation stage.

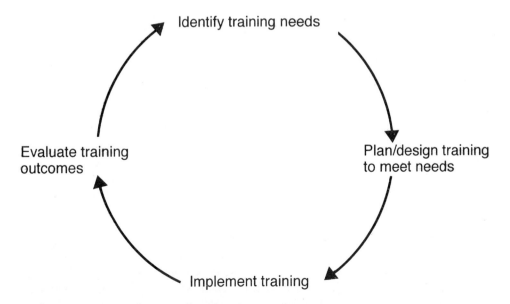

Figure 4.2 Simple systematic training cycle

More comprehensive and sophisticated approaches have been developed. These are, in essence, expanded versions of the basic systematic cycle (see Figure 4.3). In the *assessment* phase, the need for training is determined and the objectives of the training are specified. The training is then *planned*, *designed* and *implemented* on the basis of these objectives. The *evaluation* phase is crucial and focuses on measuring how well the training accomplished what it originally intended to do.

4.7 Identifying training needs: the assessment phase

Training is largely designed to help the organisation accomplish its objectives. Determining training needs is the diagnostic phase of setting training objectives. The ability to identify areas in which training can make a real contribution to organisational success is crucial. This is a method of 'gap' analysis; it is aimed at determining the difference or gap between actual and required performance. The inherent assumption, which must be tested, is that the shortfall in performance is caused by deficiencies in knowledge, skills or attitude.

For over 30 years the dominant framework for identifying training needs has been McGehee and Thayer's (1961)[31] three-category needs analysis approach: *organisational analysis, occupational analysis* and *personal analysis*. In reality, costs and other resource constraints may determine a more specific interventionist strategy rather than a blanket and costly coverage. Accurate learning objectives derived from real needs should underpin blanket or *ad hoc* strategies.

Organisational analysis

Needs assessment should diagnose present problems and future challenges which are to be met through training and development. For example, changes in the external environment may present an organisation with new challenges and to respond effectively, employees may need training to deal with these changes. Sometimes a change in the organisation's strategy can create a need for training; for example, the introduction of new products or services usually requires employees to learn new procedures. As part of the organisation's strategic human resource planning, it is important to identify the knowledge, skills and abilities that will be needed for employees in the future as both jobs and the organisation change. Both internal and external forces that will influence the training of workers must be considered.

Assessing organisational needs can isolate problems which may indicate the need for training of groups of employees or of particular individuals. The first way of diagnosing training needs is through *organisational analysis*, which considers the organisation as a system. Goldstein (1986) described organisational analysis as the study of 'the system-wide components of an organisation that may have impact on a training program(me) ... [including] an examination of the organisational goals, resources of the organisation, climate of training, and internal and external constraints present in the environment'.[32]

Organisational analysis can be undertaken using a variety of sources of information: human resource data can show training weaknesses; departments or areas with high turnover, high absenteeism, low performance or other deficiencies can be pinpointed, and their specific training needs investigated. Specific sources of information for organisational level needs analysis may include grievances, accident records, observations, exit interviews, customer complaints, waste/scrap quality control data, etc.

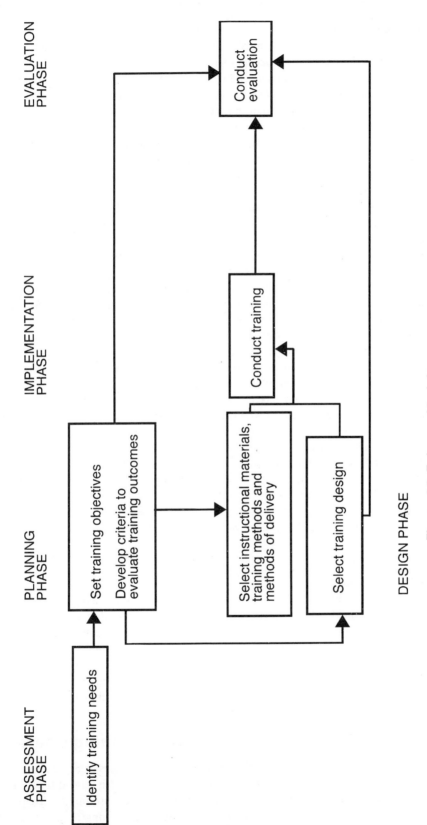

Figure 4.3 Enhanced training process

ASSESSMENT
PHASE

PLANNING
PHASE

IMPLEMENTATION
PHASE

EVALUATION
PHASE

Identify training needs

Set training objectives

Develop criteria to
evaluate training outcomes

Select instructional materials,
training methods and
methods of delivery

Select training design

Conduct training

Conduct
evaluation

DESIGN PHASE

Occupational analysis

It is generally accepted that some examination of the job itself should be carried out in order to determine what should constitute an appropriate training programme. It is also accepted that this involves a description and a breakdown of the tasks which make up a job into elements of some kind. However, no general agreement exists as to how this should be accomplished as there are a number of different approaches and techniques which may be adopted.

An examination of the training literature and discussions with people in the field reveals that genuine difficulties exist over terminology. This is perhaps most apparent in the analysis of activities to derive training content. The terms *job, skills* and *task analysis*, which might be used interchangeably, represent different processes, or even refer to different stages within the same process.

Job analysis is 'the process of examining a job in detail in order to identify its component tasks. The detail and approach may vary according to the purpose for which the job is being analysed, for example, training, equipment design, work layout'.[33] There are those who have suggested that the term 'job' is person-oriented[34] and that for training purposes the more specific term 'task analysis' is preferred.

Skills analysis relates to a detailed analysis of the skilled physical movements involved in manual operations and although they are useful in some training situations, their range of application is limited, particularly in supervisory and management roles.

Task analysis is probably the most important form of analysis for training purposes. It focuses on the objectives or outcomes of the tasks that people perform and provides an extremely flexible and useful method for analysis. This includes a detailed examination of each task component of a job, performance standards of a job, methods and knowledge the employee must use in the performance of job tasks and the ways in which employees learn these methods and acquire the needed knowledge.[35] In other words, task analysis 'results in a statement of the activities or work operations performed on the job and the conditions under which the job [or group of similar tasks] is performed'.[36]

In order to undertake an occupational analysis (be it job, task or skills analysis) effectively, it is necessary to know what the job requirements in the organisation are. Job descriptions and job specifications provide information on the performances expected and details necessary for employees to accomplish the required work. By comparing the requirements of jobs with the knowledge, skills and abilities of employees, training needs can be identified.

Personal analysis

Personal analysis focuses on individuals and how they perform in their jobs. Such information can be obtained from a variety of sources, for example, directly observing job performance, reviewing supervisory evaluations of performance, using diagnostic tests such as written ability tests, comparing behaviour of well performing employees with those of poorly performing employees, and discussing with employees their individual job performance and factors that may inhibit that performance. The use of performance appraisal data in undertaking this individual analysis is the most common approach.

4.8 Setting training objectives: the planning phase

Once the mismatch between actual and required performance has been identified, the question *Is training the answer?* needs to be asked. Is the mismatch related to a learning situation? Often, if care is not taken, situations which require counselling or disciplinary action are handed over as training situations to be resolved. Training is not always the answer to every managerial problem, and should be treated as a development opportunity giving individuals time to learn, rather than remedial action. It is true, however, that there are times that retraining someone whose training has not been adequate in the first place is required. Training and development should be a part of the overall training strategy of the business and germane to those objectives. It should not be treated as a shot in the arm to deal with an immediate situation when other solutions, perhaps less palatable, are available.

When the need for training has been identified, the next stage in the systematic training process is to set training objectives. An objective is a specific outcome that the training programme is intended to achieve. These are typically set for the trainee rather than the organisation, though the outcome of training should ultimately lead to the achievement of organisational goals. Training objectives define performance that the trainee should be able to exhibit after training. They should be stated explicitly, and answer three questions:[37]

1. What should the trainee be able to do after training?
2. Under what conditions should the trainee be able to perform the trained behaviour?
3. How well should the trainee perform the trained behaviour?

Explicit objectives serve a number of purposes. One of the most important is that they assist in developing the criteria to be used in evaluating the training outcome.

Furthermore, these explicit objectives must be aligned to the overall strategic objectives of the business. Training is a cost centre, if only in terms of the time taken away from the job by both trainer and trainee. Therefore, it is important that any training undertaken meets individual, departmental and organisational objectives. This is also true of long-term development of staff, which should be in line with the organisation's human resource plan.

4.9 Selecting training design and methods: the design phase

Once the question *Who needs training?* has been answered by conducting an analysis of training needs, and training objectives have been set, appropriate training design and methods can be selected. However, there is a need to think beyond simply sending someone on an off-the-job training course either internally or externally.

It is at this stage that thought should be given to the trainees, who they are and what they know already. What follows is a checklist of questions and activities which could be used in designing training and selecting appropriate training methods, in order both to maximise the learning experience and the cost effectiveness of the training opportunity.

In deciding the most appropriate content and design, it is important to ask the question – *What is the purpose of the training?* The purpose will dictate, to a large extent, the design and training methods adopted.

An introduction to a job or function (induction)

As well as following naturally from recruitment and selection, induction should also consider the initial training and development that anyone needs on joining either the new organisation or taking on a new function within it.[38] As well as dealing with the initial knowledge and skills needed to do the job, in the case of a new organisation, it should also deal with the structure, culture and activities of the organisation.

Basic understanding of a job or function

Effective job analysis[39] should result in a list of key tasks which are the core components of the job. Initial training of this kind would be separate from the induction process but would follow on from it immediately.

Provision of skills to carry out the job

Some jobs have key skills elements attached to them, for example, working in a customer interface situation would require not only knowledge about dealing with complaints but also the key behavioural skills of the likely interactions. This acquisition of skills is a separate entity from acquiring knowledge and should be considered as such. It is likely to be far less quantifiable and also take longer to train and practise, requiring feedback from coach or mentor to help the development process.

Developing specialist knowledge

This area could cover the specialist skills required in particular functions, for example, accounting or human resource management itself, or alternatively knowledge about particular customers who are key account holders. It is likely that this is development which will need to be acquired over a longer period and will necessitate progress checks at regular intervals.

Broadening knowledge of the business

This allows training and development into the wider context beyond an individual's job or function. It allows for commitment to the goals and mission of the organisation as a whole and is often achieved through guided reading as well as off-the-job seminars and conferences.

Changing attitudes about a job or function

This type of training objective is becoming increasingly important as organisations go through significant changes and attempt, in line with these, to change their organisational culture.

Will both content and method be suitable for employees' learning styles?

We have talked earlier in this chapter about the importance of establishing individuals' learning preferences before designing and undertaking any training.[40] Every time training takes place, it is important that this information is reviewed and methods used are compatible with the individual's preferences. This will also be true of the person doing the training.

We have already looked at how people learn, and have suggested that for some learning styles, off-the-job training would not provide the best environment in which to learn. What are the alternatives to formal off-the-job training? There are several alternatives including:

- *Individual coaching:* To be effective this method of training needs to be planned and executed with thought. First, this means providing the person who is going to be the coach with training in coaching skills and then providing time slots in their own schedule for coaching to take place. They can then identify opportunities in their own and others' daily work as *development* opportunities, helping the other person learn how to do the job and providing continuous feedback as to progress. This can also be seen as a learning opportunity for the coach.[41]

* *Prescribed reading:* Manuals or books may be available through open learning centres in organisations which cover particular facets of an individual's job which may be helpful for individuals to be aware of. As with coaching, time needs to be set aside for individuals to complete the task outside daily work. Short pieces of text about key tasks could be created which could then be given to individuals to use and keep for future reference.

* *Open learning:* Open learning texts and courses are available in the marketplace, which enable people to study in their own time, and at their own pace, a subject area which both interests them and at the same time enhances their training in the workplace. This is particularly true of management and supervisory training and more and more opportunities are presenting themselves in areas such as customer service. Alternatively, organisations may have an open learning centre which either provides a library of such texts or may be able to produce material germane to the individual's area of work if it does not exist already, or to adapt existing specific material.

* *Project work:* One of the ways in which new skills can be acquired is through specific project work. From time to time, opportunities will exist to move staff on a specific project which while being part of the department's work is not necessarily normally part of the individual's work. This gives the opportunity to acquire new skills, and to manage a whole project from start to finish.

* *Job rotation:* In departments where a wide variety of jobs are being done, it is possible to rotate individuals through them. This has the advantage of widening the skills base of individuals as well as ensuring that everyone is familiar both with whole tasks (if they normally work on parts of sequential tasks) and for covering when there is sickness and absence. Of course, at the same time there is a need to ensure that the right on-the-job training or coaching takes place in order that people can complete the new tasks. Principles of job design[42] suggest that skills variety, task identity and task significance contribute to motivating employees. Thus having the opportunity to see whole tasks through and learn a variety of new skills and tasks through this medium not only enhances learning but also motivation.

* *Job attachments:* This is a similar form to job rotation, in that people are given the opportunity to learn new tasks. In this case, however, they will be attached to another department or particular job other than their own for an extended period, usually from three months to a year. During this period they would be expected to do the other job as if it were their own, thus taking advantage of other training methods in order to enhance their knowledge and skills in this new role.

* *Further education courses:* There are many job-related and professional courses available at universities and tertiary colleges which will enhance knowledge and skills. These can also lead to qualifications or can qualify for some professional bodies' continuous professional development (CPD) schemes.

* *Computer aided learning:* Many learning packages have now been created for use on personal computers. These give people the opportunity to work at their own pace and in their own time on their training, in the same way that open learning does in a non-digital environment.

* *Mentoring:* Mentoring as a form of training opportunity has increased in popularity. A mentor is someone, usually a colleague, at the same or from a higher level in the organisation, but who is not in a line management relationship with the individual being mentored. They then become someone with whom the individual can go and discuss work-related issues and in particular their own career development. The advantage of this system is that it is outside the normal work relationship and so an overview can be

given without prejudice. The mentor's role is to encourage the protégé and to use their own experience to help manage difficulties which may arise. Many organisations are now investing in formal mentoring schemes, in particular for graduate trainees or high-flyers. In the informal sense, individuals may have more than one mentor to whom they can go for advice dependent on the situation.[43]

- *Sitting with Nellie:* This form of training is perhaps the oldest and most common form to be found in organisations and was particularly popular in production or manufacturing organisations. The trainee is assigned to an experienced member of staff in a similar way to coaching. More often than not though they do not have the training to coach. They are expected to pass on what they know as quickly as possible in order to make the trainee effective at the job.

4.10 Conducting the training: the implementation phase

Training is a partnership between the manager, the trainer and the person being trained. Unless agreement is arranged, it is unlikely that the learner will be sufficiently motivated to undertake the training, nor will the person doing the training be clear about what needs to be achieved. Thus all parties need to sit down and agree objectives for the training as well as clarify why the training is being undertaken. This may be as a part of an annual review of training needs or part of a performance management or appraisal scheme operating in the organisation as a whole. At this meeting, agreement should be reached about the timescale under which the training is to take place as well as how the training will be monitored and evaluated.

Consideration with regard to the timing of the training should be made. When the training should start and finish and, in relation to this, what the best time of day would be to take time away from the workplace. It is important to find a venue away from the normal place of work so as to avoid interruptions. Making sure that any equipment that might be needed is available, checking that it works and changing the seating arrangements in order to make people feel more comfortable with their surroundings are also important considerations.

There are other practical issues which should be borne in mind while conducting the training, for example, ensuring that the most appropriate yet varied methods are chosen to put material across. Some 75 per cent of information is taken in visually and *learning by doing* is by far the best method of all. Trainers should work with methods that they are most familiar with in order to ensure that the delivery keeps people alert and interested. Preparing thoroughly and rehearsing the session before the event, particularly if the trainer is inexperienced, is essential. This should include practising any exercises included in the programme to ascertain how and why they work.

If people are coming from other than the immediate area, sending out instructions for the venue beforehand and briefing people as to the aims and objectives of the session before the event so that they have time to think about it and prepare themselves is important.

Stating the objectives clearly at the start of the session is vital so that everyone knows what is going to happen, and why they are being trained for this particular task. In good presentation style, 'Tell them what is going to be said, say it, then tell them what has been said'.

The trainer can develop the content by expanding existing knowledge and skills through explanation and demonstration. They can check and recap for any knowledge after the session by providing trainees with the opportunity to undertake a practical exercise. The old adage 'How do you eat an elephant?' – 'in bite-size chunks' is a useful one. Little and often helps people to absorb knowledge and skills.

Trainers should look for and use feedback from learners to make sure that understanding has taken place. Watching body language and checking by asking questions helps. On the basis of this feedback, trainers may need to modify their approach. In other words, no amount of planning and design can compensate for the receptiveness of a trainee. Adapting to learners' needs is the key to successful implementation of a training programme.

4.11 Evaluating training outcomes

Evaluating training outcomes cannot be said to be simple, since nothing which involves the measurement of human behaviour, or even the results of human behaviour, is ever simple. Evaluating training is an attempt at determining what changes take place in *skills, knowledge* and *attitudes* of employees as a result of training and how far these changes are beneficial to the organisation's objectives.

Although there are many approaches and styles to evaluation, there is quite a high degree of consistency about what is considered to be the primary purpose underlying evaluation activities. Advocates of evaluation agree that it is an attempt to *improve* the quality of training, and that it might involve, therefore, mechanisms to *prove* that this is done as well as determining what learning has taken place.[44] Emphasis of these three purposes has changed over the years and has roughly parallelled the historical development of evaluation.

Proving

Proving the worth and impact of training was historically the first primary function of evaluation.[45] This form of evaluation has been popular as a mechanism for proving to the organisation that training and development add value to its strategic direction by linking back to strategic goals and contributing to the identification of training needs at an organisational level. As Shipman (1983) stated, 'It should be telling someone whether action has been successful and where fresh investment should be made'.[46]

In addition, the cost–benefit analysis of the training function is important as internal training departments increasingly compete with outside providers. The ability to demonstrate that the training is not only effective but also less costly than other alternatives is important to organisations where outsourcing of peripheral functions is becoming the norm. Training and development delivery is an easy option to outsource as the number of outside providers grows.

Improving

The improving purpose has been stressed partly as a reaction to the difficulties of proving anything about the effects of training. Thus, the 'primary purpose of gathering evaluation data is to provide the trainer with information which will help him increase their subsequent effectiveness'.[47] Hamblin (1974) concurs with this sentiment and adds that the purpose of evaluation 'is not to determine if desired changes did occur but rather determine what should happen next'.[48] This is the most common form of evaluation undertaken usually by the training function itself in the form of end-of-course or post-course questionnaires. The purpose of the exercise is to ask participants in training events to comment on the provision in terms of its strengths and weaknesses in order for the training itself to be changed or improved the next time it takes place. The problem with this sort of immediate response is that it may simply be a knee-jerk reaction to the process rather than a considered approach. One would also need to consider at what point and by what response one would make changes to the provision, i.e. does what one course or group of people say necessarily constitute a representative sample?

Learning

Perhaps the most important, and in most organisations the most under-used, form of evaluation is that of measuring the learning which has taken place as a result of the training. One of the reasons for this, is that it is the most difficult to achieve. This brings into force the relationship between setting specific objectives as a result of the identification of training needs and changes in performance as a result of the training. An advantage of this type of evaluation is that it embraces the relationship between the training function and the trainee's line manager. Strategies for accomplishing this include pre- and post-discussion. This includes setting objectives and measuring the result, often as a part of an ongoing performance management system, or the setting of specific project work which is reviewed at a distant point after the course. A potential problem with this is that it often means a somewhat subjective approach unless the training is skills-based, in which case, increases in productivity are more easily measured. More difficult is the measurement of changes in behaviour, although the increase in the use of 360 degree feedback is helping this process.

It is clear that all training and development has a purpose, thus the evaluation of that training should also have a purpose and should form an integral part of the training process.

4.12 Conclusions

Training aims to change behaviour at the workplace in order to increase efficiency and higher performance standards. In turn, learning is seen as the vehicle for this behavioural change. One of the themes running through this chapter is that the benefits and the responsibility of training rest with the organisation as well as the individual. Therefore, commitment to training is required from both.

Applying the principles of learning and adopting a systematic approach to training based on the identification of training needs as well as a programme, designed and evaluated on the basis of these needs, are all necessary commitments that the organisation needs to make. Likewise, individuals need to match this commitment with positive motivation towards training. It is only when this duality of purpose is achieved that the real benefits of training for both the organisation and the individual come into play.

4.13 References

1. Department of Employment. *Training for jobs*. Cmnd 9135, London: HMSO, 1984.
2. Department of Education and Science. *Better schools*. Cmnd 9469, London: HMSO, 1985; Department of Employment and Department of Education and Science. *Working together: education and training*. Cmnd 9823, London: HMSO, 1986; Department of Education and Science. *Higher education: meeting the challenge*. Cmnd 114, London: HMSO, 1987; Mangham IL, Silver MS. *Management training: context and practice*. Bath: ESRC/DTI, School of Management, University of Bath, 1986; Constable J, McCormick J. *The making of British managers: a report for the BIM and CBI into management training, education and development*. Corby: BIM, 1987; Handy C. *The making of managers: a report on management education,*

   training and development in the USA, West Germany, France, Japan and the UK. London: National Economic Development Office, 1987; Department of Trade and Industry. *Competitiveness: helping business to win.* Cmnd 2563, London: HMSO, 1994 (First Competitiveness White Paper); Department of Trade and Industry. *Competitiveness: forging ahead.* Cmnd 2867, London: HMSO, 1995 (Second Competitiveness White Paper); Department of Trade and Industry. *Competitiveness: creating the enterprise centre of Europe.* London: HMSO, 1996 (Third Competitiveness White Paper).

3. O'Brien R, Manpower Services Commission, Chairman, 1982.

4. *Training for jobs.*

5. Finegold S, Soskice D. The failure of training in Britain: analysis and prescription. In: Esland G ed. *Education, training and employment: volume 1: educated labour: the changing basis of industrial demand.* Wokingham: Addison Wesley, 1991.

6. Royal Commission on Trade Unions and Employers' Associations. 1965–1968. London: HMSO, 1968; National Economic Development Office. *Management education in the 1970s.* London: HMSO, 1978; Manpower Services Commission. *Skills monitoring report.* Sheffield: MSC Evaluation and Research Unit, 1986; *Skill needs in Britain.* London: Public Attitude Surveys, 1995.

7. Daly A. *Education, training and productivity in the US and Great Britain.* London: NISR, no. 63, 1984; Worswick GD. *Education and economic performance.* Aldershot: Gower, 1985; Steedman H. Vocational training in France and Britain: the construction industry. *NI Economic Review* May 1986.

8. MSC. *A challenge to complacency: changing attitudes to training: a report to the Manpower Services Commission and National Economic Development Organisation.* Sheffield: MSC, 1985.

9. Department of Trade and Industry. *Competitiveness: forging ahead.*

10. Hogarth T, Siora T, Briscoe G, Hasluck C. The net costs of training to employers: initial training of young people in intermediate skills. *Labour Market Trends* 1996; **104**(3): 121–6.

11. Hogarth *et al.* Net costs.

12. Hogarth *et al.* Net costs.

13. Park A. *Individual commitment to learning: individuals' attitudes.* Sheffield: Department for Employment and Education Research Series, no. 32, 1994.

14. Gallie D, White M. *Employee commitment and the skills revolution: first findings from the Employment in Britain Survey.* London: PSI, 1993.

15. Department of Employment. *Glossary of training terms.* London: HMSO, 1971.

16. Hesseling P. *Strategy of evaluation research in the field of supervisory and management training.* Assen: Van Gorcum, 1971.

17. Oatey M. Economics of training with respect to the firm. *British Journal of Industrial Relations* 1970; **8**(1): 1–21.

18. Manpower Services Commission. *Glossary of training terms.* London: HMSO, 1981.

19. Wexley KN, Latham GP. *Developing and training human resources in organisations.* London: Scott Foresman, 1981.

20. Goldstein IL. *Training in organisations: needs assessment, development and evaluation.* Pacific Grove, CA: Brooks/Cole, 1986.

21. Bass BM, Vaughan JA. *Training in industry: the management of learning.* London: Tavistock, 1966.

22. Campbell JP, Dunnette MD, Lawler EE, Weick KE. *Managerial behavior, performance and effectiveness.* New York: McGraw-Hill, 1970; Laird D. *Approaches to training and development.* Reading, MA: Addison Wesley, 1983.

23. Campbell *et al. Managerial behaviour*; Laird, *Approaches.*

24. Campbell *et al. Managerial behaviour*; Laird, *Approaches*; Digman LA. Management development: needs and practices. *Personnel* 1980; **57**, July–Aug.: 45–57.

25. French WL, Bell CH Jr, Zawacki RA eds. *Organisational development: theory, practice and research.* Burr Ridge, IL: Irwin, 1994.

26. Bass and Vaughan, *Training in industry.*

27. Herzberg F. *Work and the nature of man*. Cleveland: World Publishing Co., 1966.

28. Kolb DA, Rubin IN, McIntyre JM. *Organisational psychology: an experimental approach*. London: Prentice Hall, 1974.

29. Honey P, Mumford A. *Using your learning styles*. Maidenhead: Peter Honey, 1986.

30. Silverman RE. Learning theory applied to training. In: Otto CP, Glaser RE eds. *The management of training: a handbook for training and development personnel*. London: Addison Wesley, 1970.

31. McGehee W, Thayer PW. *Training in business and industry*. New York: Wiley, 1961.

32. Goldstein, *Training in organisations*.

33. Department of Employment, *Glossary*.

34. Annet J. Learning in practice. In: Warr P ed. *Psychology at work*. Harmondsworth: Penguin, 1974.

35. Mager RF. *Preparing instructional objectives*. Belmont, CA: David S Lake, 1984.

36. Goldstein, *Training in organisations*.

37. Mager, *Preparing*.

38. Thompson R. *Managing people*. Oxford: Butterworth-Heinemann, 1993.

39. Hackman JR, Oldham GR. Motivation through design of work – a test of theory. *Organisational Behaviour and Human Performance* 1976; **16**: 250–79.

40. Honey, Mumford, *Learning styles*.

41. Thompson, *Managing people*.

42. Hackman, Oldham, *Motivation*.

43. Clutterbuck D. *Everyone needs a mentor: fostering talent at work*. London: IPD, 1991.

44. Easterby-Smith M. *Evaluation of management education, training and development*. Aldershot: Gower, 1986.

45. Odiorne GS. The need for economic approach to training. *Journal of the American Society of Training Directors* 1964; **18**(3).

46. Shipman MD. Parvenu evaluation. In: Smetherham D ed. *Practising evaluation*. Nafferton Books, UK, 1983.

47. Warr PB, Bird M, Rackham N. *Evaluation of management training*. Aldershot: Gower, 1970.

48. Hamblin AC. *Evaluation and control of training*. New York: McGraw-Hill, 1974.

5 | Culture, organisation development and change

Allan Williams

The most pressing problems facing today's leaders are those associated with change. Government, industry, unions and professional bodies are all having to adapt to their changing environments. The fortunate ones have been able to adapt by voluntarily managing a process of incremental or fundamental change. The less fortunate ones have been forced into unpopular change decisions involving downsizing and mergers in order to survive. Today's leaders continue to seek strategies which will enable their organisations to cope with the need to change while satisfying a range of financial and social criteria. Organisation development (OD) represents a body of knowledge to help them in this task.

Although there is a vast literature on OD, its definition and boundaries are unclear. This is all to the good, because it is a sign of a growing and dynamic field of knowledge, and one which has been adapting to new research findings and theories. What help can OD give to those managers who are trying to improve the effectiveness of their organisations in a changing environment? Or to put it another way, the competitiveness of their organisations?

This chapter attempts to answer these questions by doing the following:

1. identifying the main influences which have shaped the emergence and development of OD;
2. presenting a framework which clarifies the nature of the conceptual and methodological resources which OD makes available to the manager;
3. outlining some ways in which these OD resources can be most effectively utilised by management.

5.1 Main influences on OD

OD theorists and practitioners are continually trying to find valid answers to two basic questions: What changes do organisations need to make to their culture, and to the way in which they organise and manage themselves, in order to remain competitive? How should organisations go about introducing these changes so as to achieve their objectives efficiently and effectively? These *content* and *process* issues have been particularly influenced by the concepts and approaches outlined below.

Open socio-technical systems model

A system is an orderly grouping of different components for the purpose of achieving some given objective. The essential difference in thinking of an organisation as an open rather than a closed system is that due emphasis is given to its dependence upon the environment for its continued existence. Closed system thinking tends to encourage the adoption of a problem-solving approach which focuses attention on internal causes of stress, rather than those causes stemming from an organisation's relationship with its external environment.

The open system model of an organisation is basically very simple. The organisation is seen as:

- importing energy from its environment (in the form of labour, materials, finance and equipment);
- transforming this energy into some product or service which is characteristic of the system (e.g., paper products, financial services);
- exporting the product or service into the environment;
- re-energising the system with further resources from the environment.

Thus the open system model highlights the need for an organisation to adapt to changes in its environment. This model has led OD theorists to research and propose those characteristics which are likely to increase the capacity of an organisation to adapt to environmental change. The term organisational effectiveness, as opposed to organisational efficiency, is often used to denote the goal of enabling organisations to grow and survive over time, rather than achieving short-term efficiency or profitability. OD is very much concerned with organisational effectiveness, and therefore with those organisational properties which are conducive to adaptability, flexibility, and innovativeness. Another term which is increasingly being used to convey a similar idea is 'the learning organisation'.[1] This highlights the capacity of an organisation to learn in the process of doing, i.e. to learn how to do things better as a result of experience.

The socio-technical component of the open system model has its origins in the pioneering work of the Tavistock Institute for Human Relations in London. Their research in British coal mines and in Indian textile mills demonstrated the interdependence of the social and technical sub-systems within an organisation.[2] Mechanisation inevitably had repercussions on roles in the social system, and re-structuring had implications for the efficiency of the technical system. The main lesson to be learned was that when introducing changes to the workplace, the needs of both the technical and the social system have to be taken into account. Ignoring or misunderstanding social needs will eventually be reflected in such criteria as productivity, quality of output, accidents, absenteeism and turnover.

Subsequent research has increased our insight into the relationships between technology, organisations and their environments. In the well-documented study of the electronics industry in Scotland, Burns and Stalker[3] found that while the less successful organisations tended to be 'mechanistic', i.e. a greater reliance placed on formal rules and procedures, narrow spans of control, and decision-making at the highest levels, the successful organisations were more 'organic', i.e. less emphasis on formal procedures, wider spans of supervisory control more common, more decisions taken at lower levels. The explanation for these findings was that organically structured organisations were able to adapt to change more quickly, and a better match therefore for changing times.

Similarly, in a study of 100 firms in South East Essex, Woodward[4] found that as the technology changed, so certain structural characteristics changed (e.g. the span of control of the chief executive). She found also that different technologies imposed different kinds of demands on organisations, and that these had to be met by an appropriate structure. Organisations with structural characteristics close to the pattern for their particular technology tended to be more effective.

A refinement to the organic/mechanistic model came from the work of Lawrence and Lorsch,[5] who further elucidated the complexity of the relationship between an organisation and its environment. They drew attention to the fact that different parts of an organisation may interact with quite different environments. Thus while an organic structure and climate may be appropriate for the R&D department, a mechanistic structure better suited the production department.

Human psychology and human relations

OD has been particularly influenced by certain values associated with humanistic psychologists such as Abraham Maslow and Carl Rogers which stress the importance of developing human potential, giving individuals opportunities to influence their work environment, providing them with interest and challenge in their work, and recognise their unique and complex needs. These values were very visible in the pioneering OD activities of such Americans as Chris Argyris and Douglas McGregor. They received new impetus through the almost missionary zeal of Thorsrud, Cherns and others in Europe.[6] The latter found expression in the industrial democracy (ID) and quality of working life (QWL) movements. In the UK a visible sign of their success is the promotional and advisory activities of the Advisory, Conciliation and Arbitration Service (ACAS) whose mission statement emphasises 'as part of our approach we seek to help organisations to become more effective by improving the quality of working life'.[7]

The human relations movement was influenced by the value systems referred to as well as those studies which highlighted the importance of social relationships, group membership and leadership style in determining the performance and well-being of people at work. Seminal studies included: the Hawthorne studies;[8] Lewin's studies[9] of the benefits of group decision-making; Coch and French's study[10] of the superiority of a participative approach to change. Of particular importance to OD were the early group approaches to individual learning and change as developed by the National Training Laboratories, and referred to as T-groups or sensitivity training. Most of the early OD giants such as Bennis, McGregor, Argyris and Schein, were all heavily involved in T-groups.[11]

Force field model

One of the most enduring conceptual models in OD was originated by an American social psychologist, Kurt Lewin.[12] In order to cope with various forces which can facilitate or inhibit change, Lewin formulated his 3-step model.

1. Organisations have an inherent capacity to maintain the *status quo* by a balance of driving and restraining forces. In order to introduce change, one must disturb this equilibrium by introducing new forces, removing old ones, or both. This *unfreezing* process can be achieved by making people feel dissatisfied with the present state of affairs, and motivating them to seek improvements.
2. Once the unfreezing process is well under way the *changing* process can be initiated, and participants encouraged to seek new solutions to old problems.
3. The final phase is to *refreeze* or stabilise the forces operating in the new situation. This involves ensuring that the changes are legitimised and integrated into the organisation so that their maintenance is not dependent upon temporary forces, such as the presence of an external consultant.

The value of this unfreezing/changing/refreezing model is that it encourages those responsible for managing change to identify those forces which are supporting the desired change, and those opposing it. A systematic analysis of these opposing forces is more likely to result in a successful strategy for change.

Action research

The action research approach to change was another valuable contribution made by Lewin.[13] He argued that research in the behavioural sciences would have only limited impact if the researcher was involved solely in the research process (i.e. developing hypotheses and gathering information), and not in the subsequent action process (i.e. planning, implementation and evaluating subsequent actions). Pioneering studies of the action research mode include: Lewin's work on changing food eating habits, Coch and French's study on overcoming resistance to change, and Jaques' studies[14] in the Glacier Metal works in the UK. Many OD practitioners continue to adopt this process model when intervening in organisations.

Change agents

Initially OD change agents were the internal or external consultants who intervened in the processes of organisations in order to bring about certain changes as effectively as possible. Well versed in psychology or the behavioural sciences, their style of intervention was very much that of a joint problem-solving approach. To illustrate this pioneering style, and the reasons for it, it is helpful to compare and contrast three types of role relationships which a consultant can adopt towards a client system: the *expert*, the *teacher* and the *counsellor*.

The expert: The client system experiences a problem; it approaches a consultant with the expectation that the latter will diagnose and prescribe a solution. The consultant, put in the position of expert, plays a fairly directive role. Often the client prejudges the problem by approaching a consultant who is an expert in a given type of solution, e.g. management by objectives, assessment centres, autonomous work groups. This sort of relationship has many attractions: the solutions applied have usually already been researched and developed by other organisations, thus reducing cost and risk of failure; the employment of an expert generates confidence in what is being done, and provides a feeling of security; if the consultant's solution is not attractive or is threatening, it can often be rejected or shelved with the minimum of disturbance to the client system.

Possible drawbacks include:

1. Superficial diagnosis and treatment. Sometimes the function of the expert is merely to provide additional authority to introduce changes which top management see as desirable.
2. The non-participative style of many experts may arouse unnecessary resistance to change, particularly where this involves breaking social norms.
3. The expert's terms of reference may severely limit the area of the client system within which he or she can operate. Thus the changes proposed or introduced may be incompatible or threatening to other sub-systems.
4. Solutions applied may be the result of a consultant's sales ability or of current fashion, rather than the outcome of a proper diagnosis of the problem.

The teacher: Here the consultant is primarily concerned in bringing about change through the transmission of knowledge and skill. The immediate target for change is the individual and his or her problem-solving behaviour, rather than the structural and technological variables affecting behaviour. Learning usually takes place at internal or external formal courses where simulated rather than real life problems are tackled, although in recent years formal learning experiences are increasingly being designed to be built around actual problems. The advantages of this approach include:

1. A high degree of control can be maintained over what is learned.
2. Large numbers of individuals can be exposed to new thinking at relatively low cost.
3. It is not too difficult to design formal learning situations to which participants will react favourably.

Potential weaknesses include transfer of knowledge and skills to on-the-job behaviour often being negligible (particularly where attitudes or managerial style are concerned), and individuals can find themselves on courses, especially external courses, which neither match their needs nor those of their organisation.

The counsellor: Sometimes a consultant takes on a role very similar to that of a counsellor in a therapeutic situation, i.e. a joint problem-solving approach where the counsellor does not try to impose a particular solution on the client, but encourages the client to arrive at a joint solution for which the client shares responsibility. While the counsellor is non-directive with respect to the solution, he or she does guide the problem-solving process through its various stages: the client will be encouraged to undertake a thorough diagnosis of the problem before thinking about solutions, and to choose a solution only after exploring a range of alternatives. Where an OD consultant adopts this role in relation to a client, the mechanics of the process are different since the client is part of a larger system; thus the problem-solving stages leading to change must involve those individuals, groups, or their representatives, with vested interest in the problem and the power to implement or to frustrate a proposed solution.

It is this counselling model which comes closest to describing the typical role played by a consultant in an OD intervention. The origins of this counselling approach can be seen in the thinking of Carl Rogers, in action research and in T-groups.

Learning theory

At this point there is a strong case for learning theory to be highlighted. There are two particular theories which inform the thinking and behaviour of change agents: Skinner's reinforcement theory[15] and Bandura's social learning theory.[16] In its simplest terms the former states that it is the consequences of behaviour which determine whether the behaviour will be repeated. Thus if openness in communicating with clients results in better cooperation and less resistance to change, then change agents are more likely to display this behaviour in their future interactions with clients. Reinforcement theory explains a good deal of our learning, much of which may occur without our conscious intervention. In contrast, social learning theory recognises the role of cognitive abilities in the process of learning. This theory accounts for human learning which occurs through a process of modelling or imitation. Change agents may model their behaviour when interacting with clients on Schein's[17] process consultancy approach because they are convinced that this approach is most likely to lead to a successful intervention. Similarly, their clients may be prepared to follow 'good practice' by learning from the experiences of their successful competitors as the British motor industry did of the Japanese.

Kolb's[18] model of experiential learning has also influenced and been influenced by OD. He defines learning as the process whereby knowledge is created through the transformation of experience. The iterative process of his model follows the sequence of concrete experience, reflective observation, abstract conceptualisation, and active experimentation. This is very similar to Lewin's model of action research, and Kolb acknowledges his debt to Lewin. It is now generally agreed that an active, experiential approach to learning is far more effective than other more passive alternatives. This is particularly so when OD practitioners are trying to facilitate change in the belief systems underlying moribund cultures, or overcome resistance to change.

5.2 OD interventions and technology

Gaining insight into the main influences on OD is the first step towards learning to use this resource for competitive gain. The next step is to become more aware of the available technology, and the situations or context in which they are likely to be valuable. Table 5.1 is a framework for exploring these issues.

Table 5.1 Intervention goals and OD technology

Basic approaches	Intervention goals	OD models and technology
process-oriented	improving organisational effectiveness and health	Changing job attributes e.g. job redesign
technostructural	improving organisational learning capacity	Changing team attributes e.g. team development role analysis intergroup development
integrated	improving the match between corporate strategy and organisational culture	Changing organisational attributes e.g. managerial grid sociotechnical system analysis survey feedback human resource development

Intervention goals

Many of the early accounts of OD included the goals of improving organisational effectiveness or health. These terms were often used to differentiate between economic criteria applied to organisations (e.g. input–output efficiency measures), and the socio-psychological criteria which emphasised the softer variables of job satisfaction, innovativeness, flexibility, organisational loyalty and commitment, and so on. Implicit in the latter criteria was the notion that certain types of behaviour were more conducive to an organisation successfully adapting to changes and new competition in its environment. Developing these desirable characteristics became a goal of many OD programmes.

An example of an influential model of these characteristics was Likert's System 4 or 'participative management'.[19] Key features of this ideal management system were: high performance goals; an overlapping network of cohesive teams (the linking pin structure); a climate of openness; and a supportive managerial style (individuals felt that their needs for self-esteem, etc., were being met). An extensive research programme provided the evidence which encouraged managers to develop their organisations along these lines through an appropriately designed OD programme.

One of the terms used in the OD literature is that of organisational self-renewal. This is the idea that it is not sufficient for organisations to change only in response to planned OD efforts, but that a climate for change needs to become an inherent characteristic of the organisation. This is a powerful idea given the rate and continuous nature of environmental change. As already pointed out, a similar idea is being promoted under the label of the *learning organisation*. An organisation which is continually able to transform itself as the need arises has an obvious competitive edge over others. From their own research and a review of the relevant literature Pedler *et al.*[20] identify eleven characteristics of the learning organisation: learning approach to strategy; participative policy-making; information; formative accounting and control; internal exchange; reward flexibility; enabling structures; boundary workers as environmental scanners; inter-company learning; learning climate; self-development of all. Underlying this framework, and other major contributors to learning organisations such as that of Senge,[21] are the OD values and systems thinking we have already mentioned.

One dimension which has aroused considerable interest in the management literature is that of *organisational culture*. This has been stimulated by such best-sellers as Peters and Waterman's *In Search of Excellence*,[22] which highlighted the key role of culture in achieving organisational success. By culture we are referring to the relatively stable and commonly held beliefs and values which underlie many aspects of behaviour displayed within an organisation. The importance of culture within the context of implementing strategic plans is clear when we consider the importance which many organisations are now attaching to quality and customer care. These attributes of products and services will only be consistently achieved if they become embedded in the culture of the organisation, hence the recent spate of organisational change programmes to bring culture into line with corporate strategy.[23] Many of these programmes may be labelled 'total quality management' and 're-engineering', and therefore may not appear to come out of the OD stable. It is true that they do not necessarily share the same value system as traditional OD (particularly when re-engineering is a euphemism for downsizing!), but many certainly draw on the proven methods of OD in the process of managing change (e.g., use of appropriate consultants as change agents, sponsorship of top management, data collection and action research, use of teams as a major driver of change).

Basic approaches

Table 5.1 lists three basic approaches: process-oriented, technostructural and integrated. Process-oriented interventions are those which are primarily directed at changing attitudes, values, norms, goals and relationships influencing behaviour. Technostructural interventions, on the other hand, are primarily directed at changing technological and structural variables influencing behaviour. Integrated interventions are those which combine both approaches. In the early days of OD the first approach dominated practice, but evaluation studies revealed its limitations and the strengths of the technostructural approaches. Now it is generally acknowledged that for effective change to take place an integrated approach is needed. Such an approach is also consistent with the principles of systems and learning theories.

Changing job attributes

Many behavioural scientists have criticised the person/job relationship which exists for the majority of people at the lower levels of organisations. These criticisms are usually based on theories of motivation, on the values underlying the quality of working life philosophy, and on certain aspects of sociotechnical systems thinking. The result is that various theorists and practitioners have arrived at certain principles of 'good' job design which it is argued will not only lead to greater individual job satisfaction, but to benefits to the employing organisation (e.g., better quality performance, lower turnover and absenteeism) and even to society itself in the form of improved mental health of its working citizens.[24]

Some OD interventions are aimed at developing the person/job relationship in the direction of normative job design principles. Thus consultants guided by Herzberg's motivation–hygiene theory will seek to enrich jobs by building into them more opportunities for experiencing achievement, recognition, interesting work, responsibility, and advancement. Consultants attracted by features of sociotechnical systems thinking may want to redesign production systems along the lines of autonomous work groups, i.e. operators divided into cohesive teams which match the technology they are using, given meaningful units of work to perform (e.g. servicing all the needs of a client or assembling complete television receivers), and allowed significant autonomy in organising and monitoring their work (e.g. determine their own work pace, distribute tasks among themselves, carry out their own quality control).

There are now many examples of interventions of this nature. Buckingham[25] describes a programme where job enrichment principles were successfully applied in restructuring the role of foreman in nine factories in a tobacco manufacturing firm. Most of the successful interventions reported in the UK have seen the early involvement of workers and their union representatives in the change processes.

Changing team attributes

Improving team effectiveness is an important objective of organisations, since much of the work is accomplished through teams and it is recognised that work-team culture has a significant effect on individual behaviour. McGregor was typical of an early group of psychologists who tried to identify the characteristics which differentiated the more effective managerial team from the less effective team. Table 5.2 incorporates these criteria into a form which he used in an intervention activity at the Union Carbide Corporation. This form was borrowed from Bennis.[26] Individuals are asked to analyse their team by rating it on a scale from 1 to 7 with respect to each of the variables. The whole team is then asked to discuss in depth the situation with respect to each variable, and to formulate ideas as to why these perceptions exist. The objective is to try and get the group to agree on those characteristics which require improvement, to formulate action plans, to implement the plans, and to evaluate the value of the team development exercise.

The above is just one example of a technique used to build or develop effective teamwork. There are a host of others. Some are primarily designed to improve teamwork in an established group, some more useful for building up the effectiveness of a newly formed team. An example of the latter is the role analysis technique. This intervention is aimed at clarifying the role expectations and obligations of team members, and is particularly useful where role ambiguity or confusion exists. The assumption behind the intervention is that consensual determination of the content of roles for individual members of a team will lead to more satisfying and productive behaviour.

Often the creative and productive energy of an organisation is sapped by intergroup conflict. The factors which contribute to intergroup conflict (e.g. competition), and the consequences of conflict, are well understood in the literature and have been succinctly summarised by Schein.[27] The consequences include: each group develops negative stereotypes of the other; interaction and communication between them decreases, and when it takes place, information is distorted; each thinks that it is better than the other with respect to its products, methods of work, and so on. These consequences are less likely to occur where the groups can identify a common enemy, where the nature of their tasks forces them to interact and communicate with each other frequently, or where a higher goal exists which transcends conflicting interests but is only attainable through cooperation. The problem is, how does one go about creating the conditions when intergroup conflict is the norm rather than the exception?

Table 5.2 Team development scale

Stage	Initial position			Final position
1.	Degree of mutual trust: High suspicion_____			High trust
	(1)		(4)	(7)
2.	Communications: Guarded, cautious_____			Open, authentic
	(1)		(4)	(7)
3.	Degree of mutual support: Every man for himself_____			Genuine concern for each other
	(1)		(4)	(7)
4.	Team objectives: Not understood_____			Clearly understood
	(1)		(4)	(7)
5.	Handling conflicts within team: Through denial, avoidance, suppression, or compromise_____			Acceptance and 'working through' of conflicts
	(1)		(4)	(7)
6.	Utilisation of member resources: Competencies used by team_____			Competencies not used
	(1)		(4)	(7)
7.	Control methods: Control is imposed_____			Control from within
	(1)		(4)	(7)
8.	Organisational environment: Restrictive, pressure for conformity_____			Free, supportive, respect for differences
	(1)		(4)	(7)

Source: Bennis, *Organisation development*

The development of techniques to improve sub-systems larger than single teams was a major advance within OD. The most influential model of intergroup development is that of Blake, Shepherd and Mouton.[28] The following steps are typical of the process:

1. The two groups (or their leaders) meet to discuss ways of improving intergroup relations.
2. If commitment is obtained, the intervention process proceeds by asking each group to prepare two lists, working independently of each other. One list describes their perceptions of the other group; the second how they think the other group will describe them.
3. The groups come together to share the information on the four lists. Discussion is limited to questions of clarification.
4. The groups separate again, to complete two tasks: to discuss what they have learnt about themselves and the other group; to list the priority issues which need to be resolved between the two groups.

5. The groups come together to share the information on the lists, create a joint list of issues to be resolved in order of priority, generate action plans, assign responsibilities.
6. Sometimes a follow-up meeting is organised to evaluate progress on action plans and implementation.

This type of intervention has been carried out in order to improve collaboration not only between functional groups within an organisation (e.g. marketing and production), but also between representatives of head office and a field sub-system, between union and management representatives, and between representatives of merging organisations.[29]

Changing organisational attributes

Although the popularity of the managerial grid OD programme[30] has declined, it is worth describing since it incorporates the classic features of OD. It is designed to change an organisation's culture so that it moves from its present state to an ideal state as indicated by an influential body of knowledge. It is a good example of what may be called a 'packaged' OD programme, since it is mainly run by internal change agents and is structured around printed learning materials. Table 5.3 summarises the six phases of the grid; each phase consists of several days' intensive study directed by line managers, themselves under the guidance of a skilled OD coordinator.

Table 5.3 The six phases of the managerial grid

Phase	Development
Phase 1	Introduces individual managers to a 9 × 9 grid (showing concern for production on the horizontal axis and concern for people on the vertical axis) which is used to present assumptions underlying five main managerial styles. Managers learn to recognise the gap between their own style and the ideal style, and through standard exercises are encouraged to acquire new behaviours to reduce the gap.
Phase 2	A team or 'family group' examines itself in terms of grid theories, barriers adversely affecting its performance are identified and plans made to overcome them.
Phase 3	Key managers heading interdependent teams are brought together so that grid learning can be applied to resolve problems preventing cooperation between divisions, departments, etc.
Phase 4	Top management contrast current objectives and culture of their organisation with a model of what it would be like if it was truly excellent. Objectives are identified to bring the organisation nearer to this ideal model.
Phase 5	Stated objectives in phase 4 are implemented.
Phase 6	Overall accomplishments of grid OD are reviewed and the need for further change identified.

Source: Blake *et al. Managing intergroup conflict*

On paper, grid OD is an excellent example of applying behavioural science knowledge to change. Attractive features of this approach are: the organisation-wide perspective; it attempts to change in a logical sequence the basic sub-systems of an organisation; it gives managers a large part of the responsibility for directing formal learning experiences; plans for change are the result of joint problem-solving; the unfreezing/changing/refreezing model underlies the structure of the learning activities; it is based on a coherent management philosophy. It is therefore not surprising that many organisations have made use of the grid. However, few have gone through all six phases, since this would involve several years of commitment for large organisations. It is perhaps significant that the most frequently quoted evaluation of the grid was published when it was first being widely marketed,[31] and that apart from British–American Tobacco[32] there are few examples of UK organisations having made systematic and extensive use of grid OD. It is not on methodological but on ideological grounds that the grid can be criticised. Its strong value system may be appropriate for some American companies, but not for all American companies nor for other cultures.

Survey feedback

This is an OD technique which has been in use for many years and is flexible enough to remain popular. It is an intervention technique which managers can readily comprehend since it has grown out of a fairly traditional management tool – the attitude survey. The latter is a systematic attempt to assess attitudes of organisational members to their jobs, and to existing and proposed company policies and practices. This information is used to aid management problem-solving. There are a number of reviews in the literature which amply demonstrate the potential value of attitude surveys as diagnostic instruments for throwing light on problems of morale, turnover, absenteeism and performance. On the other hand, their contributions to organisational change have often been fairly limited. It has been common practice for the full report on the survey to be treated as confidential and restricted to top management in its uncensored form. The pressure to *unfreeze* and change is slight, and the report can always be shelved if it threatens the *status quo* or criticises policies or practices which are regarded with favour by senior management.

The model which OD consultants most frequently refer to when talking about survey feedback has been described by Mann.[33] The data is collected on an organisation-wide basis, fed back to top management, and then down the hierarchy through the medium of functional teams. At each feedback meeting the superior takes the chair, and together with subordinates they interpret the data, make plans for desirable changes and for introducing the data at the next level. Because of the overlapping nature of functional teams within an organisation (through the dual membership of the superior), the outcome of discussions is fed both up and down the hierarchy. Thus a head of department who is in a subordinate position at a plant meeting will report to subordinates at a departmental meeting the outcome of discussions at the plant level, and report to his or her superior at a plant meeting the outcome of discussions at the departmental level. The data fed back to a given functional team will be relevant to the problem-solving activities of that group. Thus the top management team would see the data relating to all departments and sections of the organisation, but the marketing department may only see data relating to that department and, for comparison, the average organisational responses to those questions which were also asked of other departments (comparative data can encourage the unfreezing of attitudes by creating dissatisfaction with one's own showing).

The consultant usually attends the meetings and serves as a resource person and 'counsellor'. Sometimes the consultant may have an important role to play in preparing a superior for a meeting, particularly if the data is critical of the management team and the superior not accustomed to joint problem-solving sessions with subordinates. The consultant may also see his or her role as encouraging the team to analyse the problem-solving processes used during the feedback sessions. This process consultation is intended to help the team learn more effective problem-solving behaviour from its own experiences – a sort of team development exercise.

There are studies to suggest that in the right cultural setting survey feedback can be a successful intervention technique.[34] However, it has its limitations. The objective of survey feedback is to induce the organisation to change itself; this removes from the consultant's shoulders the responsibility of deciding what structural and functional changes should be made. The disadvantage of this is that an organisation may reinforce its present mode of operation even if this had certain basic defects. Thus a non-union organisation is likely to remain a non-union organisation even after a survey feedback exercise. The changes made therefore are likely to be in the form of mild reform, and there are unlikely to be fundamental shifts in information flow, power handling, or basic structure. The goal of the consultant is not to suggest actions, but to enable individuals and groups to identify important problems and their solutions. This takes place in the feedback sessions. These are often voluntary; unfortunately it is the supervisors with the most problems who are least likely to hold them.

These two examples of applying OD techniques to changing organisational attributes are primarily process-led interventions. In a sociotechnical systems analysis, structural change becomes a prime target. With these and other theoretical frameworks in mind, a consultant can enter into a collaborative relationship with a client system based on the action research model. Clark describes a project of this nature.[35] Over a period of three years the project was concerned with the organisational aspects of designing an advanced and technologically integrated factory that was intended to replace three semi-autonomous factories. For the most part the client consisted of a specially constituted design team drawn from R&D, production, industrial relations, finance and engineering services. The consultants did not see their task as trying to push any particular solution, but tried through jointly conducted projects in the existing factories to re-educate the client; that is, to help them to re-appraise some of the design-related beliefs they held in the light of alternative designs and their accompanying consequences.

The human resource development model

Another management model which is less clearly structured and theoretically bound than others, has been exerting considerable influence on management action and on academic research.[36] This may be referred to as the human resource development model. It is characterised by renewed importance being attached to line managers becoming skilled in human resource management, by an attempt to develop human resource policies which are compatible with and reinforce corporate strategies, and by aiming to achieve high levels of employee involvement, commitment and self-development. There are many ways in which an organisation can attempt to bring about these attributes. To do it effectively in most organisations will involve changing their culture, since the changes will mean a fundamental shift in shared beliefs about the ways in which human resources are managed. Few organisations may attach the label of OD to these activities, because of the emphasis on technostructural rather than process approaches.

5.3 Effective use of OD resources

Now that we have discussed some of the intervention goals associated with OD, and some of the approaches and techniques being applied to achieve these goals, it remains to provide a few guidelines on the effective use of OD resources. The manager who is seriously interested in learning more about OD resources than is appropriate to describe here, will find it rewarding to study French and Bell[37] or one of the other detailed texts on OD. By OD resources I include the conceptual models which have been developed to guide managers as to the direction in which change should be made (content issues), the tools and techniques which have been developed to effect change successfully within organisations (process issues), and the skills of OD consultants (professional change agents).

The interactive model of factors influencing planned change in Figure 5.1 is a convenient structure for this discussion.

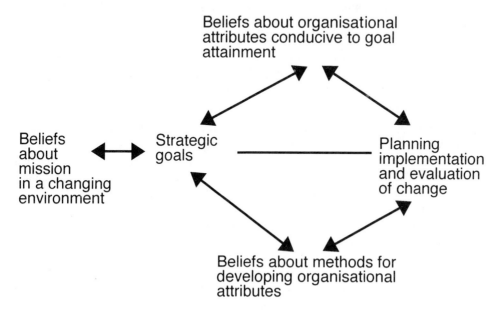

Figure 5.1 An interactive model of factors influencing planned change

1. *Mission and strategic goals:* One of the weaknesses of many early OD efforts was that they tended to become an end in themselves rather than being closely linked to the organisation's strategic plans. To indulge in OD in order to 'make the organisation more effective', or to follow the lead of competitors, is a luxury to be dropped as soon as finance is tight, the senior manager sponsoring the programme leaves, or the novelty value of the programme wanes. For a successful change programme to be initiated, more enduring forces need to be operating such as: agreed change objectives to support the business strategy; informed decision-making by the chief executive officer and his or her team when committing themselves to particular change objectives, and the means of achieving these objectives; adequately resourced and skilled coordinators to oversee the development and implementation of plans. Planned change must be an integral part of the strategic plans of an organisation. An OD intervention should not be seen as a means of changing the internal environment of an organisation to conform to an ideal state, but as a means of establishing a better fit between corporate strategy and the internal environment.

2. *Attributes conducive to goal attainment:* As we have seen in our discussion of the main influences in the development of OD, research in the behavioural sciences has led theorists and practitioners to believe that certain attributes of jobs, teams and organisations will lead to certain consequences. Accumulated research findings have meant that some of these beliefs have had to be radically modified, others have only needed fine tuning. We now know more about the conditions (e.g. dominant technology used by the organisation, national culture) under which certain types of solutions (e.g. participative management) are likely to achieve expected outcomes. Managers initiating planned change

need to be well informed, or to have access to appropriate experts, before selecting given behavioural science solutions to achieve their strategic goals.

3. *Methods conducive to change:* Our knowledge in this area is substantial. We have some proven models to help us in managing the process of change (e.g. force field model). We have a range of reliable and valid techniques for arriving at action plans, and for ensuring commitment to implementation (e.g. action research, survey feedback). We know about the importance of giving the ownership of change to those who have to implement it and make it work, and that this relationship is more likely to hold in certain situations than others (e.g. in Western democratic cultures). We know about the techniques which will facilitate individual and group learning (e.g. modelling). We know the key role of power in bringing about change, and hence the importance of the chief executive officer leading a major change effort.

One of the factors accounting for the limited success of many of the early OD efforts was the weak power base of the external consultant, a feature which was exacerbated by the value system of many OD consultants. Considerations of ownership and power have led many current OD interventions to become more management-centred and less consultant-centred. This is particularly noticeable in current attempts to change organisational culture.[38] Consultant-driven change is more likely to occur where a packaged programme such as the *managerial grid* is used, or where a prestigious consultant is employed to steer through the programme. The switch to more management-driven OD recognises the source of power within the client system, the need for more flexible and less value-laden change programmes, and the fact that a key task of general managers in any organisation is managing change. For change programmes to support corporate strategy, management-driven OD is essential. This is even more so where fundamental rather than incremental change is being considered. By fundamental change one is referring to situations where an organisation re-aligns its mission and strategy to cope with new external forces. As Beckhard and Pritchard[39] point out, this requires a change strategy which is built around top management's clear vision of the end state of the whole organisation. This vision must be used to diagnose what needs to be changed, and for managing and integrating the process of change. They emphasise the importance of adopting a learning mode, where both learning and doing are valued. This learning mode is more difficult to adopt than managers think, and it is here that the special process skills of the OD consultant can play a key role.

There are clear implications here for the training of senior managers and consultants. Managers must learn to use the latter in the most appropriate way. Consultants need to be trained not only to acquire the traditional process skills of the OD practitioner, but also to have an understanding of the relationship between a business and its environment and the range of applicable solutions open to the client. Nowadays the OD consultant needs to master both process and content issues if OD is to survive as a form of consultancy which is valued by client organisations.[40]

5.4 References

1. Pedler M, Burgoyne J, Boydell T. *The learning organisation: a strategy for sustainable development.* London: McGraw-Hill, 1991.
2. Trist EL, Higgin GW, Murray H, Pollock AB. *Organisational choice.* London: Tavistock, 1963.
3. Burns T, Stalker G. *The management of innovation.* London: Tavistock, 1961.
4. Woodward J. *Industrial organisation.* Oxford: Oxford University Press, 1965.
5. Lawrence PR, Lorsch LW. *Developing organisations: diagnosis and action.* Reading, MA: Addison-Wesley, 1969.
6. Davis LE, Cherns AB. *The quality of working life.* New York: Free Press, 1975.

7. ACAS *QWL News and Abstract* 1996; **127**, Summer: 2.
8. Roethlisberger FJ, Dickson WG. *Management and the worker*. Boston, MA: Harvard University Press, 1939.
9. Lewin K. Group decision making and social change. In: Swanson GE *et al. Readings in social psychology*. New York: Holt, 1952.
10. Coch L, French JRP. Overcoming resistance to change. *Human Relations* 1948; **1**: 512–32.
11. Bennis WG. *Organisation development: its nature, origins and prospects*. Reading, MA: Addison-Wesley, 1969.
12. Lewin K. Frontiers in group dynamics: concept, method and reality in social science; social equilibria and social change. *Human Relations* 1947; **1**(1): 5–42.
13. Lewin K. *Field theory in social science*. New York: Harper and Row, 1951.
14. Jaques E. *The changing culture of a factory*. London: Tavistock, 1951.
15. Skinner BF. *About behaviourism*. New York: Vintage Books, 1976.
16. Bandura A. *Social foundations of thought and action: a social cognitive theory*. Englewood Cliffs, NJ: Prentice-Hall, 1986.
17. Schein EH. *Process consultation: volume II*. Reading, MA: Addison-Wesley, 1987.
18. Kolb DA. *Experiential learning: experience as the source of learning and development*. Englewood Cliffs, NJ: Prentice-Hall, 1984.
19. Likert R. *New patterns of management*. New York: McGraw-Hill, 1961.
20. Pedler *et al. Learning organisations*.
21. Senge P. *The fifth discipline: the art and practice of the learning organisation*. London: Century Business/Doubleday, 1990.
22. Peters TJ, Waterman RH. *In search of excellence*. New York: Harper and Row, 1982.
23. Williams APO, Dobson P, Walters M. *Changing culture: new organisational approaches*. London: Institute of Personnel Management, 2nd edition, 1993.
24. Warr P. *Work, employment and mental health*. Oxford: Oxford University Press, 1987.
25. Buckingham GD, Jeffrey RG, Thorne BA. *Job enrichment and organisational change: a study in participation at Gallaher Ltd*. Aldershot: Gower, 1975.
26. Bennis. *Organisation development*.
27. Schein EH. *Organisational psychology*. Englewood Cliffs, NJ: Prentice-Hall, 3rd edition, 1980.
28. Blake RR, Shepherd HA, Mouton JS. *Managing intergroup conflict in industry*. Houston: Gulf, 1965.
29. Blumberg A, Wiener W. One from one: facilitating organisational merger. *Journal of Applied Behavioural Science* 1971; **7**(1): 87–102.
30. Blake RR, Mouton JS. *The managerial grid*. Houston: Gulf, 1964.
31. Blake RR, Mouton JS, Barnes L, Greiner L. Breakthrough in organisation development. *Harvard Business Review* 1964; **42**(6): 133–55.
32. Hutchinson C. Organisation development in BAT Ltd. In: Hacon R. *Personnel and organisational effectiveness*. London: McGraw-Hill, 1972.
33. Mann FC. Studying and creating change. In: Bennis WG *et al. The planning of change*. New York: Holt, 1961.
34. Bowers DG. OD techniques and their results in 23 organisations: the Michigan ICL study. *Journal of Applied Behavioural Science* 1973; **9**: 21–43.
35. Clark PA. *Organisational design: theory and practice*. London: Tavistock, 1972.
36. Storey J. The people–management dimension in current programmes of organisational change. *Employee Relations* 1988; **10**(6): 17–25.
37. French WL, Bell CH. *Organisation development*. Englewood Cliffs, NJ: Prentice-Hall, 4th edition, 1990.
38. Williams *et al. Changing culture*.
39. Beckhard R, Pritchard W. *Changing the essence: the art of creating and leading fundamental change in organisations*. San Francisco: Jossey-Bass, 1992.
40. Williams APO, Woodward S. *The competitive consultant: a client-oriented approach for achieving superior performance*. London: Macmillan, 1994.

From personal to professional development

Creating space for growth

Peter Critten

6.1 Personal development: a historical perspective

For the purposes of this chapter 'personal' development is taken to be synonymous with self-development[1] and means that learners take the primary responsibility for choosing what, when and how to learn.[2] What and how they choose to develop may or may not be related to their organisation's needs. But organisations themselves need to understand the power and implications that accrue from personal development so that they can reap its benefits.

Self- or personal development emerged in the 1970s and 1980s as an antidote to the 'systematic' training approach that was adopted by the Industrial Training Boards (ITBs) (following the Industrial Training Act 1964). The rationale of 'systematic training' was that each organisation be required to specify the skill requirements of its workforce, identify who needed to be trained/developed to meet necessary standards, plan and implement appropriate training as required and finally evaluate whether identified needs had been met.

But while such an approach was appropriate to specific jobs where knowledge and skill could be specified, it was less easily adapted to the fields of supervisory and management development. The appearance in 1978 of Pedler, Burgoyne and Boydell's *A manager's guide to self-development*[3] was the first of a number of works which provided companies with alternatives to the 'systematic' approach which was organisation-led and mediated by training officers.[4,5,6] The key shift was from trainer/manager-led training to learner-led development. In the 1980s the UK government recognised the need for individual development and made funds available for the development of open learning materials which enabled individuals to choose and learn what they wanted to learn.

By the 1990s the UK government's Investors in People scheme was going to capitalise on the development of the individual in relation to the needs of the business as a whole and although this has led to a more strategic approach to development (in contrast to the rather piecemeal way training for individual jobs was rewarded earlier by the ITBs), the focus for development is still organisation/management rather than individual-led. This highlights the differences in interpretation which persist as to the meaning of 'personal development' as a comparison of two journal extracts, appearing virtually concurrently has shown: *Training Officer*, September 1995: 'Personal Development programmes should be inextricably linked to the needs of the organisation. No organisation can afford to waste time and resources on unfocused development.'[7] Contrast this statement with the following from

Personnel Today, June 1995 (quoted from Peter Heriot of Institute of Employment Studies): 'You can no longer specifically target training and development now that organisations have fewer layers and people don't stay long enough to target them for development.'[8]

These contrasting themes emerged from an Institute for Employee Studies (IES) survey of the practice of 'personal development plans' by eight national companies,[9] the majority of whom saw 'personal development' in the context of an employee's current or future job skills rather than a function of the 'whole person'. 'From the employee's perspective it can be seen as a contradiction in terms to be encouraged to think about their own development in their own way but then be told to concentrate only on those needs in relation to the current job.'[10] Is it reasonable that an organisation should pay for its employees to develop themselves in whatever way they like? This is a principle Tom Peters[11] has long supported, in so far as, if it leads to more motivated staff who are encouraged to take responsibility for their own learning, it has got to be good for the business too. Similarly, in the UK John Harvey-Jones[12] has identified the need for companies to cater for 'people's true inner needs which they may even be reluctant to express to themselves'.

Before examining some practical ways open to organisations to facilitate personal development, below are three principles which I would argue need to be applied if real personal development is to be promoted.

6.2 Principles underpinning personal development

Principle 1

> There can be no 'personal' development without an individual taking ownership for his/her own development and choosing how such development will take place.

In his best-seller *The seven habits of highly effective people: powerful lessons in personal change*, Steven Covey throws new light on what the word 'responsibility' means: he suggests it literally means 'response-ability', i.e. the ability to be able to choose the response to make to a particular stimulus or experience.[13] It is salutary, perhaps, to reflect that much of the rationale for 'effective' training derives from the behavioural psychology of the 1950s and early 1960s[14] which sought to build a world around 'shaping' correct responses to given stimuli – choice didn't come into it.

But it is also true, as the IES survey points out, that 'taking ownership for one's own development' does not fit comfortably within the UK culture in that it 'is not merely by self but also of self'.[15] On the one hand, Knowles argues that all individuals are naturally self-directed learners, albeit needing help to get started[16] while Abbot and Dahmus[17] are of the view that individuals will vary as to their 'preparedness' for self-directed learning. But either way the individual is the only person who can take responsibility for his/her learning – however it occurs.

Over the last decade there has been increasing interest by companies in 'personal development plans' but these very often are seen as but an extension to *the* training plan whereby an individual's 'personal' needs are as prescribed by others as is the training programme to meet the company's objectives,[18] or they are an add-on at the foot of the appraisal form with little time given by the appraiser to address them.[19] A personal development plan must start and finish with the individual.

Another recent trend has been increasing recognition of learning from experience and accreditation of prior learning (APL).[20,21] These initiatives have moved the focus of attention away from the trainer and the company towards an individual's own experience and the learning derived from that. However, when assessing APL, all too often the main attention is given to the evidence of the experience itself rather than the learning derived from it and where that leads.

Huxley (quoted in Pye)[22] maintained that 'experience is not what happens to a man, it is what a man does with what happens to him'. Pye makes the point that learning is an active and essentially integrative process continually trying to make sense of experiences in a context within which the learner is both patient and agent. While we tend to think of reflection as a very individual and private process, the fact is that reflection only makes sense with reference to action or context which is located at a time in history. Thus, reflection is a social process. This takes us on to principle 2.

Principle 2

If learning is a 'social' process, individual and personal development plans can only be realised in and through developing with others.

the individual is necessarily enmeshed in a world of others. The eternal dilemma for individuals is that, once they embark upon social relationships, this very act demands the surrender of their individuality – to some degree.[23]

The paradox here is that 'Persons can only be persons in relation'.[24] Heron goes on to say:

Following the path of self-development is not simply to take an inward turning, it is to go in and to go out. The clear implication is that an organisation will not be responsive, innovatory and self-renewing on the outside unless we are able to nurture and release the energy of those on the inside. This is the vision of the learning organisation.

Unfortunately it is a vision that few organisations which aspire to be 'learning organisations' have fully realised. Most have the right intentions – to provide the necessary support and resources to 'facilitate' individual development – but what they fail to do is to become fully enmeshed in and identified with the kind of development they seek to promote. Adlam and Plumridge[25] sought to simulate just how an organisation might come to terms with 'self-developers'. At a conference on self-development they created two groups: one group was encouraged to focus on issues of self-development while the other was to consider itself as the parent organisation who had to find ways to accommodate and support the self-development group. Though they devised appropriate strategies of support, nothing prepared them for the reality of coming to terms with the very personal nature of the experiences the self-development group enjoyed. This led them to this basic premise: 'Unless those responsible for supporting the growth and development of others in the organisation are themselves actively engaged in their own self-development, they cannot actually tune in to the quality of the experiences of self-developing others.' Organisations trying to come to terms with the dilemma between supporting individual development (in whatever direction that might lie) and development to achieve corporate goals might well reflect upon the following:

It is in the very act of trying to help others that we are likely to be allowed a sense of their inner selves – of their thoughts, values and feelings; and that process unlocks for us many insights into our own selves . . . This opening of others to self and self to others is a perquisite for reciprocal behaviour and therefore the foundation stone of our own growth and development. Opportunities for such behaviour are constantly with us if we choose to take them.

This leads on to principle 3.

Principle 3

> In opening up our own development to and with others a reciprocal process takes over whereby others are drawn to us in ways we had not previously anticipated.

Not so many years ago such a notion might have been thought to border on the mystical but in the 1990s what Jung called 'Synchronicity'[26] appears as a central theme in a range of works both populist[27] and of the more 'management guru' kind.[28,29] Covey observes:

> the more authentic you become, the more genuine in your experience, particularly regarding personal experiences and even self-doubts, the more people can relate to your experience and the safer it makes them feel to express themselves. That expressing in turn feeds back on the other person's spirit and genuine creative empathy takes place, producing new insights and learnings and a sense of excitement and adventure that keeps the process going.

Such a sentiment is not new. It is embedded in existentialist philosophy and psychology[30,31] but though 'tacitly' understood it has not really been translated into best practice. Carl Rogers tried to break the mould in 1969 with the publication of *Freedom to Learn*[32] and in 1987 Roger Harrison took a great risk (for the time) by publishing a paper sub-titled 'a strategy for releasing love in the workplace'.[33]

The current preoccupation with the concept of an organisation as a learning organisation might be thought to provide a context for such a principle to be put to the test but there is little evidence of this happening. I would argue that the main reason is that in seeking to envisage and espouse something 'out there' called a learning organisation we have lost sight of what, at heart, an organisation actually is – relationships between individuals. If, as we have suggested, personal development can only take place in relationship with others might this not be a start on the learning organisation journey?

6.3 Translating principles into practice

A personal development plan for all

The starting point must be for each individual to put together their own personal development plan which needs to cover:

1. Goals and aspirations.
2. An indication of resources/methods/support needed to achieve these goals.
3. An indication of a time in the future when the goals will be realised.
4. An indication of how these goals will be recognised by others.

Though organisations tend to reserve PDPs for managers and high-flyers, David Clutterbuck makes the point that there should be 'a personal development plan for every citizen'[34] which should include goals and achievement that are not confined to the workplace but encompass domestic, leisure, sport, community and long-term career prospects.

It is also in keeping with what has been called 'organisational citizenship behaviour'[35] which draws attention to the breakdown of the 'normal contractual relationship between employer and employee'. In its place they suggest the growth of a 'covenantal relationship which is characterised by open-ended commitment, mutual trust and shared values'. Perhaps this is the 'new bonding agent' Simon Caulkin is seeking:

> Put brutally, individuals are asking themselves: if the company no longer represents a career, a pension or a 'safe job' what am I doing here? If the organisation can't provide a satisfactory answer to this existential question – if it hasn't found a new bonding agent to replace the deferred gratification of the next job or a secure old age . . . it will fall apart at the first touch of pressure.[36]

Caulkin envisages a new kind of organisation called 'ME plc' where 'the workers' take control of all that is left to them to control – their own development. He quotes Robin Linnecar, partner at KPMG Career Consultancy: 'The only way to keep them [employees] is to risk losing them. You have to give them more room to develop, which at the same time makes them more marketable. But, ironically, that's how you create loyalty'.

A question for managers to address, then, is what scope can they give every employee to develop themselves in whatever way they choose? There is a tendency for many PDPs to be too narrowly focused, reinforced by a work ethic which is reflected in the way they are encouraged to think that 'personal' relates to personal behaviour in the workplace. If we are really serious about expanding individuals' horizons in the hope that they may contribute to expanding an organisation's horizons too (at least while they are still employed there), we must encourage employees to 'dig deeper': 'Our task is to encourage people to think as widely as possible about their attributes'.[37] One way of doing this is through the creation of a 'personal portfolio'.

Portfolios for development

As we shall see when we review trends in professional development, the use of the portfolio as a vehicle for recording evidence of an individual's continuing professional development (CPD) has become widespread. But in my experience there is often an underlying assumption that putting together a portfolio is simply a matter of following a few guidelines. In my work with healthcare practitioners,[38] despite there being a number of 'do-it-yourself' portfolios on the market, they were unable to answer two fundamental questions: why am I putting together this portfolio and where do I start?

Besides being used for charting professional development, the portfolio is also a useful vehicle for exploring one's personal development. But where do you start? Warren Redman has a very useful five-stage approach to building up a portfolio starting with the creation of what he calls 'The Index'.[39] 'The aim of this is to begin to establish the range of experiences that a person has . . . These are brief reminders of a whole range of things that someone has done, or events that have taken place that have some significance for the portfolio-builder.' This is a different approach from the usual one of starting by encouraging an individual to identify their strengths and weaknesses. Redman suggests that it is often difficult for individuals to look objectively at their strengths and weaknesses and suggests we take a more 'neutral' approach by enabling them to focus on their 'experience before we can usefully get them to recognise what their qualities are'.

By first jotting down three or four significant experiences (e.g. 'the birth of my son', 'being made redundant', 'running a training course for trainers'), Redman argues that an individual can get 'some insights into their own abilities and how they can extend themselves'. The next part of this first stage is to take each experience and describe what happened, to tell a story. Various other techniques can help an individual focus on significant areas of life's experiences which can be a basis for a portfolio's 'index': producing a biography; charting ups and downs on a 'lifeline'; domain mapping; repertory grid.[40,41] Stage two is to discover what is to be learned from this experience. Redman suggests that this be done in conjunction with others. Again, the summary should be written down. Stage three is at the heart of the portfolio: producing evidence of what was learned from the experiences described. Evidence may be in the form of photos, certificates, letters, reports, notes, designs. Producing evidence is a critical part in anyone's personal development as it externalises an internal process to enable it to be recognised and corroborated by others.[42] Thus our perception of ourselves is reinforced by the way others see us.

In many schemes of accreditation of prior learning and certainly in so far as assessment of National Vocational Qualifications (NVQs) is concerned, stage three must be the ultimate aim of the portfolio – to produce evidence able to be assessed by others in recognition of a claim for accreditation against vocational, academic or professional standards. But Redman adds two other steps to justify his claim that portfolios can be used for development purposes as well as vehicles for accreditation. Having derived learning from a particular experience and provided evidence of this, stage four asks, 'What do I still need to improve in this area?' Redman describes it as taking ownership for development needs for the future. Finally, stage five brings us back to the personal development plan. First, what action am I going to take to improve in the way I have identified in stage four and what resources and support will I need to do it and by when? Second, stage five reviews whether 'I have taken up the learning opportunities identified' and asks what has been the outcome/consequence of that learning. It follows that this might lead on to another cycle of development.

Although I have suggested that the production of a PDP is the starting point, others have recognised the need to help individuals 'engage' in a personal planning process which the creation of a portfolio in the way Redman describes helps to facilitate. We can summarise the two stages so far identified in helping individuals' personal development as two *interlinking* routes the starting point for which could either be a PDP or a portfolio, as shown in Figure 6.1.

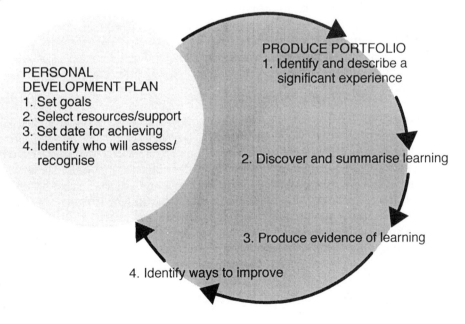

Figure 6.1 Stage 1 of a personal development plan

Involving others

Principle 2 stated that learning is a social process and that individual and personal development plans can only be realised in and through developing with others. Thus the development manager has a role in trying to help individuals create the kind of support network around them which will not only help them develop but will also enable others to develop with them. Personal development has to be part of reciprocal relationships. 'Persons can only be persons in relation'.[43]

But just as it is not always easy to sit down and produce a personal development plan without going through some of the exercises we have explored, so it is advisable that individuals first do some personal reflections about the kind of people who have influenced them in the past so that they can better identify the kind of person who will be helpful in the future. A simple way of doing this is to put oneself in a circle in the middle of a page and then identify 'significant' other people that have been of help to you in the past and the present: e.g. your partner; particular colleagues; tutor on a training programme, etc.

The next stage is to identify who can help with what. A useful way of doing this is to select the objective to be worked on, list appropriate individuals on the left and the kind of help/support being sought on the right. Here's an example:

| OBJECTIVE: | To have submitted and had approved budget by end of financial year |

WHO CAN HELP	HOW
Mary from Central Services	By installing new spreadsheet package and coaching me until I can produce report from input data
Tom in Accounts	By giving me feedback on first draft

Finally, negotiate with each person and perhaps arrive at individual learning contracts. Some people may be able to act as mentors.[44] But colleagues can support other colleagues in a variety of ways. The aim is to encourage dialogue and 'learning conversations'.[45] Individuals can come together on a regular basis for no other purpose than to support each other's development. But there must be clear objectives which each person is trying to achieve – so individual PDPs would be useful data on which the group can plan how to help one another.

Depending on just how task or process oriented the group is, it could be classified as a learning support group or an action learning group. Action learning has received considerable attention in recent years, mainly in relation to management training, 40 years after its founder Reg Revans first introduced the idea of building up a degree of trust between a group of professionals, each of whom wished to solve particular problems. The idea was that the group encouraged each person to articulate their problem and take on board comments and criticism from the others before committing themselves to action which would then be reviewed at the next meeting.[46,47]

Support groups of this kind usually begin by drawing up ground rules to govern the way they will work with each other. Some commonly accepted principles underpinning action learning are:

- respect for each other;
- trust in each other;
- non-competitive;
- take risks;
- confidentiality;
- listen and give full attention;
- say what you feel;
- value each other's contribution;
- all members to participate;
- be honest;
- don't interrupt;
- feel free to challenge.

Such groups are ideal for self-development because there is no formal theory or content to shape their course. They exist solely to help individuals achieve their task and in the process become aware of the learning needed to fulfil the task.

We can now add the various ways of 'involving others' to the first two ways of going about self-development. It provides a third route which can start with the PDP and be reflected upon in the portfolio (see Figure 6.2).

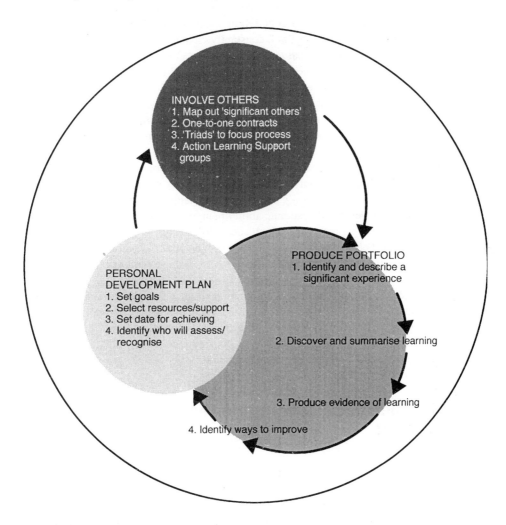

Figure 6.2 Stage 2 of a personal development plan

6.4 Professional development – a historical perspective

Having sought to explore reasons for managers to promote personal development – not least because of the consequences for interpersonal as well as organisational learning, we now turn to what might be thought a safer area, *professional* development. This is a typical dictionary definition of 'profession': 'A vocation or calling, especially one that involves some branch of advanced learning or science (the medical profession).'[48]

The Standard Occupational Classification regards a professional as someone with a degree and post-graduate qualification.[49] Defined thus, 'professionals' would currently represent about 15 per cent of the workforce. By the end of the decade it has been estimated there will be over 10 million people classified as managers, professionals or associate professional, and involved in knowledge-intensive work and requiring a high level of education and continual professional development throughout their careers.

In recent years most professional bodies have recognised that merely 'having' qualified at a given time to meet the knowledge requirements imposed by a profession is not sufficient for a practising professional in a constantly changing world. Hence the emphasis on CPD – continuous professional development – whereby each profession requires its members to demonstrate that they have kept themselves abreast of changing theory and practice.[50] Unless a member seeks upgrading of membership it is difficult to monitor the success of such a policy but at least it is becoming a recognised policy. More and more professions are providing their members with the means of recording such development (e.g. Institute of Personnel & Development 1995; Institute of Management 1996) as evidence of their CPD.

Implicit in the Standard Occupational Classification definition of 'professionalism' is that a professional will have not only a first degree but also a post-graduate qualification (appropriate to a particular profession's domain of knowledge/expertise). Therefore 'professionalism' implies a degree of academic ability being recognised. This is in contrast to the notion of 'vocational' competence which seems to be aligned with a perception of a level of skill that falls below that of professional. This perception has done much to colour the debate about another UK government initiative, the establishment of NVQs. Is there a way of bridging this divide?

To find out, we need to understand a little more about the nature of professional knowledge and the context within which it can be acquired. As in the first section, we will explore three principles we believe underpin the nature of 'professionalism' and then suggest a framework within which such principles can be put into practice, building on the guidelines already proposed for facilitating personal development.

6.5 Principles underpinning professional development

Principle 1

The professional is continually developing his/her practice by reflecting on experience of new and changing contexts.

There is a paradox here which Richard Winter explores.[51] On the one hand, just what the professional does may be difficult to verbalise but, on the other hand, unless the process is made explicit in some way, how can the professional and other professionals learn?

Donald Schon has done much to focus attention of academics and managers alike on the way professional people actually learn to become professional.[52,53] He contrasts the way colleges 'teach' would-be professionals against 'validated' rules with the way the professional learns his/her trade in practice, building up a 'repertoire' of past examples as precedents to deal with any particular situation. In this sense the would-be professional draws as much upon intuition as to what feels right in a particular context. In examining how architects, musicians, psychoanalysts and counsellors learn their profession Schon feels that the context in which they learn is more akin to a 'studio' than a classroom.[54] He sees two processes at work: 'knowing-in-action' and 'reflection-in-action'. 'Knowing-in-action' would describe the knowledge implicit in being able to carry out some skilled performance (e.g. driving a car; carrying out an operation) but which the professional wouldn't normally be able to 'verbalise' at the time: 'The knowing is in the action'.[55]

Schon would argue that we are unable to explain what it is we are doing or why we do it until something happens to make us question and reflect on what we are doing. This could be as the result of a surprise remark, action or error or somebody simply asking 'Why?' or 'What if?'. This leads to what he calls 'reflection-in-action': 'the rethinking of some part of our knowing-in-action leads to on-the-spot experimentation and further thinking that affects what we do in the situation at hand and perhaps also in others we shall see as similar to it'.[56] It is this 'iterative' process of engaging in a dialectical process of learning which characterises the nature of professional 'knowing' as we build up a body of knowledge appropriate in a particular context. Winter produces a list of ten propositions which together form 'a unified process linking professional practice, knowledge, understanding, skill, commitments and self-knowledge' which I would suggest provide a useful framework within which managers can recognise and actively promote professional development.[57] These ten propositions on the nature of professional work are reproduced below:

1. The nature of professional work is that situations are unique, and knowledge of these situations is therefore never complete.
2. It follows that, for professional workers, a given state of reflective understanding will be transformed by further experience of practice.
3. Professionals will draw upon a repertoire of knowledge derived from comparison of a multitude of different contexts and the way their practice has changed.

An implication that follows from such principles is that, regardless of whether a manager has or has not got a particular management qualification, for example, there should be something new for him/her to learn from every situation involving management decisions and judgements. How are your managers or any other 'professional' encouraged to 'reflect' on their practice and record such 'continuing development'?

4. Professional work involves commitment to a specific set of moral purposes, and professional workers will recognise the inevitably complex and serious responsibilities which arise when attempting to apply ethical problems to particular situations.
5. The responsibility for equitable practice which characterises the professional's role commits professional workers to the comprehensive, consistent, conscious, and effective implementation of 'anti-oppressive' non-discriminatory principles and practices.

This has particular implications for managers responsible for the development of all their staff, some of whom may seek development which you, as their manager, consider inappropriate. How do you help managers come to terms with such decisions and how can they be helped to learn from them?

6. Authoritative involvement in the problem areas of clients' lives inevitably creates a complex emotional dimension to professional work, and professional workers therefore recognise that the role involves understanding and managing the emotional dimension of professional relationships.
7. Consequently, professional workers recognise that the understanding of others (on which their interpersonal effectiveness depends) is inseparable from self-knowledge, and consequently entails a sustained process of self-evaluation.

Again, what support do you give to managers, fellow professionals, to cope with situations in which they have become 'personally engaged'? How do you help them to use the situation (for example, having to break the news to someone that they have been made redundant) to enhance their own learning?

8. The incompleteness of professional knowledge (see 1. and 2.) implies that the authoritative basis of judgements will always remain open to question. Hence, for professional workers, relationships with others will necessarily be collaborative rather than hierarchical.
9. Professional workers will be aware of available codified knowledge – e.g. concerning legal provisions, organisational procedures, resources and research findings – but they will recognise that the relevance of the knowledge for particular situations always depends on their own selection and interpretation.

Underpinning both of these principles is the recognition that, contrary to what the text books may say, there are no right, absolute answers to all situations. The professional has to look at each situation differently although it is the hallmark of professionalism that the professional draws on his/her experience to make the most appropriate decision in a given context. Again, how are your staff encouraged to identify such situations and learn from them?

10. The process of analytical understanding which professional workers will bring to their practice involves creative tension between making sense of different contexts, synthesis of varied experiences into a 'unified overall pattern', ability to relate a situation to its context, understanding of a situation in terms of its tensions and contradictions.

Common to all of these skills is the capacity to make sense of a variety of changing and often conflicting situations.

I wonder how many professional bodies take these propositions into account in their recommendations for CPD. The emphasis has tended to be on what Winter calls 'codified knowledge' rather than on 'the relevance of the knowledge for particular situations' which will always depend on the manager's 'own selection and interpretation'. Hartog used the same argument to comment on IPD's modular professional education scheme.[58] She argues that there isn't sufficient scope for developing individuals' 'capability' which can only come from some kind of 'Action Learning' in the company of fellow professionals. Similar views about the need for 'reflection-in-action' have been put forward to develop professional practice amongst teachers[59] and physiotherapists.[60]

This brings us to a key criterion of 'professionalism' which underpins Principle 2.

Principle 2

To be recognised as 'having' professional expertise requires that one's knowledge and competence are recognised by others themselves recognised to be professionals in a particular context.

'A professional's knowing-in-action is embedded in the socially and institutionally structured context shared by a community of practitioners.'[61] It is the 'context shared by a community of practitioners' which is at the core of professional knowledge and an area where managers can play a key role in helping create the kinds of networks in which professionalism can be nurtured. In a previous work Schon referred to this as 'public knowing'[62] but it is also a form of 'public testing'. Only when you are prepared to test out your ideas and have them validated (or refuted) by the wider 'academic' community can you be said to be a professional researcher, for example. Again, it is the *professional* context which gives your work meaning.

In the final principle we examine the nature of 'transferability' of the core knowledge and experience which underpin all professional activity irrespective of context.

Principle 3

> Underpinning professional competence are a core set of values which, whilst being needed to demonstrate professional competence in a particular context, have universality of application wherever professionalism is required.

The paradox is that, on the one hand, professional evidence needs to be related to a particular context from and within which it is given credibility and validated but, on the other hand, the professional learning derived from that evidence goes beyond the present and has a universality, the essence of which can be transferred to other situations.

This was a basic principle which led Richard Winter to evolve what he calls a 'general model for practice-based professional education'[63] in what is known as the ASSET programme (Accreditation for Social Services Experience and Training). This was a programme which resulted from a collaboration between Anglia Polytechnic University and Essex Social Services Department to provide a qualification for social workers which reflected both academic standards (through getting a degree through Anglia) and professional standards as recognised by the Central Council for Education and Training in Social Work (CCETSW) (now replaced by the Social Care Council).

The model developed was based on the evolution of competences through the NVQ-preferred route of functional analysis. This involves starting with the 'purpose' of an occupation and continually asking the question 'What needs to happen for this purpose to be achieved?' For a full explanation of the role of functional analysis in the development of NVQs, see Mansfield and Mitchell.[64] But Winter felt that the normal process of assessment against performance criteria of separate elements did not reflect the 'holistic' way that professionals worked; nor did it meet the kind of criteria we have examined under Principle 1. Winter therefore decided to arrive at a set of what he called 'Core Assessment Criteria' which social workers used in judging qualities of their professional colleagues.

As a result, seven additional criteria were derived:

1. commitment to professional values;
2. continuous professional learning;
3. affective awareness;
4. effective communication;
5. executive effectiveness;
6. effective grasp of a wide range of professional knowledge;
7. intellectual flexibility.

In demonstrating their competence, social workers had to show evidence of their meeting each of the competences (as they would under any NVQ assessment) but, in addition, they had to choose one core competence and show how their evidence met that criteria also.

As Winter acknowledges, his model is not the only one to be concerned about the emphasis on 'lists of specific behaviour' rather than taking a more 'holistic' approach to assessment of underpinning core values. The Management Charter Initiative (MCI)'s management standards, for example, have a 'Personal Competence Model' over and above the functional units, which covers processes of 'optimising results' by planning, managing others and managing oneself, and 'using intellect'. But because they are a separate unit they are not automatically integrated within the assessment process though assessors are required to take account of them. This has led to calls for their integration.[65]

The Care Sector Consortium's standards for care include what they call a 'Value Base Unit' which are the basic standards of good practice which all healthcare practitioners should observe in their professional work: e.g. anti-discriminatory practice, confidentiality of information, individual rights and choice, etc. But again, though assessors are reminded of appropriate values to be taken into account in assessment of each element, Winter's point is that no other scheme has made assessment of core values such an integral feature to the extent that they provide a framework within which evidence is selected in the first place.

It is perhaps ironic that although NVQ standards are presented as long lists of performance criteria against each of which a candidate has to provide evidence in practice (as anyone who has assessed NVQs would confirm), an assessment is made of *overall* performance using the criteria as exemplars of the kind of behaviour the assessor should be looking for.

We have covered a wide range of theoretical principles in this chapter. At the beginning of the chapter we speculated about how to bridge the divide between what is perceived as vocational and what is perceived as professional. To illustrate just how the three principles we have discussed might help managers do just this, I include an example based on a manager helping colleagues better manage their teams.

Let us suppose you are asked to help a manager develop their team of staff. A starting point might be using the Management Charter Initiative's NVQ accredited standards for managers, a unit of which focuses on how to 'Develop and improve teams through planning and activities'. This specifies separate 'performance criteria' against which managers would be required to demonstrate competence at being able to develop their team. Equally, you may have your own company criteria for team development. Either way there are criteria against which competence can be assessed.

But Winter would argue that 'professionalism' is more than meeting pre-designated criteria. Using the three principles we've introduced we can see ways in which professionalism might be developed and accredited.

According to Principle 1, professionals develop and refine their expertise in a range of situations from each of which they would be expected to learn and review their practice ('reflection-in-action'). You might therefore require your managers to keep a log of situations where they contributed to their team's development and how reflection on what they achieved has informed their practice. Furthermore, taking account of Winter's ten propositions characterising professional work, you might also want them to identify particular situations where they have had to cope with ethical and personal dilemmas (e.g. having to negotiate with a group to 'include' a member of staff they are seeking to 'exclude').

According to Principle 2 there is a requirement that their professional behaviour is recognised by other professionals. Thus you might stipulate that the achievement of your managers in developing their respective teams is recognised by other managers in other departments and by the HRM department.

Finally, according to Principle 3 you might want to check out the extent to which skills in one situation can be transferred to others. For example, 'affective awareness' was one of the core professional competences Winter identified. What evidence is there of your manager being able to 'empathise' with others – a quality which should be evident to staff in his own team but which also becomes a part of his 'professional' behaviour which is demonstrated in a variety of contexts?

I hope this gives you a feel for how professionalism can be fostered amongst your staff. Now let's look at some other practical ways of putting these principles into practice.

6.6 Translating principles into practice

Creating professional groups

A key principle for professional development is that professionalism is not just about acquiring what Winter calls 'codified knowledge' but depends on 'reflection-in-action' in the company of other professionals. What role, if any, has a manager in facilitating such a process?

In the first section we argued that helping individuals to become aware of and take ownership of their personal development can create a different kind of trust between employees and the organisation which goes far beyond the job for which they are employed. Though there is a risk – as there is with any form of development – that individuals will take their new knowledge and expertise elsewhere, the very engagement in such a process cannot but add value not only to the individual but to the organisation as a whole because, if the development takes place at work, the individual's development must take place in an organisational context. It is up to the organisation if it chooses to see personal development as an altruistic act or as adding value to the organisation as a whole.

If investment in personal development is a risk which may be difficult to evaluate at the level of the organisation, then investment in professional development has a more immediate pay-off. But, I would argue, you cannot have one without the other.

In personal development the individual is primarily learning from and with others for their own development. In professional development the individual is also learning from and with others but this time is able to give something back such that the professional group and wider community as a whole benefit. Once we see professional work as going beyond the traditionally recognised boundaries set within 'codified knowledge', we are in a position to explore new connections between an individual's work and contribution to the organisation as a whole.

Within the ten propositions there are five key themes which, I would suggest, give us a clue as to how to recognise professional work when we see it. The same principles could be used to create professional groups within the organisation. Work that is professional will demonstrate the following characteristics:

1. It will involve a unique situation in which knowledge within a group is pooled but recognised as incomplete and requiring the collaboration of the whole group.
2. Through a process of reflection relating to the issue/problem under review the group arrives at an extension of/addition to the knowledge it possesses.
3. The group recognises the responsibilities and rights of all parties involved.
4. The group is sensitive to and able to manage inherent contradictions and tension in the situation and emotional consequences.
5. The group possesses recognised knowledge and expertise which members are able to draw from a wide range of separate experiences.

Put thus, you might well wonder if a Quality Control Group, a Learning Support Group or an Action Learning Group might not be considered to be a 'professional group'. The answer is undoubtedly yes, if it can be seen to meet the above criteria. Professional development in the past has been too much focused on 'content' (codified knowledge) rather than the context within which that codified knowledge can be given shape.

One way of changing the balance would be for development managers to recognise what groupings potentially could give rise to such work. It is likely that in the majority of organisations work is organised according to functions and accountability largely within a hierarchical framework. Suppose now that you were to create alternative groupings which are built around individuals' contributions to an organisation's objectives. It is likely that the nature of an organisation's business will determine the kind of professional development it would seek to encourage. Thus, a marketing company would be likely to encourage CPD leading to membership of the Institute of Marketing, an engineering company would look to accreditation of professional engineers. It is also likely that such professional routes would only be open to employees with appropriate technical background who have appropriate jobs and positions in the hierarchy within which such knowledge can be applied and developed.

Thus the proper CPD route for a Sales Manager might be to get accreditation for a management competence and/or recognition through the Institute of Marketing. On the other hand, an employee who merely 'sells' to the public (either a retail assistant in a shop or a catering assistant serving up chips in the company's restaurant) is unlikely to be a member of a professional group designated as 'selling'. If they do get development it is more likely to be seen to be 'vocational', an NVQ level 1 or 2, for example. But may they not also be considered 'professional' according to the criteria listed above and be developed as such? We would argue that the route from vocational to professional is a function of being recognised as having a contribution to make which is recognised within a group of professionals.

So, when the chef leaves his kitchen he leaves his 'whites' behind, dons a suit and joins a group of fellow professionals who are not discussing menus but company-wide services. The technical assistant leaves her workshop and joins a professional group exploring new ways of improving manufacturing design. The 'secretary' switches off his PC and joins fellow professionals to help design a company-wide communication system.

I suggest that every employee in any organisation could become a member of a 'professional' group which cuts right across the job they happen to be in at any one time. Despite attempts to create the 'flexible firm' and 'organic networks',[66] most organisations reflect principles of management and control appropriate to a different age.[67] My suggestion is that development managers have a role in not just encouraging CPD within the familiar professional groupings (Accounting, Marketing, Personnel, etc.) but across vocational boundaries so that everyone can work towards a profession, even when the jobs they were trained for no longer exist.

Creating a context within which professionalism can grow in the company of other professionals is the first step. The next step is to ensure that the group engages in what Schon calls 'reflection-in-action' in such a way that reflection on practice leads not only to improved practice but genuinely new knowledge which both adds value to the organisation and can potentially contribute to the profession as well.

Facilitating 'reflection-in-action' that leads to new knowledge

In his book *Portfolios for development* Redman has chapters on the use of portfolios for both team development and for organisation development.[68] In the latter case he reports on work carried out at Sutcliffe Catering in which I was also involved. The objective was to 'create a culture of learning within one particular profit centre' involving all 1000 staff.

To do this we designed a portfolio in which everyone, from the Operations Director down to catering assistants, was asked to record evidence of learning from a customer. As Sutcliffe was a 'Service' business it was thought appropriate to use this as the focus for learning. But in order to demonstrate how individual learning could be picked up by respective groups in the hierarchy, individual employees were encouraged to share their learning with colleagues at a number of levels: unit level staff shared with each other and their manager who in turn took ideas on to a meeting of unit managers chaired by an Area

Manager (as well as sharing his/her own learning). The Area Catering Supervisor then reported upwards, and so on.

In retrospect, the aim of 'creating a learning culture' by this means was extremely optimistic[69,70] but the method of using a portfolio to record not just individual learning but also group learning, I suggest, can be used to help groups of professionals (as described above) collect and have their own learning corroborated.

In the Sutcliffe project each individual was asked to identify what it was that others could learn from what he/she had learned. This is what was shared with the work group. The group then commented on the outcome, as a result of which an original idea was likely to be modified in some way, leading to the building up of new knowledge which the group as a whole could own and take responsibility for developing further. In this way what may have begun as personal development can become the basis for professional development depending on the group involved (see Principle 1) and extent to which the group engages in reflection-in-action which in turn leads to new knowledge (Principle 2).

So, a lesson for the development manager might be that it is not enough to create a professional grouping in the way suggested above; the group must also be seen to be 'reflecting' on their practice in such a way that the outcome can in some way add knowledge to the organisational bank. We can now add this dimension to our model (see Figure 6.3).

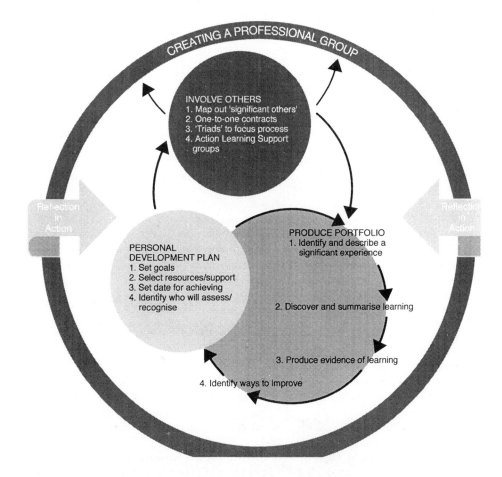

Figure 6.3 Stage 3 of a personal development plan

6.7 Conclusions

In this chapter I have suggested some ways in which development managers can help facilitate the process of personal development. I have argued that by taking care of personal and professional development the conditions are created whereby learning can be recognised and facilitated that will lead not only to a learning organisation but to a learning society. By following the kinds of practice suggested in this chapter, the development manager will be helping employees of the future adjust to a different view of their jobs, their career and their development which is well expressed in this final extract:

> Perhaps we need to develop a new orientation, a new psychology of aspiration that fits better with the harsher, more competitive conditions. Rather than assuming each new job is ours until we choose to leave it, we should assume it is temporary until it proves permanent. Rather than assuming a lifetime of corporate ascent we should seek a lifetime of interesting experiences. Rather than planning personal development in relation to a defined coherent career path, we should perhaps ensure we remain flexible and develop skills and abilities in relation to the best map we can draw of society's future rather than follow an extrapolation of our own past.[71]

6.8 References

1. Pedler M, Boydell T. *Managing yourself.* London: Collins, 1985.
2. Megginson D, Pedler M. *Self-development: a practitioner's guide.* London: Kogan Page, 1992.
3. Pedler M, Burgoyne J, Boydell T. *A manager's guide to self-development.* New York: McGraw-Hill, 1986.
4. Pedler, Boydell, *Managing yourself.*
5. Reeves T. *Managing effectively: developing yourself through experience.* Oxford: Butterworth-Heinemann, 1994.
6. Anderson A, Barker D, Critten P. *Effective self-development: a skills and activity-based approach.* Oxford: Blackwell, 1996.
7. Young C. Personal development: part of a happy family. *Training Officer* 1995; September: 202–3.
8. Hagerty S. Self-service. *Personnel Today* 1995; 6 June: 25–6.
9. Tamkin P, Barber L, Hirsch W. *Personal development plans: case studies of practice.* London: Institute for Employee Studies, 1995.
10. Tamkin *et al., Personal development plans.*
11. Peters T. *Thriving on chaos.* New York: AA Knopf, 1987.
12. Harvey-Jones J. *Making it happen.* London: Pan, 1989.
13. Covey S. *The seven habits of highly effective people: powerful lessons in personal change.* London: Simon & Schuster, 1992.
14. Skinner BF. *Analysis of behaviour.* New York: McGraw-Hill, 1961.
15. Tamkin *et al. Personal development plans.*
16. Knowles M. *The adult learner: a neglected species.* London: Gulf, 1978.
17. Abbott J, Dahmus S. Assessing the appropriateness of self-managed learning. *Journal of Management Development (UK)* 1992; **11**(192): 50–60.
18. Young, Personal development.
19. Tamkin *et al. Personal development plans.*
20. Kolb D. *Experiential learning.* Englewood Cliffs, NJ: Prentice Hall, 1984.
21. Simosko S. *APL (Accreditation of Prior Learning): a practical guide for professionals.* London: Kogan Page, 1991.
22. Pye A. Past, present and possibility – an integrative appreciation of learning from experience. *Management Learning* 1994; **25**(1): 155–73.
23. Adlam R, Plumridge M. Organisational effectiveness and self-development: the essential tension. In Pedler M, Burgoyne J, Boydell T, Welshman G eds. *Self-development in organisations.* London: McGraw-Hill, 1995.

24. Heron J. *Catharsis in human development*. Human Potential Research, Surrey: University of Surrey, 1977.
25. Adlam, Plumridge, Organisational effectiveness.
26. Vaughan A. *Incredible coincidence: the baffling world of synchronicity*. New York: J B Lippincott, 1979.
27. Redfield J. *The Celestine philosophy*. London: Bantam Books, 1994.
28. Covey, *Seven habits*: 267.
29. Jaworski J. *Synchronicity: the inner path of leadership*. San Francisco: Berrett-Koehler, 1996.
30. Macquarrie J. *Existentialism*. Harmondsworth: Penguin, 1973.
31. Maslow A. *The farther reaches of human nature*. Harmondsworth: Penguin, 1971.
32. Rogers C. *Freedom to learn*. Columbus, OH: C E Merrill, 1969.
33. Harrison R. *Organisation culture and quality of service: a strategy for releasing love in the workplace*. London: Association of Management and Education Development, 1987.
34. Clutterbuck D. A personal development plan for every citizen. *People Management* 12 September 1996: 23.
35. Van Dyne L, Graham J, Dienesch R. Organisational citizenship behaviour: construct redefinition, measurement and validation. *Academy of Management Journal* 1994: **37**(4): 765–802.
36. Caulkin S. The New Avengers. *Management Today* November 1995: 48–52.
37. Redman W. *Portfolios for development: a guide for trainers and managers*. London: Kogan Page, 1994.
38. Critten P. *Developing your professional portfolio*. Edinburgh: Churchill Livingstone, 1995.
39. Redman, *Portfolios*.
40. Pedler, Boydell, *Manager's guide*.
41. Critten, *Developing your professional portfolio*.
42. Critten, *Developing your professional portfolio*.
43. Heron, *Catharsis*.
44. Clutterbuck D. *Everyone needs a mentor: fostering talent at work*. London: IPD, 1991.
45. Harri-Augstein S, Thomas L. Self-organised learning for personal and organisation growth. *Training and Development UK* 1992; **10**(6): 19–21.
46. Revans R. *The origins and growth of action learning*. Bromley: Chartwell Bratth, 1982.
47. Wynstein K. *Action learning: a journey in discovery and development*. London: HarperCollins, 1995.
48. *The Concise Oxford Dictionary of Current English*. 9th edition, Oxford: Clarendon Press, 1995.
49. Clyne S. *Continuing professional development: perspectives on CPD in practice*. London: Kogan Page, 1995.
50. Clyne, *Continuing professional development*.
51. Winter R, Maisch M. *Professional competence and higher education: the ASSET programme*. London: Falmer Press, 1996.
52. Schon D. *The reflective practitioner*. New York: Basic Books, 1983.
53. Schon D. *Educating the reflective practitioner*. San Francisco: Jossey-Bass, 1987.
54. Schon, *Educating the reflective practitioner*.
55. Schon, *Educating the reflective practitioner*.
56. Schon, *Educating the reflective practitioner*.
57. Winter, Maisch, *Professional competence*.
58. Hartog M. Shortfalls in professional education for the personnel and development practitioner. Paper given at HEC Conference on Capability and Professionalism, London, January 1996.
59. Fish D. Reflection on theory and practice – a holistic approach to professional education. *BDA Conference Papers* 1991.
60. Titchen AC. Design and implementation of a problem-based continuing education programme. a guide for clinical physiotherapists. *Physiotherapy* 1987; **73**(7): 318–23.
61. Schon, *Educating the reflective practitioner*.
62. Schon D. *Beyond the stable state*. London: Temple Smith, 1971.
63. Winter, Maisch, *Professional competence*.
64. Mansfield B, Mitchell L. *Towards a competent workforce*. Aldershot: Gower, 1996.

65. Fowler B. *Management Charter Initiative personal competence model: use and implementation.* Sheffield: Employment Department, 1994.

66. Handy C. *The age of unreason.* London: Hutchinson, 1989.

67. Taylor FW. *The principles of scientific management.* New York: Harper & Row, 1911.

68. Redman, *Portfolios.*

69. Redman, *Portfolios.*

70. Critten P. *Investing in People: towards corporate capability.* Oxford: Butterworth-Heinemann, 1993.

71. Inkson K. Managerial careers: facing the new reality. *Professional Manager* 1993; July: 14–15.

SECTION III

EMPLOYEE RELATIONS: THE LEGAL FRAMEWORK OF EMPLOYMENT AND EQUAL OPPORTUNITIES

Introduction

The significance of collective bargaining between management and unions had already begun to diminish at the time when the second edition of this book was published in 1990, and this trend has continued, along with continuous erosion of the membership base of trade unions. However, this has not diminished the significance of employee relations, but has rather transferred the emphasis to attempts to achieve greater cooperation between management and employees in the battle to maintain market share, profits, and jobs in the face of greater international competition, privatisation, and the trend to downsized, decentralised, and delayered organisations. The legal framework of employment has likewise responded to changed circumstances, notably the need to take on board a steady flow of European Community (now European Union) directives, in addition to continuous and on-going litigation and legislation within the UK.

The issue of equal opportunities is of particular concern in the workplace, and the third chapter in this section is dedicated to an examination of key issues, and the range of practical measures which managers can take to ensure the potential benefits which can arise from the diversity of employees who now make up the workforce in the UK.

7 Employee relations

Phil James

7.1 Introduction

This chapter aims to provide readers with an introduction to the systems and management of employee relations in the UK and some of the key developments taking place concerning them.

Major changes have occurred in the last decade which have impacted on employee relations. Higher levels of unemployment and structural changes in the economy have affected employment patterns, management strategies, and trade union organisation, membership and bargaining power. Thus strike activity has declined significantly, while new legislation has increased the legal liabilities of unions and their members. Alongside these developments innovative collective agreements have been concluded incorporating 'no strike' provisions and espousing closer links between pay and performance, extensive labour flexibility, and harmonised terms and conditions of employment for all employee grades. One must take care not to overstate the scale of the changes which have evolved. Thus management–union relations in some organisations may continue to retain significant elements of those which existed during the 1970s, but pressure from global competition is everthreatening, and constant commitment to change through continuous improvement must be the only route for survival and growth.

This chapter attempts to capture this combination of continuity and radical change. Its contents are presented under four broad, but inter-related, headings: managing employee relations; collective bargaining structure; the conduct of bargaining; and the assessment of employee relations. A brief final section considers likely future developments in employee relations by reference to recent and future trends in union membership and recognition.

7.2 Managing employee relations

As with many tasks of management, there is no one correct way of managing employee relations. Organisations need to develop policies and strategies best suited to individual circumstances. Many factors are likely to play a part. These may include: type of product and labour markets in which an organisation operates; type of technology in operation; internal structure and organisation culture; and the degree and nature of trade union organisation within it.

Employee relations policies not surprisingly vary considerably between organisations. Two leading academics, John Purcell and Keith Sisson, have attempted to classify them into four 'ideal typical' styles of management: *traditionalist, sophisticated paternalist, sophisticated modern* and *standard modern.*[1]

Traditionalists, according to Purcell and Sisson, adopt a policy of 'forceful opposition' to trade unions and an often overtly exploitative approach towards their employees. Sophisticated paternalist, a category held to include companies like Hewlett-Packard, Marks & Spencer and Kodak, also tend to be non-union, but differ from traditionalists in that they spend considerable time and money developing personnel policies which ensure that unions are seen as unnecessary and inappropriate by their employees.

Sophisticated moderns, such as Ford, by contrast, adopt a rather more positive approach to trade unions, legitimising their role in certain areas on the grounds that they can help maintain stability, promote consent, assist management–employee communications and help the process of change. Finally, the standard modern category is considered to be the largest and characterised by an approach to employee relations which is essentially pragmatic or opportunistic. While they may recognise unions and employ specialists to handle employee relations, they tend to view it as primarily a 'fire-fighting' activity.

In arguing that the standard modern category is the most common, Purcell and Sisson highlight the fact that most UK employers do not tend to approach employee relations in a particularly strategic manner. A recent study of practice in 175 large multi-establishment enterprises found that, while over 80 per cent of firms claimed to have an overall employee relations philosophy, only half said this was written in a formal document and even fewer that a copy of this was given to employees.[2] The authors concluded that the general weight of evidence seemed to confirm that most UK-owned enterprises remain pragmatic or opportunistic in their approach to the management of employees.

Moreover, the presence of a particular philosophy or policy at corporate level does not necessarily mean that it is actually implemented. Managers within companies differ in terms of both the work they do, and their attitudes, philosophies and personal experiences. These differences inevitably influence how they personally approach the management of their employees. Research on the impact of initiatives introduced to promote greater employee empowerment or involvement illustrates the importance of this point. A variety of studies have found that such initiatives often fail as a result of resistance or failings on the part of junior and middle managers.[3] Such findings highlight the importance of providing managers and supervisors with sufficient training so that they are knowledgeable about the procedures they are to operate, understand and support the philosophy underlying them, and possess the skills and competencies needed to carry out the duties relating to them.

7.3 Collective bargaining structure

Collective bargaining arrangements vary in terms of who they cover, the subject matter they encompass, the form they take (procedural and substantive elements) and the levels at which they operate.

Collective bargaining coverage

For collective bargaining to occur trade unions need to be recognised for bargaining purposes. Such recognition has a number of potential advantages and disadvantages for management. On the negative side, unions will inevitably restrict the freedom of management to organise work and reward employees in the way they wish, and this may be considered undesirable in relation to organisational efficiency and costs. Employers may also fear that recognition will lead to the creation of an 'us and them' division within the company and necessitate considerable amounts of management time being tied up in negotiations. On the positive side, managements, particularly in larger organisations, may see unions as providing a valuable means of two-way communication with employees. Moreover, collective bargaining may be considered a useful means of gaining workforce commitment, particularly to change, and a relatively efficient way of altering the employment contracts of large numbers of employees simultaneously.

The previous discussion of the differing styles of managing employee relations points to the fact that widely differing views are held regarding the relative strengths of these two sets of arguments. It is clear that in recent years employers, against a background of union weakness, have generally found the arguments against recognition to be the more persuasive. Consequently, there has been an increased unwillingness to grant recognition and a noticeable rise in cases where employers have chosen to derecognise unions, either completely or in respect of particular groups of workers.[4]

The effect of this change in employer attitude has been accentuated by two further developments. First, a shift of employment from traditionally highly unionised areas of the economy, like manufacturing, to sectors such as retailing, and hotels and catering, where union recognition has historically been limited.[5] Second, a reduction in the size of employment units, stemming in part from this shift in the distribution of employment as well as the more general growth of small businesses.

At the same time collective bargaining remains an important feature of the UK economy. Findings from the 1990 Workplace Industrial Relations Survey indicated that in workplaces with 25 or more employees, collective bargaining covered around 54 per cent of employees, and had formed the basis of the most recent pay increase for manual workers in 48 per cent of workplaces and for non-manuals in 43 per cent.[6] These average figures, however, conceal marked sectoral variations in the extent of union recognition. For example, the same survey found that whereas unions were recognised in nearly 90 per cent of public sector workplaces, the corresponding figures for the private manufacturing and services sectors were 44 per cent and 36 per cent, respectively.[7]

The subject matter of bargaining

The subjects covered by management–union negotiations can be considered under two broad headings: *procedural rules* – which lay down the regulatory framework within which management–union relations are to be conducted; and *substantive provisions* which lay down the terms and conditions under which workers are employed.

Procedural rules: These can cover a wide variety of issues including: types of workers covered by collective bargaining; composition of the machinery through which management–union discussions and negotiations are to take place; appointment and constituencies of shop stewards; shop stewards' rights, facilities and training; subject matter to be discussed and negotiated; and procedures to be followed when attempting to resolve or handle particular issues.

Where more than one union is recognised, a not uncommon situation in the UK, particularly in the public sector, separate procedural arrangements will frequently be agreed with each union. This is particularly likely to occur where both manual and non-manual unions are recognised. But it may also apply where more than one manual union is present. (Traditionally, in manufacturing, unions representing production workers frequently bargain separately from those representing craft workers.)

The Donovan Commission which reported on trade unions and employers' associations in the UK in the 1960s revealed that multi-unionism, and the multiplicity of bargaining units frequently associated with it, had long been a criticised feature of UK industrial relations.[8] It was seen to have a number of potential drawbacks for employers. Inter-union disputes over the right to recruit particular types of worker, demarcation disputes over whose members can do particular work, inefficiencies arising from job demarcations, and the greater complexity of bargaining arrangements were among the problems highlighted. Thirty years on in multi-union workplaces employers have sought to minimise such problems by persuading different unions to negotiate together, thus reducing the number of bargaining units.

This process of rationalisation has also seen the creation of single-table bargaining arrangements under which all unions bargain jointly. Organisations which have taken this route include British Steel Strip Products, Midlands Electricity, Thames Water and a number of NHS Trusts.[9]

Where organisations set up operations on 'greenfield sites' they are frequently seeking to avoid the problems associated with multi-unionism by recognising just one union, if they are willing to concede recognition at all. Such single union agreements have been established in a number of Japanese companies, including Nissan, Sanyo Industries, Toshiba, Hitachi and Komatsu, as well as on new sites opened by companies which have long had operations in the UK.

Many of these 'single union deals' contain a number of distinctive features.[10] These include: harmonised terms and conditions of employment for all staff (including a common grading structure); incremental pay structures and appraisal systems covering all employees (see also Chapter 12); wide-ranging labour flexibility provisions, and negotiating and consultative machinery involving the workforce rather than union representatives. Such features are now also becoming a feature of agreements concluded on older 'brownfield' sites.

Substantive provisions: The substantive content of collective agreements can encompass a vast array of issues: hours of work, holidays, staffing levels, payment systems, pensions, gradings, redeployment, environmental conditions, job content and pay are just some of the topics that may be covered. Some firms negotiate longer-term pay deals as a way of creating a more predictable and stable employee relations environment. Such agreements, which generally still provide for annual pay increases, usually last either two or three years. Longer-term agreements are not unknown. For example, a five-year agreement covering distribution drivers has recently been signed at Blue Circle. This provides for greater work flexibility, contains a management commitment not to make compulsory redundancies or engage in any further contracting out of haulage work during the period of the agreement, and establishes a pay review body to determine pay increases during the final three years of the agreement by reference to 'industry standards'.[11]

Organisations have also, against a background of greater competitive pressures and declining union power, secured significant changes in the substantive content of collective agreements.[12] Grading structures have been simplified to remove restrictive distinctions between different categories of jobs, sometimes as part of harmonisation programmes; closer links have been established between pay and performance; working practices have been reformed to acquire greater labour flexibility by breaking down demarcations between different types of craft worker and making production workers responsible for inspecting the quality of their work and carrying out routine maintenance. Working hours have been reformed and greater use made of part-time, temporary and sub-contract staff, to achieve a better match between labour supply and demand. New patterns of working hours include changes to shift patterns, the use of 'min–max' contracts under which employers are able to vary the number of hours an employee works during a particular week up to a specified maximum, and annual hours schemes which enable the number of hours worked in a defined period, for example where the work has seasonal fluctuations, to be varied in relation to a given number of working hours per year.

Employers have been active in taking initiatives to improve management–worker communication, and to involve employees more closely in decision-making, at least at the level of their job.[13] A variety of different means has been used to achieve these objectives including videos, in-house newspapers, employee reports providing information on the employer's financial results, team briefing, profit sharing and share option schemes, quality circles and team working.

A recent agreement covering craft and process workers at Castle Cement provides a good illustration of these developments. This provides for the replacement of existing job demarcations with a system of multi-skilled team working; the introduction of an annualised hours scheme; the establishment of a grading structure encompassing fewer and more broadly defined job grades; and the creation of harmonised arrangements for redundancy and sick pay.[14]

Levels of bargaining

Collective bargaining can take place at industry level through the medium of employers' associations as well as in individual organisations. Within individual organisations it can take place at different levels, such as company, division and establishment levels.

Industry-wide bargaining has been of declining importance throughout the past 50 years.[15] As we approach the millennium it now covers less than one in ten of those employees covered by collective agreements.[16] Such bargaining continues to operate in a number of sectors, including electrical contracting, local government and the printing industry. The agreements concluded generally set only minimum rates of pay which are often considerably exceeded following negotiations conducted within individual organisations, although terms concerning matters like overtime premium, sick pay, hours of work and holidays are usually followed.

This decline in the importance of multi-employer bargaining has been compounded in recent years by developments stemming from the government's policy of privatisation, its creation of an internal market in the National Health Service and resultant NHS Trusts, and the introduction of compulsory competitive tendering (CCT) in local government. The privatisation of the electricity and water industries prompted the demise of the previously existing systems of national bargaining and their replacement by individual company-based arrangements,[17] while the advent of NHS Trusts has led to attempts to reduce the importance of centralised pay negotiations and increase the role of local pay determination.[18] In a similar vein, CCT has in some cases resulted in local government Direct Labour Organisations (DLOs) moving away from national agreements in order to establish terms and conditions of employment that would enable them to win contracts.[19]

Management must take into account a wide variety of factors and considerations when deciding the level at which to bargain within their organisations.[20] Both centralised and decentralised bargaining arrangements have potential advantages and disadvantages. Centralised arrangements can make labour costs more predictable, enable a common approach to be adopted towards union recognition, and ensure that negotiations are carried out by skilled and experienced negotiators. They also ensure consistency between workplaces thereby avoiding jealousies and rivalries between them and the comparability-based pay claims that these may generate. On the other hand, central negotiations can be very time-consuming and lead to delays in resolving disputes. They may also mean that pay rates have to be set at the level sufficient to recruit and retain labour in the most expensive labour market in which the employer operates. Moreover, it is difficult to take account of differences in the performance of different workplaces and the types of work they carry out, and to engage in detailed discussions about ways of improving efficiency. A further potential problem is that where negotiations 'break down', any resultant dispute is likely to affect the whole company rather than just one part of its operations.

A number of factors need to be considered when assessing the relative strengths and weaknesses of these arguments. These include: internal management structure, existing patterns of union representation and collective bargaining, payment system in use, geographical location of plants, nature of labour and product markets, and types of work carried out.

In practice, companies have been moving away from highly centralised bargaining arrangements and seeking to negotiate at divisional or workplace level. Philips, Royal Insurance, Courtaulds, GEC, Pilkington and the privatised regional electricity companies are among those organisations that have gone down this road during the last decade or so. The trend appears to be very much associated with a change in corporate strategy and business policy towards local profit centres, and the granting of greater autonomy to management at unit level.[21] It is also seen to reflect the greater emphasis being placed on the cost-effective use of human resources.[22]

Decentralisation of bargaining does not, however, mean that local managers are given a completely free hand on employee relations matters. In fact, rather the opposite appears to be true. The study of multi-establishment companies mentioned earlier, for example, found that two-thirds of those with establishment-level bargaining had a policy on pay settlements or issued pay guidelines and a similar proportion indicated that there were consultations with management at higher levels before the start of negotiations.[23] Only 17 per cent of establishments surveyed in the study indicated no such higher-level policy, guidelines or consultation.

7.4 The conduct of bargaining

Collective bargaining conduct is considered under four headings: the context of negotiations; the nature of negotiations; the bargaining encounter; and disputes procedures.

The context of negotiations

Collective bargaining is part of an ongoing relationship between management and unions. This needs to be borne in mind during negotiations, and care must be taken to ensure that relatively minor short-term gains are not obtained at the cost of harm to the long-term relationship. Nevertheless, disagreements will inevitably occur which will prove difficult, if not impossible, to resolve in a way that is reasonably acceptable to both management and union.

Negotiations involve a combination of coercive and persuasive strategies. The latter encompass both threats and arguments; the former, the application of direct sanctions intended to inflict harm on the opposing side and prompt it to shift its negotiation position.

Threats and arguments can take a number of different forms and those used will inevitably be influenced by the issues under discussion and the particular circumstances surrounding those discussions. In the case of pay negotiations union claims will often be supported by reference to one or more of the following: rises in the cost of living, improvements in productivity, trends in company profitability, the level of settlements negotiated elsewhere in the industry or the economy, and the earnings of other employee groups, either inside or outside the company. Notions of equity, fairness and justice will frequently underpin, either implicitly or explicitly, union arguments put forward concerning pay and other issues. For example, in discussions over a disciplinary matter, union representatives may well argue that the proposed penalty is out of all proportion to the offence committed, or that management is guilty of inconsistency in that a lesser penalty had been imposed when a similar situation occurred in the past. It is important not to underestimate the importance of such notions when handling such issues.[24]

Threats involve one party threatening to impose sanctions on the other unless a more favourable settlement is offered. Sometimes these threats may be meant. On other occasions they may involve an element of bluff. A crucial task for the other party is to try and assess which of these situations apply. Sanctions can be imposed by both sides. Management may, for example, threaten to lock the workforce out, cease negotiations and impose a pay settlement unilaterally, dismiss any workers taking industrial action, or close the workplace down. Union-initiated sanctions can include strikes, go-slows, work-to-rules, overtime bans and the withdrawal of cooperation.

Calculations about the ability of members to take effective action will influence the willingness of unions to impose sanctions on a particular issue. These in turn will reflect assessments of the degree of support among members and the capacity of those members to disrupt their employer's operations. The nature of the employer's products, the position the workers occupy in the work process, and in particular the immediacy and extent to which they can affect the supply of goods and services, and the ability of the employer to find alternative means of meeting customer demand – such as through the use of alternative labour or production from another plant – are some of the more important factors which will influence the disruptive potential of particular employee groups.[25]

The nature of negotiations

The process of negotiation has been defined by Gottschalk as 'an occasion where one or more representatives of two or more parties interact in an explicit attempt to reach a jointly acceptable position on one or more divisive issues'.[26] Various models have been put forward to analyse management–union negotiations. One of the most influential is that developed by Walton and McKersie who argue in their model that negotiations consist of four sub-processes: *distributive bargaining, integrative bargaining, attitudinal structuring* and *intra-organisational bargaining*.[27]

Distributive bargaining exists where the function of the negotiations is to resolve conflicts between the parties, the resolution of which requires by definition one party to win, the other to lose. Walton and McKersie argue that this form of bargaining is the dominant activity in management–union negotiations.

Integrative bargaining, in contrast, refers to negotiations over issues which are not marked by fundamental conflicts of interest and hence are capable of solutions which benefit both sides to some degree, or at least do not result in the gains of one side representing equal losses for the other. The productivity bargaining carried out in the 1960s and 1970s under which employees agreed to accept more efficient working practices in return for improved terms and conditions was a good example of this type of bargaining.[28] The same is true of some of the flexibility agreements signed in the 1980s.[29]

While most bargaining situations will involve elements of both distributive and integrative bargaining, they will generally approximate to one or other of these two 'ideal types'. According to Walton and McKersie, 'integrative bargaining is tentative and exploratory and involves open-communication processes, whereas distributive bargaining involves adamant, directed, and controlled information processes'.[30] Integrative bargaining is consequently facilitated by a supportive and trusting climate which encourages the negotiators to behave spontaneously without fear of sanctions.

Attitudinal structuring is more concerned with the process by which one party to the negotiation attempts to influence the attitudes of the other in a way favourable to itself. Attitudes can be influenced both during negotiations and before they start. For example, management and unions may try to influence the expectations of the other side with regard to forthcoming negotiations during discussions in forums like joint consultative committees.[31] Management may also try to influence attitudes in the build-up to negotiations by the provision of information on financial performance, trading prospects and likely future developments in the enterprise. Here it should be noted that under the Trade Union and Labour Relations (Consolidation) Act 1992 officials of independent, recognised unions have a right, on request, to be provided with information without which they would be 'to a material extent impeded' in carrying out collective bargaining. Employers have a similar obligation to provide information which it would be in accordance with good practice to disclose for the purpose of such bargaining (see Chapter 8). An ACAS Code of Practice provides guidance on the types of information that employers should disclose in order to meet their statutory requirements.[32]

Intra-organisational bargaining, the final sub-process distinguished by Walton and McKersie, reflects the fact that those directly involved in negotiations are acting as representatives of their respective parties. Consequently, an important aspect of negotiations is the process of discussion and debate that goes on within each of the parties involved in order to reach consensus on matters like the offer which should be made to the other side, the tactics to be employed during negotiations and the acceptability of a proposed settlement. As one writer has observed, 'when two organisations are party to negotiations, it takes, in effect, three agreements to achieve a negotiated settlement between the parties: an agreement within each party and between them'.[33] In the public sector this process of intra-organisational bargaining can be particularly complex since the government will frequently try, either formally or informally, to influence the policies and strategies adopted by management.

Negotiators need to bear in mind these intra-organisational considerations. A sensitivity to, and awareness of, the internal political pressures which the negotiators 'on the other side' are under can be helpful in the search for the compromises and packages necessary to resolve disputes. Moreover, management negotiators need to appreciate that even if their union counterparts find an offer acceptable, they may have to reject it because of the views of their members.

Negotiations may involve union full-time officials, shop stewards or a combination of the two. Shop stewards are elected by union members in a particular location, department or section to represent their interests. Traditionally they were associated with manufacturing industry and manual workers, their widespread appointment developing first in the skilled engineering trades during the nineteenth century.

Today it is estimated that there are more shop stewards in the public sector than in the private, and that there are nearly as many representing non-manual employee grades as manual. Shop stewards are found in the majority of workplaces where unions are recognised and where two or more stewards are present, they may appoint senior stewards, and/or conveners. Committees representing stewards from one or more unions may also exist. Consequently, when negotiating, stewards have to take account not only of the policies of the national union, and the expectations and aspirations of their members, but also the views of their fellow stewards.

The nature of the relationship between stewards and the members they represent will reflect the composition of the workforce and their own personality and opinions. A study of steward organisation in a car factory distinguished four different types of steward based on the extent to which they espoused trade union principles and the nature of the relationship they had with their members.[34] The most important distinction was that drawn between what they termed *leader* and *populist* stewards. Leader stewards adopted an initiator role in decision-making, actively shaping the issues raised on behalf of members, and sought to achieve objectives supportive of wider trade union principles. Populists, in contrast, saw themselves more akin to a delegate whose role was to carry out merely the wishes of the membership, whatever these might be. Interestingly, Batstone found populists to be more common among white collar groups and leaders among manual workers.

The bargaining encounter

Negotiations can range from relatively informal discussions between a supervisor and a shop steward to a large set-piece affair involving a number of representatives from each side. In this second situation, it is important to clarify the roles to be played by each member of the negotiating team before the start of negotiations. Roles commonly distinguished are those of chief negotiator, the person who does most of the talking, the secretary, who is expected to keep notes and look for any verbal or non-verbal signals from the other side, and the analyst, whose role is to scrutinise and analyse what is being said and to summarise the

issues, if and when this is appropriate. Negotiating teams may also include one or more specialists with technical knowledge and experience relevant to the issues under discussion.[35]

It is vital to ensure that team members do not give contradictory messages, since this is
not only confusing, but may give the other side an opportunity to exploit any differences of
opinion that exist. Disagreements within a negotiating team should be discussed during
adjournments, an important part of negotiations. Adjournments give negotiators time to
consider the arguments and offers put forward by the other side, to re-appraise their bargaining tactics and to seek clearance from senior management if a change in bargaining
objectives is thought desirable.

Good preparation is an essential prerequisite for effective negotiations. Each side needs
to consider carefully what its negotiating objectives are to be, including fallback positions,
and the arguments to be used to support them. Where a number of issues are to be discussed, it may be useful to allocate the various objectives to one of three categories: essential, desirable and optimistic.[36] Negotiators should give thought also to the objectives likely
to be pursued by the other side, and the arguments that they may use to support them. They
must also consider the necessary bargaining tactics, for example, management may choose
to make a relatively generous opening offer which leaves little subsequent room for
manoeuvre, or it may adopt the opposite approach.

Once negotiations start, the convention is that the party seeking the negotiation should
open the encounter. In the case of a pay claim, the union will start the process by outlining
its claim and the rationale underlying it. At this stage management listens carefully to what
is being said, seeks any necessary clarification and makes sure that what the union is asking for is fully understood. Indeed, these three techniques should be used throughout negotiations. Research by Rackham and Carlisle has found that 'skilled negotiators' tend to
seek more information, and more frequently to summarise and test understanding, than
'average negotiators'.[37]

Agreement by definition only becomes possible if one or both sides are willing to make
concessions and move from their opening positions. But both sides may be wary of offering concessions for fear that they will not be reciprocated. The use of what has been called
signalling can be used to try and 'break out' of circular and non-conclusive argument in a
way that minimises this danger. Signals are qualifications placed on a statement of position
indicating a willingness to consider alternative proposals. An example is where a negotiator adds the phrase 'in its present form' to a statement that 'we will never agree to what you
are proposing'.[38] More generally, when negotiating, it is important to think creatively about
how the various issues on the bargaining table can be combined or packaged in a manner
acceptable to both sides.

As far as possible, exchanges that could be perceived as personal attacks by the other
side's negotiators should be avoided since this is unlikely to be helpful to the discussions
and could have adverse implications for future negotiations. Similarly, where a party
makes a concession it may be sensible to help them do this without losing face.

Once agreement has been reached, it is important to clarify exactly what has been agreed.
One way of doing this is to prepare a detailed summary which both sides then agree. A
further important point is that union negotiators will frequently have to refer agreements to
their members for approval before they can agree them formally. Management should seek
an undertaking that they will recommend acceptance by their members.

Disputes procedures
When negotiations become deadlocked the parties will usually register a failure to agree
and refer the issue to the next stage of the disputes procedure. It is normally understood, if

not explicitly stated, that both sides will refrain from taking any industrial action until all stages of the procedure have been exhausted. Nevertheless, unconstitutional action, that is, action in breach of procedure, can occur.

Disputes procedures are intended to aid the resolution of disputes by enabling them to be processed through a series of hierarchical stages, each of which involves the introduction of more senior personnel from both sides who are less directly involved with the issues under discussion. Survey evidence shows that the majority of workplaces with 25 or more employees have formal, written procedures and that they are almost universal in establishments with workforces of over 500.[39] The absence of a formal procedure does not, however, mean that an organisation does not have any standard means of processing disputes.[40]

When devising procedures only those levels of management able to play an effective role in resolving disputes need to be involved, to avoid their becoming unduly cumbersome and time-consuming. An important issue is whether individual grievances and collective disputes should be covered by the same procedure. Where a combined approach is adopted, it is common with collective disputes for the procedure to provide for certain of its early stages to be omitted.

Procedures vary considerably both in relation to the number of stages they contain and the identity of those to be involved at each stage.[41] Three main levels or stages can be distinguished, although each of these may in turn include a number of different stages. These are the department, the establishment and the external. An additional corporate level stage may be distinguished in some multi-plant companies.

Not all procedures formally provide for issues to be referred outside the organisation. Where provision is made, it may take the form of reference to an industry-wide disputes procedure if the employer concerned is a party to the relevant set of industry-level negotiations. Alternatively, the matter may be referred to an independent third party.

Independent third party intervention, often organised in the UK under the auspices of ACAS, can take one of three main forms: *conciliation, mediation* and *arbitration*. With conciliation the third party supports the negotiating process by assisting the parties to identify the nature of their differences and possible ways of resolving them. Mediation, in practice often difficult to distinguish from conciliation, permits a rather more interventionist stance in that the third party puts forward recommendations for settlement, although the parties are free to accept, reject or amend the terms proposed. Finally, arbitration involves an even greater degree of intervention in that the third party has to make an award which is binding on the parties.

Procedures which include provision for third party intervention differ in terms of how the process is to be triggered. In some cases this can only occur with the joint agreement of the two parties. In others, one party may have the right to refer an issue to a third party. A third possibility is for the procedure to provide for an issue to be automatically referred once a failure to agree has been registered internally. Moreover, it is possible for procedures not only to specify more than one type of intervention, but to lay down different procedures regarding how they are to be initiated. For example, an agreement may provide for joint reference to conciliation, but unilateral reference to arbitration.

Procedures which provide for automatic recourse to arbitration were central to the debate about 'no strike' or 'strike-free' deals. This was because, when combined with the normal obligation not to take action in breach of procedure, they effectively precluded a union from calling unconstitutional industrial action. Optical Fibres, NEK Cables, Toshiba and Hitachi are among the companies with agreements of this type.[42]

Arbitration can provide a valuable means of resolving disputes without costly industrial action, but it does have several potential drawbacks since, by definition, it involves management allowing a third party to decide issues which could have considerable implications for internal costs and efficiency. It may also act to undermine the collective bargaining process in two important ways: first, because it provides the parties with a way of 'getting off the hook' without having to work out their own solutions; second, because arbitrators can choose compromise solutions somewhere between the final negotiating positions of the two sides. As a result, it is argued that negotiators are encouraged to hold back their final negotiating stances on the grounds that they have 'something to give' at the arbitration stage. In the USA this is referred to as the 'chilling effect'.

Such potential drawbacks have prompted considerable interest in the concept of 'pendulum' or 'last offer' arbitration, a feature of most of the 'strike-free' deals referred to above. Used widely in the USA to resolve public sector disputes, this type of arbitration differs from that traditionally used to resolve disputes over issues like pay in that the arbitrator cannot make an award somewhere between the final negotiating positions of management and union. In other words, the arbitrator has to opt for one or other side.

It is argued that pendulum arbitration serves to support rather than undermine collective bargaining since it encourages the parties to narrow their differences as far as possible in order to avoid the 'all or nothing' character of the process and minimise their chances of losing if an issue does go to arbitration. But it does have certain potential disadvantages compared with 'traditional arbitration'.[43] These include the difficulties surrounding what constitutes the final negotiating positions of management and union; the fact that it precludes arbitrators from considering the long-run implications of their awards for industrial relations; and the rather crude nature of the process where the dispute concerns a complex set of negotiations covering several different issues such as pay, holidays and hours of work.

7.5 Assessment of employee relations

Disputes procedures are intended to help management and unions to resolve disagreements without recourse to costly industrial action. However, they must guard against assessing the quality of their employee relations solely by reference to the amount of such action experienced.

Effective management–union relations take place within the context of the employment relationship more generally. Both parties to this relationship, management and workers, have objectives which they want to fulfil. Employees, for example, are likely to see their work as a means of meeting their aspirations on, for example, pay levels, employment security, hours of work, and promotion. Similarly, organisations employ people to enable the enterprise to further its commercial and/or public service objectives.

As seen by the employer, the ultimate test of effectiveness should be whether their management–union relations enable the organisation to operate in a way conducive to the achievement of both its short- and long-term objectives. Relevant questions to consider are whether they are helping or hindering the achievement of high levels of output and productivity, satisfactory labour recruitment and retention, the maintenance of an atmosphere supportive of change, and the presence of a committed and motivated workforce.

Organised conflict can dramatically harm an employer's operations in each of the areas mentioned. This is certainly not what any employer wants. On the other hand, a low level of conflict is not necessarily a sign that relationships are satisfactory. It is quite possible for low levels of conflict to exist alongside high levels of absenteeism and labour turnover, inflexible working practices, and widespread resistance to change. As has been pointed out by Fox, 'overt and palpable expressions of conflict are no more a reliable indicator of low morale than their absence is of a clean bill of health'.[44]

7.6 Future developments in employee relations

The future coverage of collective bargaining in the UK is inexorably linked to developments in union membership and recognition. As already noted, the past 15 years have seen unions experiencing reverses in both of these areas.

Back in 1979 union membership in Britain had reached an all-time record level of 12.6 million, or 55 per cent of the employed workforce. Since then it has declined both continuously and dramatically. Indeed, data from the Labour Force Survey indicates that by the autumn of 1993 membership had fallen by over 4 million to 7.7 million covering 31 per cent of those in employment.[45]

A variety of economic and structural factors have contributed to this decline in membership.[46] These include the existence of relatively high levels of unemployment combined with generally rising real incomes; a shift of employment away from highly unionised industries, such as mining, manufacturing and the docks, to the less well-organised private services sector; an increase in the number of white collar and female workers; and a growth in self-employment and temporary and part-time work.

The effects of these developments have in turn been compounded by changes in employer and government attitudes towards trade unions. Successive governments since 1979 have introduced a host of legislative changes which have both made it harder for unions to secure recognition and increased their vulnerability to legal action.[47] For example, the previously existing statutory recognition procedure has been repealed; secondary (sympathetic) action and the enforcement of closed shop arrangements have been made unlawful; the inclusion of union-only clauses in commercial contracts has been prohibited; and employers have been given the right to seek damages from unions in respect of industrial action which has not been approved by a membership ballot. At the same time, and partly as a result of these legislative developments, employers have been considerably less willing to recognise unions and in some cases have decided to withdraw recognition, either completely or in respect of particular groups of staff.[48]

One response of unions to these developments, and the loss of subscription income associated with them, has been to merge as a means of obtaining greater institutional security and economies of scale. As a result the number of unions in the UK dropped from 454 in 1979 to 268 in 1992.[49] New unions created as a result of mergers during this period included Manufacturing, Science and Finance (MSF), the Amalgamated Engineering and Electrical Union (AEEU), the Graphical, Paper and Media Union (GPMU) and UNISON, the public services union.

Another union response has been to improve the organisation and resourcing of their recruitment activities. For example, new legal and financial services have been made available to members and attempts made to increase recruitment among part-time, temporary, and even self-employed workers.[50] There is considerable debate as to how far activities of this type can succeed in securing an expansion of union membership.[51] However, it would seem questionable whether they can significantly reverse recent membership trends in the absence of an economic and political environment which is more conducive to union organisation.

It is a matter of speculation whether, and to what extent, such an environment will become a reality. At the time of writing, it appears that a more supportive political climate may develop as a result of the election of a Labour Government committed to re-introducing a statutory union recognition procedure. In addition, it is possible that union attempts to increase membership and recognition will be assisted by European Union developments relating to the establishment by employers of consultative representative bodies.

The European Works Council Directive currently requires over 200 UK multinationals to establish such bodies in respect of their operations elsewhere in the European Union and it appears that most of these will choose to include representatives of their home workforce in the arrangements they establish. Moreover, the number of companies affected by the Directive will increase further should a subsequent government elect to sign the Social Protocol attached to the Maastricht Treaty. The establishment of bodies of this type in companies which do not recognise unions for all (or parts) of their UK workforce could provide unions with another forum to push for recognition rights. This would perhaps be even more true of any future European requirements concerning the creation of domestic, rather than transnational, consultative arrangements.[52]

7.7 References

1. Purcell J, Sisson K. Strategies and practices in the management of industrial relations. In: Bain GS ed. *Industrial relations in Britain.* Oxford: Blackwell, 1983. Also see Purcell J. Mapping management styles in employee relations. *Journal of Management Studies* 1987; **24**: 533–48.
2. Marginson P, Sisson K. The management of employees. In: Marginson P *et al. Beyond the workplace: managing industrial relations in the multi-establishment enterprise.* Oxford: Blackwell, 1988.
3. Geary J. New forms of work organisation: the case of two American electronics plants. *Economic and Industrial Democracy* 1993; **14**: 511–34.
4. Gregg P, Yates A. Changes in trade union and wage setting arrangements in the 1980s. *British Journal of Industrial Relations* 1991; **29**: 361–76; and Claydon T. Union derecognition in the 1980s. *British Journal of Industrial Relations* 1989; **27**: 214–24.
5. Lucas R. Industrial relations in hotels and catering: neglect and paradox? *British Journal of Industrial Relations* 1996; **34**: 267–86.
6. Millward N *et al. Workplace industrial relations in transition: the ED/ESRC/PSI/ACAS surveys.* Aldershot: Dartmouth, 1992.
7. Millward *et al., Workplace industrial relations*: 71.
8. Royal Commission on Trade Unions and Employers' Associations 1965–68. *Report.* Cmnd 3623, London: HMSO, 1968.
9. Single-table bargaining: an idea whose time has yet to come? *IRS Employment Trends* 1995: **577**, February: 10–16.
10. Bassett P. *Strike free: new industrial relations in Britain*, revised edition, London: Macmillan, 1987.
11. *IDS Report*, January 1997.
12. See e.g. Brewster C, Connock S. *Industrial relations: cost effective strategies.* London: Hutchinson, 1985.
13. Marchington M *et al. New developments in employee involvement.* Employment Department Research Paper No. 2, London: Department of Employment 1992.
14. A firm foundation: Castle Cement's new deal. *IRS Employment Trends* 1997: **628**, March: 11–16.
15. Brown W, Walsh J. Pay determination in Britain in the 1980s: the anatomy of decentralisation. *Oxford Review of Economic Policy* 1991; **7**: 44–59.
16. Brown W. The contraction of collective bargaining in Britain. *British Journal of Industrial Relations* 1993; **31**: 189–99.
17. Ogden S. Decline and fall: national bargaining in British water. *Industrial Relations Journal* 1993; **24**: 44–58; and James P. Reforming industrial relations in electricity supply. *IRS Employment Trends* 1992; **521**, October: 6–12.
18. Bach S, Winchester D. Opting out of pay devolution? *British Journal of Industrial Relations* 1994; **32**: 263–82.
19. Keenan P, Gaunt C. Recession storm shakes building. In: Jones G ed. *Local Government Management Agenda.* London: ICSA, 1993.
20. See e.g. Commission on Industrial Relations. *Industrial relations in multi-plant undertakings.* Report No. 85, London: HMSO, 1974; and Jackson M *et al. Decentralisation of collective bargaining: an analysis of recent experience in the UK.* London: Macmillan, 1993.

21. Purcell J. How to manage decentralised bargaining. *Personnel Management* 1989; May: 53–5.
22. Brewster, Connock, *Industrial Relations*.
23. Edwards PK, Marginson P. Trade unions, pay bargaining and industrial action. In: Marginson *et al. Beyond the workplace*: 123–64.
24. Hyman R, Brough I. *Social values and industrial relations*. Oxford: Blackwell, 1975.
25. Batstone E, Boraston I, Frenkel S. *The social organisation of strikes*. Oxford: Blackwell, 1978: 27–44.
26. Gottschalk A. The background to the negotiating process. In: Torrington D ed. *Code of personnel administration*. Aldershot: Gower, 1973.
27. Walton R, McKersie R. *A behavioral theory of labor negotiations*. New York: McGraw-Hill, 1965.
28. See e.g. McKersie R, Hunter L. *Pay, productivity and collective bargaining*. London: Macmillan, 1973.
29. Marsden D, Thompson M. Flexibility agreements and their significance in the increase in productivity in British manufacturing since 1980. *Work, Employment and Society* 1990; **4**: 83–104.
30. Walton, McKersie *Behavioral theory*: 166.
31. Marchington M, Armstrong R. A case for consultation. *Employee Relations* 1980; **3**: 10–16.
32. *ACAS Code of Practice: disclosure of information to trade unions for collective bargaining*. London: HMSO, 1977.
33. Singh R. Negotiations. In: Towers B ed. *A handbook of industrial relations practice*. London: Kogan Page, 3rd edition, 1992: 137–51.
34. Batstone E, Boraston I, Frenkel S. *Shop stewards in action*. Oxford: Blackwell, 1977.
35. Useful texts on the negotiating process include: Atkinson G. *The effective negotiator*. London: Quest, 1977; and Kennedy G, Benson J, McMillan J. *Managing negotiations*. London: Hutchinson, 2nd edition, 1984.
36. Kennedy *et al., Managing negotiations*.
37. Rackham N, Carlisle J. The effective negotiator – Part 1. *Journal of European Industrial Training* 1978; **6**: 7–14.
38. Kennedy *et al., Managing negotiations*: Ch. 5.
39. Millward *et al. Workplace industrial relations*: 189–90.
40. Thomson A, Murray V. *Grievance procedures*. London: Saxon House, 1975.
41. Singleton N. *Industrial relations procedures*. London: HMSO, 1975.
42. No-strike deals: are they different? *Industrial Relations Review and Report* 1988; **414**, 19 April.
43. Wood J. Last offer arbitration. *British Journal of Industrial Relations* 1985; **XXIII**: 415–24.
44. Fox A. *Industrial sociology and industrial relations*. Royal Commission on Trade Unions and Employers' Associations, Research Paper No. 3, London: HMSO, 1967: 9.
45. See Waddington J, Whitson C. Trade unions: growth, structure and policy. In: Edwards P ed. *Industrial relations: theory and practice in Britain*. Oxford: Blackwell, 1995: 151–202.
46. See e.g. Disney R. Explanations of the decline in trade union density in Britain: an appraisal. *British Journal of Industrial Relations* 1990; **28**: 165–77.
47. Dickens L, Hall M. The state: labour law and industrial relations. In: Edwards P ed. *Industrial relations: theory and practice in Britain*. Oxford: Blackwell, 1995: 255–303.
48. See Gregg, Yates, *Changes*; and Claydon, Union derecognition.
49. Waddington J, Whitson C. Trade unions: growth, structure and policy. In: Edwards P ed. *Industrial relations: theory and practice in Britain*. Oxford: Blackwell, 1995.
50. Mason B, Bain P. Trade union recruitment strategies: facing the 1990s. *Industrial Relations Journal* 1991; **22**: 36–45.
51. See e.g. Mason B, Bain P. The determinants of trade union membership in Britain: a survey of the literature. *Industrial and Labour Relations Review* 1993; **46**.
52. Wedderburn Lord. Consultation and collective bargaining in Europe: success or ideology? *Industrial Law Journal* 1997; **26**: 1–34.

8 The legal framework of employment

Brenda Barrett

A manager with responsibilities for human resources cannot ignore the legal framework of employment. There is a great volume of employment law and it is both complex and subject to frequent change. This chapter can only outline the law sufficiently to alert managers to the circumstances in which they may need to seek expert advice. It must be understood that the broad rules set out here may be subject to qualifications which might modify their operation in particular situations.

8.1 The legal system in Britain

To understand employment law it is necessary to have some knowledge of the legal system. Strictly speaking, laws are enforceable only within the jurisdiction to which they apply and within the UK there are three distinct jurisdictions, namely, (a) England and Wales; (b) Scotland ((a) and (b) together make up Great Britain); and (c) Northern Ireland. However, as the three jurisdictions share one Parliament, and the Appellate Committee of the House of Lords is for most purposes the highest appeal court for each, there are few major regional differences. Moreover, the development of the European Union has already brought a high level of harmonisation of laws throughout the Member States.

Sources of law

Laws stem from two important sources: litigation and legislation.

Litigation: In former times this was the more important source of English law. Centuries ago judges decided disputes according to local custom; in time, through reporting of judgements, some customs became common to the whole country and provided the foundation of the 'common law' system whereby the decisions of the higher courts create precedents which are binding in future litigation. Today good reporting ensures that the majority of significant judicial decisions are published.

A number of cases are cited in this chapter so it may be helpful to explain the referencing system which lawyers employ to denote where a case can be found in a law library. For example, the citation *Gascol Conversions Ltd* v *Mercer* [1974] ICR 420 indicates that this case (which incidentally bears the names of those involved in the litigation) is reported at page 420 of Industrial Cases Reports for the year 1974. Other important modern series of reports are:

QB   Queen's Bench ⎱ The (i.e. Incorporated Council) Law Reports
AC   Appeal Cases ⎰
WLR   Weekly Law Reports
All ER All England Reports
IRLR   Industrial Relations Law Reports

Managers may subscribe to IRLR: quality daily papers usually carry brief reports of the more important of the previous day's hearings as part of their news service. *The Times* reports are available on the Internet.

The development of legal rules through decided cases has limitations since, on the one hand, it depends on the fortuitous occurrence of situations which provoke litigation and, on the other, the system of precedent can produce rules which cannot easily be adapted as society changes.

Legislation: Since the beginning of the twentieth century the UK Parliament has increasingly legislated to direct the development of the law although the foundations of modern employment law were laid in the nineteenth century. In the UK because legislation has developed pragmatically to deal piecemeal with defects in the law, there is no single Act of Parliament constituting a code in which all rules relating to employment are contained. Most of the legislation currently in force originated in the 1970s but such has been the pace of change that barely a year has passed without major amendments being made. The position has been somewhat simplified in the 1990s by two major consolidation statutes: the Trade Union and Labour Relations (Consolidation) Act 1992 (hereafter TULR(C) Act) and the Employment Rights Act 1996 (hereafter ER Act). The first of these brings together trade union law, including individual worker rights in relation to trade union membership and activities, and the latter replaces the Employment Protection (Consolidation) Act 1978.

Other major statutes which will be considered in some detail here are:

Equal Pay Act 1970 (as amended)
Health and Safety at Work Act 1974
Sex Discrimination Act 1975 (as amended)

Subordinate legislation: So complex has society become that Parliament has not for many years attempted to legislate in detail; the detail has been spelt out in regulations made subordinate to the framework legislation.

Codes of Practice: Statutes may also enable, or even direct that a Code of Practice be made to provide guidance as to a proper mode of conduct in given circumstances within the scope of the statute's provisions. The Code of Practice is a regulatory device which enables legislation to be fleshed out without introducing the rigidity of subordinate legislation, for unlike statutes and regulations, compliance with Codes of Practice is not mandatory. Codes may be of evidential value in a court of law, and in reality it is very hard to justify why the relevant code has not been followed. There are a number of Codes of Practice relevant to employment law: a very important example is the Code of Practice on *Disciplinary Practice and Procedures in Employment.*

Europe: When the UK joined the European Community in 1973 it became immediately bound by the founding treaties, particularly the 1957 Treaty of Rome – cornerstone of the European Economic Community – (some Articles of this Treaty, such as Article 119 on equal pay, are very important to employment law) and by any laws made further to the Treaties.

The European Union (EU), since 1993, most frequently legislates by adopting Directives to further the purposes of the Treaties: a Directive is, as its name suggests, an instruction to the Member States. It requires them to implement its provisions, within a stated time. In the UK Directives are sometimes implemented in Acts of Parliament (e.g. the Sex Discrimination Act); sometimes by regulations made under an existing statute, e.g.

the Framework Directive (89/391/EEC) to encourage improvements in the safety and health of workers at work, was implemented in Great Britain by the Management of Health and Safety at Work Regulations 1992, which were made under the Health and Safety at Work Act 1974. It is also possible for regulations to be made under the European Communities Act 1972, an Act of the UK Parliament passed to facilitate the UK's entry into the European Community. The troublesome Transfer of Undertakings (Protection of Employment) Regulations 1981 were made in this way to implement the Acquired Rights Directive (77/187/EEC). The UK response to Directives is often to make separate provision for the various jurisdictions which make up the UK, e.g. the Sex Discrimination Act 1975 does not apply to Northern Ireland.

If experience proves that UK legislation has failed to capture the intention of the EC, further amending legislation may be necessary: thus the Equal Pay Act 1970 was amended by the Equal Pay (Amendment) Regulations 1983 to introduce the concept of work of equal value into the Act of 1970.

Interpretation: Words used in legislation often require interpretation: indeed, there is an Interpretation Act 1978, which interprets words frequently used in legislation, for example, 'he' used in a statute normally includes 'she' (a lawyer's discriminatory practice employed in places in this chapter!). In spite of this Act much statutory interpretation is left to courts, and case law which develops in relation to an Act of Parliament can considerably influence the impact of the legislation; therefore the legal practitioner relies less on a Stationery Office copy of a statute than upon text books which incorporate subsequent judicial interpretations of that legislation. In recent years the interpretations of the European Court of Justice in litigation concerning other Member States have had an effect on the interpretation of UK laws.

Deregulation: In the 1990s the UK government has been committed to reducing the amount of detailed regulation, but it is proving difficult to reconcile this objective with the commitment of the EU to producing detailed rules in order to harmonise the law of the Member States.

Criminal and civil law

Rules of law fall into two main categories: criminal and civil.

Criminal law: This aims to regulate society, and imposes sanctions, such as fines and imprisonment, on those who do not observe the rules. Criminal cases are normally brought to court by the police (through the Crown Prosecution Service) or by a special enforcement agency such as the Health and Safety Executive's inspectorate. Criminal law is enforced in England through the magistrates' courts and the Crown Court. Minor criminal charges are tried summarily in magistrates' courts; serious offences are tried upon indictment, before a jury, in a session of the Crown Court, but only after a preliminary enquiry has been conducted in a magistrates' court to determine whether there is a case to answer. Appeal may lie from decisions of the Crown Court to the Court of Appeal, and thence to the House of Lords.

The criminal law plays a relatively unimportant role in employment matters, with the notable exception that breaches of occupational health and safety laws are usually criminal offences, but management will, no doubt, cooperate with the police should it appear that criminal offences, for example theft, have occurred at the workplace. Also, industrial disputes have a regrettable tendency to encourage violence; for example, picketing has often provoked police intervention with resultant criminal prosecutions. The rules invoked in such situations will normally be drawn from the general body of the law, rather than employment law.

Civil law: This is intended to give parties the opportunity to obtain redress from the person or organisation who has injured them. In England most civil disputes are determined in county courts, but cases which are very complex or involve a lot of money are tried at first instance (i.e. initially) in the High Court. Appeals go to the Court of Appeal and finally to the House of Lords. There are different courts in other parts of the UK.

European Court of Justice (ECJ): Where there appears to be a difference between UK and Community law the matter may be reviewed in the ECJ. The ECJ is empowered to hear references from national courts for interpretation of Community law (Article 177 of the Treaty of Rome and s.3(1) of the European Communities Act 1972): it is also concerned with actions alleging failures by Member States to fulfil the obligations of the Treaty of Rome (Article 170). The UK has been brought to account on several occasions, for example in *Commission* v *United Kingdom (safeguarding of employees' rights in the event of transfers of undertakings)* [1994] ICR 664, the ECJ found the Transfer of Undertakings (Protection of Employment) Regulations to be deficient because they did not provide for consultation with employees where there was no relevant recognised trade union. Consequently, UK law was changed by the Collective Redundancies and Transfer of Undertakings (Protection of Employment) (Amendment) Regulations 1995.

Even an industrial tribunal (see below) may refer a question to the ECJ for interpretation. However, the European Communities Act 1972 directs UK courts to interpret the laws before them in accordance with any relevant Community laws and so judges give a 'purposive' interpretation of UK statutes to give effect to EU law wherever possible (see *Pickstone* v *Freemans PLC* [1989] 3 WLR 265 – where the House of Lords granted a women's equal pay claim even though there was a man employed on the same work).

The rights of the individual employee to apply to the court for interpretation of employment provisions are complex: they depend on the nature of the rule in dispute and whether the employee is in public or private employment. Article 119 (on equal pay) being unequivocal can be directly relied on by employees (see *Marshall* v *Southampton & SW Hants AHA* [1986] 2 WLR 780).

Industrial tribunals

Employees (and in some cases workers more generally) have, since the late 1960s, by statutes been granted rights (such as the right not to be unfairly dismissed) which are enforceable only through industrial tribunals. Such rights are additional to common law rights (such as those relating to wrongful dismissal) which were formerly, and remain even today, enforceable in county courts and the High Court. While these statutory rights are not themselves enforceable in common law courts, common law rules may influence the decision reached in cases concerning such rules. Tribunals are empowered by the Industrial Tribunals Extension of Jurisdiction (England and Wales) Order 1994 to hear most claims for common law damages which are outstanding on the termination of an employee's contract of employment.

Appeals from an industrial tribunal lie on a matter of law to the Employment Appeal Tribunal (EAT) (a special court of High Court status); further appeal lies with the Court of Appeal and finally to the House of Lords. Since the higher appellate courts are common law courts they also tend, some believe wrongly, to infuse principles of common law into the statutory system and, unlike industrial tribunals, they (including the EAT) provide binding precedents on statutory interpretation.

Originally it was imagined that industrial tribunals would provide a swift and cheap resolution of employees' complaints; so complainants are not entitled to legal aid. Experience has shown that issues can be complex and when cases are appealed it may be a long time before a dispute is finally resolved. The rules of operation of industrial tribunals are now largely contained in the Industrial Tribunals Act 1996. Industrial tribunals are likely to be renamed employment tribunals and alternative methods of dispute resolution may be introduced (Employment Rights (Dispute Resolution) Bill).

Advice, conciliation and arbitration

Legislation (currently the TULR(C) Act), has provided for an official Advisory, Conciliation and Arbitration Service (ACAS) to promote the improvement of industrial relations, and in particular to encourage the extension of collective bargaining. ACAS is empowered to provide, free of charge, advice to employers, employers' associations, workers and trade unions on any matters concerned with industrial relations or employment policies. It may also publish general advice on these matters. In addition, it may issue Codes of Practice containing practical guidance to promote the improvement of industrial relations. Its most significant code is that on disciplinary practice and procedures. It is also empowered to inquire into any question relating to industrial relations generally, or in any particular industry or undertaking and (with certain safeguards) publish its findings.

ACAS's mission is to improve the performance and effectiveness of organisations by providing an independent and impartial service to prevent and resolve disputes. Thus ACAS's statutory functions include the provision of assistance in the settlement of workplace disputes. An ACAS conciliation officer will offer assistance (merely to facilitate a settlement) where any complaint has been filed with an industrial tribunal.

Parties to an agreement may always include in that agreement a provision that in the event of dispute they will ask a particular person, or institution, to arbitrate: even if the original agreement did not make provision for use of arbitration, the parties may elect to go to arbitration when a dispute has actually arisen. Arbitration has not traditionally featured strongly in UK employment law, though it may be used to determine a dispute which has arisen out of a collective agreement. Where there is a strike or one is threatened, ACAS may, at the request of one or more of the parties to the dispute, and with the consent of all, refer the matter to the Central Arbitration Committee (CAC).

It is possible, in theory, for disputes between an individual employee and employer to be resolved by arbitration but this has not been customary in the UK, though there has been some support for such systems to be used instead of the present statutory procedures involving industrial tribunals. However, as the law *currently* stands, this could only be done if there was a special dismissal procedure (see ER Act s.110), otherwise any arrangement for arbitration would be likely to fall foul of the rule prohibiting persons from bringing proceedings before an industrial tribunal (ER Act s.203).

Collective and individual employment law

Common law considered the employment relationship as essentially an individual arrangement between employer and employee, creating personal, and non-assignable rights and duties for the parties to it (*Nokes v Doncaster Amalgamated Collieries Ltd* [1940] AC 1014). Today the ability of the parties to negotiate contractual terms is somewhat restricted by statutory controls: for example, the very rule as to the personal nature of the relationship has been largely undermined by the Transfer of Undertakings (Protection of Employment) Regulations 1981, which are intended to protect the employee from suffering termination of contract when the employer transfers the business to another employer (Regulation 4A entitles the employee to refuse transfer but 4B intends that in the event of refusal the employee will be treated as having voluntarily terminated the contract).

The significance of personal relationships in employment is also likely to be reduced where a trade union negotiates employment terms for a class of employees with an employer or its representative association. Individual contracts of employment may then incorporate collectively bargained terms. Any study of employment law has therefore to consider both the contractual relationship between the employer and employee and the relationship between the employer and trade union(s).

A third aspect is the relationship between the trade union and its individual members but this is beyond the scope of this chapter.

8.2 Individual employment law

The contract of employment at common law

Contract has played an important part in the development of English common law and there are many contractual rules which are applicable regardless of the context in, or the purposes for which, a contract has been formed; but, in addition to this general law, a number of specific rules have developed to govern that particular kind of contract known as a contract of employment. From 1970 onwards the contract of employment has been increasingly governed by statute, but arguably, in the recent past, legislation has for a number of reasons been less relevant and the role of common law has again become more prominent.

Identifying the contract of employment

It is important at the outset to distinguish a contract of employment from other contractual relationships, including other kinds of contracts for the performance of work, because both common law and statutes have distinguished the employee, i.e. the worker who has a contract of employment, and given such workers and their employers rights and duties which are at the core of employment law, and which distinguish employment from other commercial arrangements, like those for the provision of services or the sale of goods.

An employer who requires the outside of a building to be painted might negotiate in one of two ways for the performance of this work. He might either indicate the work to be done and ask another to quote a price for the job or, alternatively, he might ask someone to work for a certain wage until the task was completed. In this example the law would probably hold a contract arising out of the first arrangement to be a 'contract for services' because the parties to the contract might be regarded as contracting as separate business enterprises, so that the worker would be an independent contractor: the second arrangement would most probably be a 'contract of service', that is to say the worker would be held to be an employee and the relationship formed would be a contract of employment. The position in the first example would be unambiguous if the person tendering for the work were an employer of labour, or a person who had a large capital investment in plant whose use would significantly contribute to the performance of the task. Difficulties might arise in both situations if the worker engaged had only labour to offer but wished to be treated as 'self-employed' with an organisation separate from that of the employer. In such circumstances the law, rather than the contracting parties, would determine the nature of the contract and would tend to classify the arrangement as a contract of service, weighing the intention of the parties as only one of a number of relevant factors.

No single perfect test has been devised by the courts for the identification of the distinction between the two types of contract, in spite of the many cases which have been heard.

One of the major problems is identifying a test which might be applied for whatever reason the contract might be under scrutiny. The worker's status is relevant not only to determine the rights and duties contained in the contract, but also to determine the extent of the employer's liability to third parties for injuries caused to them by the worker. It also determines assessment for income tax, though in recent years for some marginal situations, regulations have set out arrangements for payment of income tax independently of consideration of the type of contract under which work was performed. The Inland Revenue may thus have taken away one of the incentives for claiming self-employment status.

The courts have always held that the more the employer is able to control the activities of the worker, the more likely it is that that worker is an employee. However, there are many circumstances in which, although it is inappropriate for an employer to exercise any real control over a worker, there is no dispute that the worker is so 'integrated' into the employer's organisation as to be an employee (servant). The courts therefore regard the 'control test' as only one factor in determining whether the contract is one of employment. The matter was analysed thus by Mackenna, J. in *Ready Mixed Concrete (South East) Ltd* v *Minister of Pensions and National Insurance* [1968] 2 QB 497:

> a contract of service exists if the following three conditions are fulfilled: (i) the servant agrees that in consideration of a wage or other remuneration he will provide his own work and skill in the performance of some service for his master (ii) he agrees, expressly or impliedly, that in the performance of that service he will be subject to the other's control in a sufficient degree to make that other master (iii) the other provisions of the contract are consistent with its being a contract of service.

The contractual provisions will not be consistent with there being a contract of employment if the worker is taking the chance of making a profit and running the risk of making a loss out of the sale of labour rather than offering personal service for a wage which will be paid regularly whether or not there is profitable employment.

This chapter is concerned with the attributes of the contract of employment, since it remains the principal employment relationship. In particular, modern statutory regulation of employment, such as social security law and unfair dismissal law, is primarily concerned with the protection of the employee rather than the self-employed person.

Legally binding agreement

A contract of employment is (as Mackenna, J. reaffirmed) a legally binding agreement. It is created by agreement, and while it exists it imposes rights and duties on the parties to it. In due course it is terminated.

Formation of the contract of employment

No person (whether employer or worker) in the UK is under any legal obligation to enter into a contract of employment: in a free society there is neither a right nor a duty to work, and conversely there is neither a right nor a duty to employ labour; but parties who elect to make contracts enter into obligations that they will normally be bound by law to honour, incurring liability if they fail to do so. Thus if persons enter contracts which promise employment 'starting 1st of next month', but learn on or before that date that they are not required, they may sue for damages, even though they have not actually earned their pay by doing the work (*Sarker* v *South Tees Acute Hospitals NHS Trust* (1997), *The Times* 23 April). On the other hand, if a person performs a task without previously entering an agreement under which the other party promised to pay for the work, no claim for payment will be possible (*Lampleigh* v *Braithwait* [1616] 80 ER 155). It will be unlawful discrimination, if a person intending to contract, refuses to do so with a particular person on grounds of race, sex or on grounds of being, or not being, a trade union member.

There are certain situations in which, although the parties have made an agreement, they will not have entered into a legally binding contract:

1. *There is no intention to create legal relations*. Where parties are negotiating in a commercial environment the courts will presume an intention to make a contract unless they have expressly said that they are not so doing, or that they are not may be implied from their conduct. The rule is not significant in regard to the contract of employment but explains why there is no litigation between employer and trade union for enforcement of the collective bargain; the customary rule that the collective bargain is presumed not to be intended to be legally binding (see *Ford* v *Amalgamated Union of Engineering and Foundry Workers* [1969] 2QB 303) is now enacted in TULR(C) Act, s.179.

2. *The parties lack the legal capacity to make a binding contract*. Certain persons are not allowed to incur normal legal obligations, for example, persons under the age of 18 have only a limited contractual capacity and can only be bound by contracts of employment which are beneficial to them. In former days this rule was important. Today there is a greater reliance on statutory protection enforced in the criminal courts (e.g. while the UK is reluctant to implement some of the provisions of the Directive on the Protection of Young People at Work (94/33/EC) the health and safety provisions are implemented under the Management of Health and Safety at Work Regulations 1992). There are few constraints on capacity which are important in the employment contract today: for example, although it is doubtful whether the Crown may bind itself contractually, civil servants have the same right as other employees to bring a complaint against their employer if they are unfairly dismissed (ER Act, s.191).

3. *The agreement is tainted by illegality*. The courts will not assist in the enforcement of an agreement which is tainted by illegality. It would be difficult to identify all the situations in which a contract of employment might become unenforceable because of some illegality associated with its formation or performance. It is only possible to give examples here. Contracts in restraint of trade, that is contracts which unreasonably restrict the freedom of the employee to sell his labour to another employer, are illegal: such restraints are more likely to be considered unreasonable if they are to continue after the termination of the contract. Similarly unenforceable are contracts to evade income tax by classifying part of wages as expenses (see *Napier* v *National Business Agency Ltd* [1951] 2 All ER 264). Normally the courts refuse to assist a party to enforce any of his contractual rights where the contract is tainted by illegality, but in employment contracts sometimes they will sever the illegal aspects and enforce the remainder.

4. *There is no consideration*. The courts will not enforce an agreement in which there are not mutual obligations; each party must have agreed to make payment for what the other party is promising. Nevertheless, the courts do not normally investigate the adequacy of the bargain so an employee will not usually be able to repudiate employment because the agreed wage is below the 'going rate' for the job, especially while the UK does not have statutory minimum wage rates.

5. *Form of the contract*. There is no requirement that a contract of employment be made in writing, but writing provides valuable evidence of what was agreed. The disadvantage is that such a document is itself constraining, for it is difficult to persuade a court that more was actually expressly agreed than is in the document. A court would not, for example, be sympathetic towards the argument that, while the document referred to a 30-hour week, it was verbally agreed that a further 10 hours a week overtime were to be

worked as a contractual obligation (see *Gascol Conversions Ltd* v *Mercer* [1974] ICR 420). The importance of having on record what was intended is now recognised by the statutory requirement that the employee receive written particulars of employment. As a consequence of the statutory requirement the majority of employers now purport to give a full written contract.

Agreed terms of the contract

Terms may be incorporated into a contract in one of two ways: by express agreement and by implication.

Express terms: The common law allows the parties freedom to determine the terms on which they will form the contract, and the courts will not require them to observe terms which they have not expressly or impliedly incorporated into their contract, unless the matter is governed by statute. An agreement between employer and union as to the terms of a contract of employment will not become part of an individual's contract of employment unless the collectively agreed terms have been expressly or impliedly so incorporated (see *National Coal Board* v *Galley* [1958] 1 WLR 16).

In the past, employment law contracts tended to be rather terse and the parties had a regrettable tendency not to make express provision for many of the situations which might reasonably be expected to arise. This problem is largely alleviated by statute, now so phrased as to comply with the Proof of an Employment Relationship Directive (91/533/EEC).

Implied terms: The courts are prepared to imply a term into a contract to give business efficacy to that contract, or because it is obvious to a bystander that it was the intention of the parties to include such a term. In addition, they will imply a term into an employment contract because it is usual for such a term to be implied in employment contracts generally, or because the term is one which it is customary to include in an employment contract with the particular employer or in the particular industry. A term which is completely contrary to what the parties have actually said, or may by their conduct be deemed to have intended, will never be implied. As a result of case law it has long been recognised that there are duties to be implied in a contract of employment on the part of both the employer and the employee.

The duties of an employer are:

1. To pay the agreed wages when they have been earned. If an employee is unable to work because of illness the employer will certainly be bound to make payments of sums due under social security legislation but there may also be a duty to provide the employee with contractual pay (but see *Mears* v *Safecar Security Ltd* [1982] IRLR 183. In the case of a salaried employee, there is an implied term that wages will be paid during illness until the contract is terminated (*Orman* v *Saville Sportswear* [1960] 1 WLR 1055).
2. To provide the opportunity to work if the wage depends on the provision of work (*Turner* v *Goldsmith* [1891] 1 QB 544); the usual view is that the employer is entitled to retain a worker on full pay without provision of work (*Collier* v *Sunday Referee Publishing Co Ltd* [1940] 2KB 647) although this was doubted by Lord Denning in *Langston* v *Amalgamated Union of Engineering Workers* [1974] ICR 180.
3. To reimburse the employee for expenditure properly incurred by the employee in the course of employment.
4. To take reasonable care to provide the employee with a safe system of work.

In the absence of agreement there is no duty on an employer to provide an employee with a reference. An employer who does provide a reference must take care to give an accurate one, otherwise there may be liability to pay damages to the employee (if the reference is defamatory) or to either the recipient of the reference (*Hedley Byrne & Co.* v *Heller & Partners Ltd* [1964] AC 465) or the employee (*Spring* v *Guardian Assurance Co.* [1994] 3 All ER 129) where the reference is incorrect due to negligence. There might also be liability to compensate the employee if reference is made to 'spent' criminal offences (see Rehabilitation of Offenders Act 1974).

The duties of an employee are:

1. to perform contractual duties personally: their performance may not be delegated;
2. to obey reasonable orders; but a single act of disobedience is unlikely to be serious enough to warrant dismissal (*Laws* v *London Chronicle Ltd* [1959] 1 WLR 698);
3. to account to the employer for money received for the employer (*Reading* v *Att. G* [1951] AC 507);
4. to indemnify the employer for loss caused by incompetent performance of contractual obligations, e.g. by negligence (*Lister* v *Romford Ice & Cold Storage Ltd* [1957] AC 555). As a result of a gentlemen's agreement between insurance companies this duty is unlikely to be enforced (but see *Janata Bank* v *Ahmed* [1981] IRLR 457).
5. to respect the employer's trade secrets.

Breach of an implied term may lead to an action in a common law court for damages for breach of contract; in practice it is more likely to be evidence in either wrongful or unfair dismissal proceedings to justify or dispute the termination of the contractual relationship.

Statement of particulars of employment

Sections 1–7 of the ER Act require the employer to give the employee a written statement of particulars of employment not later than two months after the beginning of employment, and, if the contractual arrangements are subsequently changed, a new statement must be provided within a space of a month of the change. In essence the statement must give:

1. the names of the employer and employee;
2. the date when the employment began;
3. the date on which the employee's continuous employment began (taking into account any relevant employment with a previous employer);
4. the scale or rate of remuneration;
5. the intervals at which remuneration is paid;
6. any provisions relating to hours of work;
7. any provisions relating to:
    (a) holidays;
    (b) sickness;
    (c) pensions;
8. the notice required to terminate the contract;
9. the title of the job;
10. (where relevant) the expected duration of the employment;
11. the place of work;
12. any relevant collective agreements;
13. (where relevant) information about employment outside the UK.

The statement is also required to include (except in small firms) a note specifying any disciplinary rules or referring to a document which specifies such rules. It must also identify a person to whom the employee can apply if dissatisfied with any disciplinary decision and a person to whom to apply for redress of any grievance, the manner in which any such application should be made, and what, if any, further steps are consequent upon that application.

These requirements encourage employers positively to address the matters set out above, though there is no need to make provision for every one of these matters. Unfortunately, while well-informed employers comply with the statute, there is no effective means of ensuring that all employers are aware of and meet their obligations. There is no penalty for failing to provide these particulars but an employee who has not received an appropriate statement may complain to an industrial tribunal (ER Act 1995 s.11; see also *Mears* v *Safecar Security Ltd* [1982] IRLR 183).

The Act does not affect the common law rule that a contract of employment may be created orally, and care should be taken to ensure that a document which is given with the intention of achieving a minimal compliance with the Act is not unintentionally elevated to the status of a written contract. An employer could give the statutory statement this status by giving it to an employee stating that it was that employee's contract of employment (see *Gascol Conversions Ltd* v *Mercer* [1974] ICR 420).

Termination at common law

At common law a contract is usually terminated by *performance*; each party carries out the contractual obligations and the contractual relationship ends. It has always been exceptional for a contract of employment to be terminated by performance though it is possible to create employment of this description by employing a person on the agreement, preferably recorded in writing for clarification of statutory rights, that the contract is for a *fixed* term (see now ER Act ss.95 and 197) or for a specific task.

The great majority of employment contracts are made for an indefinite period and are, at common law, terminated by *variation, notice, breach* or *frustration*.

Variation: The parties may agree to alter the terms of the contract (thus terminating it) and make a new one to have immediate effect: this is a negotiation of no practical importance in employment since the law presumes the total employment period is one continuous contract (ER Act s.210). It used to be thought that if either of the parties did not agree to accept a contractual variation which the other sought to impose unilaterally, the contract would be terminated. Case law has indicated that it may be possible for the aggrieved party to resist the variation (see e.g. *Rigby* v *Ferodo Ltd* [1988] ICR 29) but this may not be of great assistance in saving the contract on its original terms, in the long run, since the other party could respond by giving notice to terminate it (see *notice* below and also *unfair dismissal*).

Notice: The contract will be terminated if either party gives notice of wishing to terminate and that notice duly expires; alternatively, the employment may sometimes be terminated forthwith by the employer giving wages in lieu of notice. It is now necessary to give at least the statutory period of notice (ER Act s.86). The employee who has been continuously employed for 1 month or more is required to give the employer 1 week's notice. The employee's entitlement varies in length in accordance with the period for which that employee has been continuously employed by that employer:

Employment of over 1 month and under 2 years = 1 week's notice.
Employment of over 2 years and under 12 years = 1 week's notice for every year of service.
Employment of over 12 years = at least 12 weeks' notice.

Now that an employee has statutory rights in relation to redundancy and unfair dismissal, it is unusual for an employer to be able to terminate by notice the contract of an employee with two or more years' continuous employment without incurring further liability.

Breach: The contract will be terminated if one of the parties fails to fulfil the contractual obligations and the other party demonstrably regards this repudiatory conduct as a termination of the contract (see *London Transport Executive* v *Clarke* [1981] ICR 355). If the wrongful conduct is sufficiently serious for the injured party to be released from contractual obligations that party has no need to give notice to terminate the contract (ER Act s.86(6)).

The courts will not issue an order (i.e. specific performance) requiring the parties to continue an employment contract when one of them has indicated the wish to sever the relationship, but occasionally an injunction will be granted to prevent an employer carrying out an intention to terminate the contract, particularly if the employee concerned has had long and satisfactory service with that employer (*Hill* v *CA Parsons & Co Ltd* [1972] Ch 305).

Frustration: In certain rare circumstances a contract will be deemed to have terminated by operation of law because an event has occurred, beyond the control of the parties, which makes its further performance impossible or futile, always providing that this event is not one expressly provided for in the contract. Occasionally contracts of employment have been deemed to have been frustrated by outbreak of war, more frequently because of a long incapacitating illness (see *Condor* v *Barron Knights Ltd* [1966] 1 WLR 87) suffered by, or a prison sentence (see *Hare* v *Murphy Bros. Ltd* [1974] ICR 603) served by, the employee. The occurrence of the frustrating event immediately releases both parties from further contractual obligations. If an employee suffered a serious incapacitating accident it would seem that the relationship would be severed from the moment of the accident, but in the case of prolonged illness or imprisonment, the courts have not identified the exact time at which the relationship has ended and have in the past been content to hold that the contract has ceased to exist by the time that the employee seeks to return to work. Nowadays there is reluctance to see a case put outside the rules of unfair dismissal by an employer establishing that the contractual relationship was ended by frustration rather than by dismissal and judges have expressed the view that, if the contract is to be fairly terminated, the employer ought to note what has happened by formally dismissing the employee (see *London Transport Executive* v *Clarke* (see above)). Since the Disability Discrimination Act 1995 s.6, placed a duty on employers to make reasonable adjustments to accommodate a disabled employee, it may be more difficult for an employer to claim that an employee's accident or illness has frustrated the contract.

Common law rights and remedies

If loss is suffered because the contract of employment is either broken or wrongfully terminated, an action for damages will lie in either a county court or the High Court but since 1994 industrial tribunals have some jurisdiction to deal with common law issues (see above). A common law action for wrongful dismissal may be attractive to the manager with an exceptional contractual entitlement to notice; but for most employees, since dismissal with notice is lawful, and damages will be limited to the sum, if any, due to compensate for an inadequate period of notice, and loss of fringe benefits, the common law provides little satisfaction (see *Addis* v *Gramophone Co* [1909] AC 488). The Court of Appeal has held that where a contract provides for wages in lieu of notice, the employee is entitled to payment for the full notice period: there should be no deduction in respect of earnings in the notice period (*Abrahams* v *Performing Rights Society Ltd* [1995]).

The unsatisfactory common law led to statutory reforms in the 1960s and 1970s to give employees protection against redundancy and unfair dismissal. However, the adequacy of these statutory remedies is questionable: they are dependent on the employee concerned having 2 years' continuous employment before dismissal, and they are of little satisfaction in times of depression when alternative employment is hard to find. For these reasons there has been something of a revival of the use of common law courts both as a means of establishing contractual rights (e.g. *R* v *BBC, ex p Lavelle* [1983] IRLR 404) and as a means of preventing or postponing dismissal (*Hill* v *Parsons*, see above).

8.3 Statutory protection

Since the nineteenth century, but increasingly after 1970, legislation has provided workers, particularly employees, with protection during the performance of their work and in relation to the termination of that employment. Some of these statutory provisions have already been identified (e.g. the right to receive particulars of employment) but in the following sections the most important of the remainder will be indicated.

Equality of opportunity

The common law rules of contract are based on the assumption that the contractual parties have equality of bargaining power; they therefore proved unhelpful to minority groups whose bargaining power was weak. Women and racial minorities are especially vulnerable and it has proved necessary to legislate to make it unlawful to discriminate against a person on sexual (Equal Pay Act 1970 and Sex Discrimination Acts 1975 and 1986) or racial grounds (Race Relations Act 1976). The legislation, which (Equal Pay Act apart) is not confined to employment issues, has the positive objective of achieving equal opportunities, and the sex discrimination legislation, while predominantly concerned with eliminating discrimination against women, also outlaws discrimination against men. The sex discrimination and equal pay statutes are intended to implement the EU requirements for equal opportunities.

In addition, a variety of provisions have addressed employment-related discrimination against persons on grounds of trade union membership and activities, or because of their other roles and activities at the workplace. In relation to trade union membership (or non-membership), it is unlawful to refuse employment (TULR(C) Act s.137), or to take action short of dismissal (s.146), or to dismiss an employee (s.152). In the case of employees the statute expressly states that the discrimination must not be on account either of membership/non-membership or union-related *activities*. Similar protection against discrimination during employment, or by dismissal, are granted to safety and other employee representatives, employees refusing Sunday work and employee trustees of occupational pension schemes. Recently the Disability Discrimination Act 1995 has addressed disability on grounds of physical or mental impairment. It remains lawful to discriminate on grounds which are not expressly prohibited, notably on grounds of age, unless such discrimination in fact amounts to sex discrimination (e.g. *Price* v *Civil Service Commission* [1978] ICR 27; *James* v *Eastleigh Borough Council* [1990] 2 AC 751).

The nature of discrimination: Sexual or racial discrimination may be direct or indirect. *Direct* discrimination is treating a person less favourably than another on grounds of sex or race. *Indirect* discrimination occurs when a person applies to one person the same requirement or condition which he applied to another but:

(a) which is such that the proportion of women (persons of the racial group) who can comply with it is considerably smaller than the proportion of men (persons not of that racial group) who can comply with it; and

(b) which he cannot show to be justified irrespective of the sex (colour, race, nationality or ethnic or national origins) of the person to whom it is applied; and

(c) which is to (her) detriment because (she) cannot comply with it.

Mostly direct discrimination is easily recognised but surprisingly in *James* v *Eastleigh* (see page 139) it was found to be direct discrimination to charge a 60-year-old man to use a swimming pool, whereas a woman could enter free at this age: this was so even though the apparent discrimination was a reflection of the age at which the old age pension became available.

Indirect discrimination sometimes occurs through practices which are so deeply embedded in culture and tradition that their discriminatory character is hard to recognise. It might, for example, be indirect discrimination to offer employment or promotion opportunities only to persons with a record of continuous full-time employment if it were established that only white men could comply with this requirement (see *Price* v *Civil Service Commission,* page 139). Indirect discrimination may be exonerated if it is established that there is a justification, but the courts are not sympathetic to explanations related merely to matters of practice or convenience (see *Steel* v *Union of Post Office Workers* [1978] ICR 181).

Discrimination in employment: Legislation makes discrimination unlawful in a number of specific situations related to the formation and execution of the contract of employment. It is unlawful for an employer to discriminate in the arrangements made for the purpose of determining who should be offered employment. This very wide provision could cover placing and wording of advertisements, the contents of application forms, and the procedure of selecting for interview.

It is unlawful to discriminate in the terms on which employment is offered or by refusing or deliberately omitting to offer employment. It is also unlawful to discriminate in respect of access to opportunities for promotion, transfer or training, or to any other benefits, facilities or services, or by refusing, or deliberately omitting, to afford access to them. It is unlawful to discriminate by dismissing or subjecting a person to any other detriment.

Discrimination in the matters outlined may be lawful if sex or race, as the case may be, is a 'genuine occupational qualification'. Each Act includes a list of circumstances in which exceptionally discrimination may be allowed, as, for example, where the job involves participation in a dramatic performance and a particular type of person is required for reasons of authenticity.

Harassment (including harassment on grounds of sexual orientation) may amount to unlawful sex discrimination but dress codes may be lawful if circumstances require them, provided comparable rules are imposed for both sexes. In the recent past dismissal in relation to childbirth has been contested under both UK and EU laws (see *Webb* v *Emo Air Cargo (UK) Ltd* [1994] IRLR 482) but this form of discrimination may occur less in future, given it is now unlawful to dismiss a person merely on grounds of pregnancy.

It is also unlawful to discriminate in relation to pay. The Equal Pay Act 1970 deals with inequality between the sexes, a broadly similar provision to be found in the Race Relations Act 1976. The 1970 Act had the broad objective that where men and women were doing the same work, they should receive equal pay, but the enactment of a statutory formula to achieve this objective proved difficult and the original Act was revised.

Under the present law the terms of a woman's contract are deemed to include an 'equality clause' which relates to both pay and other contractual terms so that it is not, for example, lawful to require a woman to work longer hours for the same pay as her male colleagues receive. The equality clause applies:

(a) where the woman is employed on like work with a man in the same employment;
(b) where the woman is employed on work rated as equivalent with that of a man in the same employment; and
(c) where a woman is employed on work which, not being work in relation to which (a) or (b) applies is, in terms of the demands made on her (for instance, under such headings as effort, skill and decision), of equal value to that of a man in the same employment.

In spite of the restriction in (c), the House of Lords has allowed an equal value claim to be made even though there was a man employed on like work: in the view of the House, to have decided otherwise would have defeated the objectives of Article 119 of the Treaty of Rome (*Pickstone v. Freemans PLC* [1988] IRLR 357). Certainly, any other decision would have invited employers to suppress wage rates by ensuring that there was at least a minimal representation of both sexes on the payroll.

An employer may avoid the requirements of the equality clause by proving that a variation in pay is genuinely due to a material factor (gmf) which is not the difference of sex. It is controversial how far 'market forces' can be used in this context. In *Rainey* v *Greater Glasgow Health Board* [1987] AC 224 the House of Lords was prepared to allow this as a lawful explanation of the lower pay rate for women as compared to men. But in *Enderby* v *Frenchay HA* [1994] 1 All ER 495, the European Court held that the burden was on the employer to justify the lower pay of the women and did not accept that it was a sufficient justification that the rates were determined in collective bargaining. In *Ratcliffe* v *N. Yorks CC* [1995] IRLR 439, the House of Lords found for dinner ladies who had been dismissed and re-engaged at lower rates in order to enable their employer to tender competitively.

Matters of sex discrimination and equal pay are often difficult to distinguish but they are areas in which there has frequently been reference to the European law and in these circumstances it is especially important to identify the basis of the complaint, for if it can be based on Article 119 of the Treaty (equal pay), the claimant can rely on direct enforcement of the decision regardless of whether the employer is in the public or private sector (see *Jenkins* v *Kingsgate* [1981] ICR 715). Claims concerned with inequality in age of retirement (*Marshall* v *Southampton & SW Hants AHA* [1986] IRLR 140) and pensionable age (*Barber* v *Guardian Royal Exchange* [1990] ICR 616) have been found to be equal pay claims within Article 119.

Equal pay and sex discrimination claims are presented by way of complaint to an industrial tribunal. 'Equal value' claims are subject to a complex procedure, under which an independent expert is appointed to investigate the claim. Hearings therefore tend to be protracted, but interesting comparisons have been pursued (see e.g. *Hayward* v *Cammell Laird Shipbuilders Ltd* [1988] IRLR 257 – comparison between a female cook and male shipyard workers). The impact of the Act generally is limited in that there is no provision for class actions, so claims are made only for individual, rather than groups of, workers. However, where the provisions of a collective agreement stipulate different contractual terms for employees according to sex, either party to the agreement may refer it to the CAC which has powers to direct that the agreement may be suitably amended. The Equal Opportunities Commission has now introduced a Code of Practice guiding employers in the implementation of equal value.

Both the Race Relations and the Sex Discrimination Acts contain provisions making it unlawful for bodies other than the employer to discriminate; in particular it is made unlawful for a trade union to discriminate in relation to membership.

The Commissions: Under each principal Act there is established a Commission which is charged with working towards the elimination of discrimination; for this purpose it is empowered to investigate where discriminatory practices appear to exist and to serve a 'non-discrimination notice' on any person whom the Commission is satisfied is committing, or has committed, unlawful discrimination. The notice requires the person on whom it is served to refrain from the discrimination and may require positive action to rectify the situation. If the notice is not complied with, the Commission may apply to a county court for an injunction: breach of such a court order would be contempt of court and could result, in the last resort, in imprisonment. The Commissions have used their powers to issue Codes of Practice relevant to employment.

Enforcement: The major responsibility for ensuring that unlawful discrimination is subject to legal process rests with the individuals who have suffered discrimination. It is frequently difficult for a complainant to obtain the information on which to base a complaint so the legislation has authorised a form by which the aggrieved person may question the respondent's reasons for acting as alleged. Not only will the answers thus received help to determine whether a complaint should be made, but the document may constitute evidence at the hearing of a complaint. The Commission may assist a claimant, when a case is complex or involves an important matter of principle.

Positive discrimination and quotas: UK law, like EU law (see *Kalanke* v *Frei Hansestadt Bremen* [1995]) does not generally favour positive discrimination and has little sympathy for quotas. It does not permit a person to refute an allegation of discrimination by demonstrating operation of a 'quota system', but the production of employment records which showed a reasonable distribution of men and women and of racial groups might be evidence of lack of intention to discriminate in a particular case. Such evidence might be valuable in cases of indirect discrimination. These records are also likely to be valuable aids to management monitoring performance and evaluating policies (see recommendations of Equal Opportunities Commission's Code of Practice).

The Disability Discrimination Act 1995: This came into effect in January 1997, with the objective of protecting anyone with a physical or mental impairment which has a substantial and long-term effect (i.e. for at least twelve months or is terminal) on ability to carry out normal day-to-day activities. The Act is by no means a mirror image of the sex and race discrimination legislation: it does not expressly address indirect discrimination but does allow justification of direct discrimination. It prohibits discrimination in recruitment, promotions, transfer, benefits, dismissal and 'any other detriments'. Employment-related claims lie in industrial tribunals. The effectiveness of the Act depends on regulations and codes of practice now being introduced to spell out its framework provisions such as *Guidance on matters to be taken into account in determining questions relating to the definition of disability* and *Code of Practice for the elimination of discrimination in the field of employment against disabled persons or persons who have had a disability*. A National Disability Council will advise the government.

Other major statutory rights during employment

The 1970s saw the introduction of a statutory floor of rights for employees during the course of their employment. In the years since, sometimes as a result of EU Directives, these rights have been further developed and amended. It is only possible to refer to them briefly here.

Terms relating to wages: These terms are as follows:

1. *Protection of wages.* The Wages Act 1986 (now ER Act ss.13–27) gave workers certain rights to complain to an industrial tribunal in respect of problems related to payment of wages. The employer's power to make deductions from wages or require payments from workers is restricted. Broadly, the employer may make only deductions where these are required by statute (e.g. PAYE) or there is an actual agreement between employer and worker. There is also special protection for those in retail employment: deductions for cash shortages must not exceed 10 per cent of the gross wages payable when the deduction fails to be made, though the deficit may be carried forward to the following pay day, and when the employment ends there is no limit to the amount the employer may deduct or demand. However, the Act does not permit an employer to make a deduction for over-payment of wages: a dispute on this matter must go before a county court. These provisions have much increased the workload of tribunals even though, in *Delaney* v *Staples* [1992] 1 AC 687, the House of Lords held that payment in lieu of notice was damages not wages (payment during 'garden leave', i.e. suspension during notice, is wages!). This distinction may not be important now that tribunals have jurisdiction to hear claims for common law damages.
2. *Itemised pay statement.* The employer is required to supply at or before the time at which wages are paid, a written statement showing the gross amount of wages, the amount and purposes of deductions, the net amount of wages payable and where different parts are paid in different ways, the amount and method of payment of each part payment (ER Act s.8).
3. *Guarantee payments.* An employee who has been continuously employed for at least one month, but has no contractual right to receive full wages when laid off because there is no work, must be paid according to the provisions of the statute. A guarantee payment is not due where the absence of work is caused by a trade dispute involving any employee of the employer or associated employer. Nor will an employee who has refused suitable alternative work, or failed to comply with reasonable requirements imposed by the employer, be entitled to payment. The amounts payable are relatively small so it is unlikely that the employee will obtain normal wages (ER Act ss.28–35). These provisions are not relevant to salaried employees who are entitled to full pay, even though there is no work for them to do.
4. *Suspension from work on medical grounds.* An employee who has to be suspended from normal work by his employer by reason of a statutory provision (and there is no suitable alternative employment) may not be dismissed; and is entitled, while suspended, to be paid for up to 26 weeks. These provisions apply to a few situations where a harmful substance, such as lead, could cause illness: they do not apply if the employee is in fact ill, and therefore entitled to sickness payments (ER Act ss.64–65).

Time off from work: These terms are as follows:
1. *Time off for trade union duties.* An employee who is an official of an independent trade union recognised by the employer is entitled to take paid time off during his working hours for:

(a) negotiations with the employer related to those aspects of collective bargaining for which the trade union is recognised by the employer; or

(b) undergoing training relevant to these duties (TULR(C) Act s.168).

There is a Code of Practice concerning the amount of time an employee should be permitted to take off.

2. *Time off for trade union activities.* An employer must permit an employee who is a member of an appropriate trade union to take time off during working hours to take part in trade union activities (TULR(C) Act s.170).

3. *Time off for public duties.* An employee who performs certain specified public duties, such as being a justice of the peace, is entitled, subject to certain provisos, to take time off for the purpose of those duties (ER Act s.50).

4. *Time off to look for work or training.* An employee given notice of dismissal for redundancy is entitled to reasonable time off to look for new employment or make arrangements for training for future employment (ER Act s.52).

5. *Time off for ante-natal care.* A pregnant employee is entitled to time off for ante-natal care (ER Act s.55).

Pregnancy and childbirth: Rights in pregnancy and childbirth have been considerably strengthened following the EC's Protection of Pregnant Workers Directive (92/85/EC), but the UK was not involved when the Parental Leave Directive was initially discussed by the other 14 Member States.

The ER Act provides that a woman may not be dismissed on grounds of pregnancy (s.99) and one who is suspended from employment on maternity grounds is entitled to remuneration (s.66). A woman absent from work on maternity leave is entitled to the terms and conditions of employment – except remuneration – which would have been applicable if she had not been absent (e.g. she maintains her seniority) (s.71). She is entitled to at least 14 weeks' maternity leave (s.73), but she may not return to work until two weeks after the birth and, if necessary, leave will be extended to cover this. Maternity leave may begin as early as the 29th week of the pregnancy but will begin on the first day after the beginning of the 6th week before the expected week of childbirth (ewc) on which she is absent from work because of the pregnancy. Entitlement to leave depends on notification to the employer, not less than 21 days before the intended start of the leave, and the employer may request a medical certificate (ss.74/75). An employee who has 2 years' continuous employment by the beginning of the 11th week before the expected week of childbirth, has the right to return to work after the end of her maternity leave and up to 29 weeks after the childbirth, provided that she informs her employer at the same time when she informs him of the intention to take maternity leave (s.79), and complies with the other statutory requirements as to re-affirming her intention after the birth of the child.

Pay entitlement during maternity leave depends partly on statutory provisions and partly on the contract. Regulations provide that a woman who has 26 weeks' continuous service by the 15th week before the ewc, who has had average earnings above the threshold for payment of National Insurance contributions for the 8 weeks ending with the qualifying week and (unless not reasonably practicable) given 21 days' notice that she intends to stop work because of pregnancy, is entitled to 18 weeks' statutory maternity pay: 6 weeks at 90 per cent of normal earnings, 12 weeks at sick pay rate. Her contract may give her a further entitlement related to her salary.

Occupational health and safety

The law has two roles in respect of occupational health and safety: it provides compensation for victims of industrial accidents and diseases and it provides operational standards with the objective of eliminating from the working environment the hazards which may cause accidents and ill-health.

Compensation: An injured person (quite apart from claiming social security benefits) may bring an action for damages, claiming both for loss of income and for 'non-pecuniary' loss such as pain and suffering. This is equally true whether the accident occurs at the workplace or elsewhere, even in the victim's home. However, persons who suffer injury while at work, or as a result of work activities, were in practice more likely to succeed in their claims than were other categories of litigants; today the organisation's responsibility to members of the public is virtually the same as to its employees (*Margereson and Hancock* v *JW Roberts Ltd* [1996]), though historically the employer owed a special responsibility to employees, based on an implied term in their contract. The desirability of employers providing compensation for injuries to their employees, where the employer is legally responsible, is recognised by the Employers' Liability (Compulsory Insurance) Act 1969: it requires the employer to be insured against liability for such accidents if they arise out of and in the course of the employee's employment.

To succeed in a claim for damages the plaintiff (victim) must prove either that the defendant has committed the tort of negligence or that he has broken a statutory duty.

Negligence When claiming in negligence the plaintiff must prove that the defendant owed a duty of care; that this duty was broken by negligent conduct; and that this breach caused the injury.

The courts today take a liberal view as to the existence of duty situations and few claims for personal injury fail because the plaintiff cannot establish the defendant's duty to take care. Thus the plaintiff's decision as to who to sue is largely determined by considering which of a range of possible defendants is likely to be able to pay any damages awarded, and what evidence there is of negligent conduct causing the injury. For the employee, the employer is likely to be the most attractive defendant, both because of the insurance requirement and because litigation has spelt out that employers must provide their employees with a safe system of work, including safe plant and equipment, a safe working place and instruction and training. Where the employer is a small sub-contractor, the plaintiff may prefer to sue a more substantial organisation, such as a head contractor, in the justifiable belief that the courts expect a high standard of care from large organisations.

Breach of statutory duty Sometimes a plaintiff can identify a statutory duty imposed upon a person (usually an employer) for the protection of persons such as the plaintiff, and show that this duty has been broken and that its breach has caused the plaintiff to suffer the alleged injury. The rules governing such claims are complex, but these actions have become less usual with the development of the tort of negligence and because modern statutory provisions lend themselves less to this form of litigation than did the legislation which pre-dated the Health and Safety at Work Act 1974.

Vicarious liability An employer is liable (even if not personally at fault) for the injuries caused by the wrongful acts of his employees in the course of their employment. So if one employee injures another (or a member of the public) by negligent conduct, the victim may claim damages from the employer (see *Mersey Docks & Harbour Board* v *Coggins & Griffiths (Liverpool) Ltd and McFarlane* [1947] AC 1).

Prevention: It is recognised that it is better to avoid industrial accidents and work-related ill-health than to compensate for them; so statutory codes have established standards for the workplace and special inspectors are appointed with powers to enter premises to investigate whether these standards are being observed. These statutory duties are enforced in the criminal courts. There were by 1970 more than 30 statutes concerned with safety at the workplace, perhaps the best known of which was the Factories Act 1961; in addition there were more than 500 regulations.

The Health and Safety at Work etc. Act 1974 was a reforming Act. It was an enabling, or framework Act with the objectives of securing the health, safety and welfare of all persons at work and of protecting the public against risk arising out of the activities of persons at work. This legislation has now been underpinned by a number of sets of Regulations, many of them to implement Directives adopted under Article 118A of the Treaty of Rome. It will be noted that the Act extends protection to workers generally rather than just to employees: there is often some room for dispute whether EC Directives which do not usually use the word 'employee' are looking beyond the narrow interpretation of the employment relationship.

The 1974 Act set up the Health and Safety Commission and gave it a general responsibility for occupational health and safety. The tasks of inspection and enforcement were entrusted to the Health and Safety Executive and the inspectorates were brought under the control of the Executive. Many offences became triable upon indictment, and, in addition, the inspectorate was given new powers of enforcement through improvement and prohibition notices.

Improvement notices are orders from inspectors requiring persons upon whom they are served to carry out specific tasks to comply with their statutory duties. A prohibition notice is an order that a certain activity shall cease, on the grounds that it involves a risk of personal injury. It is a criminal offence to fail to comply with an order but the validity of the order may be disputed in an industrial tribunal.

General duties: The general duties contained in the 1974 Act (ss.2–9) aim to establish safe systems of work, and for this purpose they identify, and impose duties upon, those involved in the work activity. They are very broad but are of a high standard; for the most part they impose absolute liability for unsafe situations unless the accused can prove that it was not reasonably practicable to do more to achieve safety (e.g. *R v British Steel PLC* [1995] 1 WLR 1356).

Regulations may be made to create specific standards in respect of specific situations but although important regulations have been made, many incorporating EU standards (e.g. Control of Substances Hazardous to Health Regulations 1994), it seems unlikely that the general duties will ever be fully discharged by observing all the relevant regulations, since they encompass the total operational system.

It is fundamental to compliance with the 1974 Act that safety be seen as a matter of safe systems and related to the proper management of people. The principal responsibility for safety at the workplace falls upon employers and the Act requires them to do all that is reasonably practicable to ensure the health, safety and welfare at work of all their employees (s.2) and of other workers and the general public (s.3 e.g. *R v Board of Trustees of the Science Museum* [1993] 1 WLR 1171). The Act also places general duties on controllers of premises (s.4, see *Mailer v Austin Rover Group PLC* [1989] 2 All ER 1087) and those who supply articles and substances for use by people at work (s.6).

Section 7 imposes a duty upon employees while at work to take reasonable care for their own health and safety and that of other persons who may be affected by their acts or omissions at work and to cooperate with their employer and other persons to enable them to discharge their statutory obligations in respect of health and safety. EC Directives (reflected in British regulations) give some content to this duty, e.g. the Manual Handling Operations

Regulations 1992, regulation 5 requires 'Each employee while at work shall make full and proper use of any system of work provided for his use by his employer'.

Supplementary to, and in explanation of, the general duty imposed on the employer in s.2(1) of the Act, s.2(2) requires:

(a) the provision and maintenance of plant and systems of work that are, so far as is reasonably practicable, safe and without risks to health;

(b) arrangements for ensuring, so far as is reasonably practicable, safety and absence of risks to health in connection with the use, handling, storage and transport of articles and substances;

(c) the provision of such information, instruction, training and supervision as is necessary to ensure, so far as is reasonably practicable, the health and safety at work of his employees;

(d) so far as is reasonably practicable as regards any place of work under the employer's control, the maintenance of it in a condition that is safe and without risks to health and the provision and maintenance of means of access to and egress from it that are safe and without such risks;

(e) the provision and maintenance of a working environment for his employees that is, so far as is reasonably practicable, safe, without risks to health, and adequate as regards facilities and arrangements for their welfare at work.

As part of his duty, the employer is also required to provide a written statement of his safety policy, and the organisation and arrangements for the time being in force for carrying out that policy and to bring this statement and any revision of it to the notice of all his employees. The arrangements which are set out should relate to the findings of the risk assessment which the employer is now required to make under the Management of Health and Safety at Work Regulations 1992.

Both the Act itself and regulations to comply with EC Directives (e.g. the Management of Health and Safety at Work Regulations and the Personal Protective Equipment at Work Regulations 1992) stress the need to provide instruction and training of workers. A relatively early decision of the Court of Appeal held that s.2(2)(c) obliged employers to provide information to sub-contractors' men so that they did not endanger their own employees, and s.3(1) required them to provide information to the visiting workers for their own safety (*R* v *Swan Hunter Shipbuilders and Telemeter Installations Ltd* [1981] ICR 831). Subsequent cases have stressed the responsibility of employers to control the work of contractors and their employees (e.g. *R* v *Associated Octel Ltd* [1994] IRLR 540).

EC Directives require worker involvement in safety matters. The Safety Representatives and Safety Committees Regulations 1977 provide for recognised trade unions to appoint safety representatives. These regulations set out the functions of such representatives and the ways in which the employer is required to cooperate with them. Their principal functions are to carry out regular inspections of the workplace, to consult with the employer, to represent their constituents, to inspect documents and to receive information both from the employer and the inspectorate. They are also entitled to investigate accidents and must be consulted where changes are to be introduced at the workplace. Two safety representatives may require that the employer set up a safety committee, but there are no regulations as to the constitution and functions of such a committee. The regulations are not mandatory but represent a set of rights with which the employer with a recognised trade union may be required by the union to comply, in default of any alternative negotiated arrangements. Further regulations have now given slightly less generous rights to employees in workplaces where there is no recognised trade union.

The general duties may not be used in civil actions for compensation and they are enforceable in the criminal courts only by the inspectorate. Employers, the performance of whose duties to provide safe systems will often depend on the conduct of others, will need to rely on contractual arrangements to ensure that safety is maintained by these other people: under the contract of employment the employee whose conduct is unsafe may be disciplined; commercial contracts with other organisations may give the employer rights to monitor the conduct of these contractors and their workers; and purchase contracts may relate to the safety of the products to be supplied.

8.4 Statutory protection at dismissal

Unfair dismissal

Statutory provisions (now ER Act ss.94–135) give many employees the right not to be unfairly dismissed; the principal exceptions are most employees who have not the qualifying 2 years' employment, and those who, at the time of dismissal are over retirement age.

There are no moral connotations in the term 'unfair dismissal'; it has a statutory meaning and qualified employees are entitled to the statutory remedies even though their cases are without merit, but the complainant without merit may be denied compensation (see *Devis & Sons Ltd* v *Atkins* [1977] AC 931).

The employee who considers that (s)he has been unfairly dismissed may present a complaint to an industrial tribunal within three months of the effective date of termination of the employment, that is within three months of the last day on which the employment relationship subsisted (e.g. when working out notice, the date on which the notice to terminate expires). The general rules concerning effective date of termination might lead to hard cases (see *Dixon* v *Stenor Ltd* [1973] ICR 157), as for example where an employee is required to leave immediately and so reduce the qualifying period of service – in such cases employees are treated for the purpose of service as if they had worked out their notice.

The burden is on the employee to satisfy the tribunal that there has been dismissal, the burden then shifts to the employer to establish that the dismissal was for one of the reasons permitted by the statute. The statute provides (s.95(1)) that an employee shall be treated as dismissed if, but only if:

(a) the contract under which he is employed is terminated by the employer (whether with or without notice);
(b) he is employed under a contract for a fixed term and that term expires without being renewed under the same contract; or
(c) the employee terminates the contract under which he is employed (with or without notice) in circumstances in which he is entitled to terminate it without notice by reason of the employer's conduct.

The Transfer of Undertakings (Protection of Employment) Regulations 1981 provide (subject to exceptions related to economic, technical or organisational reasons) that a transfer of an employing undertaking from one person to another shall not operate so as to terminate the contract of any person (with qualifying service) employed by the transferor immediately before the transfer. Any person whose contract is terminated (or has terms unilaterally altered) has a right to bring a claim of unfair dismissal against the transferee.

These regulations, and the Directive on which they are based, have been interpreted very broadly, so that they apply to most situations in which a business changes ownership (see *Litster* v *Forth Dry Dock and Engineering Co Ltd* [1989] ICR 341); they apply to most competitive tendering, and may cover the provision of labour-only contracts, such as cleaning or catering (for a full discussion see *Dines and Ors* v *Initial Healthcare Services and Pall Mall Services Group Ltd* [1994] IRLR 336) and can apply where only one service worker is involved (see *Schmidt* v *Spar und Linkasse* [1994] IRLR 302). An employee who is not aware of the identity of the transferee may be protected (*MRS Environmental Services Ltd* v *Dyke and Another* [1997]); but the Directive does not necessarily protect the workforce where a contract for services (e.g. cleaning) is transferred from one contractor to another (*Süzen* v *Zehnacker Gebäudereinigung BmbH Krankenhausservice (Lebarten GmbH, partly joined)* [1997] ECJ).

An employee claiming that the employer's conduct amounted to constructive dismissal will only succeed if the claim shows that the employer's conduct was in breach of the contract: thus an employer is entitled to behave unreasonably if the contract gives an express right to do so, e.g. withhold pay as a disciplinary penalty (*Western Excavating (ECC) Ltd* v *Sharp* [1978] QB 761). An employee might claim to have been constructively dismissed if the employer attempted unilaterally to change the terms of the contract, e.g. reduce the wages.

It follows that there are a number of circumstances in which a contract of employment may come to an end without there being a dismissal within the statutory definition: for example, if a contract is terminated by a frustrating event, or because the employee gives notice to take up an appointment elsewhere.

Grounds for dismissal

In order to establish that a dismissal was fair, the employer must satisfy the tribunal that the reason for the dismissal was one of the permitted statutory reasons or some *other substantial reason* of a kind such as to justify the dismissal of an employee holding the position which that employee held. The tribunal must also be satisfied that, having regard to equity and the substantial merits of the case, the employer acted reasonably in treating it as a sufficient reason for dismissing the employee.

The employer may support the dismissal by showing:

(a) it relates to the capacity or qualifications of the employee for performing work of the kind which he was employed to do; or
(b) it relates to the conduct of the employee; or
(c) it is that the employee was redundant; or
(d) it is that the employee could not continue to work in the position which he held without contravention (either on his part or on that of his employer) of a duty or restriction imposed by or under an enactment (ER Act s.98).

Unfair dismissal cases form a large part of the workload of industrial tribunals. While tribunal decisions are not binding precedents they have been frequently appealed and, as a result, the statutory provisions have been much interpreted by the courts.

The catch clause 'other substantial reason' has been interpreted generously in favour of the employer; dismissals in the interests of the business have been allowed, as for example where the employee was unacceptable to a major customer (*Scott Packaging & Warehousing Co Ltd* v *Paterson* [1978] IRLR 166) or the employee was unable to secure a fidelity bond (*Moody* v *Telefusion Ltd* [1978] IRLR 311).

Except in misconduct cases, an employer is unlikely to be able to justify a dismissal without considering finding alternative employment for the employee. Thus if an employee is incapable by reason of sickness or incompetence, the employer should consider whether there is less exacting employment suitable for this person (see *Spencer* v *Paragon Wallpapers Ltd* [1977] ICR 301); similarly, if the employee can no longer lawfully be employed in his/her present occupation, as might be the case where a vehicle driver became disqualified from driving, the employer should consider whether that person might be employed about the employer's premises rather than on the road (see also *Sutcliffe & Eaton Ltd* v *Pinney* [1977] IRLR 349). A dismissal for redundancy may be unfair, for example where an employer has not observed procedures for selection (*Polkey* v *AE Dayton Services Ltd* [1987] IRLR 503).

Polkey's case came as a salutary reminder that in dismissal cases the employer must have regard to procedural matters, giving proper warnings, carrying out necessary consultation and, in most instances, terminating with notice. Before dismissing for misconduct the employer must take care to ascertain the full facts, giving the employee the opportunity to tell his/her story (see *Earl* v *Slater and Wheeler (Airlyne) Ltd* [1973] 1 All ER 145). The employer should have regard to the ACAS Code of Practice on *Disciplinary Practices and Procedures*, for any organisation not observing it has to persuade a tribunal that it operates a satisfactory alternative system.

It is only in relatively rare cases of gross misconduct that a single act of misconduct will warrant dismissal and, even then, the employer ought initially to suspend the employee on full pay (unless the contract expressly allows suspension without pay: *Western Excavating (ECC) Ltd* v *Sharp*) and dismiss only if an investigation confirms that there has been serious misconduct. In less serious cases the wrongdoer should initially be warned, and dismissed only for repeated offences. An employee will have no claim if dismissed while taking part in unofficial industrial action and, in the case of official action, only if the employer has discriminated between employees in failing to dismiss (or by re-engaging) other employees in like position to the claimant (TULR(C) Act s.237).

Dismissal will automatically be unfair in some cases, including: where no reason is given; where dismissal or selection for redundancy occurs for reasons of trade union membership/non-membership and activities; for reasons of sex, race, pregnancy, or assertion of statutory rights. Worker representatives are also protected.

Remedies

When an industrial tribunal considers a complaint of unfair dismissal to be well founded it must explain to the complainant what order for reinstatement or re-engagement may be made and ask whether the complainant wishes the tribunal to make such an order. An order for reinstatement is an order that the employer is to treat the complainant as if there had been no dismissal; an order for re-engagement is an order that the complainant be engaged by the employer in employment comparable to that from which there was dismissal and the tribunal in making such an order is required specifically to state the terms on which re-engagement is to be effected.

Where reinstatement or re-engagement is not ordered (the usual position), or although ordered does not occur, the complainant (who is not above the age of retirement) will receive a monetary award. There are three elements in an award:

1. *Basic award.* This is calculated by reference to the claimant's age, length of service (up to 20 years) and weekly wage (up to the current allowable maximum), which provides an entitlement calculated:

(a) one and a half weeks' pay for each year of employment in which the employee was not below the age of 41;

(b) one week's pay for each year of employment between the ages of 41 and 22;

(c) half a week's pay for each year of employment when the employee was aged less than 22.

Where the dismissal was solely for being an employee representative (ER Act ss.100(1) (a) and (b), 102 and 103) or on trade union grounds (TULR(C) Act ss. 152 and 153), the basic award (before reductions) must not be less than £2770 (NB: this and other monetary awards are subject to annual review). An award will be reduced if the employee was between the ages of 64 and 65 at the time of dismissal and it will also be reduced, by such amount as the tribunal considers just and equitable (and may be denied entirely), if the tribunal finds that the dismissal was to any extent caused or contributed to by the action of the complainant. The award will also be reduced by the amount of any redundancy payment awarded by the tribunal.

2. *Compensatory award.* The tribunal is required to make such compensatory award as it considers just and equitable having regard to the loss sustained by the complainant in consequence of the dismissal in so far as that loss is attributable to the employer – the loss to include any expenses reasonably incurred by the claimant in consequence of his dismissal, and any benefit which he might reasonably be expected to have had but for the dismissal. The award may not exceed £11 300 and the tribunal may take into account whether the complainant might have mitigated his loss and also whether his actions have caused or contributed to his dismissal.

3. *Special awards.* Where the employer has failed to comply with an order to reinstate or re-engage and cannot satisfy the tribunal that it was not practicable to comply with it, the tribunal must make an additional penal award in favour of the complainant. Where the dismissal was in violation of the protection given to worker representatives, or in relation to trade union membership or activities, and any order for reinstatement or re-engagement has not been complied with, the special award may amount to between £13 775 and £27 500; otherwise up to 156 weeks' pay (at least £20 600) will be awarded. There is no limit to the award which may be made in sex and race discrimination cases: the claimant is entitled to the actual loss suffered.

An employee who complains of being unfairly dismissed for being a worker representative, under ER Act, or for trade union matters under TULR(C) Act may apply to the tribunal, within 7 days of dismissal, for interim relief pending the full hearing. The tribunal will give an early hearing to the application and if it appears to be well grounded, will ask the employer to reinstate or re-engage the employee pending the hearing: if the employer is not prepared to assist, the tribunal must make an order for the continuation of the employee's contract of employment until the full hearing.

Redundancy

The Redundancy Payments Act 1965 provided for severance payments to employees dismissed as redundant. The Act gave no security of employment, merely providing compensation. Subsequently, the wider and more generous provisions in respect of unfair dismissal have tended to overshadow the redundancy scheme, for the person who is made redundant is normally only entitled to the basic award outlined above. The statutory provisions are now in ER Act ss.135–154 and TULR(C) Act s.153. TULR(C) Act ss.188–198 (as amended in 1995 by regulations) provides for consultation with recognised trade unions and other workers about redundancies.

Entitlement: An employee is entitled to a redundancy payment if he has been continu-ously employed by his employer for two years since he reached the age of 18 and he is dismissed by that employer by reason of redundancy or is laid off or kept on short time. An employee who has reached retirement age or who might lawfully be dismissed for misconduct or other reasons (e.g. taking part in a strike or other industrial action) is not entitled to a redundancy payment.

The dismissal of a person is for redundancy when it is attributable wholly or mainly to:

(a) the fact that his employer has ceased, or intends to cease,
  (i) to carry on the business for the purposes for which the employee was employed by him; or
  (ii) to carry on that business in the place where the employee was so employed; or
(b) the fact that the requirements of that business
  (i) for employees to carry out work of a particular kind; or
  (ii) for employees to carry out work of a particular kind in the place where he was so employed, have ceased or diminished or are expected to cease or diminish (ER Act s.139).

For the purposes of this definition, the business of the employer and associated employers are treated as one.

The definition of dismissal is set out (s.136) in the same words as are used in the context of unfair dismissal.

An employee is not entitled to a redundancy payment if his employer has made an offer (before the ending of the contract) to renew employment, or to re-engage under a new con-tract to take effect either immediately on the ending of employment or after an interval of not more than four weeks thereafter. If the employer makes such an offer and as to the terms and conditions of employment, would not differ from the corresponding provisions of the previous contract, or, though the terms do differ, the offer constitutes suitable employment, then an employee unreasonably refusing that offer is not entitled to a redun-dancy payment. Where the new contract differs from the previous one there is, however, additional to any contractual entitlement, a trial period of four weeks beginning with the date on which the employee starts work under the contract as renewed, and if the new con-tract is terminated within this period, the employee will retain such rights to redundancy as he had under the earlier contract.

Case law demonstrates that entitlement to a redundancy payment often depends on a very careful interpretation of the terms of the contract in order to determine how much flex-ibility it gives to the employer to change the circumstances of the employment in a redun-dancy situation, without changing the terms of the contract. There is no more right under statute than at common law for a party to make unilateral changes in the terms of the con-tract and in this context such changes will amount to dismissal (*Marriott v Oxford and District Co-operative Society* [1970] 1 QB 186). In some contracts it may not be possible to require the employee to move from one building to another in the same neighbourhood, or to work at the same place at a different time of day (but see *Lesney Products & Co Ltd v Nolan* [1977] ICR 235) while in others it may be possible to require working in another part of the country (see *O'Brien v Associated Fire Alarms Ltd* [1969] 1 All ER 93), or transfer from the day to the night shift, without varying the terms of the contract of employ-ment. It must, however, be remembered that variation of contractual terms and redundancy are not by any means identical concepts: thus to ask an employee to change working hours may be a variation of that worker's contract, but if the same number of employees is needed to carry out the same amount of work there will be no redundancy situation, though there might well be an unfair dismissal.

In these days of rapidly changing technology it may frequently be necessary to consider, when planning introduction of new plant and equipment, the extent to which the employer is entitled, within the contractual terms, to require the employee to change work methods (*North Riding Garages* v *Butterwick* [1967] 2 QB 56) but courts do expect employees to adapt to change (*Cresswell* v *Board of Inland Revenue* [1984] IRLR 190).

Consultation

In compliance with EU law it is necessary for an employer to consult with employee representatives when proposing to dismiss as redundant 20 or more employees at one establishment within a period of 90 days or less. The consultation must take place in good time and in any event where the employer is proposing to dismiss 100 or more employees, at least 90 days (otherwise at least 30 days) before the first dismissal. The employee representatives may be those elected by the employees or, where there is a recognised trade union, they may be representatives of that trade union. The consultation must include discussion about ways of avoiding the dismissals, reducing the number of employees to be dismissed and mitigating the consequences of dismissals, and shall be undertaken by the employer with a view to reaching agreement with the representatives.

If an employer fails to comply with these requirements the appropriate employee representatives may present a complaint to an industrial tribunal. The employer may escape a sanction if he can satisfy the tribunal that there were special circumstances which did not render it reasonably practicable for him to comply with the statutory provisions and that he had taken all such steps as were reasonably practicable in those circumstances. Where the tribunal finds a complaint well founded it must make a declaration to that effect and may also make a protective award. This is an order that the employer pay remuneration for a protected period to those employees described in the award, who have been dismissed or whom it is proposed to dismiss as redundant. The award will be for a period specified by the tribunal but may in no case exceed 90 days.

8.5 Trade unions, collective agreements and trade disputes

Trade unions

TULR(C) Act s.1(1) defines a trade union as an organisation:

> which consists wholly or mainly of workers of one or more descriptions and whose principal purposes include the regulation of relations between workers of that description or those descriptions and employers or employers' associations; . . .

> and whose principal purposes include the regulation of relations between workers and employers or between workers and employers' associations.

There is no special procedure for creating a trade union. However, many statutory provisions refer to *independent* and/or *recognised* trade unions. To establish its independence the union must first be placed on the Certification Officer's list of trade unions and then make a further application for a certificate that it is independent. Whether it is deemed independent will depend upon whether, in the view of the Certification Officer, the trade union is one which:

(a) is not under the domination or control of an employer or group of employers or one or more employers' associations; and

(b) is not liable to interference by an employer or by any such group or association (arising out of the provisions of financial or material support or by any other means whatsoever) tending towards such control (TULR(C) Act s.5).

A union is recognised when it has recognition by an employer to any extent for the purpose of collective bargaining (TULR(C) Act, s.178). Since there is no statutory procedure for recognition, a union may have difficulty in establishing that it is recognised.

Collective bargaining means negotiating for the purposes of reaching collective agreement. TULR(C) Act s.178 spells out the matters which the law recognises as matters for collective agreement. It does so using virtually the same words as are used in other sections of the Act (ss.218 and 244) to define 'trade dispute'.

Trade dispute is defined in s.244 as a dispute between workers and their employer which relates to one or more of the following:

(a) terms and conditions of employment, or the physical conditions in which any workers are required to work;

(b) engagement or non-engagement, or termination or suspension of employment or the duties of employment, or one or more workers;

(c) allocation of work or the duties of employment between workers or groups of workers;

(d) matters of discipline;

(e) a worker's membership or non-membership of a trade union;

(f) facilities for officials of trade unions; and

(g) machinery for negotiation or consultation, and other procedures, relating to any of the above matters, including the recognition by employers or employers' associations of the right of a trade union to represent workers in such negotiations or consultation or in carrying out of such procedures.

Thus the definition covers both disputes of interest and disputes of right and both the content of the employment relationship and the procedures for negotiation.

Containment of trade disputes

The collective bargaining process is a sensitive one and liable to break down, either at the stage of negotiating new terms (disputes of interest) or subsequently when one or other party allegedly fails to honour the negotiated agreement (disputes of right). Additionally, disputes between individual workers and their employers may escalate into collective disputes, so it is not entirely accurate to associate industrial unrest solely with the collective bargaining process.

Breakdowns in industrial relations result in disruption at the workplace with either the workforce withdrawing labour (striking) or the employer refusing to allow workers to carry out their work (lockout). Disruptions of this nature, which may well involve large numbers of workers, can have serious consequences for the economy and may cause great inconvenience to the public at large, particularly if, as is often the case, the breakdown occurs in a public sector service industry.

It is for these reasons that much of employment law is concerned with trying to prevent the occurrence of trade disputes. Statutory mechanisms for this include:

(a) legislative machinery for promoting the improvement of industrial relations;
(b) individual employment rights, which the worker may pursue, in an industrial tribunal if necessary;
(c) systems for informing the workforce, and for involving them in the making of decisions which relate to the operation of the organisation for which they work;
(d) procedures which have to be followed by trade unions before strike action in order both to protect their members and to avoid liability for damage caused.

The legislative machinery for assisting industrial relations and individual employment rights have already been outlined.

8.6 Worker involvement

UK governments of the 1970s held the view that industrial harmony could best be promoted by encouraging recognition by employers of trade unions and much of the legislation of that time gave rights to recognised trade unions. Important provisions concerned disclosure of information, safety representatives (see the Safety Representatives and Safety Committees Regulations 1977) and consultation in relation to redundancies and transfer of undertakings. Subsequent events, including amendments to legislation, have very much reduced the power of trade unions and so the legislation became much less effective.

In the meantime the EU adopted Directives which require worker participation in addressing the specific issues to which they relate. These Directives assume, but do not require, the European model of worker participation through Works Councils. It became clear that the UK system of giving participation rights only to recognised trade unions did not meet the requirement of the Directives. As has been noted, the ECJ has declared this in respect of the transfer of undertakings and those regulations (and the statutory provisions on redundancy) were, following the ECJ rulings, altered in amending regulations. Similarly, the requirements on the Framework Directive on health and safety have led to new regulations to provide for safety representatives where there is no recognised trade union (the Health and Safety (Consultation with Employees) Regulations 1996). It remains questionable whether these regulations meet the expectations of the EU: the revised redundancy and transfer of undertakings provide for consultation only where at least 20 employees are to be made redundant and the new safety regulations are less favourable than are the 1977 regulations, which continue to apply where there is a recognised trade union.

Most controversial was the UK's disassociation from the Directive on the Establishment of a European Works Council (994/45/EC) which was adopted under the Social Protocol Agreement operated by the other Member States following the UK refusal to accept the Social Charter. The main provision of this requires organisations which have over 1000 employees working in the EU, with 150 in each of two or more Member States, to establish a European level information and consultation procedure (or European Works Council). In practice many UK-based organisations operating in other Member States had decided to institute a European Works Council and include UK employees in its operations before the Labour Government was returned to power.

The 20-year-old provision for disclosure by an employer of information relevant to collective bargaining at the request of the representatives of trade unions it recognises remains in force (TULR(C) Act ss.181–187). Disclosure must be of all such information relating to the employer's undertaking as is in its possession (subject to certain exceptions) for the purposes of all stages of collective bargaining, which is both information without which the trade union representative would be to a material extent impeded in bargaining, and information which it would be in accordance with good industrial relations practice that they should receive.

A recognised trade union which has not received information to which it is entitled may complain to CAC, which may, if other means of settlement fail, make an award that the employer must observe the terms and conditions specified.

8.7 Liability for strikes

Common law gave trade unions no special rights to organise labour, and it proved very difficult for labour to be withdrawn by employees without liability being incurred by them in either contract or tort: in contract, liability was attached to individuals for breach of their personal contracts of employment; in tort, there might be liability for conspiracy or for interfering with, or inducing the breach of, the contracts of other persons. Moreover, since normally the trade union could not itself be sued, individual members and officers of the union were brought to court, to meet claims for damages, or, much more frequently, to be served with an injunction whose intent was to produce a return of the strikers to work.

This century there have been numerous Acts of Parliament modifying the common law to adjust the balance of power between labour and capital. Judges have had the invidious task of interpreting statutes and applying them to particular strike situations. Successive governments of left or right have amended the legislation to redress what they have perceived as imbalances of power inherent in then existing legislation passed, and judicial interpretations of it. Since 1979 Conservative governments have radically changed trade union law, removing the immunity of the trade union itself from liability, laying down rules for the internal management of unions, and setting out procedures which must be followed before industrial action takes place.

The statutory rules now set out the framework for liability for both persons and trade unions. A person is given immunity from liability for an act done in contemplation or furtherance of a trade dispute (the so-called 'golden formula', which, over the years has itself been much interpreted) 'on the ground only':

(a) that it induces another person to break a contract or interferes or induces another person to interfere with its performance; or
(b) that it consists in his threatening that a contract (whether one to which he is party or not) will be broken or its performance interfered with, or that he will induce another person to break a contract or interfere with its performance. (TULR(C) Act s.219).

There are special rules relating to picketing (which must normally only be carried out by a limited number of persons at their own place of work), and picketing in circumstances not allowed by the statute may result in civil liability (TULR(C) Act ss.219 and 220). Picketing which involves any violence is likely to incur criminal penalties.

For a trade union the rule is that: 'An act done by a trade union to induce a person to take part, or continue to take part, in industrial action is not protected unless the industrial action has the support of a ballot' (TULR(C) Act s.226). This simple statement is fraught with problems. First, the rules for the conduct of the ballot are complex: everyone entitled must have the opportunity to vote (raising questions about the accuracy of the register of members), and any action taken as a result of the ballot, must be called by the person specified in the ballot, strictly in accordance with the proposition voted on, and started within the statutory time limit (4 weeks) of the ballot. The voting paper must bear the words 'If you take part in a strike or other industrial action, you may be in breach of your contract of employment.'

There remains the question of whether in any particular circumstances the act of a trade union official is the act of the trade union itself (i.e. is the official the agent of the union?): this can be of crucial importance if the union is to avoid liability for unofficial action (see *Heaton's Transport (St Helen's)* v *TGWU* [1973] AC 15).

A controversial issue is whether 'secondary action' should be permissible in the course of a trade dispute (i.e. interference with the commercial activities of an organisation by persons other than the workers who are involved in the trade dispute, or actions by the strikers against persons other than their own employer). The present position (TULR(C) Act s.224) is that such action is not protected, unless (exceptionally) the action is lawful picketing. Section 224 confirms, indeed may go beyond, cases such as *Express Newspapers* v *McShane* [1980] AC 672, where journalists employed by provincial newspapers went on strike, causing their employers to obtain copy from the Press Association and leading to those journalists who were both NUJ members and employed by national newspapers being told to boycott Press Association copy. The Court of Appeal (the House of Lords took a different view) found the involvement of national newspapers to be so remote from the strike as to be unlawful secondary action.

While there have been relatively few strikes in recent years, it would be rash to conclude that this is due to the law: it could be at least as much to do with other factors such as changes in the nature, and availability of, employment and the associated reduction in trade union power.

The legislation is still superimposed on the general common law rules for civil liability and not the least of the problems is still the lack of clarity in the common law.

8.8 Conclusions

Anyone who has followed the analysis in this chapter will appreciate the warning in its first paragraph as to the complexity of employment law; particularly since English law has had EU law superimposed on it. As far as reasonably possible, references to sources have been cited, but even in these situations it should not be assumed that the material printed here is an exact citation: often, in the interests of brevity, it has been necessary to paraphrase, and this, of course, may be at the expense of complete accuracy. Those who need the accuracy of the fine detail should refer to the source itself.

8.9 Further reading

Textbooks
Barrett B, Howells R. *Cases and materials on occupational health and safety law*. London: Cavendish Publishing Limited, 1995.
Kidner R. *Statutes on employment law*. London: Blackstone, 1996.
Lewis D. *Essentials of employment law*. London: IDP, 1996.

Selwyn N. *Employment law*. London: Butterworths, 1996.

Smith I, Wood J. *Industrial law*. London: Butterworths, 1996.

Sweet & Maxwell's *Employment law manual*. London: Sweet & Maxwell (ongoing loose leaf).

Journals

Industrial Law Journal, Oxford University Press.

Industrial Relations Law Bulletin, Industrial Relations Service.

9 Equal opportunities
Delia Goldring

9.1 Introduction

In the economic climate of the late 1990s many authors advocate that organisations should behave in strategic, pro-active ways in order to gain competitive advantage and thereby survive as effective operations. The principles of managing human resources indicate that competitive advantage can only be achieved through the efficient utilisation of employees at all levels.

The fundamental starting-point must be to ensure that, in the first place, a balance of different types of people are recruited into an organisation and once inside are developed, promoted and retained. To achieve this 'balance of diversity' there must be available a pool of applicants for all vacancies (external or internal), open to everyone equally, and there should be no discrimination against individuals who may be disadvantaged due to their belonging to a specific group. Disadvantaged groups who traditionally suffer discrimination include women, disabled people and people from certain racial groups or ethnic backgrounds that are in the minority within the potential workforce, and older workers.

An organisation made up of diverse groups, containing a wide range of abilities, experience and skills, is more likely to be open to new ideas and different possibilities than one which is more homogeneous in terms of worker background and experience. While the ethical case for equal opportunities is a strong one, it will be the economic case that will be the deciding reason for organisations to take note of equal opportunities and implement effective policies.

The real issue for the future is not whether any particular group achieves equality, but whether the UK can compete successfully internationally if all groups of people are not treated as equal. Statistics produced by the Commission for Racial Equality (CRE) and the Equal Opportunities Commission (EOC) indicate that in the future, not only will there continue to be high unemployment but also a parallel skills shortage in Great Britain. The reasons for this shortage of skill development in our current and potential workforce are complex and not discussed here. However, continued lack of availability of appropriate skills will force employers to look at traditionally under-utilised groups, whether they are groups such as women, ethnic minorities, disabled or older workers. This latter group are currently not protected by employment legislation in the UK.

There are two ways in which action can help to overcome the disadvantages these groups suffer. One is to influence attitudes and preconceptions held by our society about them and the other is to introduce and implement legislation to prevent discrimination. Influencing attitudes is a very slow process. It may take more than one generation to filter through society. Indeed, the debate relating to whether it is possible to change attitudes and behaviours *at all* fills many chapters in texts about organisation behaviour.

Legislation has been introduced intermittently since the mid-1970s in an effort to reduce the disadvantages these groups experience. But as Ross and Schneider (1992)[1] point out, statistical evidence over the past 20 years indicates that the law is not a particularly effective vehicle for influencing change in attitudes or in practice. The future labour market situation may leave organisations with little alternative but to alter traditional thinking. Their approach reflects the assumption that the law merely sets out minimum standards and that there are compelling business reasons for embracing equal opportunities.

In 1991 Joanna Foster,[2] in her role as chair of EOC, said, 'Equal Opportunities in the 1990s is about economic efficiency and social justice', and while the case for equal opportunities has been argued on moral and ethical grounds, economic reasons are central, with the law providing the *modus operandi*. The law has played a valuable role in defining and outlawing discrimination against particular groups. Some discussion of legislation relating to equal opportunities is set out later in this chapter. This should be read in conjunction with Chapter 8 which covers all key aspects of UK law on equal opportunities.

Both CRE and EOC have played and continue to play important law enforcement and campaigning roles. Let us hope that the newly formed National Disability Council (NDC) will aid the implementation of the recent disability legislation – Disability Discrimination Act 1995.

In view of these developments, we can but wonder why in practice so little progress has been made in equal opportunities. Cooper and White (1995)[3] believe that the reasons may be related to the fact that the positions of power in UK organisations are dominated largely by white males. 'Therefore those who are in the best position to promote change have no personal experience of discrimination.' This view is supported by an EOC report (1995)[4] showing that in specific employment sectors, such as banking, building societies and post offices, men in managerial positions totalled 68 per cent of all managers. Similarly, only 31 per cent of medical practitioners were women. Latest figures[5] for the total UK workforce show that 45 per cent of the workforce is female. Nevertheless, women's earnings have begun to increase. In 1975 they were at 71 per cent of male earnings; by 1995 this figure had improved to 80 per cent of male earnings – a modest improvement perhaps when we consider that equal opportunities legislation has been in force for over 20 years.

Women employees

There are over 5 million part-time workers in the UK, 87 per cent of whom are women and the numbers are rising. Pay for part-time work is often lower despite the Equal Pay Act. Recent changes to part-time employees' employment protection enforced by European Community legislation will perhaps begin to have an impact shortly and we should see an improvement in women's pay relative to that of men. However, we should also realise that over 2 million female part-time workers earn so little or are so sporadically employed that they do not pay National Insurance, have no entitlements to unemployment benefits, sickness pay or state pensions, and therefore the true picture of equality is rather blurred by official statistics since they do not feature in them.

Disabled employees

Estimates are that there are 3.9 million people, over 10 per cent of the potential UK workforce, with some impairment or disability affecting their ability to gain employment.[6] It is expected that employment legislation under the Disability Discrimination Act, which came into effect in January 1997 to protect disabled people, will have a positive effect on the numbers of disabled employed over the next decade.

The law has nevertheless impacted on some areas of discrimination, most notably in the area of recruitment advertisements. The incidence of discriminatory practices in recruitment advertising has reduced dramatically over the past 20 years. It is, however, more difficult to ascertain the degree of change in equality of opportunity for the female work-force in relation to training and promotion practices within organisations. Firm evidence to support the belief that discrimination is diminishing for women within organisations would require detailed national research. In the absence of this, however, it is clear from material appearing in the national press as well as details held at Companies House for limited companies and also published annual company reports that there are more female directors in businesses now than was the case 20 years ago.

Ethnic minority groups

Unemployment among ethnic minority groups is notably higher than that of the white population; indeed, it currently stands at 'about double that for the white population, even when age, sex and level of qualification were taken into account'[7] and when employed, a far higher proportion of ethnic minority groups work in unskilled manual jobs than do the white population. Thanks to monitoring figures, many organisations now have data showing that they employ more ethnic minority employees than they did 20 years ago. But research carried out by O'Neilly (1995)[8] shows that these employees are often discriminated against when seeking promotion opportunities: 'there is a real danger, not only that an organisation will fail to make the best use of its prime resource, but that future cohorts of good ethnic minority recruits will look at the workforce, read the message and take their talents elsewhere'. This echoes my earlier comments that to succeed in business we must promote equality of opportunity to all.

This chapter outlines the legal framework and regulatory bodies set up to support the legislation within the UK, considers aspects of diversity and discusses equal opportunity policy and practice with reference to some of the organisations who have been working to reduce discriminatory practices in the workforce.

9.2 The legal framework and regulatory bodies

Legislation aimed at eliminating or vastly reducing inequalities of opportunity in employment was first introduced in the UK in 1965 and 1968 with the Race Relations Acts, later replaced by the Race Relations Act 1976. 1970 saw the introduction of the Equal Pay Act, followed by the Sex Discrimination Act 1975. More recently the Disability Discrimination Act 1995 was introduced. By joining the European Community (EC) in 1973, the UK accepted the terms of the Treaty of Rome. This had some impact on our equal rights legislation. Subsequently, certain amendments have been made to UK law where appropriate.

In brief, the current legal position in the UK is that organisations are required not to discriminate against individuals on grounds of race, sex, marital status or disability in selection for employment. In addition, the law states that employees be treated equally in respect of rewards including benefits, training and promotion once they have been employed. Also if the situation should arise where redundancies or short time working are under consideration by an employer, all employees regardless of race, sex, marital status or disability should be treated equally and not be subject to discrimination.

The nature of discrimination

Racial or sexual discrimination can be *direct* or *indirect*. Direct discrimination occurs when a person is treated less favourably than another person on grounds of sex or race. *Indirect* discrimination occurs when a person (employer) applies to one person (employee) the same requirement or condition which he applied to another but:

1. which is such that the proportion of employees in that racial group who can comply with the condition is considerably smaller than the proportion of people not of the employee's racial group who can comply with it; and
2. which is to the employee's detriment because he/she cannot comply with it; and
3. which the employer cannot show to be justified irrespective of the sex (colour or ethnic or national origins) of the person to whom it is applied.

Indirect discrimination is well illustrated by the case of *Manila* v *Dowell Lee* [1983] IRLR 209, where the complaint resulted from a requirement for male school children to wear school caps. It was a requirement with which a smaller proportion of Sikhs could comply than could non-Sikhs because Sikhs customarily wear turbans. The schoolboy in this case could physically comply with the requirement but, in practice, for religious reasons, was unable to do so.

Positive discrimination

Both the Sex Discrimination Acts 1975 and 1986 and the Race Relations Act 1976 make it lawful to encourage and provide training for people of one sex or racial group who have been under-represented in particular work in the previous 12 months. However, although advertisements can explicitly encourage applications from one sex or racial group, all other applicants must also be treated fairly and no discrimination must be allowed to take place.

Equal pay

The Equal Pay Act 1970, as amended by the Equal Pay (Amendment) Regulations 1983, and the Sex Discrimination Act 1986, established the right of women and men to be treated equally with regard to terms and conditions of employment when they are employed on the same or broadly similar work or work which, though different, has been given equal value under a job evaluation scheme, or work which is of equal worth in terms of the demands of the job. It applies equally to men and women and to full-time and part-time employment.

Of course there are different jobs within the workplace, some of which may justifiably be paid at a higher rate and the lower paid jobs may by coincidence be carried out by women. So that even when it is proved that the woman is doing similar work, she will have no right to equal pay if an employer can show that there is a material difference, not based on sex, between the two employees which justifies the difference in payment. What constitutes a material difference in one instance, may be irrelevant in another; as is usual, it all depends on the facts of each case.

Sex discrimination

The Sex Discrimination Act 1975, as amended by the Sex Discrimination Act 1986 and the Employment Act 1989, makes it unlawful to discriminate on grounds of sex or marital status in a number of specific situations related to the employment situation, for example, in the recruitment and selection process; in the provision of access to promotion, transfer or training, or to any other benefits, facilities or services normally provided to employees.

Sex discrimination is not unlawful where a person's sex is a 'genuine occupational qualification' for the job. Each Act includes the specific circumstances in which discrimination may be permitted, for example, in a single sex prison or hospital or where there is a need for certain welfare, educational or similar services to be provided by a person of a particular sex. Further details are given in Chapter 8.

Sexual harassment

Although sexual harassment is not mentioned specifically in the legal provisions relating to sex discrimination or unfair dismissal, complaints may be brought to an industrial tribunal under either of these of these headings in certain circumstances. Sexual harassment was defined by the European Commission Council of Ministers in 1990[9] as

> conduct of a sexual nature, or other conduct based on sex, affecting the dignity of women and men at work, including conduct of superiors and colleagues if:
>
> - such conduct is unwanted, unreasonable and offensive to the recipient;
> - a person's rejection of or submission to such conduct is used explicitly or implicitly as a basis for a decision which affects that person's access to vocational training, access to employment, continued employment, promotion, salary or any other employment decisions; and/or
> - such conduct creates an intimidating, hostile or humiliating work environment for the recipient.

Complaints of sexual harassment may constitute sex discrimination where it is established that the claimant has been treated in a way which would not have been applied to someone of the opposite sex in the same circumstances, and that this treatment has resulted in some loss such as disciplinary action, dismissal (actual or constructive), transfer or failure to promote or train.

Race discrimination

The Race Relations Act 1976 makes it unlawful to discriminate against a person, directly or indirectly on grounds of race, in the field of employment. Discrimination occurs when, on racial grounds, a person is treated less favourably than others would be treated, or is segregated from others and there is ostensibly equal treatment in that a requirement or condition is applied to all people, but the number of people in a particular racial group who can comply with it is proportionately smaller than the number of people outside it who can comply, and the employer cannot justify the requirement as necessary to the job.

Indirect discrimination can occur where, for example, employers require higher language standards than are needed for the safe and effective performance of the job.

Although generally prohibiting discrimination in employment, like the Sex Discrimination Act, this Act allows race discrimination in certain circumstances such as genuine occupational qualification of the job, for example, in modelling, photographic work, welfare services to a particular racial group and in public restaurants where authenticity requires members from a particular racial group.

Racial harassment

Racial harassment can be a form of racial discrimination concerned not with practices and procedures but more with individual behaviour of one person towards another. Employers must ensure that their employees are not racially harassed either by their colleagues or by the public and any other external contacts, while carrying out their duties.

Racial harassment may involve racist insults and ridicule, jokes, display of racist literature, the use of racist names, and so on.

Disability Discrimination Act 1995

The Disability Discrimination Act 1995, which came into force in January 1997, makes discrimination against disabled people for a reason related to their disability unlawful in the field of employment and places a duty of 'reasonable adjustment' on employers with more than 20 employees, to help overcome practical difficulties caused by employers' premises or working practices. The Act applies to employees, job applicants and contractors who are disabled physically or mentally.

The Code of Practice accompanying the Act provides general guidance and outlines the reasonable steps required by employers as 'reasonable adjustment'. Although not a legally binding document, the Code will have a strong influence on the operation of industrial tribunals who will have to consider the practicalities of making adjustments to premises, working methods, hours of work, etc. as well as the costs (to the employer) of making these changes, and the degree of usefulness of any such changes to the disabled employee. A company may be justified in refusing to make high cost adjustment for a temporary employee but would be expected to meet such a cost for a permanent member of staff.

It is too early to estimate the Act's impact on the employment of disabled people, but it will certainly affect the way organisations view disabled people and their employment. As James and Bruyere (1995)[10] observed – the Act imposes new obligations on employers with regard to the management of workplace disability and 'the challenge of the new Act demands much more than the review and development of appropriate policies and procedures but also that organisations improve the coordination existing between all of those involved in the prevention and handling of disability at work, including occupational health staff, safety advisers, line managers, human resource management, safety representatives'.

National Disability Council

Introduced in tandem with the Disability Discrimination Act 1995, to advise the government, the National Disability Council (NDC), unlike CRE and EOC, has not been given the status of an Employment Commission and cannot represent individuals at industrial tribunals. Litigation is thus in the hands of disabled individuals who may or may not be able to afford to fight a claim, or feel confident to do so by virtue of their disability. We may find that employment lawyers will be willing to take the first few test cases for disabled clients without fee so that they can become the 'experts' in disability industrial tribunals. The change in government in May 1997 may see the Council upgraded to Commission status with more power to exert some influence in this area. Only time will tell.

Age discrimination

The protection of older workers is not covered by legislation in the UK in spite of attempts by some politicians to introduce legislation. By the year 2000, 26 per cent of the total UK population will be aged over 55, yet latest national figures available[11] show that the participation rate of older people in economic life is declining.

Although a handful of firms in the UK have operated successful policies to attract older people (e.g. B&Q over-50s' advertising campaign) as employees, it is still the practice of many organisations to place advertisements or include a maximum age in their selection criteria for job applicants. At present, much of the debate about age discrimination concerns treating older workers less favourably, but it may also be discriminatory to treat younger employees less favourably. As we move towards the millennium, it may depend on UK government policy, or stronger influence by the European Union to alter the situation with regard to legislation on age discrimination.

Equal Opportunities Commission

The Equal Opportunities Commission (EOC), established in 1976, works towards the elimination of discrimination, promotes equality of opportunity and keeps under review the Sex

Discrimination Act 1975 and the Equal Pay Act 1970. It further promotes research and activities of an educational nature and in consultation with the Health and Safety Commission, keeps under review certain health and safety legislation which requires men and women to be treated differently. It has produced a *Code of Practice* which gives guidance on the steps considered reasonably practicable for employers to take to promote equality of opportunity and to eliminate discrimination in employment. In 1996 EOC published a Code of Practice on Equal Pay to provide practical guidance and to recommend good practice on pay provision in organisations. This has drawn on decisions from the UK courts and the European Court of Justice (ECJ) as well as good practice known to EOC. The Code gives guidance on drawing up an equal pay policy as well as a suggested policy outline.

The Commission may also represent an individual claiming discrimination on grounds of sex against an employer at an industrial tribunal.

Commission for Racial Equality

The Commission for Racial Equality (CRE) was set up by the Race Relations Act 1976 to work towards the elimination of discrimination, to promote equality of opportunity and good relations between persons of different racial groups and to keep under review the working of the Act.

The Commission has issued a *Code of Practice on Employment*. It has powers to institute formal investigations where there is some evidence of discrimination and can issue a non-discrimination notice following an investigation and obtain an injunction from a County Court if a non-discrimination notice is not being complied with within 5 years of its issue.

It has also produced a 'Standard for Racial Equality for Employers' with the aim of helping employers develop racial equality strategies and to measure their impact. While the Standard does not have legal status, it seeks to provide a link between the *Code of Practice on Employment* and the broader strategies favoured by employers when working with communities and clients.

The Commission may also represent an individual claiming discrimination on grounds of race against an employer at an industrial tribunal.

Monitoring

Monitoring signifies checking, recording and analysing data. It is of necessity a bureaucratic system but if it helps employers to recognise and deal with discrimination, whether on grounds of race or sex or both, then it achieves its purpose. The CRE Code of Practice states that employers should regularly monitor the effects of selection decisions and personnel practices and procedures in order to assess whether an equal opportunities policy is being achieved.

The EOC recommend that employers retain records of the breakdown of applications received from men and women, the breakdown of successful appointees as well as the breakdown of staff and seniority of staff within their organisations. At the recruitment stage, both CRE and EOC suggest that records of applicants and interviewees be retained for three years, so that if an employer is challenged by a candidate complaining of discrimination, the gender and racial breakdown of external applicants and those within the organisation can be provided for any investigations. Both Commissions recommend that ethnic and sex monitoring information be kept separate from the application forms or curriculum vitae when processing candidates and the names of candidates should not be known to the people responsible for short-listing as names could indicate the sex or racial origin of candidates.

For monitoring to succeed, candidates need to know why information is sought by prospective and current employers. For example, the reasons for asking ethnic questions should be stated on job application forms and on staff surveys for ethnic monitoring purposes and confirmation that any details given will be protected from misuse must be made clear to those completing such forms. Recommended methods of keeping and collecting monitoring data are available from both Commissions. The National Disability Council (NDC) recommends that similar activities be carried out by organisations for the monitoring of disability in employment.

9.3 Diversity or equal opportunity?

The terms 'diversity' and 'equal opportunity' are used, often interchangeably, to describe initiatives which can help to remove barriers to employment for people in society. Diversity and managing diversity are increasingly used by employers, not only as an alternative, broadly equivalent term to equal opportunity, but also as a redefinition or redirection of equal opportunity policy development.

Managing diversity relies on the concept that the workforce consists of a diverse population of people. Diversity recognises that people differ, not just in the more obvious ways of gender, ethnicity, age and disability but in visible and non-visible ways including background, personality, culture, work styles and approach, etc. Kandola and Fullerton (1994)[12] clarify the difference between equal opportunity and diversity as being that equal opportunity theories of the 1960s and 1970s were more concerned with assimilation and integration of minority groups, whereas diversity recognises that harnessing people's differences will create a productive environment in which everybody feels valued and where their talents are being fully utilised and in which organisational goals are being met. This is summarised in Table 9.1.

The concept of diversity has aided managers as they strive for long-term change in organisations. The value that it places on the differences between people has helped to motivate employees and to increase productivity.

Table 9.1 Differences in approach between diversity and equal opportunity policies

Managing diversity	Equal opportunity
• Ensures all employees maximise their potential and their contribution to the organisation	• Concentrates on issues of discrimination
• Embraces a broad range of people; no-one is excluded	• Perceived as an issue for women, ethnic minorities and people with disabilities
• Concentrates on issues of movement within an organisation, the culture of the organisation and meeting business objectives	• Less of an emphasis on culture change and the meeting of business objectives
• Is the concern of all employees especially managers	• Seen as an issue to do with 'personnel' and human resource practitioners
• Does not rely on positive/ affirmative action	• Relies on positive action

Source: Kandola, Fullerton, Diversity

Comments on diversity from the Institute of Personnel and Development have focused on ways of maximising individuals' potential and contribution to organisations. Worman (1996)[13] states 'managing diversity is not just about concentrating on issues of discrimination, but ensuring that all people maximise their potential and their contribution to the organisation ... it is a concept which embraces a broad range of people'.

Commentators on 'diversity' and 'equal opportunities' have remarked that they are not and should not be seen as an alternative to equal opportunities. The two concepts are interdependent. For example, Ford (1996)[14] points out that equality and diversity have an impact on all people management processes, from the nature of the employment contract, hours and place of work, through compensation and benefits, to employee behaviour and attitudes that welcome rather than fear differences. Ford feels that whatever definition an organisation uses for equality and diversity, the important fact is that, by adopting such a strategy, the organisation is working for commercial success.

The CRE (1996),[15] while welcoming the concept of diversity as a positive overall objective with equal opportunities as an essential and integral part, has anxieties about diversity policies in general. 'If diversity policies produce no progress towards racial equality we will continue to champion the need for specific equality measures to achieve this. Diversity policies which produce no racial equality impact will also be producing little that is of real benefit to their employees.'

Different but equal: diversity in practice

Organisations such as SmithKline Beecham have adopted diversity as a way forward; recruitment advertising in 1996 states:

> Make no mistake about it, discrimination is a major part of SmithKline Beechams' employment strategy; what's more, we're proud of it. After all, we want to ensure that only the best people join us. So we ruthlessly reject anyone who doesn't make the grade. But gender, colour, race, religion, nationality, disabilities or sexual orientation don't come into it. Why should they, unless they affect your ability to do the job? Because that's what concerns us when we receive an application. In other words we are more interested in individual qualities like commitment, talent, energy and creativity.
>
> The company benefits hugely from an integral diversity and equality policy. It's not merely a matter of legislation; it's sound business strategy. We realise that people from different backgrounds bring individual skills and approaches. Besides, we want a workforce which accurately reflects the community.

Bernard Fournier, managing director, Rank Xerox has explained his company's policy in the following terms:

> Equality and diversity are about creating an environment where everyone is treated equally, whatever their race, religion, sex, colour or any other type of difference. I see differences as a source of enrichment. To be successful we have to be creative and apply diverse perspectives to business problems. Everyone should be able to contribute and should progress in the company in relation to his or her ability.

Rank Xerox[16] describes its objectives as qualitative and quantitative. It aims to:

- create an environment where management can respond positively to differences in the people who work for Rank Xerox, its potential employees, its customers and its suppliers;
- encourage everyone to contribute to their full potential – based solely on their ability, competence and performance;

- challenge the traditional workplace culture and work patterns to eliminate barriers;
- introduce measurable goals for a more diverse workforce profile that reflects the skills, talents and experience available.

9.4 Equal opportunities policies

Recommendations from the CRE, EOC and NDC are that organisations should develop written equal opportunities policies embracing recruitment, promotion and training, all of which should be clearly linked to the aims and objectives of the organisation. They also stress the importance of communicating the policy to employees and their representatives, where applicable, to applicants and potential applicants, customers and clients, share-holders, suppliers of goods and services as well as external bodies such as Training and Enterprise Councils and the public.

To create a written policy, a step-by-step approach is advisable:

1. Develop outline draft policy.
2. Prepare an action plan including targets for senior management, detailing responsi-bilities for policy implementation, resources for any changes necessary to fulfil the policy, timetables for action and implementation and intended methods of measuring effectiveness.
3. Arrange consultation with all employees and their representatives and any external specialist advisory bodies.
4. Provide training for all employees including all senior managers to ensure consistency of approach and an overall understanding of the importance of equal opportunities. Arrange specific training for those people responsible for recruitment, selection, appraisal interviewing and training.
5. Carry out an audit to review current procedures for recruitment, selection, appraisal or performance review, disciplinary and grievances, promotion, training, health and safety, selection criteria for redundancy, transfer and redeployment.
6. Write clear and justifiable job criteria for each job in the organisation to ensure that they are objective and job-related.
7. Consider pre-employment training, where appropriate, to prepare job applicants for selection tests and interviews.
8. Examine the feasibility of flexible working schemes such as career breaks, job sharing, flexitime, shift work, childcare, prayer breaks or areas for prayer, etc.
9. Set up monitoring systems adjusting documentation for recruitment accordingly, to collect appropriate information as necessary for monitoring.
10. Larger organisations should introduce an Equal Opportunities Committee to maintain a positive approach to the issues surrounding equality of opportunity and to review equal opportunity in practice.
11. Finally, agree the equal opportunities policy and set a regular review date to ensure that it is kept up to date.

Managing equal opportunities

Over 25 years have now passed since the first legislative steps were taken to eliminate unfair discrimination in the workplace and we have seen a vast range of different approaches unfolding within organisations. The public sector was the first to respond and some rather bureaucratic systems were implemented which sometimes served to make the situation more complex than it needed to be. Many organisations now have separate policies for racial strategy, equal opportunity on grounds of sex, disability equality, and diversity policies. There is no right or wrong approach. It is up to each organisation to design policies and procedures to fit with their individual approach to business operations and culture while adhering to the spirit and intention of legislation.

One organisation to have implemented equal opportunities strategies for business reasons is Frederick Woolley Ltd, a Birmingham manufacturing firm, investigated by Parkyn and Woolley (1994).[17] In 1991 the organisation was facing both the effects of recession and demands for increased quality from customers. The company developed an equal opportunities programme which became an integral part of its strategy for survival as it took steps to move from traditional methods of production. The firm was family-owned and run by an all-male management team with 36 per cent of its workforce being female. These workers were under-utilised and under-valued by the firm. The company had to involve and empower its employees in order to develop an appropriate change strategy to meet the new philosophy of continuous improvement.

They recruited their first female director and an equal opportunities programme was instituted to demonstrate how positive action could increase women's participation in employment, especially in non-traditional female areas *including* management. They set up an equal opportunities project steering group to highlight the traditional, restrictive ways of deploying women, together with a summary of how these limitations had been affecting the bottom line of the business. Many changes were made to implement the new ideas from the project team including targeted training for women, assertive communication skills for both sexes, new recruitment and promotion procedures. The equal opportunities strategy was a most successful part of the overall new approach to business strategy and the financial position of the company improved dramatically as a result of the many initiatives put in place.

A different approach which worked well was introduced by the WH Smith Group who conducted an Employee Profile Audit in 1995,[18] to collect accurate employee data on all 30 000 UK employees. They started by publishing explanatory articles in the in-house magazine, then team briefings took place around the group and question and answer leaflets were prepared for managers. Next, they issued personal information forms to employees asking them to check the accuracy of personal data such as date of birth, grade, and so on. In addition, employees were asked to state their ethnic origin and whether they considered themselves disabled. Some 84 per cent of the forms were returned showing the importance that staff themselves attached to this audit. Following the audit, the company produced a very practical working document containing a number of checklists suggesting ways in which the businesses in the WH Smith Group could take action to improve the diversity of their workforces. The report will be updated and reviewed regularly.

The Group has also supported many initiatives such as one to help unemployed ethnic minority young people find permanent employment. Pre-employment training has also been introduced for a group of unemployed people in London. They have revised their application forms which are now regularly monitored and each business within the group has set up 'diversity action teams', consisting of senior line managers and staff representatives, to plan and monitor further action.

Another example is in the financial sector: Midland Bank has introduced 8 weeks' paid summer work experience for ethnic minority students at the end of their penultimate year at university,[19] offering an insight into banking and an opportunity to develop particular skills. High calibre participants are encouraged to apply for entry to the bank's graduate programme. Midland Bank have publicised the project extensively in the national and ethnic minority press and radio, and all university career offices now have application forms.

The bank now organises induction and development training to introduce candidates to Midland Bank and the graduate recruitment process uses assessment facilities to provide instruction in interview techniques as well as written exercises, with feedback on performance.

For Midland Bank the benefits are that they now receive more applications from ethnic minority graduates, a group previously under-represented and untapped as a source of supply of highly educated labour. In addition, managers within Midland have increased their own cultural awareness with the added benefit that this must bring to all staff.

A further example of interest is British Petroleum (BP)[20] whose equal opportunities policy handbook highlights the purposes of the policy:

> An equal opportunity policy is important for the individual. But it is also important for the company. Such a policy helps to identify, attract and make the best use of the skills and talents we need to conduct our business efficiently, wherever these may be available. In essence, race, religion, colour, nationality, ethnic or national origins, sex or marital status must not influence, directly or indirectly, the way in which a person is treated.

The policy goes on to detail each employee's responsibilities in relation to equal opportunities as well as mechanisms for dealing with situations of perceived inequality.

Finally, in British Gas[21] the approach to equal opportunity policy is to break it down to embrace different aspects of equality and provide specific actions the organisation has taken to redress the balance of race and sex. For example, the policy relating to women's issues revolves around 'family friendly' approaches; for example, childcare vouchers issued to female employees; career breaks with a guaranteed job after a 2-year break and preference over external applicants given to returners after a 5-year break. Flexible working arrangements such as variable hours, flexitime and job sharing have also been introduced. Similar policies exist for other equal opportunities issues.

Evaluating equal opportunities policies

In order to achieve success, policies must be supported by senior management and trade union leaders and not simply become 'top-down' initiatives or simply the concern of specific groups. Leiff and Aitkenhead[22] make the point that, 'Equal opportunities policies are often said to fail because they are not promoted enthusiastically enough or are not implemented in a comprehensive enough manner.' It is vital that any equal opportunities policies introduced into an organisation not only have the support of all employees but must be seen as a necessary and beneficial activity to the organisation. As already mentioned, influencing attitudes is a slow process and not always easy, but sound policies for equal opportunities and supportive training programmes may do much to influence behaviour and may, over a period of time, alter attitudes. Clearly there has been much progress in the moves towards equalising opportunities in the workplace thanks to the initiatives of companies leading the field.

9.5 The future of equal opportunities

The essence of much of the work involved in managing human resources effectively, according to Torrington and Hall (1995),[23] involves discrimination between individuals but the essence of equal opportunity is to avoid *unfair* discrimination.

As this chapter has attempted to convey, equal opportunity is not only about meeting legal and social responsibilities but also about attaining organisational effectiveness. The 'diverse organisation' of the future will be part of the formula for success if the UK is to be competitive on an international basis.

Every organisation will need to develop and build on its own particular experiences of equal opportunities and diversity and will aim for different objectives. Rather than trying to follow a single formula for success, it is up to management to initiate the best policies and practice for their unique environment. In this way will evolve changes necessary to provide the optimum climate in the firm to foster talent, performance and creativity so vital to organisational effectiveness and growth.

9.6 References

1. Ross R, Schneider R. *From equality to diversity: A business case for equal opportunities.* London: Pitman, 1992.
2. Foster J. *Launching the equality agenda.* Conference EOC, London, 1991.
3. Cooper C, White B. Organisational behaviour. In: Tyson S. *Strategic prospects for HRM.* London: IPD, 1995.
4. *Some facts about women.* London: EOC, 1995.
5. Equal Opportunities Commission. *Guidance notes for employers: setting targets for gender equality.* London: HMSO, 1995.
6. Dryden G. *Post-16 Policy, RNIB.* IPD North London Branch Meeting, 1996.
7. Equal Opportunities Commission. *Guidance notes for employers: successful positive action.* London: HMSO, 1994.
8. O'Neilly J. When prejudice is not just skin deep. *People Management* 23 Feb 1995: 34–7.
9. European Commission. *Council of Minister's Report.* Brussels: 1990.
10. James P, Bruyere S. Handling disability – implications of the new law. *Occupational Health Review* 1995; Nov./Dec.: 21–4.
11. *Labour force survey.* London: HMSO, 1996.
12. Kandola R, Fullerton J. Diversity: more than just an empty slogan? *Personnel Management* 1994; Nov.: 46–50.
13. Worman D. *Diversity: code of practice.* London: IPD, 1996.
14. Ford V. Partnership is the secret of progress. *People Management* 1996; Feb. 8: 34–7.
15. Commission for Racial Equality. *Case study no. 2.* London: HMSO, 1996.
16. *People Management* 1996; 8 February: 46–50.
17. Parkyn A, Woolley S. Learning to give women an equal input. *Personnel Management* 1994; June: 20–4.
18. *Employee profile audit.* London: WH Smith, 1995.
19. *Work experience handbook.* Midland Bank, 1995.
20. *Equal opportunity: What it means in practice.* London: BP, 1994.
21. *Equal opportunities policy.* London: British Gas, 24 December 1993.
22. Leiff S, Aitkenhead M. Assessing equal opportunities policies. *Personnel Review* 1989; **18**(1), 27–34.
23. Torrington D, Hall L. *Personnel management: HRM in action.* 3rd edition. Hemel Hempstead: Prentice Hall, 1995.

9.7 Further reading

Cassidy J. But not for the author who took on the feminists. 9 January 1994 *Sunday Times News Review Section* 4, p. 3.
Coussey M, Jackson H. *Making equal opportunities work.* London: Pitman, 1991.
CRE Case Study No. 1. London: HMSO, 1996.
CRE. *Diversity & Racial Equality.* London: CRE, 1996.

CRE. *Racial equality means business: a standard for racial equality for employers.* London: CRE, 1995.

CRE. *The Inequality Gap.* London: EOC, 1995.

Equal Opportunities Commission. *Challenging inequalities between women and men: twenty years of progress 1976–1996.* London: EOC, 1996.

Hawkins K. Taking action on harassment. *Personnel Management* March 1994, 26–29.

Janner G. *Sex and ethnic monitoring, discriminating and equal pay.* Croner: Surrey, 1984.

Leighton P. Dignity at work. *Human Resources Journal* Summer 1993, 106–9.

Little A. New disability legislation will affect all employers. *Hospitality* Oct./Nov. 1996.

McGoldrick A. *Equal treatment in occupational pension schemes. Research Report.* London: EOC, 1984.

Pye M. The War Between the Sexes. *The Telegraph Magazine*, 15 October 1995, 15–21.

Shaw M. Achieving equality of treatment and opportunity in the workplace. In Harrison R ed. *Human Resource Management.* London: Addison Wesley, 1993.

Sullivan A. The witch hunt is ending, *Sunday Times* 9 Jan 1994, News Review Section 4, 2.

Williams A. *Croner's Guide to Discrimination.* Croner: Surrey, 1995.

SECTION IV
REWARD MANAGEMENT AND THE MANAGEMENT OF PERFORMANCE

Introduction

High all-round performance is the goal. This will only be delivered by staff who are positively motivated and have a high level of commitment to what they are doing. Effective human resource management aims to bring about high levels of commitment, by means of policies and practices which motivate, and the intelligent management of rewards.

The terms which have been used in the past to describe and execute this process have possessed a negative connotation. In Britain the terms 'wages' and 'salaries' have been, and still frequently are, used to describe reward processes, and are a hangover from the days of class discrimination when blue collar manual workers earned wages, whereas white collar office workers earned salaries. American companies still use the term 'compensation', implying that work is a negative experience for which employees have to be 'compensated' for turning up! Another negative attitude to reward management which dies hard is the cost accountant's approach, which sees wages merely as a cost. Cost it certainly is, but that is an argument for using the money wisely, not for pushing for cost-cutting exercises that lower morale and motivation and hence productivity, a policy which sooner or later will impact negatively on the bottom line, quality of service, and market share. Satisfying and well-tailored rewards and high productivity lead to a lower *total* wage bill, than a low wage, low productivity approach.

Economic conditions have in recent years forced organisations to become leaner, fitter and more customer-oriented. This has been reflected in their pay structures. In the past, pay policy was often exemplified by bureaucracy, inflexibility and adherence to the *status quo*. Today, pay policy in the more successful organisations is fully integrated with corporate strategy and with an emphasis on rewarding individual and group contributions to corporate goals.

The three chapters in this section progress from a consideration of motivation theories and their practical implementation to ways of ensuring that the pay policies and practices are up-to-date and contributing to strategic goals, and conclude by outlining and examining recent developments in the quest to link performance with rewards.

10 Motivation and rewards

Alan Cowling

10.1 Introduction

Reward management aims to improve the performance of employees, and this in turn requires positive measures to ensure high levels of motivation. Most organisations try to motivate employees by offering financial rewards in return for skill, time, and effort. Financial rewards alone are generally insufficient to create sustained levels of motivation. Evidence points to the need to adopt measures that satisfy a range of desires which employees bring with them to the workplace, including the desire for satisfactory pay, job security, satisfying work, good working conditions, opportunities to maintain and improve skill levels, status, and good social relationships in the workplace.

Mention was made in Chapter 2 of the need to develop a positive employment policy in order to attract and retain quality staff. Policies in the UK need to take account of survey findings on the attitudes of British workers, such as the recent wide-ranging survey which indicated that British workers were more dissatisfied than those in any other European nation, according to a study of 400 companies in 17 countries,[1] and an opinion poll carried out for the GMB union which showed most workers did not regard pay, overtime, or fringe benefits as overwhelmingly important. They were more interested in job security and job satisfaction.[2] Basic pay ranked fourth for the men surveyed, and seventh for women. The women surveyed felt that it was more important to work for an employer whom they respected, to have a clean and healthy place to work, and to have a say in how they worked.

Pay systems need to be designed as part and parcel of a total employment package which motivates employees to strive for higher levels of performance. All too frequently company pay systems have had the opposite effect, rewarding years of service and conformity to rules and regulations rather than the employee's contribution to organisational goals, and involving a minimal expenditure of effort. By applying research findings on motivation, policies and practices can be formulated which contribute to commitment and performance.

This chapter reviews the nature of motivation, its relevance to performance, and theories of motivation appropriate to the management of rewards, as a prelude to a consideration of reward management policies and practices in the following two chapters.

10.2 Motivation

Motivation is a psychological concept related to the strength and direction of human behaviour.[3] It is frequently explained as a driving force within individuals by which they attempt to achieve some goal in order to fulfil some need or expectation. There is an implication of deliberate choice by individuals to exert effort; Mitchell defines motivation as 'The degree to which an individual wants and chooses to engage in certain specified behaviour'.[4]

In the workplace setting, motivation is concerned with the manner in which individuals choose to exert effort in pursuit of their goals, and, correspondingly, with the manner in which employers attempt to create work environments which stimulate such effort. Understanding motivation at work requires an understanding of the goals which individuals are pursuing, and the manner in which these goals and expenditure of effort are influenced by group dynamics, job design, organisation structure, and financial and other incentives.

Three theories of motivation are particularly relevant to motivating people in work situations. These are the so-called 'two-factor' theory, 'expectancy theory', and 'goal-setting' theory.

10.3 Two-factor theory

The research into motivation conducted by Herzberg in the United States over thirty years ago has been replicated on a number of occasions since, and continues to carry weight today. Based on individual responses to questions as to what provides them with the most memorable instances of happiness or unhappiness at work, people tend to indicate two different sets of factors, one contributing to happiness, the other to unhappiness. Typically, the former list includes:

- a sense of achievement;
- recognition by superiors;
- responsibility inherent in the job;
- satisfying job content;
- promotion.

By way of contrast, the negative factors typically include the following:

- company policy and administration;
- relationships with supervisors and peers;
- physical working conditions.

Pay also attracts comment, some favourable, some unfavourable. This led Herzberg to dub the second list 'Hygiene' factors, on the grounds that corrective action needs to take place before positive motivation will result, in the same way that human beings have to observe the rules of hygiene before they can progress to high levels of physical fitness and performance.[5]

These findings have led to the inference that pay is a hygiene factor, and that employers should therefore focus on achieving a well-administered pay system and erase causes of dissatisfaction among employees, before moving on to the more exciting measures that create high levels of motivation and performance. While there is a large measure of truth in this inference, and experience and research both tell us that it is extremely hard to motivate employees dissatisfied with their pay schemes, it neglects the role that money can have in achieving high levels of motivation. For a significant proportion of employees, particularly high-flying managers and sales staff, financial rewards are an important form of recognition. Money can become a goal in itself, as well as a reinforcing behaviour which leads to high performance.

Herzberg's findings on motivation are popular with many managers, who can relate to them on the basis of their own work experience, and because they provide a blueprint for action, clearly indicating areas to be tackled in order to improve levels of motivation at work. Critics of Herzberg fasten on weaknesses in his methodology, including his generalisation from a sample consisting of 203 employees in just one company, mostly engineers, accountants, and the like, and that he used a 'story-telling' *critical incident method,* held to introduce bias.[6] While further studies by other researchers replicating his methods with samples drawn from other categories of employee have provided support for his findings – and managers are frequently surprised to learn that these show that shop-floor workers also value a sense of achievement and recognition – critics argue that these are the result of the method used. It has also been pointed out that lack of recognition and achievement are also powerful 'hygiene' factors.[7] However, further studies have lent support to the idea that both *extrinsic* (hygiene) and *intrinsic* (motivational) job factors affect job satisfaction in the qualitatively different ways hypothesised by Herzberg.[8]

Two-factor theory was associated with the move to redesign and enrich jobs which gained popularity in the 1970s and has recently re-emerged with the drive to multi-skilling in many companies, referred to in Chapter 5. This move to enrich and redesign jobs was given impetus by researchers at the Tavistock Institute, leading to the popularising of the 'socio-technical' framework of job design,[9] as well as the job characteristics model devised by Hackman and Oldham[10] and the 'requisite-task attributes' model of Turner and Lawrence[11] and Cooper.[12] The principles of job enrichment are summarised in Table 10.1.

Table 10.1 A synthesis of the principles of job enrichment

Principle	Motivators involved
1. Remove some controls while retaining accountability	Responsibility and Achievement
2. Increase the accountability of individuals for their own work	Responsibility and Recognition
3. Give a person a complete 'natural' unit of work	Responsibility, Achievement, and Recognition
4. Give individuals additional authority in their work, provide job freedom	Responsibility, Recognition, and Achievement
5. Make regular performance feedback available to the worker rather than the supervisor	Recognition
6. Introduce new and more difficult tasks	Growth
7. Assign individuals specific tasks, enable them to become experts	Responsibility, Growth, and Advancement

10.4 Expectancy theory

Expectancy theory concentrates, as the name implies, on the expectations which employees bring with them to the work situation, and the context and manner in which these expectations are satisfied. The underlying hypothesis is that appropriate levels of effort, and hence productivity, will only be extended if employees' expectations are fulfilled. It does not assume a static range of expectations common to all employees, but rather points to the possibility of different sets of expectations. Rewards are seen as fulfilling or not fulfilling expectations. The basic model is illustrated in Figure 10.1.

This model emphasises that high levels of performance require clarity about work roles, the selection of workers who possess the appropriate aptitudes and abilities, and subsequent training and job knowledge. Research by Porter and Lawler indicates that the value of the reward, particularly pay, and the perception of the effort–reward relationship combine to influence effort in a positive manner.[13] Managers in their sample who perceived their pay to be related to their performance were rated more highly by their superiors than those managers who perceived little relationship.[14]

The implications for reward management[15] include the need to:

- find out what rewards are valued by each employee;
- clarify what constitutes good performance;
- ensure that performance targets can be achieved;
- be clear about the link between rewards and performance;
- check that alternative expectations are not being fostered in other parts of the organisation;
- ensure rewards and bonuses are large enough to attract interest;
- ensure the system is perceived to be fair.

Expectancy theory challenges management to demonstrate to employees that extra effort will reap a commensurate reward. The evidence of research findings and practical experience is that many employees are not convinced that if they exert more effort they will definitely achieve more, and will be rewarded commensurately. Cynicism has been reinforced by, for example, recent performance management schemes offering bonuses of less than 5 per cent in return for extra effort. The link between effort and reward needs to encompass both the pay packet and a variety of other extrinsic or intrinsic rewards. Reward schemes must therefore create a positive link between the size of the pay packet and the effort expended for employees primarily motivated by money. For others, links must be created between effort and rewards which include job satisfaction and praise and other forms of recognition.

10.5 Goal-setting theory

There exists strong evidence that setting goals for employees leads to higher performance, provided the goals are relevant and acceptable to participants. Goal-setting theories, originally propounded by Locke, have considerable relevance to motivation and reward management.[16] At a basic level, this means that all employees should:

- be clear about their individual and group goals;
- participate in the setting of these goals.

Goal choice is a function of (a) what the individual expects can be achieved; (b) what the individual would ideally like to achieve; and (c) what the individual believes is the minimum that should be achieved. For many people, a goal set and delegated by others serves as a disincentive. For goals to have their full effects it is also necessary for participants to

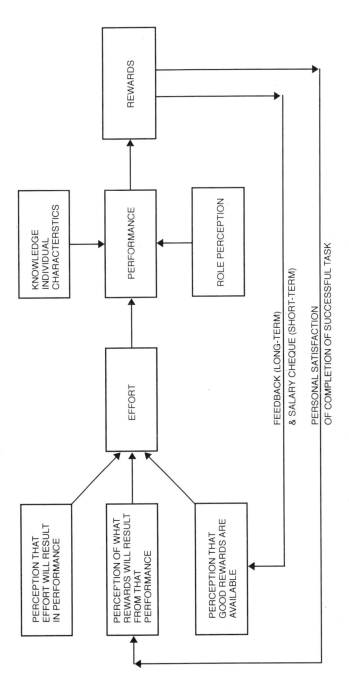

Figure 10.1 Expectancy theory of motivation – applied model

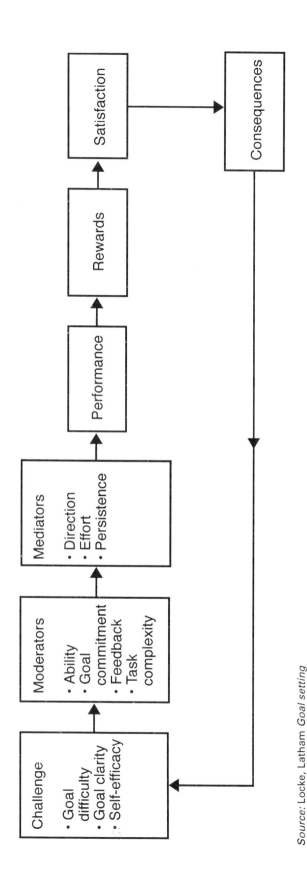

Figure 10.2 Simplified Locke and Latham goals model

Source: Locke, Latham *Goal setting*

have feedback on whether their performance has been successful. These points are brought out in Figure 10.2.

Difficult goals lead to high performance only when an individual is committed to them.[17] As commitment declines, performance also declines. Commitment to a goal can be considerably improved if employees participate in the goal-setting process. Indeed, research suggests that a goal set and delegated by others serves as a disincentive.[18] Providing feedback on performance is necessary if goals are to be fully effective.[19]

The most obvious applications of goal theory are in managerial style and the design of appraisal schemes. As management is a process of achieving results through people, successful managers will involve staff in goal setting ('management by objectives'), ensure the goals can be achieved, and provide feedback on whether goals are being achieved. The 'mushroom theory of growth' is proverbial (and not attributable!) in much of British industry – 'keep staff in the dark and shower them with shit'! Where still practised, this leads to poor quality workmanship, and is in stark contrast with the Japanese style of forms of communication and consultation. The styles of communication needed for modern forms of appraisal and performance management are described in Chapters 6 and 12.

10.6 Creating a motivating environment

This chapter has focused on three of the better known theories of motivation in order to bring out the importance of creating a motivating environment when devising reward management policies. Other theories of motivation have also made a useful contribution to current thinking on this issue, notably equity theory[20] and control theory.[21] Recent thinking about the manner in which a motivating environment at work can be created has been usefully summarised by Ivan Robertson and Dominic Cooper,[22] and includes the following characteristics:

- Employees have a realistic understanding of the links between effort and performance.
- Employees have the competence and confidence to translate effort into performance.
- Performance systems are expressed in terms of hard, but attainable, specific goals.
- Employees participate in setting goals.
- Feedback to employees is regular, informative and easy to interpret.
- Employees are praised for good performance.
- Rewards (including pay) are seen as equitable.
- Rewards are tailored to individual requirements and preferences.
- Employee psychological and physical well-being is recognised as important.
- Productivity is recognised as important.
- Jobs are designed, where possible, to maximise skill variety, task identity, autonomy, feedback, and opportunities for learning and growth.
- Organisation and job changes are brought about through consultation and discussion, not by fiat.

The various forms of pay systems and processes in common use are examined in the next chapter, but all must pass the acid test of whether they motivate and encourage effort.

10.7 References

1. Study by International Survey Research, reported in *Personnel Management* 1991; 11 January: 7.
2. *The Times*, 9 May 1991: 3.
3. Robertson IT, Smith M, Cooper D. *Motivation*. London: Institute of Personnel Management, 1992.

4. Mitchell TR. Motivation: new directions for theory, research, and practice. *Academy of Management Review* 1982; **7**(1): 80–8.

5. Herzberg F. One more time: how do you motivate employees?. *Harvard Business Review* 1968; Jan.–Feb.: 53–62.

6. Vroom VH. *Work and motivation.* Chichester: Wiley, 1964.

7. House RJ, Wigdor LA. Herzberg's dual-factor theory of job satisfaction and motivation: a review of the evidence and a criticism. *Personnel Psychology* 1967; **20**, Winter: 369–90.

8. Robertson IT *et al. Motivation*: 58.

9. Emery FE. Designing socio-technical systems for greenfield sites. *Journal of Occupational Behaviour* 1980; **1**(1): 19–27.

10. Hackman JR, Oldham GR. *Work redesign.* New York: Addison Wesley, 1980.

11. Turner A, Lawrence PR. *Industrial jobs and the worker: an investigation of response to task attributes.* Boston, MA: Harvard Graduate School of Business Administration, 1965.

12. Cooper R. Task characteristics and intrinsic motivation. *Human Relations* 1973; **26**: August: 387–408.

13. Porter LW, Lawler EE. *Managerial attributes and performance.* New York: Irwin, 1968.

14. Porter LW, Lawler EE, Hackman JR. *Behaviour in organizations.* New York: McGraw-Hill, 1975.

15. Nadler DA, Lawler EE. Motivation: a diagnostic approach. In: Steers R, Porter LM eds. *Motivation and work behaviour,* 2nd edn, New York: McGraw-Hill, 1979.

16. Locke EA. Towards a theory of task motivation and incentives. *Organizational Behaviour and Human Performance* 1968; **3**: 157–89.

17. Locke EE, Latham GP. *A theory of goal setting and task performance.* London: Prentice Hall, 1990.

18. Naylor JC *et al.* Goal setting: a theoretical analysis of motivational technology. In: Straw BM, Cummings LL eds. *Research in organizational behaviour* 1980; **6**: 95–114.

19. Erez M. Feedback: a necessary condition for the goal-setting performance relationship. *Journal of Occupational Psychology* 1977; **62**(5): 624–7.

20. Klein HJ. An integrated control theory model of work motivation. *Academy of Management Review* 1989; **14**: 150–72.

21. Greenberg J. A taxonomy of organizational justice theories. *Academy of Management Review* 1987; **12**: 9–12.

22. Robertson IT, Cooper D. Motivation: evolution or revolution?. Paper presented to Institute of Personnel Management Annual Conference, Seminar 51, 1993.

11 Pay policy, pay processes, and the management of rewards

Alan Cowling

11.1 Introduction

Reward management encompasses both extrinsic rewards, of which pay is the most important, and intrinsic rewards such as recognition and status. This chapter concentrates on pay policy and pay processes, whilst bearing in mind that pay has to be treated as part of the total employment package in the manner highlighted in Chapter 10.

Pay represents both a cost and an investment to the organisation. It is the largest cost item for many employers. Attention to budgeting and control is always important. Pay is also an investment because it represents money spent in pursuit of productivity. Ensuring that the money devoted to pay is invested wisely is the prime objective of a company's pay policy. Economic conditions have in recent years forced organisations to become leaner, fitter and more customer-oriented and this has been reflected in their pay structures. Pay policy aims to facilitate the attraction and retention of employees and to encourage effort and cooperation as well as a willingness to learn new skills and to adapt to change. At the same time, pay policy has to be administered in a manner perceived by employees to be equitable and fair.

In this chapter methods of updating policies on pay and developing rewards appropriate to organisational goals and strategy are examined. While the administration of pay has become increasingly specialised in larger organisations, pay policy is too important to be left to the specialists. Corporate strategy must provide the overall direction, with line management involved in all stages of its operation and the HRM function providing advice and support.

11.2 Market forces

Any review of pay policy must start with economic considerations: there are limits as to what organisations can afford to pay, and the objective must be to make pay increases self-financing through higher productivity. The basic price of labour in a free economy is determined largely by the forces of supply and demand in the labour market and no organisation can afford to let itself be too far out of line. Pay policy has to be incorporated into budgets which in their turn require accurate forecasts of trends in external pay levels. Employment costs consist of more than basic wages, and include pension contributions, holiday pay, sickness benefits, and a range of other benefits outlined below.

A number of sources of intelligence are available concerning the labour market. Systematic investigation is essential if the correct conclusions are to be drawn since haphazard and 'off the cuff' investigations are liable to mislead. Job titles can mislead, so accurate job descriptions are vital. The five factors of skill, responsibility, mental effort, physical effort and working conditions provide a popular and well-tried set of headings for this purpose. Systematic investigations into pay levels frequently concentrate on so-called 'benchmark' jobs. These are jobs considered to have special significance for pay structure on account of custom and practice, their use in pay bargaining, and the number of employees covered.

Useful sources of information on market rates include:

- information gleaned from job applicants;
- job advertisements in papers and journals, although these should be treated with caution as they can mislead, and may not be based on accurate job descriptions;
- private employment agencies who are usually helpful, but have a vested interest in inflating rates;
- public employment agencies, such as 'Job Centres';
- published surveys: although publishers may charge a high fee to cover costs, reputable publications such as *Incomes Data Services* provide excellent information;
- official publications such as the *Labour Market Trends* provide general information but are of limited use for local labour market information;
- inter-firm pay surveys can be an excellent source of information.

Regular inter-firm pay surveys are carried out by a large number of organisations.

11.3 Pay surveys

The financial rewards offered by most organisations embrace a complete package of basic pay plus a variety of allowances, opportunities to earn overtime, and fringe benefits. Data generated on earnings should be in a format suitable for simple statistical analysis. A wide spread of earnings is frequently found within and across a sample of organisations. This information should be further simplified by calculating respective ranges, medians and quartile statistics. Management is then in a position to decide whether to maintain or establish a position as a relatively high, average, or low paying firm. The economic state of the organisation, the need to attract large numbers or a high class of recruit, the level of labour wastage, the trade union position, and the general employment philosophy of the organisation are all relevant considerations.

11.4 Job evaluation and internal equity

The concept of a fair day's pay for a fair day's work is deeply engrained into our thinking. A fair day's pay tends to be defined by workers consciously or subconsciously by reference to what fellow workers in similar jobs are earning, particularly their colleagues at their place of work. While an internal structure of differentials is generally accepted as necessary by most workers, their feelings concerning equity and fairness demand that the size of differentials be regulated in accordance with some open and rational system. A professional approach to wage and salary administration by management likewise demands a rational and acceptable structure of differentials. These demands have given rise to the technique and widespread popularity of job evaluation.

Job evaluation is not a new technique. Most commonly found methods have been in use for the last 50 years. But in recent years there have been a number of attempts to adapt traditional methods to fit in with social and technological change, notably in the use of participation, consensus, information technology, and competencies. Exponents of job evaluation have sometimes claimed that it represents a truly scientific method of payment but this is an exaggeration. In the last resort, it can only rely upon subjective judgement. But there are many benefits that can accrue from a well-installed job evaluation scheme, including:

- cost control: where specific rates and differentials are established and maintained, labour costs can be analysed, budgeted, and controlled;
- fairness: employees can see that an impartial system is being used to establish differentials, and pay rates are not just subject to favouritism or whim;
- simplification: instead of a large number of different job rates, some perhaps only differing by a few pence, jobs can be slotted into a simple graded structure.

Job evaluation is essentially concerned with job content and not with either the individual job holder or outside market forces. In real life it is not always easy to ignore the job holder, who may in fact have had a large say in developing the scope of the job he or she occupies, nor the presence of supply and demand for particular job skills. However, management should aim for a practically useful scheme, acceptable to both management and workers, rather than one that is technically pure. The essence of job evaluation is job analysis. The successful operation of a scheme requires that thorough job studies are carried out by trained analysts. Also basic is the concept of 'benchmark' jobs – jobs accepted by all parties concerned as being fairly paid at the current time in relation to each other, and also having sufficient in common with the other jobs to be used for comparison. At the start of a job evaluation scheme considerable time needs to be spent on establishing satisfactory benchmark jobs. A method of checking on their usefulness is given under the points method outlined on page 186.

11.5 Traditional approaches to job evaluation

Different job evaluation techniques have their own peculiar advantages and disadvantages. Four techniques of job evaluation have been in use for many years. These are 'ranking', 'grading', 'factor comparison' and 'points method'. The first two are based on 'whole job' comparison and are therefore referred to as 'non-analytic' to distinguish them from the latter two that analyse job content under a number of 'factor' headings.

Ranking

The object of ranking is simply to establish a rank order or hierarchy of jobs. Pay rates will then reflect this hierarchy. Evaluation is carried out by comparing the contents of jobs with the contents on the benchmark jobs, and putting the job into its appropriate place in the hierarchy. Evaluators must use their judgement as to whether one job is to be rated higher or lower than another job. In a typical engineering factory machine shop the following rank order might emerge: tool room fitter – maintenance fitter – machine setter – semi-skilled machinist – unskilled labourer. Rates of pay will then reflect this simple hierarchy, although the actual differentials must be settled by judgement or negotiation. The principal advantage of this method is its simplicity. It is easily understood, and is not complicated to carry out. But because it is so simple it is not appropriate when a large number of jobs of varied content need to be included. For example, we would have difficulty in fitting jobs such as 'secretary' or 'sales representative' into our rank order above but where a small homogeneous 'family' of jobs is concerned, ranking can be useful.

Grading

This technique is also referred to as 'classification'. As its name implies, it is based on the establishment or maintenance of a graded, hierarchical, structure. Frequently a simple grading structure with a strictly limited number of grades is the objective. To take an example again from engineering, a company might have five basic job grades covering, in turn, highly skilled (apprenticeship plus further toolroom training), skilled (apprenticeship or equivalent), partly skilled (two years' training), semi-skilled (four weeks' minimum training) and unskilled work. These jobs are then fitted into a structure labelled grades A to E respectively, reflecting the differences in skill. Simplicity is the principal virtue of grading. It is extensively used in manufacturing industry and with white collar jobs. But as with ranking, it can only be effectively used within a homogeneous family of jobs of limited number.

Factor comparison

This method is less frequently used in practice. Jobs are compared on the basis of their relative importance under a set of job 'factors', such as 'training', 'responsibility', 'skill' and 'physical effort'. A rank order is established under each of these headings, and the factors are then weighted in accordance with the opinions of the evaluating team. For example, under the factor heading of 'physical effort', our five engineering machine shop jobs might show up in the following rank order; semi-skilled machinist – machine setter – maintenance fitter – unskilled labourer – toolroom setter. The machinist should therefore be paid more under this factor heading than the toolmaker. The rank order will of course be different under other factor headings. Translating factor comparison into actual pay is something of a headache, and so the usual way out of the dilemma is to use a quantitative approach in which factors are accorded a points value, as in the points method.

Points method

Points method achieves a system of differentials by ranking jobs in accordance with the number of points they have been awarded during a job evaluation exercise. First, a set of factors must be drawn up that will permit satisfactory analysis and comparison of the jobs in question. A weighting exercise has then to be carried out to decide what possible maximum total of points shall be permitted under each factor heading. Illustrated by the application of a points scheme to the simple list of five jobs in a typical machine shop, and using the factors of training, responsibility, skill and physical effort, a weighting exercise for each factor might give a maximum of 20 points for each factor, giving a possible grand total of 100 points. The results of evaluation might then be presented as in Table 11.1.

Table 11.1 Job evaluation: simple points method scheme

Job title	Training	Responsibility	Skill	Physical effort	Total
Toolroom setter	20	15	20	5	60
Maintenance fitter	15	12	16	7	50
Machine setter	10	10	10	10	40
Machinist	6	4	5	15	30
Labourer	2	3	2	8	15

If pay is directly related to points, it would mean in this case that toolroom setters earn four times as much per hour as labourers. As differentials of this order are not normally acceptable within a factory, this difficulty can be overcome by giving an initial allocation of 50 points to all jobs at the commencement of the exercise, giving a final differential between toolroom setters and labourers of 110:65. Thus, the toolroom setter earns £300 per 37-hour week the labourer earns £150.

This example highlights the fact that any job evaluation scheme must be tailored to individual company pay policy and practical objectives. The relationship between points and pence to be aimed for is normally a linear one with pay rising in proportion to the allocation of points. Such a points scheme can be portrayed on a graph. Graphs show up anomalies which it is the prime purpose of job evaluation schemes to correct. Figure 11.1 shows the results of an evaluation exercise which has allocated points totals to a number of jobs.

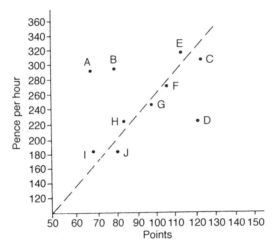

Figure 11.1 Job evaluation: a scattergram of points and money

Some of these jobs are in a correct relationship with each other and therefore fall on or near the straight line that relates points and money. A few jobs are some way from the line indicating that job holders are either being paid too much in relation to the agreed benchmark jobs (where they appear above the line) or are being paid too little (where they appear below the line). As will be seen in Figure 11.1, jobs A and B are being paid too much in relation to the points total credited to them, whereas jobs C and D are being paid too little. The remaining jobs are receiving the correct rate per hour. Strictly speaking, the pay for jobs A and B should be reduced, and that for C and D increased to bring them into line. In practice, individual rates of pay are usually only increased or maintained, never decreased. An undertaking to this effect is usually given in advance of the exercise to ensure the full co-operation of both employees and unions. Thus the rates for jobs A and B may be reduced to the appropriate level, but individuals currently occupying those jobs will be allowed to keep the higher rate, the difference between the newly adjusted rate and their own higher rate being expressed as a personal 'plus' rate in the pay records. These individuals may not share in annual cost of living or general increases until such time as the adjusted rate for the job has caught up with their hourly rate of pay, subject of course to negotiation and consultation. Frequently a job evaluation scheme is linked to a grading structure. A particular grade then includes all jobs that achieve a total of points falling within the minimum and maximum for that grade. Such a scheme is illustrated in Table 11.2, derived from a public sector job evaluation scheme.

Table 11.2 Job evaluation: an example of a points system and grade bandings structure

Points table

Factor number	Factors	%	Minimum points	Degree 1	2	3	4
1	Staff responsibility	16.66	166.6	267	367	467	567
2	Financial responsibility	16.66	166.6	267	367	467	567
3	Information/records responsibility	16.66	166.6	267	367	467	567
4	Communications	16.66	166.6	267	367	467	567
5	Complexity	16.66	166.6	267	367	467	567
6	Decision making and judgement	16.66	166.6	267	367	467	567
	Total	99.96	1000	1600	2200	2800	3400

Note: Grade bandings
Grade 1   1000–1280 points
Grade 2   1281–1560 points
Grade 3   1561–1840 points
Grade 4   1841–2120 points
Grade 5   2121–2400 points
Grade 6   2401–2680 points
Grade 7   2681–2960 points
Grade 8   2961–3400 points

11.6 Modern forms of job evaluation

A variety of hybrid forms of job evaluation have been developed that place particular emphasis on certain aspects of job evaluation. For example, the so-called 'consensus' method places emphasis on achieving consensus amongst employees on the grades to be allocated. Some are named after the firm of management consultants that promulgate them. A well known example is the 'Hay' method. This method uses just three factors to evaluate jobs:

• knowhow;
• problem solving;
• accountability.

Each factor has further sub-factors. The Hay method is not a pure job evaluation technique because it also takes account of market forces. Companies which subscribe to the system have the benefit of an information service in market trends for jobs and an indication of what value should be attached to the points allocated to each job.

Some companies incorporate competencies into their job evaluation schemes, in order to recognise the importance of job competencies. This trend is examined in Chapter 12.

11.7 Introducing and maintaining job evaluation

The practical problems of choosing, introducing and maintaining a job evaluation scheme can exceed the technical problem of understanding and choosing the best method.[1]

Starting from scratch is an expensive business, because of the time required in analysing jobs and servicing consultative committees. Union consent may need to be gained and this can lead to tough bargaining. The official trade union line is not usually hostile to job evaluation, but trade unions not surprisingly demand adequate union representation on committees supervising the project. Naturally, union representatives may try to wrest maximum financial advantage for their members. Frequently job evaluation schemes are introduced as part of a package deal with unions when bargains are struck on related matters such as manning levels and pay increases. Once a scheme has been installed there is a dangerous temptation to assume it will continue to operate successfully for many years without much effort. But all job evaluation schemes decay over a period of time, as the organisation itself changes to meet new situations. Resources have to be made available to carry out regradings as job content changes.

11.8 Criticisms of job evaluation

In spite of its apparent advantages and rationality, job evaluation has been fiercely criticised and some companies have stopped using it.[2] A major criticism used to be that it reinforced discrimination, particularly sexual discrimination, in the labour force. This was because heavier weighting seemed to be given to factors favouring men, such as strength or apprenticeship training, whereas factors covering such skills as dexterity or caring which featured in women's work were lowly weighted. This situation has now been largely rectified. Job evaluation finds favour with industrial tribunals because it creates a payment system that is open to external inspection and correction.

The most serious criticism of job evaluation arises from its bureaucratic nature.[3] Because it is based on job description, it assumes a degree of stability and hierarchy that is increasingly unrealistic in a world of rapid change. Organisations have to be flexible and responsive, and this means that staff must accept that their jobs are also susceptible to rapid change. Demarcation of jobs is a hindrance. Of late, market rates of pay have been held to be of greater significance than internal relativities by many employers. Modern forms of team working require different forms of payment.

11.9 Payment by results

For the greater part of this century, 'payment by results' (PBR) has been the term given to pay schemes which link earnings to output and attempt to motivate workers, usually manual workers, to higher levels of productivity. The term reflects the tradition of distinguishing between pay schemes for manual (or blue collar) workers and office (or white collar) workers, hence the terms 'wages' and 'salaries'. Traditionally, PBR has been seen as part of wage administration and the domain of work study engineers. Happily these status distinctions are being broken down, with the adoption of single status agreements. PBR systems remain widely used in industry – an estimated one-third of manual workers receiving some form of payment by results.[4] But modern methods offer a considerable improvement on old-fashioned piecework techniques. Traditionally, PBR was payment by unit of output. Widespread introductions of time and method study led to systems based on time allowances, arrived at by using a range of techniques, from the simple stopwatch to complex synthetic data and Predetermined Motion Time Systems (PMTS). As part of this process 'effort rating' undertaken by time study engineers may help to achieve fair time allowances, i.e. a systematic estimate of the effort being put into jobs by workers to determine the time a worker of 'effective worker standard' (EWS) should take for job completion, making due allowances for fatigue, rest pauses, and unavoidable interruptions. This can then be converted into standard minute values (SMVs), enabling workers to be measured and paid according to a standard performance scale, such as the popular 60/80 scale, or the 0–100 (British Standards Institute) scale. These scales are based on the notion that workers on payment by results are likely to work faster than workers on a time rate, and should be rewarded accordingly. Thus with the 60/80 scale the timeworker is estimated to put in a '60' performance, the PBR worker an '80' performance (i.e. 1/3 higher). Target remuneration for a PBR worker should therefore be set correspondingly higher. PBR workers have the opportunity to earn considerably more than time workers, how much more depending on the system in use. The ILO defines four types of gearing of performance to pay, namely proportional, regressive, progressive, and variable. Under a 'proportional' system payment increases in the same proportion as output. A 'regressive' scheme means that payment increases proportionately less than output. Traditional schemes such as Bedaux, Halsey and Rowan fall in this category. Because payment per unit decreases as output rises, labour costs decrease as output increases, although the worker has to work harder to increase his income. Under a progressive scheme the reverse happens, i.e. payment increases proportionately more than output. Employees are thus encouraged to achieve higher levels of output, but management encounters problems of cost control. With variable systems, payment increases in proportions which differ at different levels of output, as illustrated by Figure 11.2.

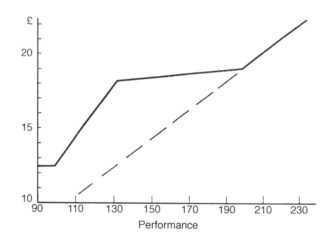

Figure 11.2 Example of 'variable' payment by results
system using BSI scale

Variable schemes may encourage higher output up to a certain level of performance, but can be complicated to install and difficult for employees to understand. Many firms operate PBR schemes which are based on 'time rate plus', i.e. workers are guaranteed a certain basic rate, and payment by results are then added to this. Frequently 'fall-back' rates also operate or other methods of guaranteeing earnings in the event of stoppages. 'Lieu bonuses' are often paid to certain categories of timeworkers, usually skilled workers such as maintenance craftsmen, to preserve differentials between them and production workers.

Group bonus and group PBR schemes operate along similar lines, but with the output targets set for groups of workers, e.g. on a production line. Bonus payments are then shared by members of the group. Such schemes may encourage group cooperation but discourage individual effort (examined further below).

Modified forms of PBR

In order to overcome some of the problems associated with traditional PBR systems, a number of modified schemes have been designed. Measured day work schemes, for example, determine the level of performance to be expected of an effective worker using work measurement techniques, and then fix an appropriate level of payment. Workers are expected to maintain this level of performance and to cooperate with management in return for guaranteed earnings and job security. Premium Payment Plan (PPP) is a graduated form of measured day work allowing workers some choice of performance level and the associated rate of pay. Under this system a worker can improve his or her pay in two ways – by achieving a higher level of performance over a specified period in the present job or by moving to a job in a higher classification.

Criticisms of PBR

As with all management systems, there are arguments both in favour and against, and once again we have to consider what is best in a particular situation. PBR can accentuate hostility between management and workers when PBR is seen as a management tool to extort more work out of workers, and when workers feel that work is being devalued to a series of hostile negotiations over money for effort. Added to this these are genuine problems of measuring effort and the risk that pressure for output will lead to poor quality work and a neglect of health and safety standards. PBR also provides opportunity for trade unions to demonstrate their support for their members by constantly arguing the toss over rates of pay, as well as providing an opportunity for workers to devote their energies to outwitting management and work study engineers rather than getting on with the job.

However, available evidence indicates that PBR can work where the scheme is well thought out, when working methods lend themselves to measurement, where industrial relations are good, and where high levels of communication and consultation take place before schemes are introduced. The introduction of PBR needs to be accompanied by support from managers at all levels, a relevant training and education programme, and a consultative approach. Evidence indicates that successful schemes have three main features in common:[5]

- They do not seek an immediate payback, but see PBR as part of an overall package of human resource initiatives designed to improve motivation and performance in the long term.
- Senior managers are committed to developing effective procedures.
- The objectives of the payment system are related to those of the organisation.

11.10 Gainsharing

Gainsharing (also known as 'value-added') pay schemes have been adopted by employers who feel strongly that employees should see a connection between the contribution their efforts make to the prosperity of the enterprise, and the rewards they receive as a share of the value added to the product or service. Thus it is felt that employees can be encouraged to identify with the fruits of their labours and to participate in improving working methods. Such schemes require a high degree of commitment by management, a willingness to disclose information, good labour relations and careful measurement.

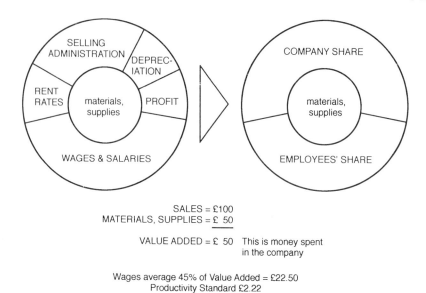

SALES = £100
MATERIALS, SUPPLIES = £ 50

VALUE ADDED = £ 50   This is money spent
in the company

Wages average 45% of Value Added = £22.50
Productivity Standard £2.22

Figure 11.3 Gainsharing: the value-added 'doughnut'

Wages are an agreed proportion of the monetary sum derived by subtracting the cost of materials and other supplies, from sales revenue. A simplified version is illustrated in Figure 11.3.

The two best-known versions of value-added schemes are the Scanlon Plan and the Rucker Plan. The first, developed in the 1930s in the USA by Joe Scanlon (an ex-steel worker and union official who wished to see a sensible conclusion to the conflict between management and employees over pay levels), focused on the whole organisation, and involved unions and employees as well as management in productivity improvements. The Plan provides for 75 per cent of gains being distributed to employees with 25 per cent going to the firm. A similar idea was inherent in the Rucker Plan except that it modified the distribution to reflect the relative contributions of labour and capital in the particular organisation. A number of successful value-added schemes are currently in operation in the USA. Typically, the successful scheme shows productivity improvements of between 5 per cent and 15 per cent in the first year of operation together with an improvement in product quality. But there have been failures too, notably associated with bonus levels which fell short of employees' expectations as well as inconsistencies in the treatment of different groups. A modified version of a value-added scheme has been in operation at Volvo's plant at Kalmar, Sweden, where gains from productivity are shared between the company and employees, all of whom receive regular briefings from team representatives. In addition plant-wide assemblies take place twice each year.[6]

11.11 Salary structures

Salary structures composed of a range of pay grades and incremental scales within each of those grades are still widely used, despite recent trends to downsizing and delayering. A typical company structure is depicted in Figure 11.4.

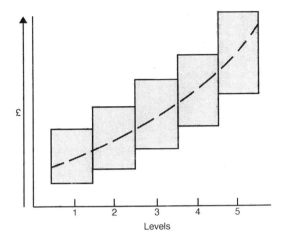

Figure 11.4 Example of graded salary structure
with varying overlap

Three fundamental decisions in developing such a structure concern the number of pay grades, the range within each grade, and the amount of overlap between each grade. Structures incorporating a large number of grades, typically found in many public sector organisations, make promotion a relatively easy matter while devaluing the significance of promotion. Conversely, a structure with relatively few grades enhances the significance of promotion but decreases flexibility. Grades with a large measure of overlap devalue the financial significance of promotion but may lead to less pressure for promotion. Grades that embrace a wide range of pay permit a large number of incremental increases (usually justified on the grounds that experience and service deserve some reward) but can mean that two persons with different lengths of service doing the same job receive widely different rates of pay. It is possible to control progression through a pay grade in order to ensure higher rewards and faster progress for staff earning good appraisal reports. This is illustrated in Figure 11.5.

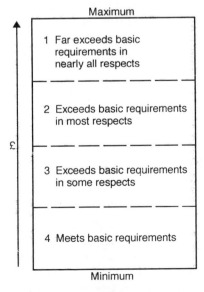

Figure 11.5 Salary grade relating progression to performance

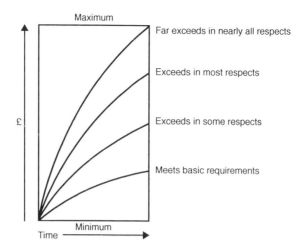

Maximum

Far exceeds in nearly all respects

Exceeds in most respects

£

Exceeds in some respects

Meets basic requirements

Minimum

Time

Figure 11.6 Salary progression curves

A system of differential rewards can be taken one stage further by use of so-called 'salary progression curves'. These curves depict the movement of employees' salaries over a period of time, and can be viewed both as a historical process and a prediction for the future, as shown in Figure 11.6.

Unified pay structures are frequently used in the public sector, covering all sections of the workforce. Whilst similar to conventional large company pay structures depicted in Figure 11.5 above, they represent the values found in much of the public sector. A typical pay spine structure is depicted in Figure 11.7.

11.12 Merit awards

Merit awards for salaried staff attempt to reward higher levels of performance. Fewer pay schemes now award annual automatic cost of living increases to all employees; instead, any pay increases are referred to as 'merit awards' and some employees receive no increase. These may be linked to some form of appraisal (examined in Chapter 12).

The evidence in favour of such merit awards is not clear-cut: while in theory they should stimulate greater effort, in practice, they can run into a number of practical problems. Staff may not be convinced that the merit awards are fairly based and the value of the awards may be insufficient to motivate staff. There is evidence that an increase of at least 10–15 per cent is necessary to stimulate greater effort.[7] In the UK such awards have averaged only 7 per cent.[8] The 'pay for performance' schemes described in Chapter 12 are now making their mark and have replaced many former merit schemes.

11.13 Team working

Team working is now becoming increasingly common among UK manufacturing companies, influenced by the successful example of Japanese companies setting up on greenfield sites in the UK.[9] It has subsequently been adopted in some large offices for white-collar workers. The flattening of management structures has widened spans of control, leading to the development of team working as a means of managing in this new environment. However, progress in developing corresponding forms of team-based pay has been rather slower. An Institute of Employment Studies survey found fewer than 10 per cent of organisations with team working had any form of team-based pay.[10] A more recent IPD study

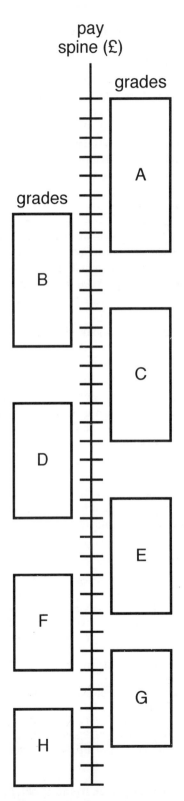

Figure 11.7 A typical pay spine

found nearly a quarter of the organisations in its study had established a formal link between team performance and pay.[11] This study found that the most popular approach was the use of team bonuses or incentive pay, but team payments were also used as part of the individual assessment process or within a competency-based pay scheme. The main reason given for developing team rewards was the need to encourage group endeavour rather than individual performance. While over half of the respondents in the IPD survey were confident that it had improved team performance, only 22 per cent could quantify the gain.

The evidence is that team-based pay must be introduced with care, and depends on the existence of well-defined and mature teams. It should not be introduced in isolation, and should be supported with non-financial rewards such as positive feedback, praise and recognition.

11.14 Employee benefits

The management of employee benefits is an important part of pay policy and reward management. The cost of benefits can amount to more than a quarter of direct pay costs, and benefits play an important role in attracting and retaining staff. Many employee benefits which are now part of the employment package started out as welfare services. As well as pensions and holidays, typical large company benefits include company cars, subsidised catering, life assurance, private health insurance, assistance with mortgages, day nurseries and social facilities. To this list some would add forms of deferred pay such as share options and profit sharing.

A philosophy of pay for performance favours 'clean cash' in preference to expenditure on benefits so as to reinforce the link between rewards and results. However, benefits are popular with many employers. The company car is now established as an important 'perk' in the UK. Some companies favour a 'cafeteria' approach (sometimes termed 'flexible benefits') for executives, allowing a degree of choice between various benefits and cash, as long as the cost to the firm remains the same.[12] This element of choice is held to increase the attractiveness of the rewards. Experience indicates that three factors in particular have to be watched carefully if cafeteria benefits are to succeed – tax law on benefits, control of the costs of administration, and communications.[13] Employee benefits should be reviewed on a regular basis to ensure that they are still achieving the desired results and that the organisation is getting good value for its money.

11.15 References

1. Fowler A. How to choose a job evaluation scheme. *IPD Personnel Plus* 1992; October: 33–4.
2. Spencer S. Devolving job evaluation. *Personnel Management* 1990; January: 48–50.
3. Wickens P. Job evaluation mitigates against change. *Personnel Management* 1988; April: 11.
4. Incomes Data Services Ltd. *Bonus schemes*. Study 547, 1994; February.
5. Kinnie M. Performance related pay on the shop floor. *Personnel Management* 1990; November: 45–9.
6. Hanck WC, Ross TL. Sweden's experiments in productivity gainsharing: a second look. *Personnel* 1987; January: 61–9.
7. Kanter RM *et al.* From status to contribution: some organisational implications of the changing basis for pay. *Personnel* 1987; January: 27–33.
8. Murlis H. The myths about performance pay. *Personnel Management* 1993; August: 18.
9. Incomes Data Services Ltd. *Teamworking*. IDS Study 516. 1992; October.
10. Thompson M. *Team based performance pay*. Brighton: Institute of Employment Studies, 1994.
11. Armstrong M. How group efforts can pay dividends. *People Management* 1996; 25 January: 22–7.
12. Incomes Data Services Ltd. *Flexible benefits*. IDS Study 481, London: IDS, May.
13. Woodley C. The cafeteria route to compensation. *Personnel Management* 1990; May: 42–5.

12 Appraising and rewarding performance

Alan Cowling

The quest to link rewards to performance has a long history. One of the earliest approaches, payment by results, was examined in Chapter 11. As jobs have come to require greater and greater amounts of discretion by job holders, and as the service sector has grown in significance, traditional forms of work measurement have become less and less relevant, and new approaches have been developed, frequently seeking to improve future performance, rather than simply rewarding what was perceived as good past performance. As a result many appraisal schemes have incorporated elements of 'management by objectives', and more recently, attention has been paid to so-called 'performance management' schemes that attempt to link individual objectives with corporate and departmental goals. At the same time many companies have been developing competency profiles for their jobs, and have consequently attempted to link rewards with the manifest capacity to carry out a good job of work. All three approaches can be found today in many organisations.

12.1 Appraisal

Carried out properly, appraisal is an essential part of good management, stimulating a two-way flow of useful information between managers and subordinates that continuously clarifies roles and objectives and engenders support in the pursuit of mutually agreed goals. Appraisal is considered in this chapter in the context of reward management, although it also has a significant role in training and development and in career planning. Opinion is divided over the use of appraisal for both pay and development purposes. Those who favour limiting its use to development argue that linking it to pay can undermine attempts to provide honest feedback and an emotion-free review of strengths and weaknesses and participative setting of targets.[1] Those who support the linking of appraisal to pay argue that pay should be seen to be linked to performance in order to increase motivation and to establish the credibility of pay decisions. There can be no right or wrong answer to this dilemma; as with most management decisions of this nature, it all depends on key variables present in the situation.

Because so many problems have arisen in the past in the design and implementation of appraisal schemes, many have questioned their worth.[2,3] The principal argument in favour of formalised appraisal schemes is that they place the process of subjective judgement onto a more objective basis, a basis moreover that is open to scrutiny. The principal arguments against formalised appraisal schemes are that a high proportion have failed to meet their objectives, and in the process have alienated both staff and management, and that the process of formalisation leads to the bureaucratisation of what should essentially be a natural process. It is possible, however, to develop appraisal schemes that avoid these mistakes, and make a really useful contribution to the objectives of the organisation, reward good performers, help all employees to do better, and enhance the personal sense of achievement of all concerned. The principal considerations, based on research evidence and examples of best practice, are enumerated below.

The first consideration is clarity concerning aims. Is the aim primarily to improve current performance, to ascertain staff development needs, or to reward high performers? The evidence from research and practice is that no system can achieve all these aims simultaneously. But the biggest mistake is to think that the introduction of an appraisal scheme can by itself rectify serious defects in the manner in which an organisation is managed. Therefore before introducing formal appraisal a management audit needs to be carried out, asking such key questions as:

- Has the organisation a clear mission and a well-thought-out corporate strategy?
- Has it communicated these to employees?
- Are managers well trained in managing people?
- Do attitude surveys indicate high levels of job satisfaction?

Having satisfied these preliminary considerations, decisions must be taken about how formalised the appraisal scheme needs to be. The critical question here is the extent to which the organisation needs to be run on bureaucratic or decentralised and flexible lines. A bureaucratic hierarchical structure requires a matching highly formalised appraisal system based on well-defined job descriptions. However, very few organisations these days can afford to be bureaucratic, because bureaucracies cannot adapt easily to change, and for most organisations the environment is undergoing rapid change. Therefore, most organisations will require appraisal systems that are both simple and flexible, and easy to operate.

The third consideration is just what is to be appraised. The evidence from research and experience is that the primary focus should be on the achievement of results, and not on personality traits. Individuals can do very little to change their personalities, but they can do much about improving their performance. This indicates that appraisal forms should focus on the results aimed for, and whether they are being achieved.

The fourth consideration is how to measure or 'appraise' performance. This requires realistic quantifiable targets, with specific time spans for their achievement. Measurement can then concentrate on the extent to which results are being achieved by a due date.

The fifth consideration is participation. To what extent should subordinates participate in the setting of performance aims? As brought out in Chapter 10, the evidence is that other things being equal, the more individuals genuinely participate in the setting of goals, the more committed they are to achieving them, the more likely they are to improve their performance.

The sixth consideration is training, both the training and development of subordinates and of superiors. Subordinates will need training and development in order to achieve targets, and superiors carrying out appraisal will need training in the skills of appraisal. Many managers do not find appraisal an easy job to carry out, and lack the skills to conduct appraisal interviews. Appropriate investment in training is essential.

The seventh consideration is timing. Should appraisals be once a year, or more frequent? Traditionally appraisal has been conducted once a year in order to coincide with the annual salary review, linked in turn to the financial year. But a one-year cycle is rarely appropriate to work tasks. Work tasks may have natural cycles that range from days to months or even years. Therefore it may be right to conduct appraisals ('performance reviews') at any time in the year to mark the conclusion of relevant tasks or projects.

The final consideration is 'ownership'. The appraisal scheme must be 'owned' by those who operate it, and this usually means line management. A scheme foisted on to managers by HRM colleagues will not work if it is not perceived as being helpful. This calls for considerable consultation and delegation, and at the same time a degree of monitoring and evaluation to ensure that schemes work well.

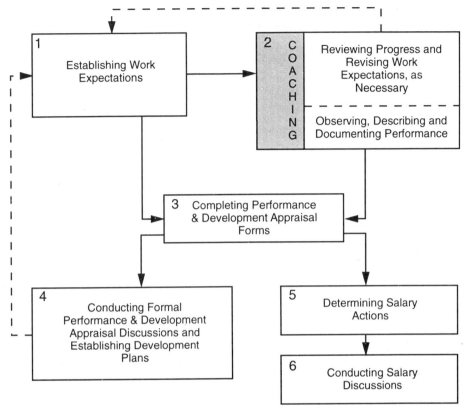

Source: Page RC, Tornow, WW, *Personnel Administrator*, January 1985

Figure 12.1 Conventional company performance appraisal process

The basis of a good appraisal system planned and administered on conventional lines is brought out in Figure 12.1.

Note the emphasis on coaching in Figure 12.1. Line management has the primary responsibility in high-performance organisations for coaching and developing their staff.

12.2 Behaviour scales

On the grounds that it is behaviour rather than personality that should be appraised and rewarded, many appraisal schemes include behaviour scales. Competency schemes, examined below, represent a form of behaviour scale.

Behaviour scales describe a range of behaviours that contribute to a greater or lesser degree to the successful achievement of the cluster of tasks which make up a job. Supervisors conducting an appraisal are asked to indicate which statements on the specially designed form most accurately describe a subordinate's behaviour. A sophisticated version of this approach is represented by 'Behaviourally Anchored Rating Scales' (BARS). Statements about work behaviour are used to create scales, which must then be tested to confirm their relevance and precision. This is a time-consuming process, and

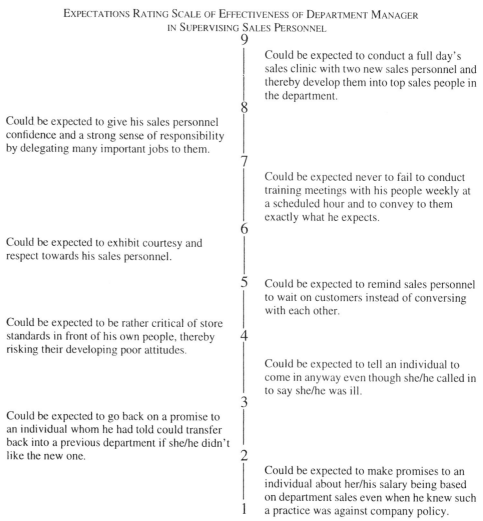

EXPECTATIONS RATING SCALE OF EFFECTIVENESS OF DEPARTMENT MANAGER
IN SUPERVISING SALES PERSONNEL

9

Could be expected to conduct a full day's sales clinic with two new sales personnel and thereby develop them into top sales people in the department.

8

Could be expected to give his sales personnel confidence and a strong sense of responsibility by delegating many important jobs to them.

7

Could be expected never to fail to conduct training meetings with his people weekly at a scheduled hour and to convey to them exactly what he expects.

6

Could be expected to exhibit courtesy and respect towards his sales personnel.

5

Could be expected to remind sales personnel to wait on customers instead of conversing with each other.

Could be expected to be rather critical of store standards in front of his own people, thereby risking their developing poor attitudes.

4

Could be expected to tell an individual to come in anyway even though she/he called in to say she/he was ill.

3

Could be expected to go back on a promise to an individual whom he had told could transfer back into a previous department if she/he didn't like the new one.

2

Could be expected to make promises to an individual about her/his salary being based on department sales even when he knew such a practice was against company policy.

1

Source: Journal of Applied Psychology 1973, **57**: 15–22

Figure 12.2 Behaviour rating scale

although a number of claims for its success have been made, further evaluation is needed.[4] An example is provided in Figure 12.2.

12.3 Multiple rating in appraisal

Traditional appraisal systems have involved just the appraiser and the appraisee. Recent developments in appraisal have seen a move away from one-to-one rating towards multiple rating, which in turn may involve lateral and upward appraisal. Flatter organisation structures, moves to empower employees, participative leadership styles, the recent emphasis on self-development rather than course attendance, and the possible trauma induced by downward appraisal in the appraisee, have led many leading companies to forms of multiple assessment. The best known version is the so-called '360 degree

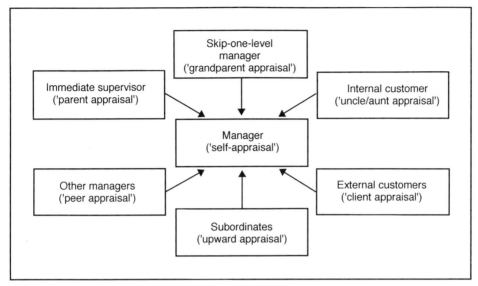

Source: Redman T, Snape E, *Personnel Review* 1992; **21**(7): 33

Figure 12.3 Potential appraisers in a multi-appraisal system for managers

appraisal', in which comment on performance is provided by subordinates and peers as well as superiors. The range of possible options is illustrated in Figure 12.3.

Typical large organisation 360 degree appraisal schemes are designed to enable the principal 'stakeholders' in a person's performance to comment and provide feedback. This may include the boss, direct and indirect reports, peers, and internal and external customers.[5] Information is usually collected through questionnaires. The locus of the appraisal thus shifts from a formal one-to-one appraisal interview situation to one where feedback is received in the less hostile environment of the normal place of work, and support by counselling and assistance is then offered as appropriate. Confidentiality for the appraisee and anonymity for the respondents is clearly very important.

Possible pitfalls include a negative emphasis, lack of confidentiality, poor communication, lack of support, and that traditional British failing, a 'flavour of the month' approach. Research evidence on the effectiveness of these types of schemes in improving organisational performance is still limited but the potential benefits of broadening the base of appraisal appeals to many companies.[6] Strong reservations are still expressed about linking multi-appraisal to pay review. A recent survey showed 81 per cent of top UK companies limiting it to staff development purposes.[7]

Another recent development has been the introduction of the so-called 'balanced score card'. This measures management performance across a range of categories, employing multiple feedback that can include both staff and customer comments. Typically, staff may be asked to complete a questionnaire concerning the performance of their management team, and this will influence the size of the pay rise accorded to their managers.[8]

12.4 Performance management

Performance management is a comprehensive term describing a process in which employees participate with their superiors in setting their own performance targets. These targets are directly aligned with the stated goals of their departments. As part of the process, employees are provided with the training and resources needed to achieve their targets, and are rewarded for achieving these targets. In this way rewards and appraisal are specifically linked into an organisation's mission and goals, in a manner rarely achieved in traditional appraisal schemes.[9]

Well-developed performance management systems will usually incorporate the following items:

- a statement outlining the organisation's values;
- a statement of the organisation's objectives;
- individual objectives which are linked to the organisation's objectives;
- regular performance reviews throughout the year;
- performance-related pay;
- training and counselling.

An example of this system in practice is shown in Figure 12.4.

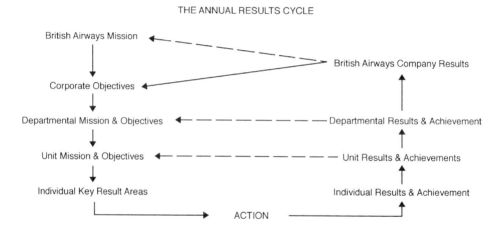

Figure 12.4 Performance management, company annual results cycle

On the face of it, performance management appears to be a sensible way of managing any organisation. However the evidence is that only one-fifth of large organisations have adopted a performance management approach.[10] The success of performance management can be restricted by any of the following:

- a reactive rather than pro-active strategy;
- insufficient involvement by line management;
- a climate of fear;
- over-emphasis on bottom line results;
- introduced simply as a performance-related pay scheme;
- too much red tape.

But when these mistakes have been avoided, or have been rectified, the results are usually beneficial.[11] It is not yet possible to demonstrate a long-term link between performance management and economic success, but when properly executed it represents a more sensible system of motivating and rewarding staff than the old-fashioned bureaucratic systems it has been replacing.

12.5 Pay for skills

Traditionally skilled workers have been paid more than their less skilled fellow workers. New technology means that unskilled jobs are disappearing rapidly and there is now an emphasis on quality, team working, and adaptability. This in turn requires new skills and new attitudes. In order to acquire and retain a workforce with appropriate skills, and support the acceptance of new values and attitudes, some employers are linking rewards directly to the acquisition of relevant skills.[12] For this to work, the amount of money attached to the acquisition and demonstration of a relevant skill needs to be sufficient to encourage employees to make the necessary effort.

Skills-based pay (SBP) is on the increase in both the manufacturing and service sectors. Nearly one-quarter of employers responding to an IPM/NEDO survey said that they had introduced changes to their payment systems in the past two years aimed at encouraging the acquisition of new skills.[13]

The two most common approaches are to pay one or more skill supplements linked to the acquisition of skill modules, or to create higher pay grades for those with extra skills. Research by Incomes Data Services established that in their case study, companies' payments per module ranged from about £200 to £700, the average being about £300.[14] The second approach is to create a separate multi-skilled pay grade. In such cases, multi-skilled status is more likely to be seen as promotion and the precise pay level may depend on the nature of the subsequent job.

Having decided on multi-skilling, an employer needs to create a training programme to equip craft workers with the requisite skills. In many cases training is linked to national NVQ or City and Guilds standards.

Experience to date indicates that it is not suitable for all situations, requires careful planning, and needs to be preceded by a more participative and open system of working. Significant resources need to be devoted to training, which includes training in new skills and in team working. Rewards need to be linked not only to the acquisition of skills but to their application, and possibly also to the performance achieved.[15]

12.6 Competency-based pay

A widely used definition of competency describes it as 'an underlying characteristic of an individual which is casually related to effective or superior performance in a job'. A working definition of competency, used in a large UK telecommunications company, describes it as 'a combination of skills, knowledge, behaviour and personal attributes which together are necessary to perform a job effectively and which provide the basis for an objective and consistent review of performance and development needs'. Competencies can include motives, traits, self-concepts, attitudes or values, content knowledge, or cognitive or behavioural skills.

At the level of the organisation, a process of isolating and measuring so-called 'core competencies' is required. It is these core competencies that can then be used for selection, training, and reward management purposes. A summary list for senior managers might include the following:

- analytical thinking;
- pattern recognition;
- strategic thinking;
- persuasion;
- use of influence strategies;
- personal impact;
- motivating.

Competency	Negative indicators	Marking	Positive indicators
Strategic Awareness – The extent to which the appraisee is aware of the Bank's competitive situation, is able to recognise business opportunities and threats and can relate these wider issues to own area of responsibility.	• Out of touch with strategic events and their results. • Infrequently identifies competitive opportunities and threats. • Sees own work in isolation from the wider context.	☐6 ☐5 ☐4 ☐3 ☐2 ☐1 Self-Appraisal Mark	• Clearly aware of strategic events occurring outside and inside the Group. • Identifies competitive opportunities and threats. • Sees how own work fits into the wider context.
Initiative – The extent to which the appraisee will promote pro-actively and take personal responsibility for the achievement of goals and changes which are beneficial to the Group.	• Takes a rigid and narrow view of own responsibilities. • Conforms to established ways of doing things without identifying improvements. • Tends to resist change or gives little help to those initiating change.	☐6 ☐5 ☐4 ☐3 ☐2 ☐1 Self-Appraisal Mark	• Expands own responsibilities to seek business opportunities. • Identifies ways of improving the way work is done. • Takes the action needed to ensure that changes happen.
Decisiveness – The readiness to take decisions and render judgements even though they may be difficult and/or unpopular.	• Reluctant to take decisions; will disown decisions. • Unable to explain or justify decisions. • Gives way too easily when pressurised or dogmatically supports decisions that cannot be defended.	☐6 ☐5 ☐4 ☐3 ☐2 ☐1 Self-Appraisal Mark	• Makes decisions and takes responsibility for their results. • Easily explains and justifies decisions. • Reviews a decision if new information makes this essential.
Technical Knowledge and Experience – The degree to which the appraisee demonstrates breadth and depth of technical knowledge and experience in the performance of his/her duties.	• Shows little evidence of technical expertise in performance. • Content to rely on basic knowledge, makes little effort to keep abreast of technical developments. • Unable to apply technical knowledge and experience in practical situations.	☐6 ☐5 ☐4 ☐3 ☐2 ☐1 Self-Appraisal Mark	• Possesses a high level of technical expertise and experience relevant to present duties. • Keeps abreast of relevant technical developments. • Applies technical knowledge and experience to enhance job performance.

Figure 12.5 Typical competency-based appraisal scheme for bank managers

These can be built into the appraisal system, and rewarded according to standards attained in each area. Linking competencies to explicit forms of behaviour ensures that they are linked to the type of performance which contributes to organisational goals. Figure 12.5 provides an example of competencies built into a company appraisal scheme.

A job family may consist of a number of competency bands, each of which constitutes a definable level of skill, competency and responsibility. Individuals move through these bands at a rate which is related to their performance and their capacity to develop.[16] There are three different types of competency-based pay structures – narrow-banded, broad-banded, and performance pay curves, all associated with job families.

Competency-based pay currently takes two different forms. One makes pay contingent on achieving certain levels of competency: if competency increases, then so does pay. The other is that of evaluating and grading jobs in relation to competency. A recent study in the UK found considerable interest in competency-based job evaluation schemes, but no wide-spread take-up. The survey also found considerable confusion and disagreement on the nature and definition of competencies, and warns against paying for the acquisition of competencies rather than their effective use in the workplace.[17]

Implementing skill-based and competency-based pay schemes requires a considerable investment in time and the establishment of procedures. Care must be taken to ensure that the cost of this investment and the imposition of over-elaborate procedures do not out-weigh the benefits of these schemes.

12.7 References

1. Fletcher C, Williams R. *Performance appraisal and career development.* London: Hutchinson, 1985.
2. McGregor D. An uneasy look at performance appraisal. *Harvard Business Review* 1957; **35**(3): 89–94.
3. Latham M. Job performance and appraisal. In: Cooper CL, Robertson I eds. *International review of industrial and organisational psychology.* Chichester: Wiley, 1986.
4. Campbell JP *et al.* The development and evaluation of behaviourally based rating scales. *Journal of Applied Psychology* 1973; **57**: 15–22.
5. Ward M. A 360 degree turn for the better. *People Management* 1995; 9 Feb.: 20–5.
6. Redman T, Snape E. Upward and onward: can staff appraise their managers?. *Personnel Review* 1992; **21**(7): 32–46.
7. Platt S. Viewed from all angles. *Personnel Today* 1996; 22 October: 45–7.
8. Littlefield D. Halifax employees to assess management. *People Management* 1996; 8 Feb.: 5.
9. Yeates JD. *Performance appraisal: a guide for design and implementation.* IMS Report No. 188. London: Institute of Manpower Studies, 1990.
10. Fletcher C, Williams R. The route to performance management. *Personnel Management* 1992; October: 45–7.
11. Incomes Data Services Ltd. *Performance management.* London: IDS Study 518, November 1992.
12. Edward E, Lawler M. Paying the person: a better approach to management?. *Human Resource Management Review* 1991; **1**(2): 145–54.
13. Cross M, Cannell M. *Skills-based pay: a guide for practitioners.* London: Institute of Personnel Management, 1992.
14. Incomes Data Services Ltd. *Skill-based pay.* IDS study 500. London: IDS, February 1992.
15. Incomes Data Services Ltd. *Paying for multi-skilling.* London: IDS Ltd, IDS Study 610, September 1996.
16. Armstrong M, Murlis H. *Reward Management*, 3rd edn, London: Kogan Page, 1994.
17. Institute of Personnel and Development. *Survey on job evaluation.* London: IPD, 1995.

SECTION V
INTERNATIONAL HUMAN RESOURCE MANAGEMENT

Introduction

Some large organisations, such as Unilever, Shell and Ford, have long been international in their scope and operations, and have developed sophisticated international HR policies and practices. Today there is a strong trend towards internationalisation as the world of commerce grows smaller, and corporations seek the benefits of global markets. This trend has been reinforced by the expansion of trade within the European Union, and it is not only the large and well-known corporations such as BT, BA, Rover and Midland Bank, which are having to face up to the new HRM implications of becoming more international. Immigration is also changing the composition of the workforce, forcing an acceptance of cultural diversity.

In Chapter 13 a useful analysis of the manner in which different cultures impact on work behaviour is provided. The implications of the changing roles of expatriate managers, appropriate forms of staffing and reward management, the transfer of management practices across national barriers, and the manner in which HRM practices and policies can best take on an international dimension, are given detailed consideration.

13 International human resource management

Wendy Banfield

13.1 Importance of international HRM

Business is increasingly being transacted across national boundaries, within a highly competitive global context. Market place competitiveness – on price/cost/value/quality/innovation – is essential for business survival and, in the long term, most companies need to aim for growth, whether in domestic or foreign markets, to survive, otherwise stronger global competitors will take over their traditional domestic markets. In countries such as the UK, domestic markets for certain goods are saturated, so companies need to look overseas for growth opportunities.

The rate of 'internationalisation' of business will increase, not decrease, so an appreciation of aspects of business internationalisation will become ever more important for a manager. Business is carried out by and through people, whether customers, suppliers or employees, so those without some appreciation of managing people in an international context start with a career handicap. Even within national boundaries, the challenge of effectively managing a multicultural workforce is exercising many organisations.

What is international HRM?

International HRM is neither copying people management practices from other countries, as cultural differences inhibit effective transfer, nor learning about the cultures of every other country and modifying behaviour accordingly, as this is too time-consuming and more than slight behaviour adaptation is hard.[1] What characterises international HRM is the interaction between the human resource functions, countries and types of employees:[2] parent country nationals (PCNs), local or host country nationals (HCNs), and nationals from neither the parent nor host country but from a third country (TCNs).[3] This creates greater complexity than is encountered when managing people within one country, plus the need for cross-cultural sensitivity.

What specifically comprises the human resource function will vary over time, between companies and countries, as will the identity of whoever – HRM specialist or line manager – executes these functions. International HRM is a fluid dynamic entity,[4] changing whenever pressures in the organisation's internal or external environment result in alterations to the business.[5]

As HRM is dynamic and context-specific, international HRM is not one theory, system or prescriptive approach to managing people, which can be applied globally. Each country and industry will have its own characteristics and thus its own HRM style. However, as some of the external environmental pressures, such as political systems, laws, economy, will influence all organisations within one country, there will be characteristics sufficiently in common to suggest national characteristics influencing HRM in that country, which can be used as guidelines by the non-national considering business there.

The areas of HRM practice which change significantly or require attention when undertaken internationally are, according to Torrington:[6]

- cosmopolitans (employing people who spend part of their time in another country);
- culture;
- compensation;
- communication;
- consultancy;
- competence (of people to work across cultural and national boundaries);
- coordination (between the parts of the organisation).

Whatever else international HRM is or is not, it also has relevance for the manager of a multicultural workforce[7] operating within one country, as it is essentially about 'managing people', not necessarily employees, from culturally divergent backgrounds and it includes developing the processes, mechanisms and links needed to do so effectively.

Variables influencing international HRM

Variables internal to the company: the organisation can choose its policies and practices, structure, and staffing approaches. Although influenced by the external environment at strategic and operational level, these are largely within organisational control.

Variables external to the company: the political, economic, sociological, technological context of the country in which the company is operating. Traditionally, these are seen from an organisational perspective as uncontrollable variables with a one-way influence on internal variables and business strategy, rather than vice versa. Over time, however, the aggregation effect of similar business strategies or HRM practices across several organisations operating in the same external environment can influence the external variables. For example, the HR practices of several companies can influence the attitude of people to what is perceived as a 'good' employer.

Competitive position: the business strategy, deriving from the organisation's competitive position, governs the nature of international HRM initiatives to some extent. If competition is largely on price, HRM initiatives which increase cost without adding positive value will be inappropriate.

A multinational enterprise (MNE) has to consider specific socio-economic, political, technical, and competitive variables and internal organisational variables in each country in which it operates. This, plus managing the 'links' between each country and an 'alien status' make international HRM and the role of its specialist HR more difficult.

Managing many variables and complexity is easier, and change speedier, if HR activities are decentralised to the units in question. This raises the issue of what to devolve. The approach taken should, in theory, match the structure of the business, which should reflect the overall business strategy; but in practice decisions are not so clear-cut. What if the organisation has many different types of business units abroad – small sales office, large and small manufacturing units, R&D facility, regional marketing centre, perhaps a couple of joint venture companies? The same approach to what is devolved may not be appropriate for all parts of the business.

Devolving all selection and promotion endangers availability of sufficiently broad-based and relevantly experienced senior staff for the future, which is why management development at middle/senior management level is seen by many organisations as too important to be left to national units. Apart from a holding company structure, the greater the decentralisation, the greater the need for integrative mechanisms, and management development can be a crucial integrating mechanism for a MNE operating globally.[8]

Philips Sound and Vision HRM is highly devolved but they pay great attention to inter-national management development and integrative mechanisms:

- international and cross-functional secondments are arranged, e.g., a marketeer from the USA might be assigned to the head office HRM department in the Netherlands;
- meetings for staff from disparate locations and functions are arranged to exchange ideas and disseminate effective practices;
- business school graduates from a range of countries are taken on placement into the head office HRM department.

To avoid becoming inward-looking, Philips' main board is not just staffed by Dutch nationals.

Convergence or divergence in international HRM practices?

The Price Waterhouse Cranfield Project[9] studies, started in 1990, to assess the impact over time of the Single European Market on HRM and the degree to which a strategic coherent approach[10] was being used (see Figure 13.1) found:

- HRM issues are similar across Europe but they are handled differently;[11]
- distinct patterns of HRM amongst Nordic, Central European and Latin countries (this had been suggested by Hofstede's 1980 national cultural values study[12]), but France did not fit easily into any of the three models;[13]
- common practices in terms of appraisal, development and job evaluation language;[14]
- increased written and verbal employee communications;
- increased usage of atypical work, part-time work and fixed-term contracts;
- the number of HR functional heads at board level varied considerably between countries but their involvement in business strategy was considerably lower than the number with board seats;[15]
- of those companies which had written HR strategies, only a half to 75 per cent turned these into action plans;[16]
- differences in the role of the HRM specialist in terms of involvement in organisational policy making and devolvement of HR practices to the line (see Figure 13.1);[17]
- devolvement tended to be of recruitment, selection and training, but not industrial relations, to line managers;[18]
- training is a key area of concern for a majority of European HRM departments;[19]
- strengths in national level centralised pay bargaining – except in the UK and France where it had decreased.[20]

The IBM/Towers Perrin Worldwide Study of HRM practices for achieving competitive advantage[21] assessed the relative importance of various HR approaches and practices at the time of the survey and as perceived by the end of the century. The perceived *future* impor-tance of the 38 HR practices surveyed, in achieving competitive advantage, was greater than at the time of the survey.[22]

These studies indicate the emergence of five groupings of countries, in terms of their approach to managing their human resources:

- the UK, Australia, the USA and Canada; with Germany and Italy moving towards this Anglo-Saxon HRM approach;
- France alone;
- Korea alone;
- Brazil, Mexico and Argentina;
- Japan.

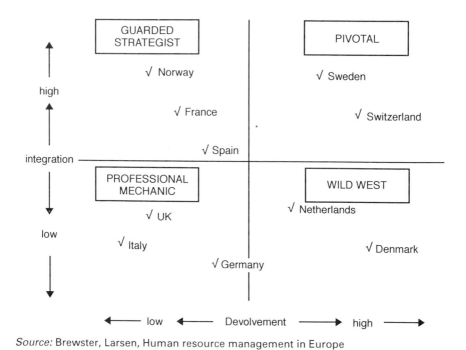

Source: Brewster, Larsen, Human resource management in Europe

Figure 13.1 The integration/devolvement matrix: models of HRM in ten European countries

13.2 Staffing the international organisation

Management and staffing approaches

Four broad approaches to managing and staffing foreign subsidiaries and senior HQ posts of an international organisation can be discerned:[23]

1. **Ethnocentric:** parent company nationals (PCNs) manage subsidiaries and staff senior HQ jobs; strategic decisions are made at headquarters.
2. **Polycentric:** subsidiaries have significant autonomy and are managed by host country nationals (HCNs) but PCNs fill senior headquarters jobs.
3. **Regiocentric:** HCNs and third country nationals (TCNs) from other countries within a geographic region are moved to senior posts within the region; significant regional decision-making autonomy.
4. **Geocentric:** a global strategy is established at headquarters; subsidiaries are managed and senior headquarters jobs are filled, regardless of nationality, by whoever has the requisite skills: PCNs, HCNs, TCNs.

The approach used must be consonant with overall business strategy and will depend on the nature of the business, its structure and resources, including the experience and skills of senior decision makers. The MNE may use different approaches in different parts of the world or in different product/service divisions.

Staff working outside their home country

An organisation needs to be clear *conceptually* about what it perceives to be the difference between the various categories of staff working internationally as this will impinge on the employment package offered. Torrington[24] (1994) sees staff who work outside their home country as falling into five general categories, each of which has distinctive HRM and acculturation needs:

1. The 'mobile worker', who is not tied to one country or company but moves around as job opportunities present themselves.
2. The 'occasional parachutist', who makes occasional brief troubleshooting/meeting attending/subsidiary inspection visits to foreign parts.
3. The 'engineer', who, home country-based, makes forays, usually unaccompanied by family and often to remote inhospitable locations, of 2 weeks to 3 months abroad.
4. The 'international manager' who, probably multilingual and cross-culturally aware, makes frequent overseas short visits abroad liaising, selling, researching business opportunities, dealing with company and government representatives, without any involvement in the internal management structures of the organisations whose representatives he meets.
5. The 'expatriate' or 'corporate transferee', who has family-accompanied or unaccompanied job postings of 2 to 3 years in a foreign business unit before returning to a job in the home country.

It costs about three times as much to use an expatriate as to hire an HCN,[25] so the organisation should carefully consider if and why expatriation is needed. Expatriate failure – the premature return of the expatriate, or sub-optimal performance in the foreign posting – is expensive; the direct costs of return and replacement may be exceeded by indirect costs: business contacts who have lost confidence in the organisation,[26] lower morale amongst staff remaining in the subsidiary,[27] and the returner's decreased confidence which may affect performance on return.[28] Particular attention should be paid to: selection and preparation for expatriation, support whilst away, and repatriation.

Selection for expatriation should be based upon: job factors, ability to relate to the other culture, motivation to expatriate, family situation and language skills.[29] Managerial or technical skill is not an indicator of cultural adaptation skill.[30] Lack of technical skill is rarely a cause of expatriate failure[31] in USA and European MNEs, but inability to adapt to the new culture is, so emphasis should be placed in selection on identifying coping skills and a positive cross-cultural attitude, bearing in mind that a positive *attitude* is not necessarily reflected in *behaviour*.[32]

Motivation of both the employee and the family to expatriate – or to sustain an unaccompanied posting – is crucial; spouse adaptation affects the employee's adaptation and hence assignment success.[33] Inability of spouse[34] or the family[35] to adapt are the most common reasons for expatriate failure amongst USA and European MNEs, although amongst Japanese MNEs it is the employee's failure to cope with larger foreign responsibilities.[36]

To minimise 'culture shock', before final appointments are made, a 'taster' visit to the proposed location helps mould realistic expectations of what living there will entail. Preparation for expatriation should include the spouse and children and, bearing in mind the problems of adjusting to international assignments which European managers cited most frequently: relationships and value differences with locals, work overload, the way business was done locally, language, and HCNs lacking appropriate skills,[37] it should cover: cross-cultural issues specific to the new environment, advice, help and support on practical matters, and language training.

When in post, expatriates need time to adjust to the local environment; up to six months is suggested,[38] so performance evaluations should allow for this. Coordinated local support facilities, including monitoring and meeting training and development needs, and the facilitation of a new social network, for the family too, both help to reduce expatriate failure.[39]

Constraints on potential expatriates are: disruption of children's education, spouse unwillingness to give up career, fear of losing visibility at the corporate headquarters and difficulty in re-absorbing the returning managers.[40] Plans need to be made *before* departure to keep expatriates in touch with developments and headquarter's 'politics' during their absence, to facilitate physical repatriation, cope with reverse 'culture shock' in work and social life and ensure repatriates will be able to return to suitable jobs.[41]

Headquarters managers need an awareness of the psychological impact, social and work life upheaval involved in expatriation and repatriation, so they can appreciate the difficulties facing returning expatriates who can take up to a year to readjust.[42] High returner turnover means organisations are suffering a significant financial and human resource investment loss.[43] 'Organisational capability' cannot be increased unless structured debriefings take place which enable both management learning to be disseminated throughout the organisation, and recognition to be given to expatriates for their experiences and learning.[44]

The 'common denominators'[45] of successful expatriation among European and Japanese MNEs are:

- a long-term orientation towards planning and performance appraisal;
- thorough preparatory training for the assignment;
- a wide-ranging support system for expatriates;
- overall suitability for working as an expatriate;
- company loyalty which restricts job mobility;
- an international orientation in the company as a whole;
- a longer history of dealing with expatriation;
- employee language skills.

Expatriation is not the only way to internationalise the organisation's experience: cross-cultural seminars, extended business trips, international networks and project teams are also useful mechanisms, and they reduce loss of visibility and power in the corporate centre. Importing foreign nationals for an expatriate spell at head office may be the most significant trend for the future.[46]

13.3 Structures of international organisations

Business decisions about the way an international organisation is structured can be enhanced if a manager has an appreciation of:

- forces precipitating change in an organisational structure;
- issues requiring consideration when changing an organisation structure;
- the fit needed between strategy, structure and organisation culture;
- the current structure, desired restructuring outcomes and what the likely secondary effects are of both the restructuring process and the new structure, in terms of customer service and staff reactions;
- the *additional* factors influencing strategy and structure in a MNE:
  - competition in several markets;
  - currency and exchange risk;

- country characteristics – cultural issues;
- trading freedoms/cross-border restrictions, affecting goods and money;
- economic imperatives requiring economies of scale but political imperatives dictating adaptation to local conditions.
- the stages in internationalisation, which impact on management and especially HRM.

In the early stages of internationalisation, organisation structures tend to evolve in response to immediate market opportunities and constraints rather than in accordance with an articulated, comprehensive and rational plan. Later, significant environmental changes or business growth trigger consideration of the appropriateness of a structure. The pressures precipitating such changes in structure are shown in Figure 13.2.

Humes[47] suggests analysing organisation structures along three dimensions:

1. **Operational distance:** the extent to which the constituent parts of the MNE are directed by the whole.[48]
2. **Interacting organisational perspectives** of: function, product, geography.[49]
3. **Controlling management dynamics** of: structure, staffing, shared values.[50]

MNEs based in different cultures and geographic areas tend to develop different combinations of the three dimensions suggested by Humes.[51]

- NORTH AMERICA: geography driven, structure stressed: control by formal systems and standards – 'formalisation'.[52]
- WESTERN EUROPE: product driven, staffing stressed: careful selection and development of key decision-makers with good interpersonal and networking skills, posted to subsidiaries – 'socialisation'.[53]
- EAST ASIA: major decisions taken at headquarters, a propensity to intervene in foreign subsidiaries – 'centralisation',[54] function driven, shared values stressed.[55]

Regardless of the 'Triad' (i.e. North America, Japan, Western Europe) power groups from which the parent MNE originated, the structural approaches to dealing with international operations have some similarities, in so far as foreign subsidiaries tend to be run as separate entities to domestic product divisions in the early stages of internationalisation; subsequently, global product divisions develop. Over time, some convergence of structural approach, towards global product divisions, supported by continental organisations can be detected.[56] When managing people across national boundaries and markets, the fact that products in some markets may be 'rising stars' but 'dogs' or 'cash cows' in others militates against a common structural and staffing approach for the whole organisation.

In terms of management mechanisms for resolving conflict between two people, national approaches vary: the British approach is to develop interpersonal skills and networks to allow the protagonists to settle the issue themselves in the context of the specific situation – the 'village market'; the French resort to hierarchy – the boss decides – the 'pyramid'; the Germans prefer comprehensive pre-set rules to govern the matter – the 'well oiled machine'.[57]

There are several forms of MNE. Porter[58] differentiates the industry types in terms of the nature of the competition they face – and thus the degree of interdependence of the parts of the MNE – on a continuum from 'multidomestic' to 'global'. Competition in one country will be independent of competition in other parts of the company elsewhere in the world in the case of 'multidomestics', so they can be structured and managed as a portfolio of several domestic industries. Retailing is an example. In 'global' industries, such as aviation, competitive status in one country will affect that in others; they need global integration in

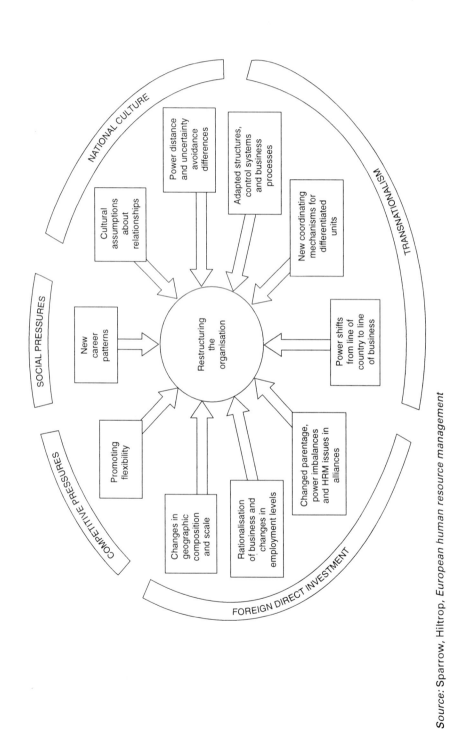

Source: Sparrow, Hiltrop, *European human resource management*

Figure 13.2 The forces precipitating changes in organisation structure in Europe

their activities to capture the intercountry linkages needed to achieve competitive advantage. Facilitating the multifarious, multi-way, multi-level links between constituent parts of the global MNE is a key HRM role.

The form and extent of business internationalisation vary widely between and within organisations, so the implications for HRM will range from administrative to strategic involvement. HRM responsibilities may be with the HRM department, line management or another department. Contextual contingent variables will be prime determinants of who does what, and what is done in an organisation. Bearing in mind the 'domestic multicultural' aspect of international HRM,[59] from an HRM perspective, organisations 'internationalise' before they establish overseas operations, as can be seen from the HRM model of internationalisation of an organisation. In practice, an organisation will not necessarily go through all the stages of the internationalisation model, and complex MNEs usually operate with a mix of several structural forms.

HRM model of internationalisation of an organisation

Conceptually, there are six stages in the full internationalisation of an organisation. At stages 1 and 2 the organisation has no foreign subsidiaries.

Stage 1 Multicultural management

- strategic focus: domestic market;
- any international sales or sourcing is via domestic-based intermediaries;
- local workforce ethnically heterogeneous, thus managers require multicultural awareness (customs, body language, etc.): HRM starts to internationalise.

Stage 2 Import/export

- strategic focus: domestic market, but some product export using overseas contacts;
- direct international resourcing of some materials/components, using overseas contacts;
- human resources may be imported to work in the domestic organisation (e.g. UK NHS imports nurses from Ireland and Finland and doctors from Germany);
- some work may be exported to people living abroad (e.g. outsourcing programming to computer programmers in India).

From Stage 3 onwards, the organisation has foreign subsidiaries. The following parts of the model delineate international organisations by their approach to control and the degree of globalisation of strategy, drawing on work by Bartlett and Ghoshal.[60]

Stage 3 International

- knowledge transfer is parent to foreign subsidiary;
- 'export' approach to strategy;
- ethnocentric staffing approach;
- parent central control.

Stage 4 Multinational or multidomestic

- portfolio of many foreign companies, run as discrete national entities;
- control decentralised on local matters, so sensitive to national differences;
- polycentric staffing approach.

Stage 5 Global

- global strategies;
- tight centralised strategic control at parent hub.

Stage 6 Transnational

- local flexibility but global integration;
- ability to manage across national boundaries;
- 'ability to link local operations to each other and to the center in a flexible way, and in so doing, to leverage of those local and central capabilities';[61]

'Networks'[62] and 'heterarchies'[63] are elaborations on the transnational form rather than new models. They feature:

- multiple strategic centres, with coordinating responsibility for specific activities[64] (e.g. design centre in Italy, information technology centre in the UK);
- a network of intra-organisational relationships at several hierarchical levels between the organisation's parts; and a network of inter-organisational relationships with competitors and stakeholders;
- a focus on coordination through interpersonal relationships, rather than just by structure and procedures;
- complex management reliant on interpersonal skills of staff.[65, 66]

A transnational is not so much a specific physical structural form, but rather, a way of thinking. As well as dealing with the HRM issues arising in earlier stages of internationalisation, developing a transnational presents special challenges for the HRM function:

- fostering global thinking in top managers;
- creating 'formal' structures which facilitate and do not impede the operation of a matrix in the mind;
- selecting and developing staff with a global mindset who are able to cope with 'cluster' rather than hierarchical structures and who have the interpersonal skills to operate in a network way;[67]
- devising effective motivation, reward, appraisal and future development programmes: encouraging a learning organisation;
- facilitating change management;
- fostering values and a structure supportive of the transnational strategy;
- developing, in conjunction with information systems specialists, appropriate systems and information flows to underpin the networking.

Joint ventures generate particular management demands:

- the creation of appropriate HRM policies, mechanisms and structures: those of one partner/a mixture/a new approach?;
- coordinating operations run by people from different companies, accustomed to their parent company way of doing things;
- developing an appropriate culture for the joint venture.

The HRM role in international HRM

For support and primary activities in the value chain, and for the value chain as a whole, the HR function undertakes direct, indirect or quality assurance activities, each of which plays a different role in gaining competitive advantage.[68] Which activity is most critical for an HR department will depend on the industry in which it is operating and the structure of the organisation, and whether the HR department is the parent's or a subsidiary's.

The role of the 'international' HR manager varies considerably according to the development stage of the international operations. HR interventions must match the needs of the organisation at the time. The more complex the organisation structure, the more the HR role tends towards focus on 'soft' HRM issues: management development, cross-cultural awareness, reinforcing corporate culture.

Schuler and Dowling[69] identified from their 1988 survey that the major challenges for the international HRM function in strategic planning included:

* identifying top management potential early;
* identifying critical success factors for the future international manager;
* providing developmental opportunities;
* tracking and maintaining commitments to individuals in international career paths;
* tying strategic business planning to human resource planning and vice versa;
* dealing with the organisational dynamics and multiple (decentralised) business units while attempting to achieve global – and regional – (for example, Europe-) focused strategies;
* providing meaningful assignments at the right time to ensure adequate international and domestic human resources.

The international HR manager needs:

* to shed ethnocentricity and think globally, and facilitate this in others, as failure to recognise HRM differences in different countries often causes major problems;[70]
* to have a broad understanding of the MNE's foreign operations and their importance to the company plus foreign experience gained in a line, as opposed to subsidiary, HRM department, role. However, international HR professionals spend about 54 per cent of their time on pay issues and only 10 per cent on strategy;[71]
* to have the abilities and personal skills to gain acceptance in involvement in strategic decision-making at corporate level.[72]

The competencies needed by international HR practitioners to develop an effective career in international HRM have been identified by the IPD from a study of 500 companies in 14 countries, and produced in a guide (1995).[73]

13.4 National cultures

National or ethnic culture is different from organisation culture. At national level cultural differences are mostly in values – absorbed during childhood from the family, rather than in practices; at organisation level, differences are mostly in practices – learnt at the workplace as an adult.[74]

All managers operating internationally, even 'occasional parachutists', need guidance on observable behavioural variables: meeting, greeting, eating, negotiating, etc., even if they have limited time to consider the underlying values which drive the behaviour. Operating cross-culturally, managers need to predict reactions to their behaviour or actions and interpret those of others: 'What will be the reactions if I manage this situation in a certain way or introduce that HR practice in our foreign subsidiaries?' Unless the gap between the cultures is small, this is not possible unless the manager appreciates the foreign contacts'/employees' underlying values, beliefs and assumptions which will govern their behaviour. In practice, understanding these requires an appreciation of how they differ from one's own cultural influences; but to use one's own ethnocentric cultural orientation as a basis for behavioural prediction or interpretation in other cultures leads to misunderstandings and business failures, as can be seen in the Lehman example. The manager needs to be able to switch from a 'self' to an 'others' orientation.

Lehman Brothers have proceeded to issue writs in the Chinese courts against two state-owned subsidiaries for non-payment of debts. In the commentaries by the parties and the media, one can be forgiven for gaining the impression that both sides in this dispute operated from a basis of trust. The Americans trusted the PRC firms would pay but the PRC firms trusted the Americans would not make insensitive demands.[75]

Characteristics of culture

Cultures are integrated, coherent, inter-related systems; if one aspect changes, it affects other aspects of the culture. Culture is not genetically inherited, but learnt. It can influence biological processes and reflexes.[76] None the less, there are certain 'cultural universals', i.e. human needs requiring satisfaction, which are common to all cultures, such as:[77]

- economic systems;
- family and marriage systems;
- education systems;
- social control systems;
- supernatural belief systems.

A greater empathy for, rather than criticism of, cultural differences, can be developed if a manager is aware of the similarities within societies; this makes criticism of the differences less likely as they are seen as environmentally determined solutions for human problems faced throughout the world.[78]

In discussing features of national cultures the distinction must be made between characteristics of the individual (personality) and characteristics which are commonly found throughout that society (culture). Individuals in every culture vary enormously one from another, so should be approached as unique human beings, and without making stereotypical judgements about them in advance. Culture does not represent the 'average citizen' or a 'model personality'; rather, it is a set of likely reactions, statistically found more frequently, in that society of people with common 'software of the mind'.[79] These generalisations about likely reactions are heuristic (general guides which help discovery and understanding) and not invariable or precise reflections of reality.[80] The normative limits of 'acceptable behaviour' are in any case hard to define.

Cultures are characterised by continual change, albeit at different speeds at different times, in response to: internal pressures of discovery, and invention; and external pressures of selective diffusion and adaptation. The speed of adoption of a new cultural item, whether it is a material object, a technology, a behaviour, a practice or an attitude will be heavily affected by five variables[81] (see Table 13.1).

Objects and technology are much more likely to be adopted than behaviour, social patterns and belief systems, because they can be seen to be useful by several people and do not necessarily threaten basic values. Imported management practices may call for changes in basic values or at least behavioural variations which are inconsistent with deeply held beliefs: they may be rejected or simply not work. For example, the introduction, into a culture with strong communitarian values, of pay related to individual performance, challenges the very fabric of the culture by introducing 'competition' between members of the 'in group', whose effective functioning has hitherto been by means of the group operating as a harmonious whole.

A practical approach to transplanting management practices across cultures requires assessing the impact of the practice on cultural values. If there is likely to be a clash, the 'Concept, Brand and Contents' approach can be used. The Concept of what the MNE wants to achieve is internationally transferable, for example, pro-active employee performance management. The Brand name or label for the practice can be varied to ensure acceptability

Table 13.1 Factors influencing the adoption of innovations

Factor	Definition
Relative advantage	The extent to which an innovation is believed to be better than whatever it replaces, and is affordable
Compatibility	The extent of perceived congruity with existing objects, behaviours and values
Complexity	The ease with which it can be understood and used
Trialability	Whether or not it can be easily tested on a limited basis
Observability	The extent to which it is perceived as offering positive benefits to several people

Source: adapted from Rogers, 1971

locally, as can the 'Contents' of the employee performance package. The 'what' that needs to be achieved is common; the 'Brand' or the 'label', plus the specific 'Contents' – means to achieving the desired outcome – can be varied.

Culture: common problems, different solutions

Hofstede,[82] analysing work-related values data, confirmed the existence across cultures of common problems but different habitual methods of problem resolution. The original four common problem areas or 'dimensions' related to:

1. Power distance. This dimension addresses the question: who is accepted as having the power to decide what?[83]
2. Individualism, with its opposite, collectivism. The USA is a highly individualistic society, Japan is collectivist (see Table 13.2).
3. Masculinity, with femininity as the other pole, is 'the desirability of assertive behavior against ... modest'.[84] Masculine societies attach importance to earnings, recognition, advancement, challenge; feminine ones to good boss and harmonious colleague relationships, employment security and living in a desirable area (see Figure 13.3).
4. Uncertainty avoidance which, poled as weak and strong, concerns the extent to which people feel threatened by unknown situations, lack of structure and ambiguity, so seek to avoid the anxiety these create by operating according to rules or diktats of superiors.[85] (See Figure 13.3).

Hofstede's first and last dimensions affect thinking about organisations themselves. The second and third dimensions concern thinking about people within organisations.[86]

The questions in Hofstede's[87] original survey reflected the 'Western' cultural bias of the survey compilers: so Michael Bond compiled a survey with questions based on Eastern values, the Chinese Value Survey (CVS). From this, a new dimension emerged, which reflected at both poles aspects of traditional Confucian values, so was named 'Confucian dynamism'.[88] Confucian dynamism has poles of long-term orientation (LTO) and short-term orientation (STO). The LTO pole reflected values seen as dynamic and future-orientated: persistence and perseverance, ordering relationships by status and observing order, thrift, having a sense of shame – and thus of obligation to carry out one's duties (see Table 13.3). The STO pole values were seen as relatively more static and past and present-orientated: personal steadiness and stability, preservation of 'face' (yours and that of others within your group), respect for tradition, meeting social obligations, reciprocation of greetings, presents and favours.[89]

Table 13.2 Individualism index (IDV) values for 50 countries and 3 regions

Score rank	Country or region	IDV score	Score rank	Country or region	IDV score
1	USA (USA)	91	28	Turkey (TUR)	37
2	Australia (AUL)	90	29	Uruguay (URU)	36
3	Great Britain (GBR)	89	30	Greece (GRE)	35
4/5	Canada (CAN)	80	31	Philippines (PHI)	32
4/5	Netherlands (NET)	80	32	Mexico (MEX)	30
6	New Zealand (NZL)	79	33/35	East Africa (*EAF*)	27
7	Italy (ITA)	76	33/35	Yugoslavia (YUG)	27
8	Belgium (BEL)	75	33/35	Portugal (POR)	27
9	Denmark (DEN)	74	36	Malaysia (MAL)	26
10/11	Sweden (SWE)	71	37	Hong Kong HOK)	25
10/11	France (FRA)	71	38	Chile (CHL)	23
12	Ireland (Republic of) (IRE)	70	39/41	West Africa (*WAF*)	20
13	Norway (NOR)	69	39/41	Singapore (SIN)	20
14	Switzerland (SWI)	68	39/41	Thailand (THA)	20
15	Germany F.R. (GER)	67	42	Salvador (SAL)	19
16	South Africa (SAF)	65	43	South Korea (KOR)	18
17	Finland (FIN)	63	44	Taiwan (TAI)	17
18	Austria (AUT)	55	45	Peru (PER)	16
19	Israel (ISR)	54	46	Costa Rica (COS)	15
20	Spain (SPA)	51	47/48	Pakistan (PAK)	14
21	India (IND)	48	47/48	Indonesia (IDO)	14
22/23	Japan (JPN)	46	49	Colombia (COL)	13
22/23	Argentina (ARG)	46	50	Venezuela (VEN)	12
24	Iran (IRA)	41	51	Panama (PAN)	11
25	Jamaica (JAM)	39	52	Equador (EQA)	8
26/27	Brazil (BRA)	38	53	Guatemala (GUA)	6
26/27	Arab countries (*ARA*)	38			

Source: Hofstede, *Cultures and organizations*

Note: Initials in brackets are country codes used in Figure 13.3 (opposite).

The importance of Hofstede's, Bond's and Hampden-Turner and Trompenaar's (1995)[90] work for HR managers is that in assessing, for example, the likely transferability of management practices and structures, rather than rely upon single country descriptions or dual country comparisons, data are available from the same base across several countries to provide the guiding heuristics a global MNE may need. Because a country scores high on one dimension, it does not mean that the characteristics of the other pole are unimportant in that culture, so can be ignored; merely that the one pole tends to be more important when forced choice questions are used. (What is involved in the relationship of a 'good' boss and a 'good' employee differs between cultures. Failure to appreciate these differences can be problematic for managers dealing with any HRM issues such as structuring, motivation, decision-making and remuneration in foreign subsidiaries, and for those managing a foreign workforce who expect loyalty systems and motivational approaches to be those they experienced back home).

The Elashmawi and Harris[91] book offers useful heuristics for three specific cultures: American, Japanese, Arab, including information about basic issues involved in dealing with people cross-culturally: meeting, greeting, letter writing styles, introduction approaches, exchanging cards, disciplining, negotiating, running training sessions, etc.

Nations vary in their view of the importance of, and the linkages between, the past, present and future. Americans view time sequentially: as having no links between the three time dimensions but with a focus on the future; Japanese and Germans tend towards a

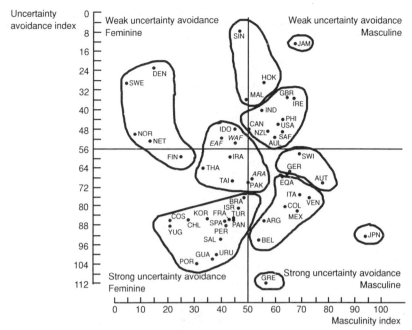

Source: Hofstede, *Culture and organisations*
Note: For country names, see Table 13.2.

Figure 13.3 The position of 50 countries and 3 regions on the masculinity/femininity and uncertainty avoidance dimensions

synchronous view of time with the three dimensions tending towards being condensed; the French place a greater importance on the past than the other two dimensions (see Figure 13.4). Circle size shows importance. Circles placed apart reveal sequential thinking. Circles overlapping reveal synchronous thinking, with a seminal future and remembered past, present, here and now. The characteristics of sequential and synchronising managers identified by Hampden-Turner and Trompenaars are given in Table 13.4.

Charles Hampden-Turner and Fons Trompenaars (1995)[92] identified seven valuing processes fundamental to wealth creation in organisations, and found national differences in how the dilemmas posed by these processes were resolved (see Table 13.5). Some cultures were 'universalist' – wanting things to be decided by universal, codified and 'one rule for all' principles – these were Anglo-Saxon and Northern European countries. 'Particularists' – France, Italy, Japan, Singapore and Belgium at the other end of the continuum – tended to value friendship and personal relationships above following rules, or rather the Japanese concept of what was the 'rule' or guiding principle for behaviour differed from the typical Western concept.[93]

The Japanese concept of organisation is a harmonious network of particular people; the American view is tasks, systems and functions. The United States is a highly analytical culture, valuing deconstruction, facts, 'the bottom line' above a holistic integrative approach which is favoured by Japan, Singapore and France. With such differences in national business values, the manager should not use norms for employee values, attitudes and satisfaction obtained in the parent country as yardsticks against which to measure foreign subsidiaries' responses in employee attitude surveys. International survey organisations have developed country-specific norms.

Table 13.3 Long-term orientation (LTO) index values for 23 countries

Score rank	Country or region	LTO score
1	China	118
2	Hong Kong	96
3	Taiwan	87
4	Japan	80
5	South Korea	75
6	Brazil	65
7	India	61
8	Thailand	56
9	Singapore	48
10	Netherlands	44
11	Bangladesh	40
12	Sweden	33
13	Poland	32
14	Germany FR	31
15	Australia	31
16	New Zealand	30
17	USA	29
18	Great Britain	25
19	Zimbabwe	25
20	Canada	23
21	Philippines	19
22	Nigeria	16
23	Pakistan	00

Source: Hofstede, *Culture and organizations*

However, Hampden-Turner and Trompenaars perceive value resolution to be a circular process with one country focusing on one aspect of a value as a *means* to achieve an *end* which another country sees as the *means* (not the end) to achieve their end, i.e. what the first country views as the *means*. This is illustrated in Figure 13.5.

13.5 Business values and ethics

If business values are accepted as being largely culturally determined, whose business values should a MNE apply? This point is important, for while business *values* can be *examined* without making judgements about whether the values are right or wrong, good or bad, business values *applied* to real situations become business *ethics*, which are prescriptive and carry with them the implication of a prior judgement of 'rightness'. The issue becomes, whose business values is it right to apply? The answer to this is far from straightforward; several options are possible.

1. Values pertaining at the parent company headquarters. This is an ethnocentric 'export' approach to ethics, workable where there is a close match between the moral ethos in the parent and host countries, but impracticable where there is a significant difference.
2. Values of the host country. This polycentric 'when in Rome do as the Romans do' approach to ethics, while sensitive to local differences, creates several different ethical approaches to business within the MNE, thus the opportunity for inconsistency, bad publicity and opprobrium in the eyes of the stakeholders who might wonder why, for example, the MNE uses child labour overseas but decries it back home.

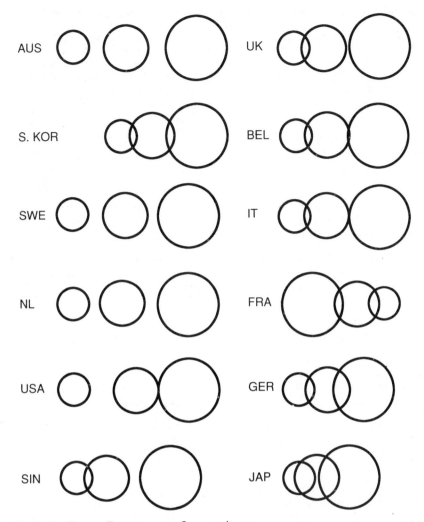

Source: Hampden-Turner, Trompenaars, *Seven cultures*

Figure 13.4 How managers in 12 nations conceived of Past (left), Present (centre) and Future (right)

3. Values generated by the MNE after careful consideration of the issues, consultation with subsidiaries and managers operating internationally. These values transcend the moral ethos in any particular country – a geocentric approach to ethics, yet have to be formulated taking into account a range of moral climates, the needs of employees operating within them, and stakeholder sensibilities.

4. Adherence to local law. Some see the aim of business as profit maximisation and what matters is law, not ethics.[94] While the rationale for this is different from the polycentric approach, potential outcomes are similar. This presupposes, incorrectly:

   (a) that all behaviour is governed by law, or any behaviour is permissible if law does not govern it; and

   (b) that it is, in fact, custom and practice for law to be obeyed in each country.

5. Ignore the issue, leave it up to employees themselves abroad to decide on how they behave. Apart from the potential for inconsistency, this seemingly empowering approach to ethics is usually an abrogation of organisational responsibility in the face of

Table 13.4 Characteristics of managers with sequential or synchronising perceptions of time

Sequential managers	Synchronising managers
• Do one thing at a time; time is tangible/divisible. • Concentrate on the job.	• Do many things at once; time is seen as intangible and elastic/flexible. • Are easily distracted/subject to interruptions.
• Regard time commitments seriously; emphasise keeping to schedule.	• Consider time commitments (schedules/agendas/deadlines) as desirable rather than as absolute objectives; emphasis on completing human transactions.
• Accustomed to a series of short-term relationships, broken without much difficulty and new ones formed.	• Accustomed to permanent links formed through a lifetime and periodically renewed in cycles of reacquaintance.
• Managers as individuals are responsible for present performance, that is, the time span coinciding with their own job occupancies.	• Managers as a group are responsible for how the past is used in the present to promote a better future.
• Time is a threat, an implacably hastening and expensive train of events that must be used fully.	• Time is a friend who keeps coming around, providing fresh opportunities for engagement on each occasion.
• Conflicts are solved by 'first come, first served' and forming lines in which each waits his turn.	• Conflicts are solved by meeting several sets of needs from a minimal set of carefully coordinated processes.
• Rationality and logic are conceived of as fault-free, direct sequences of causes and effects, premises and conclusions.	• Reasonableness is conceived of as encompassing and synchronising several aims and objectives into an inclusive process.
• Products are regarded as maturing over time, going from high novelty and profitability to routine operations, lower margins, and eventual death.	• Products are regarded as self-renewing over time, the 'genes' on one product giving life to the next generation and the next.

Source: Hampden-Turner, Trompenaars, *Seven cultures*

Table 13.5 Valuing processes fundamental to wealth creation and the dilemmas they pose

Valuing processes	Dilemma
Making rules and discovering exceptions	Universalism vs particularism
Constructing and deconstructing	Analysing vs integrating
Managing communities of individuals	Individualism vs communitarianism
Internalising the outside world	Inner-directed vs outer-directed orientation
Synchronising fast processes	Time as sequence vs time as synchronisation
Choosing amongst achievers	Achieved status vs ascribed status
Sponsoring equal opportunities to excel	Equality vs hierarchy

Source: constructed from pp. 5–12, Hampden-Turner, Trompenaars , *Seven cultures*

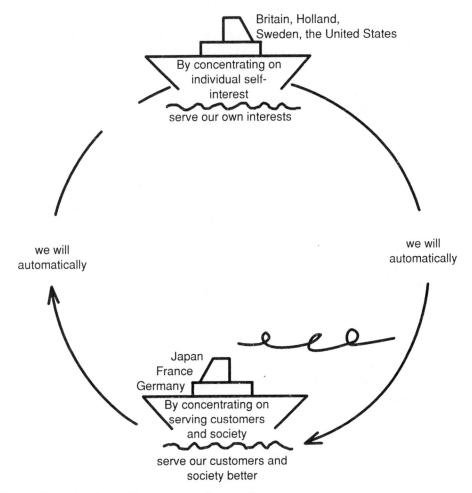

Source: Hampden-Turner, Trompenaars, *Seven cultures*

Figure 13.5 The circular nature of value resolution

'difficult' issues. For a manager operating overseas, resolving ethical dilemmas can be a lonely business, particularly in an organisation in the early stages of internationalisation, which has yet to have had enough overseas experience for managers at parent head office fully to appreciate the problems. Overseas managers can feel isolated, unsupported and 'damned if they do and damned if they don't' when their actions generate adverse publicity and a punitive MNE reaction.

MNE attitudes to supporting foreign posted staff with ethical dilemmas vary between organisations, according to their stage of internationalisation, the extent of their previous experience of operating internationally, the subject of the ethical dilemma, and the attitude of the boss back at the parent.

What constitutes appropriate ethical conduct may develop through unwritten norms evolving through group interactions; but in a MNE norms will differ between locations. Hence written codes of conduct, openly adopted, published and proactively communicated, have been developed by many companies to address ethical issues.

To be effective, they require the active involvement and support of senior managers. This means not just words for PR purposes but following through with action.

In 1987, Bob Haas, the Chairman and CEO of Levi Strauss & Co., had a top management retreat to consider the development of long-term business values and produced:

- a Mission Statement – why the company is in business;
- a Business Vision Statement – what it wants to be;
- an Aspiration Statement – how it can meet its goals.

These reflect core corporate values which, as much as cost, competition and efficiency, influence business decisions. The company's approach to difficult ethical issues is reflected in how they dealt with the issue of their Bangladesh sub-contractors employing female workers under 14. If the girls had no jobs they would be likely to become prostitutes to support their families. After discussions with the sub-contractors the issue was resolved by Levi Strauss paying for educational tuition fees, books, and school uniforms until the girls reached age 14; the sub-contractors paid the girls whilst they were attending school.[95]

A MNE could take a two-tier approach of generic global values and locally specific ones,[96] with the former perhaps including 'marketing, information policy, environmental protection, animal experiments, research policy'.[97] The two-level concept accommodates the 'think global, act local' principle but in practice may not make the issue of corruption, pervasive in many countries, any easier to deal with.

Mahoney (1995)[98] sees all commercial bribery as being bad for business, bad for the participants, bad for the society in which it occurs, but what constitutes corruption differs between societies. Managers operating abroad need some guidance on what is a 'gift', a 'bribe', an 'extortion' payment. The following distinction is helpful:

- bribing is paying people to induce them to behave unethically or to gain some particular advantage; and
- extortion is paying people to do their jobs; i.e. making payments not required by law but which individuals demand, albeit subtly, for 'the proper performance of a task not its perversion'.[99]

The former is hard to justify ethically. The latter is usually of more concern for people operating internationally. Some 'officials' with whom the business person has to deal may be poorly paid and see the only way to acquire more money as being to delay performing their job functions until given financial inducement. Paying such extortion, just to get normal business transacted is seen as less ethically reprehensible than paying a bribe, but Mahoney sees it as justifiable only if all the following four conditions prevail:

1. There is no other way of doing one's business in that country.
2. The payment is not to persuade someone to do wrong; rather, it is to stop threats or stop them from doing wrong.
3. The business person is engaged in legitimate and lawful business which is of benefit to wider stakeholders in the society and the economy, than just the immediate participants in the business.
4. Concomitantly, the business person is trying to do everything possible to prevent the practice of such extortion; for example by trying to ensure that the officials in question are paid a living wage.[100]

Snell (1995)[101] identifies four types of 'psychic imprisonment' which can restrict a manager's ability to solve ethical dilemmas.

1. limited ethical reasoning capability;
2. stereotypical assumptions about organisation structures, power and responsibilities;
3. lack of power or responsibility in the organisation;
4. a moral ethos incompatible with the individual's own stage of ethical reasoning.

The first two types of psychic imprisonment are restrictions internal to the manager, while the latter two are 'moral mazes', mainly external to the individual.

Moral dilemmas arise if the manager is pressured to enact a lower stage of ethical reasoning than her/his habitual mode. The manager's role in ethical matters could usefully include:

- identifying the real ethical dilemmas staff encounter, operating in their organisation's foreign environment;
- stimulating discussion, including the views and problems of expatriate and HCN staff, on dilemmas, possible solutions/standards, organisational support, and ethical codes;
- contributing, at senior level, to the development of appropriate ethical codes;
- code communication and explanation;
- setting an example by personal adherence to the organisation's ethical codes;
- in the case of a large organisation with substantial foreign operations or frequent buying/selling contacts overseas, pressing for the appointment of an 'ethics ombudsperson' to whom, in total confidentiality, staff could apply for guidance on code interpretation and action, in the light of specific problematic situations which have arisen;
- ensuring that appraisal, promotion and reward mechanisms, and the way they operate in practice, do not favour unethical behaviour: management mechanisms and actions must be consonant with ethical statements;
- selecting staff operating across national borders who are best able to cope with the ethical dilemmas likely to arise in the particular host cultures.

Managers may also become involved with disciplinary action against ethical code breakers. They also may have to deal with 'whistle blowers' who, adhering to the organisation's ethical code, embarrassingly publicise the unethical behaviour of others or who, personally operating at a higher level of ethical reasoning than the organisation, publicise what, from their perspective, is unethical behaviour.

Both situations pose difficult dilemmas for the manager. In an organisation operating domestically, business ethics (both personal and organisational), organisational politics, personal power/survival, and career, are not easy imperatives to balance. Managing in an international organisation, the considerations become more complex.

13.6 Culture: language and non-verbal communication

When business deals are conducted between people speaking different languages, it is vital that both parties have the same conception of what is agreed. This requires translators with up-to-date knowledge of the language, the type of vocabulary being used and its correct situational usage: speakers of 'social' Russian would have difficulty with business or engineering terms, and their misapprehensions could have disastrous consequences.

When simultaneous translation is required, the best approach is to have two translators: each to translate into their mother tongue from the foreign language. Legal documents present problems requiring specialist translators, not least because the legal concepts of one nation may not be those of another, yet the implications have to be understood by both parties.

A culture evolves words to reflect the needs of its environment so may not have the vocabulary to express a concept related to a different one. For example, in the early 1990s, the Chinese definition of 'marketing' – in a UK published Chinese/English dictionary – ill expressed the meaning of the Western concept, creating bewilderment for PRC students studying business in the UK. Before the PRC economic reforms 'marketing' was not a relevant concept to the PRC. A recommended approach, for those operating in a foreign language of which they have imperfect knowledge, and coming from a very different culture, is to look up the meaning of a word in the same language dictionary of the foreign language: the word will be explained in the context of that culture.

Just as connotations of a word vary between cultures, slang and euphemisms provide additional pitfalls. The business consequences of linguistic *faux pas* may be more serious than the wry amusement occasioned in a Moscow hotel by a notice stating: 'If this is your first visit to the USSR you are welcome to it'.[102]

'He has no power' is a typical Japanese insult about a boss, whereas 'I don't like him' is typical in some Western cultures.[103] 'I don't like him' might indicate antipathy based on objections to a boss's non-job-related personal characteristics, but it is more likely to refer to antipathy based on shortfalls in job-related interpersonal or technical skills. To Japanese managers a boss is usually characterised by power rather than job skill; but Western managers see job skill as the predominant characteristic of a boss.[104] However, the connotations of the concept of a boss's 'power' differ between nations. To the Japanese, the boss is powerful because he has harmoniously integrated the particular resources of which he has charge; this – to a UK mind – infers job skill. Hence, both phrases, while saying different things, mean the same: 'the boss is no good at his job'. However, to the Westerner, power has connotations of 'a subversive influence in which the moral order, by which the best performers rise to the top, is corrupted by the private agendas of empire builders and power seekers'.[105]

Linguistic styles vary between nations. Concise and to the point is an American preference; Arab speakers use what, to an American, seems to be an over-elaborate rhetorical style. To an American, excessive politeness, thanking and apologising characterise Japanese communication. The international manager needs to be able to interpret linguistic styles in their contexts.

Japanese has several words for 'no'. Other East Asian and Arab cultures have several ways of indicating a negative response without being as direct as saying a flat 'no'. Such circumlocution, totally understandable within their cultural contexts, where saving the other's face is a way of showing respect and maintaining harmony, can be frustrating to, or misunderstood by, many North American or UK managers. However, polite circumlocution – but different polite circumlocution – is also used in English: what does 'I'm not too keen on this idea' really mean? Elashmawi and Harris's (1993)[106] table of cultural contrasts in written business communications in America, Japan and Arab countries, offers helpful heuristics to interpreting linguistic styles (see Table 13.6).

Implicit models of boss–subordinate communications vary between cultures:

> A Western management perspective assumes that the subordinate's willingness to initiate upward communication indicates a 'healthy' relationship reflecting high trust in the boss as well as openness. This position may need to be tested in Southeast Asian organisations, which generally value authority in superior–subordinate relationships. Upward communication could also mean that the employee may criticise or challenge his/her boss's decisions. This could be perceived as not according the boss the respect attached to his/her status.[107]

Some 65 per cent of communication is non-verbal;[108] the meaning we attribute to non-verbal stimuli is defined by our culture, which leaves plenty of room for misunderstanding in cross-cultural exchanges.

Table 13.6 Cultural contrasts in written business communications

	American	Japanese	Arab
Cultural objectives	Provide information; Seek commitments and action	Seek information; Offer proposal	Information exchange
Opening	Direct to objective	Thanking; Apologising	Personal greeting
Content	Factual; Plan of action	Specific questions; Solicit information	Background information; Indirect to subject
Persuasion tools	Immediate gain or loss of opportunity	Waiting	Personal connection; Future opportunity
Non-verbal communication	Urgency; Short sentences	Modesty; Minimise standing; Letterhead or marks	Lengthy; Elaborate expression; Many signatures
Closing	Affirmative; Specific requests	Maintain harmony; Future relationship	Future relationship; Personal greeting
Applied cultural values	Efficiency; Directness; Action	Politeness; Indirectness; Relationship	Status; Continuation; Acknowledgement; Wishes

Source: Elashmawi, Harris, *Multicultural management*

Hall (1959, 1966, 1976)[109] classified cultures as:

- 'low context', where the transmission of explicit verbal messages constitutes the majority of the communication (e.g. Western societies);
- 'high context', where the physical environment, what they know and have internalised are used, as much as words, to understand the situation (e.g. Chinese culture).[110]

High context cultures tend to be polychronic, compared to Western cultures.[111]
    Non-verbal communication can include:

- paralinguistics: the non-verbal use of the voice, e.g. pitch, rate of speech, volume;
- kinesics: movements, e.g. facial expressions, hand and limb gestures;[112] gait, posture, eye contact, touching;
- proxemics: the distance between people with which those concerned feel comfortable; significant national differences exist in what is deemed appropriate for intimate, personal, social and public space between people;[113]
- silence;
- olfaction (scents or smells such as perfume);
- colour and graphic symbols;
- clothing, hairstyles, cosmetics and accessory artifacts: jewellery, fly whisks, etc.;[114]
- chronemics: the perception and use of time.[115]

In considering non-verbal communications, Ferraro[116] warns of the dangers of:

- overgeneralising;
- assuming that all non-verbal cues are of equal significance within a given culture, and apply across both genders and all social levels;
- over-emphasising the differences between cultures in non-verbal communications;
- believing the consequences of misunderstanding non-verbal cues are always catastrophic.

Divergence or convergence in national cultures?

Child (1981)[117] found that those studies indicating convergence of national cultures mostly concerned organisation structures and technology used; divergence theories focused on behavioural differences. Hofstede (1994)[118] believes the thesis 'national cultures are becoming more alike' is based on observation of the more superficial layers of culture like 'practices': the way people dress, what they buy, films they watch, sports and leisure activities they undertake; deeper values between nations continue to differ significantly.

> there is very little evidence of international convergency [in cultural values] over time, except an increase of individualism for countries that have become richer. Value differences between nations described by authors centuries ago are still present today, in spite of continued close contacts. For the next few hundred years countries will remain culturally very diverse.[119]

For many years to come, cultural awareness training will thus remain an important issue for businesses operating internationally.

Training for cultural awareness

Organisations lacking resources and time to acculturate staff operating internationally 'in house' might use bodies such as the UK-based Centre for International Briefing, at Farnham, Surrey, who offer pre-departure acculturation programmes, tailored to specific needs, covering almost any country in the world.

Who should be trained, in what, to what depth and for how long are functions of the extent of interaction required in the new culture and the similarity between the employee's own culture and the new one.[120] As for any training or development situation, there are a range of training methods which can be used. Figure 13.6 offers a framework to identify cross-cultural training needs.

In-depth country-specific immersion programmes may be suitable for expatriates and those destined to have a long relationship with a specific country, but for 'occasional parachutists'[121] likely to visit a range of different countries for short periods, information-giving sessions or an understanding of cultural components, which can then be applied to a new situation, are more appropriate.

However, as Robinson (1983)[122] points out:

> the successful international manager is one who sees and feels the similarity of structures of all societies. The same set of variables are seen to operate, although their relative weights may be different. This capacity is far more important than possession of specific area expertise, which may be gained quite rapidly if one already has an ability to see similarities and ask the right questions – those that will provide the appropriate values or weights for the relevant variables.

13.7 Labour market issues

The labour market issues which need consideration when deciding upon the location of a new foreign unit are:

- Is labour of the required type, or which can fairly easily be trained, potentially available?
- What is the employee relations climate?
- What are wage levels, associated social costs of employment, expected or required terms and conditions, and inflation rate trends?
- What local or central government laws and regulations affect employment?
- What is the prevailing attitude amongst HCNs to work, and working for a foreign company?

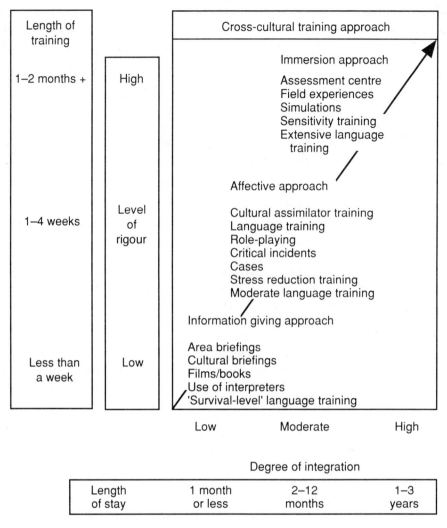

Length of training		Cross-cultural training approach
1–2 months +	High	Immersion approach Assessment centre Field experiences Simulations Sensitivity training Extensive language training
1–4 weeks	Level of rigour	Affective approach Cultural assimilator training Language training Role-playing Critical incidents Cases Stress reduction training Moderate language training
Less than a week	Low	Information giving approach Area briefings Cultural briefings Films/books Use of interpreters 'Survival-level' language training

	Low	Moderate	High

Degree of integration

Length of stay	1 month or less	2–12 months	1–3 years

Source: Mendenhall *et al., Expatriate selection*

Figure 13.6 The Mendenhall, Dunbar and Oddou cross-cultural training model

- What are the costs, advantages and disadvantages of living and working in that location for potential expatriates?
- What are the potential costs of entry and exit in the labour market in that location?
- What work permit and other restrictions affect labour mobility: both HCN mobility within the country and the ability of foreigners to work there?

For example, social costs of employment are higher in some EU countries than in others; labour mobility is restricted within the PRC; in Russia some people are oriented to work with the lowest productivity possible and are uninterested in the work to be done.

Career patterns vary between countries. In Japan, unlike the UK and the USA, staff tend to join a company from university and stay with it throughout their career: 'lifetime employment' (*shushinkoyo*). An employee who leaves the company mid-career tends to be viewed as 'disloyal' to the corporate family and is regarded with suspicion by other Japanese employers.[123] It is not easy for foreign-owned businesses to establish themselves in Japan by acquiring appropriate high calibre male staff by poaching and offering a higher salary; instead, they tend to look to women – a marginalised category in Japanese business society – or expatriates who may not have the established network relationships important to doing business. Japanese attitudes towards work as a lifetime commitment to a company are slowly starting to change;[124] new young graduates or managers who have worked overseas are more predisposed to forgo employment security and join a foreign company with a known name and reputation,'[125] particularly if slowing growth within the Japanese company – where promotion is traditionally by seniority – limits career prospects.[126]

Recruitment and selection

Recruitment through newspaper and journal advertisements is popular in many countries, as is 'word of mouth' recruitment – particularly in Greece and Ireland – which UK companies might regard askance for equal opportunities reasons. In Korea, there is a tendency for recruitment to favour people from the same geographic area (*ji-yun*) or university (*hahk-yun*) as the manager;[127] because employee loyalty tends to be to the individual manager rather than the company, a Korean manager who changes jobs may bring staff with him.[128]

In a UK or USA domestic context, gender is an irrelevant issue in selection. However, in some parts of Africa, Asia, Latin America and the Middle East women are not properly accepted – if at all – in senior roles in a business context. The organisation must take this into account in selection; whatever the domestic stance on gender, the societal values of other countries cannot be confronted head on if the objection to senior businesswomen is rooted in deeply held and widespread religious beliefs. However, some countries are merely unaccustomed to women in senior roles, rather than strongly against accepting them. In Japan, foreign highly skilled businesswomen, particularly if they speak the language, may be regarded as 'honorary men' and thus accepted.

France places great reliance on the handwritten application letter which can be analysed by a graphologist, whereas graphology, used by 97 per cent of French organisations,[129] is given scant regard because of poor validity by most UK businesses, only 3 per cent of whom admit to using it. Skills shortages, HR activities contracted out to agencies, and increasing pressure on budgets have encouraged French companies to use astrology and numerology, palmistry, phrenology and haemotology[130] to assess applicants' characters. Some countries, such as Denmark, use CVs rather than application forms.[131] The emphasis placed on aspects of the candidate's career and life history differs between countries: in the UK evidence of social and leadership skills is highly regarded; in other countries, such as Germany and France, much more emphasis is placed upon qualifications and grades.

Interviews are widely used but the types of questions regarded as 'fair', 'suitable' and 'relevant' vary between countries. The USA and EU equal opportunities approaches preclude questions about marriage intentions and children, which would be perfectly acceptable, if not expected, elsewhere. In practice, in some EU countries, such as Greece[132] and Italy: 'more searching questions may be put and expected than is normal in the UK, equal opportunity legislation notwithstanding'.[133]

Candidate behaviour at interview also varies and managers should interpret it in the light of the cultural norms of the applicant's country. A US candidate is likely to broadcast and play up his/her personal achievements and promise miracles,[134] but in other cultures such behaviour may seem like boasting or ignoring the impact of a team's effort.

Psychological tests and questionnaires, beloved selection tools in many American organisations, meet with limited acceptability elsewhere in the world. Parts of strongly

Roman Catholic southern Europe, such as Spain, disapprove of them although trade unions prefer them as a means of limiting nepotism.[135] In France, psychometric questionnaires have lost credibility and are less used than hitherto.[136] Any psychological instrument to be used outside the country and category of people on which it was norm tested needs very careful examination as to cultural validity and culturally sensitive language translation. Psychological instrument compilers Saville and Holdsworth have produced an eleven language 'International Testing System' specifically to meet this need.

A global company, seeking the best talent regardless of national origin, could establish an international assessment centre to identify employees, from a range of countries, with potential senior managerial talent. From their experiences of running a European assessment centre, BP found that participants' norm reactions vary according to nationality, and culturally determined appropriate behaviour needs careful consideration and interpretation.

Anglo-Saxon assessment centre approaches predicated on 'everyone has equal rights' would not work successfully in cultures in which this belief was not implicit.[137] The American, UK and northern European analytical, numerical and judgemental emphasis in assessment centres tends to be resisted in Latin countries and France which prefer a more 'human' and developmental emphasis.[138] Work situation observation exercises would not be acceptable in Arab countries where it is seen as an affront to dignity to be watched whilst working.[139]

The qualities of an 'effective manager' need redefinition according to the culture in which the person will be operating. The implicit meanings behind words such as 'leadership' differ between countries, making problematic both the design of exercises to test such a quality and the interpretation of outcomes. While organisation leaders in all countries need to attend to both task achievement and relationship management:

> *how* this is to be accomplished in each setting will be dependent upon the meanings given to particular leadership acts in that setting. A supervisor who frequently checks up that work is done correctly may be seen as a kind father in one setting, as task centred in another setting, officious and mistrustful in a third. The meaning of acts is given by the cultural context within which they occur. In collective cultures, the attribution of meaning is likely to be more concensually shared than would be the case in more individualist societies.[140]

Training and development

Recruitment sources for new managers and their education and training differ between countries. Evans, Lank and Farquhar (1989)[141] identified four distinctive management development approaches, heuristics to national practices which none the less vary considerably within, as well as between, countries: the 'Japanese', the 'Latin', the 'Germanic', the 'Anglo-Dutch'.

According to a 1992 survey of top managers across Europe,[142] common characteristics of management in Europe, compared to Japan and the USA, are:

- orientation towards people as individuals;
- internal negotiation within the company (not top-down orders US-style or the consensual Japanese-style of decision-making);
- managing international diversity (more tolerance for another country's culture);
- managing between two extremes – the American and Japanese approaches: short-term profit versus long-term growth; the relationship between the individual and the firm of 'hire and fire' versus lifelong commitment; the balance between individualism and collectivism in the workplace.[143]

Managers running training sessions for people from different national origins need to be aware that parent company training programmes designed for PCNs, whether managers or

Table 13.7 Cultural contrasts in training

	American	Japanese	Arab
Group composition	Medium-sized; Mixed level OK	Smallest group; Grouped for functional harmony	Largest group; Very level conscious
Time	8–5 with breaks	9–6 with breaks; May go on until 8 or continue informally after-hours	9/10–3 maximum; no lunch break
Preparation	Individually reading; Written homework	Group orientation	Not necessary or important
Getting started	Self-introductions; Random or by seating order	Intro emphasises company/belonging; Senior goes last	Introductions by status; senior goes first
Process	Emphasise 'how to' and practical applications; Self-reliance; Specialisation; More reading	Emphasis on doing/discussion; Sharing experiences; Intra-group discussion; Role play; Rotation	Memorising general skills; Coaching; Demonstration by leader; Minimal reading
Training materials	Written; Self-explanatory	Visual with group discussion by doing	Visual; coaching by team leader
Test of knowledge	Direct questions to individual; Spontaneous, open questions	Group questions; Intra-group discussions; Direct questions	No direct, individual questions; Need preparation
Cultural values	Self-reliance; Competition; Time conscious	Relationship; Group achievement; Group harmony	Seniority; Reputation; Individual achievement

Source: Elashmawi, Harris, *Multicultural management*

other staff, may not transplant without adaptation. Local systems of qualifications, education and training may make them inappropriate; the style of session which worked back home may not be effective, as norms of participation, informality, and views about the status of the teachers and their pronouncements vary. Above, Elashmawi and Harris (1993)[144] have identified approaches and dynamics of some 'typical' training sessions for different cultures (see Table 13.7).

Employment terms

The nature of the employment contract, the rights and obligations of the parties thereto, and employee and employer expectations of terms and conditions, hiring and firing and employment protections may vary considerably between countries, and may vary within a country for a range of reasons. Employment rights may be affected by whether the employer is a state or private company (PRC), the employee is a core or peripheral worker (Japan), the reasons for the termination (USA, EU countries) and length of service. Workers employed by foreign-invested enterprises (FIEs) in the PRC are said to have 'clay rice bowls', as they are not employed on the basis of lifetime employment – 'iron rice bowl'[145] – still prevalent, although now rapidly decreasing, in state-controlled enterprises (SCEs).

In Japan, employment is seen as more of a relationship than a contract and there is a disinclination to register promises in a legalistic manner in a contract document[146] as this constitutes 'alien behaviour which would meet with social disapproval (*taningyogi*)'.[147] Most 'regular' staff in Japanese companies never have a contract of employment,[148] nor are many of the obligations and expectations of employment explicitly given in the enterprise's Works Rules.[149] It is acceptable to lay off part-time staff or older 'retirees' in Japan, but a good company will go to considerable lengths, including accepting underemployment in the enterprise, to avoid making 'regular' staff redundant.[150] In Korea, during business downturns, layoffs are accepted practice at all organisational levels.[151]

Performance and reward

Foreign subsidiaries' financial results are to some extent an outcome of the MNE's approach to financial management – transfer pricing, exchange rates, accounting conventions – and global competition. Host country import levies, restrictions on profit repatriation and fiscal stance can distort the value of the subsidiary's performance to the parent.[152] Subsidiary financial results should be used with care when appraising the chief executive of a foreign subsidiary; instead, performance could be measured using 'parallel accounts' adjusted for the effect of the distorting variables, or against long-range goals such as health and safety improvements, market share and effect on the environment.[153] Each main Cable and Wireless business unit reports on: customer and employee satisfaction, business performance, productivity and growth.[154] Expatriates who are not chief executives are most appropriately assessed against criteria for their specialism and cross-cultural skills.

The best approach for appraising HCNs in foreign subsidiaries is to use host country appraisal mechanisms, but if a global approach is required, it is preferable to specify *what* must be achieved, such as:

- coaching;
- appraisal based upon accountability (group or individual);
- development discussions;
- human resource plans;
- instant feedback.

This does not specify *how* this should be done. This allows for local cultural variation.[155] Appraisal outcomes need to be evaluated in the light of cultural norms about praise and negative remarks. In Korea, where job attitude and special ability are appraised as well as performance, many managers are reluctant to give too negative an evaluation of their staff as this will undermine the much valued harmonious relationship between boss and staff; instead, staff are evaluated on a 'that's good enough' (*koenchanayo*) basis which implies tolerance and sincere appreciation of another's efforts.[156]

Values on distributive justice norms vary between countries; the philosophy underpinning reward management might be: equity, equality or needs. Equity underpins most Western approaches to rewards. It implies pay for competencies – inputs, or outputs – performance outcomes. Job holders perceived to be doing work of analogous worth, are used as pay comparators. The implication is that as inputs or outputs increase, rewards should be increased for the situation to be 'equitable'. Inequity is stressful, and an employee is motivated to reduce it by one means or another.

Equality approaches, where everyone gets the same – for example when a bonus of the same absolute amount is distributed to all staff – are emphasised more in some countries in Southeast Asia. The issue here can become delineating who is part of the 'in group' and thus who is deserving of the equal reward. In practice, even collectivist Chinese cultures tend towards an individualistic Western equity-based pay approach, the wealthier they become: individual performance and skill can dramatically affect pay in Hong Kong and Singapore.[157]

Needs-based rewards are not just found in socialist states. Expatriates are usually housed and given return home flights in accord with their needs as single or family persons.

The perceived relative value of money and other benefits varies between countries, not just because of the local fiscal policy but also because of cultural values. In France, subsidised transport, company restaurant lunches or luncheon vouchers are common and the Philippine worker values a measure of rice with better quality rice being given to skilled workers.[158] In the PRC, staff are paid in cash whatever their level, as the banking system is underdeveloped.

In the USA senior executive pay could be 100 times that of the average worker; in European countries a multiple of 12 to 15 is more common and a large disparity is seen as socially reprehensible.[159] In Japan too, the gap between top managers' pay and that of the average workers is small, relative to the USA, as a result of the Japanese emphasis on egalitarianism and togetherness.[160]

Age and seniority as well as group and company performance determine pay in Japan, but there is little differential for individual performance or exceptional skills.[161] Bonus payments, made during the two traditional gift giving seasons in Japan, can comprise as much as a third of total annual pay for an employee and large companies make them to all staff.[162]

Gomez-Mejia and Welbourne (1991)[163] using Hofstede's[164] national culture findings, derived a theoretical framework of appropriate reward strategies from the dominant values and organisational characteristics associated with the poles of each of Hofstede's four dimensions (see Figure 13.7).

They point out that:

- Each of the four dimensions and the country's placing on them will influence the extent to which the rewards strategy outlined is in fact appropriate.
- Poor reward strategy implementation and work design issues are as likely as cultural differences to create difficulties with rewards.
- Global organisations with their own strong cultures may be able to use these as a philosophical basis for rewards, irrespective of local cultural norms.[165]

13.8 Expatriate rewards

The philosophy usually stated as underpinning expatriate rewards is to keep the expatriate 'whole', i.e. no worse or better off as a result of expatriation. However, expatriates often expect to be better off as a result, and companies may need to ensure that they are if they are to tempt an employee to work abroad.

Armstrong and Murlis (1994),[166] upon whose work much of this section is based, identify three approaches to expatriate rewards:

1. Budget system
2. Balance sheet
3. Market rate.

The budget system, decreasing in popularity but still used by large paternalistic companies, involves identifying the expatriate's costs in the home country, adding the costs in the host and paying the resultant figure in host currency. Problems arise if the home or host countries have either high inflation or exchange rate volatility, as the pay needs constant adjustment. This approach can be time-consuming and thus expensive to administer, particularly when more than two countries are involved, and is rarely used for TCNs.[167]

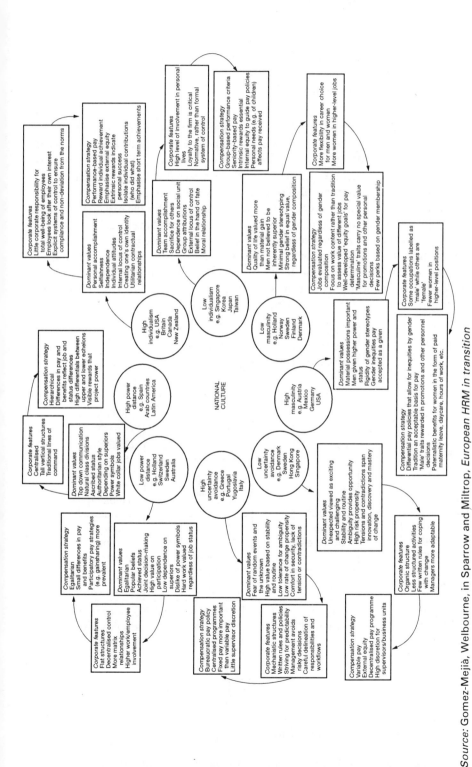

Source: Gomez-Mejià, Welbourne, in Sparrow and Miltrop, *European HRM in transition*

Figure 13.7 National cultures, organisational characteristics and compensation strategies

The balance sheet approach[168] is the most common as it is

- less time-consuming administratively;
- usually cheaper than the market rate approach;
- easier to explain to potential expatriates.[169]

It uses three elements:

- notional home salary;
- spendable or net disposable income;
- allowances.

The notional home salary, also used as a base for pension contributions, relates to the salary the expatriate would get at home after repatriation, without promotion on return. As home pay levels rise, the notional home income should be increased accordingly. The net disposable income is income after tax, pension contributions, social security payments; housing and savings commitments might also be deducted. Allowances can be made for many reasons, such as: hardship – if the working and living conditions for the expatriate will be particularly difficult or risky; clothing – where there are large climatic differences; tax equalisation; return home or rest and recreation trips; foreign service premium – usually a percentage of between 10 per cent and 15 per cent of notional home salary, paid as an incentive to move and to recompense for the disruption expatriation involves; servants allowances; provision of health care (such as for an expatriation from the UK to the USA); social security differences; standard of living (SL); cost of living (CL) (see Figure 13.8).

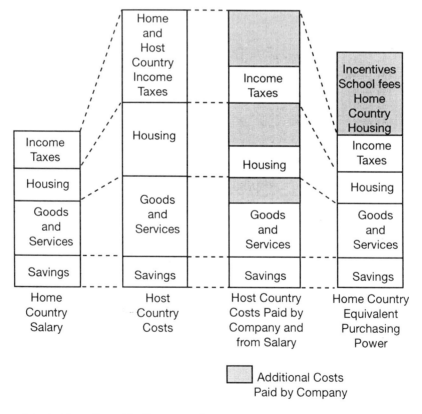

Source: Adapted from Reynolds, *Compensation*

Figure 13.8 The balance sheet approach to expatriate pay

Organisations usually determine the CL by using a CL index obtained from a specialist company that assesses the relative cost in the host country of goods and services the expatriate would use back home, so the expatriate can maintain the home country standard of living. The CL index is usually higher for the host country as many goods in the 'basket' may need to be imported. The CL index is applied to the net disposable income, to create the host country net disposable income figure which is translated into host country currency at the appropriate exchange rate.

'Plussing up' may be required to keep the employee whole in terms of tax or social security payments. Tax equalisation applies as follows: excess tax is reimbursed, usually in the home country or offshore, to expatriates in higher tax host countries; but in lower or zero-rated tax host countries the difference between home and host tax is deducted from their salary.

Standard of living (SL) is not the same as CL. For example, a manager in the host country might be paid at a level which enables her/him to afford servants or a yacht, yet a manager doing a comparable job in the expatriate's home country would neither afford nor expect these. Applying a CL index to the home country goods and services would not take these SL differences into consideration. If servants are the norm for the job in the host country, is it 'fair' to the expatriate to pay a CL equalised net disposable income, which precludes having servants? Additionally, in some countries, the visible status of the expatriate reflects strongly the way the organisation is regarded by those with whom the organisation does business in the host country, so it would not help the company's standing to be perceived as 'poor' and the expatriate as of 'low status'.

An employee moving to a higher standard of living country (HSL) paid on the CL balance sheet approach, might receive considerably less than subordinates in the host country: is this appropriate? If the employee moves to a country with a considerably lower standard of living (LSL) is it appropriate to pay the expatriate more than the host country boss? In such a case, the expatriate, whilst having rewards assessed on a balance sheet basis, might receive some pay in the host country and the rest in an offshore account.

The market rate approach to expatriate rewards can be applied where there is a large disparity between SLs in the host and home country. It is usually applied where there is a considerably HSL in the host country, and is thus a more expensive payment method for the MNE. When contemplating a market rate approach, the organisation needs to consider two aspects of SL:

1. Is the SL just different, but not higher or lower?
2. Is the SL higher, or lower?

In practice the two are intertwined, and a factor of perceptions. The approach the employer takes to coping with large disparities between home and host country SLs will depend on:

- labour supply and demand for the skills in question in both the home and host countries;
- the desirability of the expatriate posting at a particular pay level in the eyes of the potential expatriate and other appropriately skilled employees in the organisation, and thus the extent to which others could or would substitute for the potential expatriate;
- whether or not the expatriate would have the right to work in the host country if not expatriated by that employer: among the European Union countries, there is freedom of movement for workers, so no work permits are required;
- the attitude of the host government to granting work permits for staff paid significantly less or more than the host norm for that type of job;
- the perceived 'fairness' of the pay level in the potential expatriate's eyes, and hence the probable effect on the expatriate's motivation of paying at a particular level;

- the organisation's overall pay stance;
- the effect of a particular salary level on host country subordinates, boss, business and social contacts, and thus on the organisation's effectiveness.

For example, if the expatriate has no right to work in the host country outside of the subsidiary and labour demand at home is low relative to supply, the posting is 'desirable' and substitutes are available, pay rates can be lower than the host country norm, if not completely market rate. However, obtaining a work permit might be problematic as the host government is likely to object to importing cheap labour which takes work away from host country nationals.

Market rate as a basis for expatriate rewards is typically used where the expatriate has scarce skills, cannot easily be substituted, the host is HSL, host subordinates would otherwise receive more pay, or the image of the expatriate and the company are important to business effectiveness in the host.

Organisations might split expatriate payments between host country and offshore or expatriate's home country, whichever approach to calculation of expatriate pay is used. This can be particularly helpful where host country tax laws could drastically affect the intended outcome of a bonus scheme, where repatriation of funds out of the host is difficult, where there is currency volatility, or the expatriate has commitments such as school fees or mortgage payments in the home country.

Dealing with TCN expatriates presents the difficulty of deciding which country is the 'home' country for rewards purposes: that of the parent employer, or the employee. The TCN might be considerably better or worse off, according to which is chosen; just as the employer might be paying more than necessary. Using the TCN's home country as a base is administratively complex for a global company employing several nationalities and using a balance sheet approach, and it could result in two expatriates from different countries working together in one office on the same work being paid very different amounts. Market rate might thus be a better choice than a balance sheet approach.[170] 'Unfortunately, there is no perfect TCN strategy but there are companies which have applied the balance sheet or market rate successfully – and will continue to do so since the number of TCNs employed around the world is increasing all the time.'[171]

13.9 Employee relations

Employee relations need to be integrated into a global MNE's corporate strategy formulation as trade union influences can affect or delay the rationalisation of manufacturing or global integration of an MNE, or influence wage costs to the extent that competitiveness is undermined. Additionally, national legislation or trade union power can restrict the ease with which staff numbers can be varied or increase the cost of doing this.[172]

Trade unions are concerned about the power of MNEs and have pushed international organisations like the International Labour Organisation to adopt an MNE code of conduct,[173] and the Organisation for Economic Cooperation and Development (OECD) to issue guidelines[174] in 1976 regulating MNE behaviour in areas including information disclosure, employment and industrial relations and competition. Adherence to the guidelines is voluntary.

Trade unions' major concerns about MNEs' power are:

- MNEs' financial clout which enables losses in one area of the world to be offset against gains elsewhere;
- the ability to withhold investment so a unit becomes obsolete, uncompetitive and is thus closed;

- superior employee relations expertise and knowledge;
- a remote locus of authority (strategic decisions affecting the unit made at distant corporate HQ);
- dual sourcing policies which provide alternative sources of supplies, leaving MNEs less vulnerable to industrial action in one location;
- production facilities in many industries, with many product lines;
- the ability to move production facilities to other lower wage countries.[175]

Delocalisation, i.e. moving to lower labour cost countries, has to be part of the survival strategy of European companies, and is predicted to result in the loss of between 3 and 5 million jobs in Europe;[176] Muet[177] (1994) sees the European Union, with its interdependent national economic systems, gradually becoming a zone of mass unemployment.

As there are large national differences in the role of trade unions, the extent of their independence from the employer, trade union origins and coverage (craft, general, industry, company, professional, religious, white or blue collar), and what is – in practice – meant and covered by 'collective bargaining' and at what level (government, corporate or plant) negotiations occur, MNE employee relations policies need to be flexible enough to adapt to local needs. In practice, employee relations are usually delegated to subsidiaries by the parent, but with a global strategy of transnational sourcing and production a coordinated approach to employee relations is crucial to organisational success.[178]

Management and employee attitudes to trade unions also vary between countries. The USA has a low density of union membership, so American managers tend to have less experience of dealing with unions than managers elsewhere, hence tend to avoid unionisation or control union matters centrally.[179] Within Europe, decentralisation of collective bargaining is a trend, particularly noticeable in the UK and Italy, although parent companies tend to agree basic terms and conditions centrally, but leave scope for local flexibility.[180]

In countries such as Japan, the USA and the UK there is a downward trend in trade union membership, but trade union density at about 85 per cent is high in Sweden and only about 35 per cent in Germany although there is legislative support for co-determination there, via plant level Works Councils (mandatory for workplaces of five or more staff) and the corporate level *supervisory* board.

Japanese unions, established after the Second World War, are 'enterprise wide' and include all staff other than management. There is a less adversarial management/union approach than found in many Western unions, indeed, the union is regarded as a training ground for future managers.[181] Japanese enterprise unionists appreciate, perhaps because of the lifelong employment tradition, that damage to the company as a result of a work stoppage would affect them economically as well, so demonstrations may be held during lunch breaks or after working hours.[182] In Korea, worker loyalty is to the boss rather than to the enterprise, so there is mobility between companies; since 1987 when unions were allowed to organise on an industry-wide basis, Korean unions have been growing and taking an active part in negotiations for better pay and conditions.[183]

Top-down communication is a way of reinforcing corporate identity and encouraging pride in the company. Lateral communications are also required in MNEs, and are easier to establish between units which are linked through sequential workflows, than multidomestics operating as discrete local entities. The following objectives for international employee communications are suggested:

- reinforcement of organisation culture;
- letting people know what is expected of them;
- change facilitation;
- encouraging small new 'seed corn' initiatives;

* eliminate 'wheel reinventing' and encourage the exchange of information;
* prevent a 'not invented here' mentality;
* improve the organisation's PR image to the wider public, which might help with both sales and recruitment.[184]

Participation

Employee participation at work can be: financial, through profit-sharing schemes or share options; indirect, through trade unions involved in collective bargaining or corporate level Joint Consultative Councils; direct, through management/staff discussion and involvement mechanisms, which do not use union or other representatives as intermediaries. The nature and extent of employee participation vary between countries and within countries.

The Price Waterhouse Cranfield Surveys[185] have shown an increase in both direct and indirect participation efforts on the part of managements across Europe, apart from in the UK, where there was a decrease in indirect participation. In Japan, direct involvement via quality circles and teamworking is common, but decision-making is limited to local operational matters, rather than strategic involvement, and consultation is more information-giving and downward in direction; staff feel under pressure to agree with their managers.[186] Direct participative mechanisms, wherever they are used, introduced with an aim of enhancing employees' involvement and motivation and empowering them, can, as a result of internal and external pressures, be distorted into unworkable shapes which: 'from the employee point of view, [are seen as] a sinister attempt to gain more commitment, work and productivity, without the concomitant reward, control or empowerment'.[187]

The European Union and other trading blocs

The European Union (EU), more correctly still called European Community (EC) in the context of law, and sometimes still known as the European Economic Community (EEC), developed from the need perceived after the Second World War to pool Western European coal and steel resources under one authority, as these had caused conflicts, particularly between France and Germany; and to exercise control over West German industrial power which, fuelled by coal and steel strength, was seen as a factor in stimulating German nationalism and aggression in the first two world wars. The EEC aimed to develop a common market for goods and services by eliminating internal trade barriers, developing external trade policies, improving the mobility of labour, technology and capital within its boundaries. The EU aims to develop economic, monetary and political union amongst its member states.

Within the EU there is concern that unless common labour standards are adopted, jobs will move to lower labour cost countries within the EC; this is seen by some as unfair 'social dumping', preventable if member states start from a 'level playing field'.

While the EEC has always had a social policy dimension, the 1974 EC Action Programme on Social Policy aimed for:

* full and better employment: producing measures on gender equality, protection of employees' rights when there is a change of business ownership or employer insolvency, collective redundancies;
* improved living and working conditions: producing health and safety measures;
* worker participation: producing some employment rights to information and consultation, and further health and safety measures.

The European Foundation for the Improvement of Living and Working Conditions, established in 1976 aimed to encourage 'social dialogue' between the 'social partners', i.e. management, labour, trade unions and public enterprises.[188]

The more recent Community Charter on the Fundamental Social Rights of Workers, 1989, usually known as 'The Social Charter', is a broad guiding framework supporting EU social policy and covering:

- freedom of movement of workers;
- employment and pay;
- improvement of living and working conditions;
- social protection;
- freedom of association and collective bargaining;
- vocational training;
- equal treatment for men and women;
- worker information, consultation and participation;
- health and safety protection at work;
- the protection of children, adolescents, elderly persons, disabled people.

The Social Charter was not law but a statement of what the EU intended to achieve. Only a few measures have been adopted; these include:

- pregnancy and maternity rights;
- freedom of movement of workers;
- the employer's obligation to inform employees of conditions applicable to the employment/work relationship.

The 1992 Maastricht Treaty aimed to develop the existing Social Policy Chapter within the EC Treaty to put social policy-making on firmer ground than the Social Charter. The UK former Conservative government disliked the expansion of EC social policy powers and opted out of this part of the Treaty. The 1997 Labour government has now reversed this policy and will be implementing measures already in force in other member states, on European Works Councils and Parental Leave.

Within the EU, member states are not of one mind on social policy issues. Consensus is extraordinarily difficult to achieve, not least because of the different histories of member states on the following issues:

- labour relations: institutional collective bargaining arrangements differ widely between member countries, with collective agreements being legally binding in many EU countries, although only binding 'in honour' in the UK. Member states on the Council want flexibility on labour relations matters; the European Commission wants common protections of vulnerable workers.
- labour standards: within the EU 'labour standards' are variously regarded as a legitimate aspect of EU social policy and a precondition for effective EU labour market operations, or a burden on business and a matter for the individual states, not the EU, to decide (the pre-May 1997 UK government's view);
- social security: member states differ widely in their approach to what the state, as opposed to the worker, should provide in matters such as pensions, unemployment benefits, family support and health care;
- health and safety at work: different states put different parameters on this, e.g. the UK did not accept that the length of the working week or paid annual leave were health and safety matters, although they were the subject of the Working Time Directive adopted as a health and safety matter.

Other agreed or proposed EU-inspired provisions concerning employment include matters relating to: collective redundancies; acquired rights of employees in transfers and mergers; employee protection in the event of employer insolvency; equal pay; pensions; the elimination of avoidable risks to worker health and safety at the workplace and reducing the danger of unavoidable ones; atypical work; works councils; gender equality and gender discrimination burden of proof; cross-border sub-contracting; young people at work, temporary workers and extending data protection to paper-based records.

Directives need implementation in each country's national law, in a form which suits that law yet still offers the protection or right conferred by the Directive. Failure to implement, or fully implement, a Directive results in an action being brought against the member state in the ECJ. The UK has been called to answer non-implementation charges on several occasions, the best known being when it was obliged to introduce the 'equal value' amendment to its equal pay law.

The international manager operating within the EU needs to be aware of:

- which EU measures have been agreed and are proposed;
- whether or not they apply to the country in question – which may have opted out or not yet implemented a Directive, but still be within the allowed time limits for implementation;
- the effect of an EU Directive, not yet in operation in a specific country, but which could affect an MNE's dealings with its workforce across units in several European countries (for example, The Works Council Directive, while not yet formally adopted by the UK, applies to UK-based MNEs with units in other EU countries, or EU-based MNEs operating in the UK. Most such MNEs have included UK worker representatives on their Works Councils, none the less, as it seems pointless to exclude them from discussions in which their European mainland counterparts are included);
- which national law implements a specific Directive; the law may go further than the Directive;
- specific national cultural approaches to the observance of law, as in some countries the law is passed but observed more in the breach!;
- labour-related laws specific to the relevant countries;
- the institutional framework and content of collective bargaining in the relevant countries;
- the impact of Economic and Monetary Union (EMU) on the business, including pay.

The existence of a free trade association in a region needs to be considered by a manager when making decisions about the location of a foreign unit, sourcing policy, and sales potential. While the EU is currently the most integrated and well-known large supranational economic entity, other such associations are developing around the world, such as:

- NAFTA (The North American Free Trade Agreement): Mexico, Canada, USA;
- ASEAN (Association of Southeast Asian Nations), a loose political and economic arrangement, some of whose members are Brunei, Indonesia, Malaysia, the Philippines, Singapore, Thailand and Vietnam;
- AFTA (ASEAN Free Trade Association), a free trade zone of ASEAN members;
- Andean Pact, a free trade agreement of small South American countries;
- APEC (Asia Pacific Economic Cooperation), an OECD-style organisation of ASEAN members plus Australia, New Zealand, Hong Kong, Taiwan, South Korea, the USA, Canada, PRC), aiming for trade liberalisation by 2020, harmonised standards, the development of human resources to promote trade and prosperity.

13.10 Intercultural negotiations

Cultural values permeate behaviour and behavioural interpretations during negotiations, and affect:

- the number of negotiators in the team, their dress, use of language, topics of conversation, seniority and preparedness to show their feelings;
- the time taken over the whole negotiating process, including rapport establishing, information exchanging, persuading and decision-making stages;
- the level at which first and subsequent offers are pitched, the way they are put forward, and the persuasion techniques employed;
- the decision-making process, and the extent to which the negotiators are free to change an offer, or amend it once 'agreement' has been reached;
- the likelihood of direct rejection or oblique refusal; the Japanese negotiating technique of staying silent for long periods when uncertain or unhappy with a proposal, unnerves many Western negotiators;[189]
- the value placed on relationship establishment and task achievement. Cultural differences are a major reason why American negotiations with Japanese fail.[190]

Mead[191] identifies five aspects to a negotiation process, which do not necessarily occur sequentially:

- negotiating a relationship;
- finding common ground;
- persuasion;
- bargaining and conceding;
- implementation.

Graham and Herberger (1983),[192] with a different view of the stages in negotiation: non-task relationship creating, task-related exchange of information, persuasion, and concession and agreement, explain that different cultures vary in their view of the importance of each stage.

While traditional Western negotiating theory advocates separating the issue from the person, and concentrating on the issue, this is an inappropriate approach for negotiations with many Arab, East Asian and Latin cultures, where establishing a relationship of trust with the other party is an essential precursor of making a deal.

Mead[193] points out that cultures which do not have a history of intra-organisational trust need to develop a relationship with the individual; the Japanese are more concerned with establishing a long-term relationship than achieving a 'quick fix' deal.

> Many cultures, such as the Japanese and Arab, may start the negotiating process by building a relationship before moving into serious business discussions. On the other hand, most Americans and Westerners will move directly into the product/price negotiation process and worry about establishing a relationship later, if at all.[194]

The ritual greeting, flattering effusions and religious invocations (Arab)[195] or benign generalities (Japanese)[196] which precede meetings might seem superfluous to a Western negotiator but they are all part of relationship establishment and are the cultural norms. As Hampden-Turner and Trompenaars put it: 'A person who cannot wait to horse trade may not be worth trading horses with, caring more for gain than for the partnership. Such people may depart as abruptly as they arrived, thus wasting all the effort invested by their partners.'[197] (See also Table 3.8).

The Japanese tend to have more negotiating team members, who might rotate roles, than Western teams; they tend to be formally dressed and aim to develop a harmonious relationship before considering making a deal with a company. Sun Tzu, the famous Chinese military strategist whose writings have been applied to management,[198] stressed 'Know your enemy, know yourself and your victory will not be threatened. Know the terrain, know the weather, and your victory will be complete'.[199] Both the Chinese and the Japanese

Table 13.8 Contrasts in intercultural negotiations

	American	Japanese	Arab
Group composition	Marketing oriented	Function oriented	Committee of specialists
Number involved	2–3	4–7	4–6
Space orientation	Confrontational; Competitive	Display harmonious relationship	Status
Establishing rapport	Short period; Direct to task	Longer period; Until harmony is established	Long period; Until trusted
Exchange of information	Documented; Step-by-step; Multimedia	Extensive; Concentrate on receiving side	Less emphasis on technology, more on relationship
Persuasion tools	Time pressure; Loss of opportunity; Saving/making money	Maintain relationship references; Intergroup connections	Go-between; Hospitality
Use of language	Open/direct; Sense of urgency	Indirect; Appreciative; Cooperative	Flattery; Emotional; Religious
First offer	Fair +/– 5 to 10 per cent	+/– 10 to 20 per cent	+/– 20 to 50 per cent
Second offer	Add to package; Sweeten the deal	– 5 per cent	– 10 per cent
Final offer	Total package	Makes no further concessions	– 25 per cent
Decision-making process	Top management team	Collective	Team makes recommendation
Decision-maker	Top management team	Middle line with team consensus	Senior manager
Risk-taking	Calculated; Personal; responsibility	Low group responsibility	Religion-based

Source: Elashmawi, Harris, *Multicultural management*

go to considerable lengths to understand all about the other party with whom they are negotiating, and will require copious company information to be drip-fed to them on their request; during the course of this they are also assessing the relative position of the other party.

Japanese negotiators tend to take much more trouble in preparing for negotiations than Western firms take preparing to do business with the Japanese. Typically, a younger Japanese employee will accompany an older mentor on a foreign business trip to acquire background knowledge. In negotiations:

Japanese tend to think that adopting a strong initial position is akin to *yakuza* (gangster) behaviour. The Japanese side tends to listen in silence, trying to read the thoughts of the other party. This makes them seem shifty and evasive in Westerners' eyes ... The Soviet style of negotiating is characterised by threatening; in the American and European approach, logic is as important as threats. But Japanese use neither logic nor threats.[200]

Latin and Oriental cultures tend to start out with what an American or German might see as an 'unreasonably' high initial demand, although they expect to have to make considerable concessions during the negotiations.[201]

The Japanese *ringi* system of decision-making, requires all relevant people to be party to a decision; this can take what might seem to a Western negotiator an intolerable time; but impatience or a heated exchange would not be appreciated as it indicates bad manners and loss of control leading to loss of face for both parties.[202] Chinese negotiators, however, might pretend anger to force an issue.[203] (See Table 13.8).

13.11 References

1. Torrington D. *International human resource management: think globally, act locally.* Hemel Hempstead: Prentice Hall International (UK) Limited, 1994: 4.
2. Morgan PV. International human resource management: fact or fiction. *Personnel Administrator* 1986; **31**(9): 43–7.
3. Morgan, Fact or fiction.
4. Schuler RS. Linking the people with the strategic needs of the business. *Organizational Dynamics* 1992; Summer: 18–32.
5. Schuler RS, Walker JW. Human resources strategy: focusing on issues and actions. *Organizational Dynamics* 1990; Summer: 5–19.
6. Torrington D. *International human resource management:* 6–7.
7. Tayeb MH. *The management of a multicultural workforce.* Chichester: John Wiley and Sons Ltd, 1996.
8. Evans P, Lank E, Farquhar A. Managing human resources in the international firm: lessons from practice. In: Evans P, Doz Y, Laurent A eds. *Human resource management in international firms: change globalization, innovation.* Basingstoke: Macmillan, 1989: 113–43.
9. Price Waterhouse Cranfield Project (henceforth PWCP). *Report on international strategic human resource management.* Cranfield: Cranfield School of Management, 1991.
10. Brewster C, Hegewisch A, Lockhart JT. Researching human resource management: methodology of the PWCP on European trends. *Personnel Review* 1991; **20**(6): 36–40.
11. Brewster C, Hegewisch A. Personnel management in Europe: a continent of diversity. *Personnel Management* 1993; **25**(1): 36–40.
12. Hofstede G. *Culture's consequences: international differences in work-related values.* Beverly Hills, CA: Sage Publications, 1980.
13. Filella J. Is there a Latin model in the management of human resources?. *Personnel Review* 1991; **23**(6): 14–23.
14. Tyson S, Brewster C. Conclusions: comparative studies and the development of human resource management. In: Brewster C, Tyson S eds. *International comparisons in human resource management.* London: Sage, 1991.
15. Brewster C, Bournois F. Human resource management: a European perspective. *Personnel Review* 1991; **20**(6): 4–13.
16. PWCP. *Report.*
17. Brewster C, Larsen HH. Human resource management in Europe: evidence from 10 countries. *International Journal of Human Resource Management* 1993; **3**(3): 409–34.
18. Sparrow P, Hiltrop J. *European human resource management in transition.* Hemel Hempstead: Prentice Hall, 1994.

19. Brewster, Hegewisch, Personnel management in Europe: 36–40.
20. PWCP. *Report*; Brewster, Bournois, European perspective: 4–13.
21. Towers Perrin. *Priorities for gaining competitive advantage: a worldwide human resource study*. London: Towers Perrin, 1992.
22. Towers Perrin. *Priorities*; Sparrow PR, Schuler RS, Jackson SE. Convergence or divergence: human resource practices and policies for competitive advantage worldwide. *International Journal of Human Resource Management* 1994; **5**(2): 267–99.
23. Ondrack DA. International human resources management in European and North American firms. *International Studies of Management and Organization* 1985; **15**(1): 6–32; Phatak AV. *International dimensions of management*, 2nd edition, Boston, MA: PWS-KENT, 1989; Dowling PJ, Schuler RS, Welch DE. *International dimensions of human resource management,* 2nd edition, Belmont, CA: Wadsworth Publishing Company, 1994.
24. Torrington D. *International human resource management*.
25. Mayo A. *Managing careers: strategies for organizations*. London: IPM, 1991.
26. Harvey MG. The multinational corporation's expatriate problem: an application of Murphy's Law. *Business Horizons* 1983; **26**(1): 71–8.
27. Mendenhall ME, Oddou G. The overseas assignment: a practical look. *Business Horizons* 1988, September–October: 78–84.
28. Mendenhall ME, Oddou G. The dimensions of expatriate acculturation: a review. *Academy of Management Review* 1985; **10**: 39–47.
29. Ronen S. Training the international assignee. In: Goldstein I ed. *Training and career development*. San Francisco: Jossey-Bass, 1989: 430.
30. Mendenhall, Oddou. The overseas assignment.
31. Gregersen HB, Black JS. A multifaceted approach to expatriate retention in international assignments. *Group and Organization Studies* 1990: **15**(4): 461–85.
32. Gertsen M. Expatriate selection and training. In: Luostarinen R ed. *Proceedings of the fifteenth annual conference of the European international business association*. Helsinki: December 1989, pp. 1251–1280, 1257.
33. Black JS, Stephens GK. The influence of the spouse on American expatriate adjustment and intent to stay in Pacific Rim overseas assignments. *Journal of Management* 1989; **15**(4): 529–44.
34. Tung RL. Selection and training procedures of US, European and Japanese multinationals. *California Management Review* 1982; **25**(1): 57–71.
35. Evans PAL, Bartolome F. *Must success cost so much?*. London: Grant McIntyre/New York: Basic Books, 1979.
36. Tung RL. Selection and training.
37. Janssens M. Evaluating international managers' performance: parent company standards as a control mechanism. *International Journal of Human Resource Management* 1994; **5**(5), December: 853–73.
38. Zeira Y, Harari E. Managing third country nationals in multinational corporations. *Business Horizons* 1977; **19**, 83–8.
39. Tung RL. *The new expatriates: managing human resources abroad*. Cambridge, MA: Ballinger, 1988.
40. Barham K, Devine M. *The quest for the international manager: a survey of global human resource strategies*. London: Ashridge Management Resource Group/The Economist Intelligence Unit, Special Report No. 2098, 1990.
41. Conway MA. Reducing expatriate failure rates. *Personnel Administrator* 1984; **29**(7): 31–8.
42. Adler NJ. *International dimensions of organizational behaviour*. Boston, MA: PWS-Kent, 1991; Johnston J. An empirical study of the repatriation of managers in UK multinationals. *Human Resource Management Journal* 1991; **4**(1): 102–9.
43. Black JS, Gregersen H. Antecedents to cross-cultural adjustment for expatriates in Pacific Rim assignments. *Human Relations* 1991; **44**(5): 497–515.
44. Derr CB, Oddou G. Are US multinationals adequately preparing future American leaders for global competition? *International Journal of Human Resource Management* 1991; **2**(2): 227–44.

45. Tung RL. Expatriate assignments: enhancing success and minimizing failure. *Academy of Management Executive* 1987; **1**(2): 117–26.
46. Derr, Odou, Are US multinationals adequately preparing?; Derr CB, Oddou G. Internationalising managers: speeding up the process. *European Management Journal* 1993; **11**(4): 435–42.
47. Humes S. *Managing the multinational: confronting the global–local dilemma.* Hemel Hempstead: Prentice Hall, 1993: 8–15.
48. Humes, *Managing the multinational*: 8–10.
49. Humes, *Managing the multinational*: 10–11.
50. Humes, *Managing the multinational*: 15.
51. Humes, *Managing the multinational*: xviii.
52. Bartlett CA, Ghoshal S. *Managing across borders: the transnational solution.* London: Random House, 1989.
53. Bartlett, Ghoshal, *Managing across borders.*
54. Bartlett, Ghoshal, *Managing across borders.*
55. Humes, *Managing the multinational*: xviii.
56. Humes, *Managing the multinational.*
57. Laurent A. Managing across cultures and national borders. In: Makridakis, S ed. *Single market Europe: opportunities and challenges for business.* San Francisco: Jossey-Bass, 1991.
58. Porter ME. Changing patterns of international competition. *California Management Review* 1986; **28**(2): 9–40.
59. Tayeb MH. *The management of a multicultural workforce.* Chichester: Wiley, 1996.
60. Bartlett CA, Ghoshal S. Organising for worldwide effectiveness: the transnational solution. *California Management Review* Fall 1988: 54–74; Bartlett, Ghoshal, *Managing across borders*; Ghoshal S., Bartlett CA. The multinational corporation as an interorganizational network. *Academy of Management Review* 1990a; **18**(2): 603–25; Bartlett CA, Ghoshal S. Matrix management: not a structure, a frame of mind. *Harvard Business Review* 1990b; July–August: 138–45.
61. Bartlett, Ghoshal. Organising for worldwide effectiveness: 66.
62. Ghoshal, Bartlett. The multinational corporation; Bartlett, Ghoshal, Matrix management.
63. Hedlund G. The hypermodern MNC – a heterarchy?. *Human Resource Management* 1986; **25**(1): 489–514.
64. Hedlund, The hypermodern MNC.
65. Ghoshal, Bartlett. The multinational corporation.
66. Bartlett, Ghoshal. Matrix management.
67. Doz Y, Pralahad CK. Controlled variety: a challenge for human resource management in the MNC. *Human Resource Management* 1986; **25**(1): 55–71.
68. Porter ME. *Competitive advantage: creating and sustaining superior performance.* New York: Macmillan Inc., 1985: 42–4.
69. Schuler RS, Dowling PJ. Survey of SHRM/I members. Unpublished manuscript, Stern School of Business, New York University, 1988, cited in Dowling PJ, Schuler RS, Welch DE. *International dimensions of human resource management*, 2nd edition, Belmont, CA: Wadsworth Publishing Co., 1994: 43.
70. Desatnick RL, Bennett ML. *Human resource management in the multinational company.* New York: Nichols, 1978.
71. Reynolds C, Are you ready to make IHR a global function?. *HR News* Feb 1992.
72. Bhatt B *et al.* The relationship between the global strategic planning process and the human resource management function. In: Schuler RS, Youngblood RA, Huber VL eds. *Readings in human resource management,* 3rd edition, St Paul, MI: West Publishing Co., 1988: 427–35.
73. IPD, *Guide to developing an international personnel career.* London: IPD, 1995.
74. Hofstede G. *Cultures and organizations: software of the mind: intercultural cooperation and its importance for survival.* London: HarperCollins, 1994: 181–2.
75. Donleavy G. Preface: trading values. In: Stewart S, Donleavy G eds. *Whose business values? Some Asian and cross-cultural perspectives.* Hong Kong: Hong Kong University Press, 1995: xiv.

76. Ferraro, GP. *The cultural dimension of international business*. Englewood Cliffs, NJ: Prentice Hall, 1994: 20–3.
77. Ferraro, *Cultural dimension*: 23–6.
78. Ferraro, *Cultural dimension*: 26.
79. Hofstede, *Cultures and organizations*: 112.
80. Ferraro, *Cultural dimension*: 28.
81. Rogers E. *Communication of inventions: a cross-cultural approach*. New York: Free Press, 1971: 22–3.
82. Hofstede, *Culture's consequences*.
83. Hofstede, *Cultures and organizations*: 140.
84. Hofstede, *Cultures and organizations*: 80.
85. Hofstede, *Cultures and organizations*: 110–13.
86. Hofstede, *Cultures and organizations*: 140.
87. Hofstede, *Cultures and organizations*: 160.
88. Hofstede G, Bond MH. The Confucius connection: from cultural roots to economic growth. *Organizational Dynamics* 1988; **16**(4): 4–21.
89. Hofstede, *Cultures and organizations*: 165–6.
90. Hampden-Turner C, Trompenaars F. *The seven cultures of capitalism: value systems for creating wealth in the United States, Britain, Japan, Germany, France, Sweden, and The Netherlands*. London: Judy Piatkus, 1995.
91. Elashmawi F, Harris PR. *Multicultural management: new skills for global success*. Houston, TX: Gulf Publishing Co., 1993.
92. Hampden-Turner, Trompenaars, *Seven cultures*.
93. Hampden-Turner, Trompenaars, *Seven cultures*.
94. Stewart S. The ethics and the value of ethics: should we be studying business values in Hong Kong?. In: Stewart S, Donleavy G eds. *Whose business values? Some Asian and cross-cultural perspectives*. Hong Kong: Hong Kong University Press, 1995: 3.
95. Yeung A, Yeung J. Business values: a strategic imperative for the coming decades. In: Stewart S, Donleavy G eds. *Whose business values? Some Asian and cross-cultural perspectives*. Hong Kong: Hong Kong University Press, 1995: 212–13.
96. Yeung, Yeung, Business values: 179.
97. Leisinger KM. Corporate ethics and international business: some basic issues. In: Stewart S, Donleavy G eds. *Whose business values? Some Asian and cross-cultural perspectives*. Hong Kong: Hong Kong University Press, 1995: 179.
98. Mahoney J. Ethical attitudes to bribery and extortion. In: Stewart S, Donleavy G eds. *Whose business values? Some Asian and cross-cultural perspectives*. Hong Kong: Hong Kong University Press, 1995: 226.
99. Noonan Jr JT. *Bribes*. New York: Macmillan, 1984: 688.
100. Mahoney, Ethical attitudes: 251–2.
101. Snell R. Psychic prisoners? Managers facing ethical dilemmas: cases from Hong Kong. In: Stewart S, Donleavy G eds. *Whose business values? Some Asian and cross-cultural perspectives*. Hong Kong: Hong Kong University Press, 1995: 143.
102. Besner P. Watch your language. *Pace* 1982; **9**(2), March/April: 53f.
103. Holstein WJ. *The Japanese power game: what it means for Americans*. New York: Charles Scribner and Sons, 1990, cited in Hampden-Turner, Trompenaars, *Seven cultures*: 111
104. Hampden-Turner, Trompenaars, *Seven cultures*: 111.
105. Hampden-Turner, Trompenaars, *Seven cultures*: 111.
106. Elashmawi, Harris, *Multicultural management*: 124.
107. Chua Bee-Leng. The communication process. In: Westwood RI ed. *Organisational Behaviour: Southeast Asian Perspectives*. Hong Kong: Longman Group (Far East) Ltd, 1992: 334.
108. Birdwhistell R. *Introduction to kinesics*. Louisville, KY: University of Louisville Press, 1952.
109. Hall ET. *The silent language*. Garden City, NY: Doubleday, 1959; Hall ET. *The hidden dimension*. Garden City, NY: Doubleday, 1966; Hall ET. *Beyond culture*. Garden City, NY: Doubleday, 1976.

110. Bond MH. *Beyond the Chinese face: insights from psychology*. Hong Kong: Oxford Univesity Press, 1991: 49.
111. Redding SG, Martyn-Johns TA. Paradigm differences and their relation to management functions with references to South-East Asia. In: Negandhi A, Wilpert B eds. *Organizational functioning in cross-cultural psychology*. Kent, OH: Ohio State University Press, 1979.
112. Ekman P, Friesen WV. Hand movements. *Journal of Communication* 1972; **22**: 353–74.
113. Hall, *The silent language*; Hall, *The hidden dimension*.
114. Ferraro, *Cultural dimensions*: 64–5.
115. Hall, *Beyond culture*.
116. Ferraro, *Cultural dimensions*: 65–6.
117. Child J. Culture, contingency and capitalism in the cross-national study of organizations. In: Straw BM, Cummings LL eds. *Research in organizational behaviour*. Greenwich: JAI Press, 1981: 3.
118. Hofstede, *Cultures and organizations*.
119. Hofstede, *Cultures and organizations*: 181.
120. Mendenhall ME, Dunbar E, Oddou GR. Expatriate selection, training and career-pathing: a review and critique. *Human Resource Management* Fall 1987.
121. Torrington, *International human resource management*.
122. Robinson RD. *Internationalization of business: an introduction*. New York: Dryden Press, 1983: 127.
123. Min Chen. *Asian management systems: Chinese, Japanese and Korean styles of business*. London/New York: Routledge, 1995: 188–90.
124. Min Chen, *Asian management systems*: 194.
125. Min Chen, *Asian management systems*: 190.
126. Min Chen, *Asian management systems*: 190–1.
127. Min Chen, *Asian management systems*: 216.
128. Min Chen, *Asian management systems*: 221.
129. Bournois F. France. In: Brewster C, Hegewisch A, Lockhart JT, Holden L eds. *The European human resource management guide*. London: Academic Press, 1993.
130. IDS. *Recruitment*. London: IDS and IPM, 1990: 46.
131. IDS. *Recruitment*: 28.
132. IDS. *Recruitment*: 98.
133. IDS. *Recruitment*: 125.
134. Mead R. *Cross-cultural management communication*. Chichester: John Wiley & Sons Ltd, 1990: 191.
135. Shimmin S. Selection in a European context. In: Herriot P ed. *Assessment and selection in organizations: methods and practice for recruitment and appraisal*. Chichester: John Wiley, 1989.
136. IDS. *Recruitment*: 45–6.
137. Bolton M., et al. *Assessment and development in Europe: adding value to individuals and organisations*. London: McGraw-Hill, 1995: 117.
138. Bolton, et al., *Assessment and development*: 67–71.
139. Bolton, et al., *Assessment and development*: 117.
140. Smith PB, Peterson MF. *Leadership, organizations, and culture*. London: Sage Publications Ltd, 1988: 100.
141. Evans, et al. Managing human resources: 126–7.
142. Calori R, de Woot P. *A European management model: beyond diversity*. Hemel Hempstead: Prentice Hall International, 1994.
143. Calori R, Valla J-P, de Woot P. Common characteristics: the ingredients of European management. In: Calori R, de Woot P. *A European management model: beyond diversity*. Hemel Hempstead: Prentice Hall International, 1994: 31–54.
144. Elashmawi, Harris, *Multicultural management*.
145. Yun-Wing Sung, et al., *The fifth dragon*: 130–1.

146. Takezawa S, Whitehall AM. *Work ways: Japan and America.* Tokyo: The Japan Institute of Labour, 1981.

147. Akita J. Japanese industrial practices and the employment contract. In: Nish I, Redding G, Ng Sek-hong eds. *Work and society: labour and human resources in East Asia.* Hong Kong: Hong Kong University Press, 1996: 248.

148. Akita J, Japanese industrial practices: 248.

149. Akita J, Japanese industrial practices: 247.

150. Min Chen, *Asian management systems*: 190–1.

151. Min Chen, *Asian management systems*: 221.

152. Pucik V. Strategic human resource management in a multinational firm. In: Wortzel HV, Wortzel LH eds. *Strategic management of multinational corporations: the essentials.* New York: John Wiley, 1985.

153. Pucik V. Strategic human resource management.

154. Geanuracos J. *The global performance game.* New York: Crossborder, EIU, Winter 1994, as cited in Tricker RI, Dockery A. *Performance measurement that matters.* Hong Kong: Pitman Publishing Asia Pacific, 1995.

155. Fulkerson J, Schuler RS. Managing worldwide diversity at Pepsi-Cola international. In: Jackson SE ed. *Human resource management approaches for effectively managing workforce diversity.* New York: Guilford Publication, 1992.

156. Min Chen, *Asian management systems.*

157. Dowling, Schuler, Welch, *International dimensions*: 176.

158. Dowling, Schuler, Welch, *International dimensions*: 176.

159. Henzler HA. The new era of Eurocapitalism. *Harvard Business Review* 1992; **70**(4): 57–68.

160. Min Chen, *Asian management systems*: 192.

161. Dowling, Schuler, Welch, *International dimensions*: 176.

162. Whitehill AM. *Japanese management: tradition and transition.* New York: Routledge, 1991: 179.

163. Gomez-Mejia L, Welbourne T. Compensation strategies in a global context. *Human Resource Planning* 1991; **14**(1): 29–42.

164. Hofstede, *Culture's consequences.*

165. Gomez-Mejia, Welbourne, Compensation strategies.

166. Armstrong M, Murlis H. *Reward management: a handbook of remuneration strategy and practice*, 3rd edition, London: Kogan Page in association with the IPD, 1994.

167. Armstrong, Murlis. *Reward management*: 439.

168. Reynolds C. Compensation of overseas personnel. In: Famularo JJ ed. *Handbook of human resource administration,* 2nd edition, New York: McGraw-Hill, 1986.

169. Armstrong, Murlis. *Reward management*: 430.

170. Armstrong, Murlis. *Reward management*: 438–9.

171. Armstrong, Murlis. *Reward management*: 439.

172. Pralahad CK, Doz Y. *The multinational mission: balancing local demands and global vision.* New York: The Free Press, 1987.

173. ILO Code of Conduct. *Tripartite declaration of principles concerning MNEs and social policy.* Geneva: ILO, 1977.

174. Campbell DC, Rowan RL. *Multinational enterprises and the OECD industrial relations guidelines.* Philadelphia: The Wharton School, University of Pennsylvania, Industrial Research Unit, 1983.

175. Kennedy T. *European labor relations.* Lexington, MA: Lexington Books, 1980.

176. Arthuis J. *Information sur les délocalisations.* Senate, Paris, 1993, cited in Brunstein I ed. *Human resource management in Western Europe.* Berlin/New York: de Gruyter & Co., 1993.

177. Muet PA, ed. *Le chomage persistant en Europe.* Paris: Presses de la Fondation Nationale des Sciences Politiques, 1994.

178. Robock SH, Simmonds K. *International business and multinational enterprises,* 4th edition, Homewood, IL: Irwin, 1989; Hefler DF. Global sourcing: offshore investment strategy for the 1980's. *Journal of Business Strategy* 1981; **2**(1): 7–12.

179. Kochan TA, McKersie RB, Cappelli P. Strategic choice and industrial relations theory. *Industrial Relations* 1984; **23**(1): 16–39; Hamill J. The labour relations practices of foreign owned and indigenous firms, *Employee Relations* 1983; **5**(1): 14–16; Hamill J. Multinational corporations and industrial relations in the UK, *Employee Relations* 1984; **6**(5): 12–16; Hamill J. Labour relations decision making within multinational corporations, *Industrial Relations* Journal 1984; **15**(2): 30–4.
180. Marlow S. Collective bargaining. In: Beardwell I, Holden L eds. *Human resource management: a contemporary perspective*. London: Pitman, 1994: 492.
181. Min Chen, *Asian management systems*: 191.
182. Min Chen, *Asian management systems*: 192.
183. Min Chen, *Asian management systems*: 221–2.
184. Foulds J, Mallet L. The European and international dimension. In: Wilkinson T ed. *The Communications Challenge*. London: IPD, 1989: 78.
185. PWC. *Report* 1990; PWC. *Report* 1991; Holden L. Employee communications in Europe on the increase. *Involvement and Participation*. November 1990.
186. Briggs P. Organisational commitment: the key to Japanese success?. In: Brewster C, Tyson S eds. *International comparisons in human resource management*. London: Pitman, 1991.
187. Holden L. Employee involvement. In: Beardwell I, Holden L eds. *Human resource management: a contemporary perspective*. London: Pitman, 1994: 583.
188. Roney, *EC/EU* fact book, 4th edition, London: Kogan Page, 1995: 190–1.
189. Min Chen, *Asian management systems*: 244.
190. Tung RL. How to negotiate with the Japanese. *California Management Review* 1984; **26**(4), Summer: 62–77.
191. Mead, *Cross-cultural management communication*: 190.
192. Graham JL, Herberger RA. Negotiators abroad – don't shoot from the hip. *Harvard Business Review* 1983; July/August: 160–8.
193. Mead, *Cross-cultural management communication*: 191.
194. Elashmawi, Harris, *Multicultural management*: 166.
195. Elashmawi, Harris, *Multicultural management*.
196. Hampden-Turner, Trompenaars, *Seven cultures*: 36.
197. Hampden-Turner, Trompenaars, *Seven cultures*: 36.
198. Wee Chow Hou, Lee Khai Sheang, Bambang Walujo Hidajat. *Sun Tzu: war and management*. Singapore: Addison-Wesley Publishing Co., 1991.
199. Wee Chow Hou, *et al., Sun Tzu*: 17.
200. Whymant R. Japanese businessmen are 'losers at the negotiating table'. *Daily Telegraph*, 30 May 1988, cited in Mead, *Cross-cultural management communication*: 199.
201. Graham, Herberger, Negotiators abroad.
202. Min Chen, *Asian management systems*: 245.
203. Seligman SD. *Dealing with the Chinese*. New York: Warner Books, 1989: 145–6.

Index